# AI and Humanistic Management

## Aesthetics in Managerial Theory and Practice

**Edited by Michał Szostak**

Routledge
Taylor & Francis Group
NEW YORK AND LONDON

First published 2026
by Routledge
605 Third Avenue, New York, NY 10158

and by Routledge
4 Park Square, Milton Park, Abingdon, Oxon, OX14 4RN

*Routledge is an imprint of the Taylor & Francis Group, an informa business*



ISBN: 978-1-041-10293-9 (hbk)
ISBN: 978-1-041-10294-6 (pbk)
ISBN: 978-1-003-65437-7 (ebk)

DOI: 10.4324/9781003654377

Typeset in Times New Roman
by codeMantra

# Contents

# Figures

# Tables

# Prefaces

## Riding the entropy machine

*Monika Kostera*[1]

There is much talk of the AI revolution, yet there is not as much said about a slow but persistent evolution that has been going on for many years, and which has an impact much more lasting and revolutionary than the famous technology enabling the simulation of human intelligence processes by machines. Our embodiment has been gradually becoming subject to erosion and degradation, Richard Kearney (2021) observes. Indeed, we have become disembodied, excarnated. Kearney argues that increasingly many people live their lives virtually on the global Internet. That makes us interconnected and supports intersubjective sensemaking on a scale hitherto unknown. However, at the same time, there is mounting isolation and loneliness. Kearney muses on this paradox of being connected with everything and everyone but absent from where and who we are. Touch being our primordial sense, we dehumanise ourselves. It is touch that creates embodied community.

Excarnation, however, creates an aspiration to superhuman kinship. Consider the faces we show each other on social media (such as the aptly named Facebook) instead of the face that Emmanuel Lévinas (1999) speaks of as bringing unconditional responsibility for the Other. The disembodied face brings no such responsibility. In fact, the online avatar is subject to irresponsible manipulation, which then tends to permeate other aspects of our experience, bringing the new irresistible imperative to change, alter, and manipulate the persona as we go. Personas are regularly built on the outside of the human body. Like a Facebook post, words and images can be chosen and edited. What emerges is a mask, more or less in tune with other masks, more or less reflecting other reflections. But was it for no reason at all that our grandmothers were weary of mirrors and especially anxious of mirrors facing each other? Was it just a superstition to believe that they create something of a passage through which who knows what may enter, perhaps even something sinister? Is it not precisely what we have been doing with our avatars facing avatars, and screens gazing at screens, long before the "AI problem" even emerged?

Known as the "infinity mirror" effect, the continuous reflection is said to make disturbances in the flow of energy, trapping something that we cannot consciously control in the middle, even if it is just superstition, subconscious fear. What gets lost in the exchange between mirrors is just that: the ability to use the light of consciousness on things that emerge. What is controllable and controlled also changes. Some crucial elements go missing. In the virtual world, it is everything that brings "personal chemistry" or different energies from embodied meetings: facial expression, body language, movement, smell, and resonance of voice. Meetings in the real world mean that we have to act in this world at the same time – hang up the jacket, order food. Not everything that happens during an embodied meeting can be done completely on purpose. Luck, surprise, and difference are invited or at least tolerated. In virtual meetings, humans lose complexity, angularity, and unpredictability. And this: it is much more difficult to hurt someone sitting next to someone who writes something on social media. In the latter case, not only does empathy not awaken in most of us, but people actually feel morally satisfied if they have hurt or ridiculed someone, Richard Seymour (2020) observes. Ostracism on social media does not carry any real cost, so people do not feel guilt or regret. There is no responsibility or conscience involved: "It is just a comment, nothing special", even if the consequences entail despair, depression, or suicide of an Other. Here, people are truly just numbers in the end: strings of code, profile IDs. On the Internet, people live a spectral life, argues Éric Sadin (2023), which is no illusion at all – it has become a reality, an overpowering one, with real consequences. The emergence of generative AI adds special gravity to this process: it no longer manages but produces the elements and experiences that people engage in. This engagement now becomes passive rather than active, with some fundamental sense and ability delegated to machines. These machines are increasingly outsourcing disruption on the human users who cease being users and become objects, abstractions, code for the playing of roles – but roles in what? Not on stage, certainly.

According to Peter Brook's classic idea of theatre (1968), roles played on stage offer the potential to make things happen and are an invitation to fill an empty space with living performance as a way of a solid, visible, and lasting mark. Roles happen as if in another, sacred dimension, which is of highest relevance for the human condition. Roles played by Internet avatars are only superficially similar to roles played in the theatre because theatre is an embodied art form that contains and encloses them. Both actors and viewers are physically present, some on the stage, others in the audience. In social media, bodies are separated from the conversation. They offer no consolation, no transformation, no katharsis. This is no theatre: rather something like a constant marketing campaign of the increasingly fragmented persona in front of other personas. This uncannily echoes Jean Baudrillard's (1988) prophetic image of video machines watching each other's recordings. Another "infinity mirror": an endless reflection devoid of resonance.

Resonance is the very relation of the human to the world, argues Hartmut Rosa (2019), and it is being excluded by modernity's mode of communication, generation, and participation. A system of communication without resonance is an entropy machine. It creates disintegration, intensifies the time of tearing apart, and mobilises forms of engagement that carry no energy. There is no reason to change one's mind, to be enchanted, to encounter something "entirely different" that liberates the conscious mind from the imperative to spin illusions, to keep convincing, to agitate, and to fill the world with the ego. Without resonance, the answers to questions such as: *Who are we, where do we come from, where are we going?* become but simulacra. Indeed, in such a relentless space, there is no room for asking them, no room for the human condition.

Instead, humanity is promised a superhuman condition. According to Yuval Noach Harari (2015), immortality, happiness, and divine powers are the three great goals destined to be achieved in the 21st century. No wars, no epidemics. Yet ten years passed since the publication date, and we live in a world of raging, incessant wars, waged not just between armies but directed at civilians and children. The COVID-19 pandemic hit the globe, making a lasting imprint not just on human health but on the way societies are organised. The new type of Superman that Harari promised would bring a marriage of AI and biotechnology and give birth to the production of bodies, brains, and minds. Humanity would be divided into those who ride the train of progress and all the rest, devoid of knowledge and clueless. Slavoj Žižek (2023) was less than impressed by this, calling the aspiration a kind of modern hubris. Žižek comments that even those who ride the train of progress will not be able to drive it. Aurélien Barrau (2023) speaks of "the K hypothesis": an attitude leading to exponential technological growth, where science has been made abstract and reductionist, devoid of its immense poetic charge.

If humans of the late neoliberal era cannot tell the work of sets of technologies known as AI from human work, then maybe there is something wrong with humans on a much more profound level than with the technologies.

## Note

1 Professor Ordinaria in Economics and the Humanities; Elected Member of the Sociology Committee of the Polish Academy of Science; Faculty of Management at University of Warsaw, Poland; Guest Professor in Management at Södertörn University, Sweden; Professeure Invitée à L'université Rennes, France; Visiting Professor at L'Université Paris Nanterre, France; Co-Editor-in-Chief of Tamara Journal of Critical Organizational Inquiry.

## References

Baudrillard, Jean (1988). *America*. London: Verso.

Barrau, Aurélien (2023). *L'Hypothèse K La science face à la catastrophe écologique*. Paris Grasset.

Brook, Peter (1968). *The Empty Space: A book about the theatre: deadly, holy, rough, immediate.* New York: Touchstone.
Harari, Yuval Noach (2017). *Homo Deus: A brief history of tomorrow*. New York: HarperCollins.
Kearney, Richard (2021). *Touch: Recovering our most vital sense*. New York: Columbia University Press.
Lévinas, Emanuel (1999). *Totality and infinity: An essay on exteriority*. Pittsburgh, PA: Duquesne University Press.
Rosa, Hartmut (2019). *Resonance: A sociology of our relationship to the world.* Cambridge: Polity.
Sadin, Éric (2023). *La vie spectrale: Penser l'ère du Métavers et des IA génératives.* Paris: Grasset.
Seymour, Richard (2020). *The twittering machine*. London: Verso.
Žižek, Slavoj (2023). The Post-Human Desert. Project Syndicate. https://www.project-syndicate.org/commentary/ai-post-human-future-by-slavoj-zizek-2023-04

# History, Humanity, and the Hope for Humanistic Management

*David Collins*[1]

I am drafting these prefacing remarks on 9 May 2025. I am in Warsaw to meet with colleagues to discuss an edited collection that we will produce on "culture" with the support of Taylor and Francis, Routledge. And at Michal's invitation I offered a lecture on the excellence project and "bullshit" to the staff and students of Civitas University (see Collins, 2022; Collins and Collins, 2022). Yesterday, on 8 May, I visited the memorial sacred (in my mind at least) to the memory of those enclosed within Warsaw's "ghetto" and to those who rose up in opposition to the horrors perpetrated by the Nazis. I took some time to visit the nearby museum. There, I bought my wife a daffodil pin. This pin has become both a symbol of the uprising and a testimony to the courage of (learn their names) Marek Edelman, Mordechaj Anielewicz, Icchak Cukierman, Tosia Altman, and Cywia Lubetkin, who led the revolt against the Nazis.

The daffodil pin is, to my eyes, perfect as a symbol for the museum and its purpose. You see it usefully condenses the story of Marek Edelman, and the mysterious individual who, each year on 19 April, would make a gift of flowers, which were then laid by Edelman at the monument erected to honour those who lived and died in the enclosure. In this sense, the daffodil, so symbolic of spring itself, signals (re)birth, growth, and hope; the return of the light! Yet if you look closely, you will see that the stylised paper daffodils now worn by the people of Warsaw in mid-April also mirror the yellow stars that the Nazis required Jews to affix to their clothing. In this regard, the daffodil pin also reminds us that others have (and will) choose hate over humanity.

And what does this have to do with artificial intelligence (AI)? I am so glad you asked because on the 80th anniversary of the conclusion of World War II (in the European theatre at least), there are, I believe, very good reasons to suggest that AI and the large language models that feed it are – let's be diplomatic – problematic and will require careful management and regulation particularly in the context of governmental systems that are becoming increasingly brazen in their authoritarianism.

So, let me ask *you* this: when the Nazis arrived in Poland (and in Italy and France and elsewhere) how did they know where to find the Jews and the Communists and the Roma? How did they know the identities of the union leaders, the public officials and the intellectuals?

Black (2001) answers our questions. He demonstrates that subsidiaries of IBM, a company constituted to anticipate the needs of its clients had surveyed, ordered, and tabulated the world on behalf of the Nazis so that those deemed surplus to the project of the third Reich might be collected, corralled, and dispatched. And all of this, we should note was achieved (if this is the apposite term for such monstrosity) within and electro-mechanical world wherein the *Hollerith* tabulating machines were subject to regular breakdowns and indeed required, as Black suggests, IBM staff to be embedded within the very apparatus of the Nazi extermination camps.

My students returning from periods of work placement tell me that they are now expected to incorporate AI within their emerging (professional) practice. Indeed, my own Government (ahem) assures me that AI will automate 100% of routine tasks and will offer (albeit with no timeframe specified) savings of some £45 billion.

Yet, what are these routine tasks? *Palantir* owned by (let's be gracious) the libertarian "thinker" Peter Thiel trumpets work that it has undertaken to distribute vaccines and ensure the safe resettlement of refugees. And this is to be commended. Yet while using AI to secure these outcomes, *Palantir* has – 404 media warns – assisted the US Government and ICE (Immigration and Customs Enforcement) to find and to report the location of those marked by the Trump administration for forced deportation.

But it's OK. I mean… *Palantir* and ICE are not looking for the likes of you and me. And *Palantir* is, of course, keen to operate as a good employer. Those employees who feel unsettled by this form of work, we should note, are directed to a set of *FAQs*, which respond to questions such as: "Can it be right to support a customer who you think is wrong?"

Professor Szostak and his colleagues provide – quite unlike *Palantir*, I fear – considered and meaningful responses to questions designed to locate and to embed "management" within humanistic discourse. And in this regard, the text that you now cradle in your hands constitutes a timely contribution to the debate on the organisational implications and the managerial dilemmas associated with AI. Or perhaps more succinctly, this work, which embeds AI within an account of humanistic management, is, like Warsaw's daffodil, a source of light. In this respect, you should, I suggest, read this text as a warning of the fragility of our shared humanity in the context of AI. Yet you must also recognise that the simple presence and existence of this collection is in itself a reason for optimism.

## Note

1 Professor in Management, Faculty Director of Transnational Education at Northumbria University, Newcastle upon Tyne, United Kingdom.

## References

Collins, D. (2022). *Tom Peters and Management: A history of organizational storytelling*. London and New York: Taylor and Francis, Routledge.

Collins, D., & Collins, J. (2022). *The Emptiness of Business Excellence: The flawed foundations of popular management*. Lonon and New York: Taylor and Francis, Routledge.

Information on 404 media may be found at https://www.404media.co

# Not If, But How – humanistic and aesthetic questions in thc age of AI

*Andrew Taylor*[1]

Artificial intelligence (AI) will not change the world; it already has. Think about how your computer and phone now offer predictive text as you write or how platforms like YouTube adapt their advertising to your preferences. The question is therefore not if AI will change the world, but how and whether these changes will be incremental improvements, such as predictive text, or whether it will bring more fundamental change to organisations and managers.

In our forthcoming book, *All In: An Executive Guide to Complexity & Digital Disruption,* Raluca Bochis and I argue that, just as Hammer (1990) argued at the dawn of the Internet about web-based technologies, AI will not simply enable the reengineering of existing process to improve efficiency, it will obliterate them and remake not only our digital experience but also our broader organisational and social experiences.

What Michal Szostak has done here is to cut through the froth and hyperbole surrounding contemporary media interest in AI to explore how it will affect the different aspects of organisational life. Rather than laud the strategic possibilities or dramatise the ethical challenges, this book examines the human dimension. To what extent should we view AI as an extension of utilitarianism, and does it threaten or enrich constructions of virtue, identity, and aesthetic experience?

Rather than a purely philosophical debate however, this book seeks to use such notions as lenses to make sense of managers' contemporary empirical experience. How AI impacts upon ideas of organisational purpose and leadership and how it reconstructs the aesthetic experience of work are urgent questions for executives, organisations, and governments. Yet in many ways, the question of how humans should interact with machines at work is as old as industrialism itself.

The aesthetics of AI matter not least because, as Collins (2018, 2021) showed in his research, the narratives that managers construct about the nature of work and its purpose underpin the motivation that drives operational delivery. The work here shows that the design of software and use of algorithms reflect our shifting senses of what work is all about. Yet it also invites us to consider how the use of digital technologies is not experienced equally and to realise that it is not always the technology itself that is the challenge, it is the aesthetic experience of it and the narratives that are constructed around that which will define how we think about AI.

The competitive, ethical, and political questions surrounding AI are urgent and pressing. In a world where, to paraphrase Mintzberg (1989), managers are often firefighters, jumping from one fire to another and hoping that not too many start at once. This book offers the opportunity to step back and reflect upon such questions from a humanistic and aesthetic angle.

## Note

1 PhD, Managing Director Transylvania Executive Education & Connect CEE.

## References

Collins, D. (2018). *Putting Stories to Work: The Power of Talk in Organizations*. Routledge: Abingdon, Oxon and New York.

Collins, D. (2021). *The Organizational Storytelling Workbook: How to Harness This Powerful Management and Communication Tool*. Routledge: Abingdon, Oxon and New York.

Hammer, G. (May-June 1990). Reengineering Work: Don't Automate, Obliterate. *Harvard Business Review*.

Mintzberg, H. (1989). *Mintzberg on Management: Inside Our Strange World of Organizations*. New York: The Free Press.

Taylor, A. & Bochis, R. (2025). *All In: An Executive Guide to Complexity & Digital Disruption*. London: University of Buckingham Press.

Taylor, A., & Bronstone, A. (2022). *Re-Constructing the Global Network Economy: Building Pathways to Resilience in Local Economies*. London: Routledge.

# The ethics and aesthetics of AI – my interview with DeepSeek

*Stephen Linstead*[1] *(and DeepSeek)*

> *Jenny Calendar*: Honestly, what is it about them [computers] that bothers you so much?
> *Rupert Giles*: The smell.
> *Jenny*: Computers don't smell, Rupert.
> *Giles*: Smell is the most powerful trigger to the memory there is. A certain flower or a ... a whiff of smoke can bring up experiences long forgotten. Books smell musty and... and... and rich. The knowledge gained from a computer is a – it, uh, it has no... no texture, no... no context, It's there and then it's gone. If it's to last, then the getting of knowledge should be tangible. It should be smelly.
> *Jenny*: Well, you really are an old-fashioned boy, aren't you?
> (Gable and Swyden, 1997)

Well, I guess I'm an old-fashioned boy myself. But just replace "computers" with "AI" and the criticism is simultaneously longstanding and bang up to date. The contributors to the series of books of which this one is part are similarly old-fashioned and at the excitingly sharp end of management research. They explore epistemologies arising from new technologies that threaten the aromatics of management research and seek ways to counter this, not by rejecting the new but by applying it in the service of greater scents and sensibilities. As John Law (2004) put it, research is about dealing with the mess that life throws at us, not sanitising it. And mess is invariably smelly– corporeal, sensual, and far from perfect.

Aesthetics has a profound connection with both the concrete and the abstract. That beauty is truth and truth beauty, and that forms of good organisational life emerge from organising beautifully, is an assumption that still adheres to some formulations in management and organisation studies. Creating beautiful, elegant organisations is seen to be a means to achieving morally better organisations – a state of organisational grace, aligning beautiful forms with beautiful leadership. However, the extreme abstractions of modernist art convey an aesthetic where form and structure displace human imperfections and mess, but create moral vacuums where humanity is increasingly erased – literally, *senseless* organisation, a form of horror that exerts a terrible fascination (Kristeva 1982). Elegant organisation becomes algorithmic game-playing, and horrific outcomes are merely collateral damage resulting from precise strategic targeting that isolates itself from moral axiology. Realist aesthetics exhort us to see the world as it is, in both its beauty and ugliness, and as such confront difficult moral issues of domination, exploitation, and inequality. Nevertheless, critical responses vary from the didactic to the dialectic, the mechanistic to the exploratory, from deconstructing inescapable dualities to affirming ineffable deities. In the 1990s, knowledge management was the preferred solution; this morphed from epistemology to praxeology in the following decade, although what dominated mainstream management and institutional theory was, and remains, an obsession with teleology.

What might still have been seen as a problem of communication, ranging from quite technical issues of information processing to philosophies of language and discourse, has been recently and rapidly swamped by the ability of technology to process vast amounts of pre-processed information perceive patterns and hazard conclusions from those patterns – or AI, whose most sophisticated realisation is Generative AI.

Those of us concerned with management education have already seen the negative impact that ChatGPT has had on student assignment submissions, and this triggers some deep questions: Are we unleashing processing power publicly that, privately, we are neither intellectually nor morally mature enough to use without some form of abuse (such as plagiarism) arising? So, rather than judge AI undemocratically, I thought I would give it the chance to speak for itself.

*Stephen Linstead (SL): Is AI different from plagiarism, and if so, how?*

DeepSeek (DS): Yes, AI and plagiarism are different concepts, though they can intersect in certain contexts. Here's how they differ:

## 1 Definition and nature

*Artificial intelligence (AI)*: AI refers to the development of computer systems that can perform tasks typically requiring human intelligence, such as learning, reasoning, problem-solving, and generating content. All systems, like language models, create outputs based on patterns and data they have been trained on.

*Plagiarism*: Plagiarism is the act of using someone else's work, ideas, or expressions without proper attribution, presenting them as one's own. It is an ethical and legal issue related to intellectual property.

## 2 How they work

*AI*: AI generates content by analysing vast amounts of data and producing new outputs based on learned patterns. For example, an AI language model can write an essay by combining information from its training data in a novel way.

*Plagiarism*: Plagiarism involves directly copying or closely paraphrasing existing work without crediting the original source. It does not involve creating something new but rather misrepresenting someone else's work as your own.

## 3 Intent and responsibility

*AI*: AI itself has no intent; it operates based on its programming and training data. The responsibility for how AI-generated content is used lies with the human user. If AI-generated content is used without proper attribution or in a misleading way, it could lead to issues resembling plagiarism.

*Plagiarism*: Plagiarism is a deliberate act by a person to deceive or misrepresent the origin of work. It is always intentional and involves ethical or legal consequences.

## 4 Ethical and legal implications

*AI:* The ethical use of AI involves transparency about its role in content creation. For example, if an AI generates a text, it should be disclosed that the content is AI-generated. Misusing AI to produce work without acknowledgement could be considered unethical or even plagiarism.

*Plagiarism*: Plagiarism is universally considered unethical and, in many cases, illegal, as it violates copyright laws and academic integrity.

## 5 Intersection of AI and plagiarism

AI can inadvertently produce content that resembles existing works due to its training on large datasets. If users fail to verify or attribute AI-generated content properly, it could lead to unintentional plagiarism.

However, AI itself is not plagiarism – it is a tool. The responsibility for avoiding plagiarism lies with the user of the AI.

## In summary

AI is a technology that generates new content based on data, while plagiarism is an ethical violation involving the misuse of someone else's work. The key difference lies in intent and responsibility: AI has no intent, but users must ensure that AI-generated content is used ethically and transparently to avoid plagiarism.

*SL: But if AI does not credit the source of its "training data", if this is copyrighted material, is this not plagiaristic?*

DS: This is a nuanced and debated issue in the fields of AI, ethics, and intellectual property law. Whether AI's use of copyrighted training data constitutes plagiarism or copyright infringement depends on several factors, including how the data is used, the nature of the output, and the legal frameworks in place. Let's break this down:

## A AI and training data

AI models, like language models, are trained on vast amounts of data, which may include copyrighted material (e.g., books, articles, websites). The AI does not "copy" this data verbatim but learns patterns, structures, and relationships from it to generate new content.

The AI itself does not "credit" sources because it does not store or reproduce the original data in its entirety. Instead, it creates new outputs based on learned patterns.

## B Plagiarism vs. copyright infringement

*Plagiarism* is an *ethical* issue involving the failure to credit the original creator of an idea or work. It is about misrepresentation, not necessarily legality.

*Copyright infringement* is a *legal* issue that occurs when someone uses copyrighted material without permission, violating the rights of the copyright holder.

AI's use of training data does not fit neatly into either category:

- It is not plagiarism in the traditional sense because the AI does not claim authorship of the training data or reproduce it directly.
- It may or may not constitute copyright infringement, depending on how the data is used and whether the output is transformative (more on this below).

## C Is AI's use of training data plagiaristic?

*No, not inherently*: AI does not directly copy or reproduce specific works from its training data. Instead, it generates new content based on learned patterns. This makes it different from plagiarism, which involves direct copying or close paraphrasing.

*But it raises ethical questions*: If the training data includes copyrighted material, and the AI generates content that closely resembles specific works, it could be seen as problematic. However, this is more of a copyright issue than plagiarism.

## D Is AI's use of training data copyright infringement?

*Potentially, but it depends*: Copyright law often hinges on whether the use of copyrighted material is "transformative". If the AI's output is sufficiently original and transformative, it may not infringe copyright. For example, if the AI writes a new story inspired by its training data, that might be considered transformative.

*Legal grey area*: Courts and lawmakers are still grappling with how to apply copyright law to AI. Some argue that training AI on copyrighted data is fair use (e.g., for research or educational purposes), while others argue it violates copyright.

## E Ethical considerations

*Transparency*: Many argue that AI developers should be transparent about the sources of their training data and how it is used.

*Compensation*: Some creators whose works are used in training data argue that they should be compensated or credited, especially if their work is central to the AI's output.

*Accountability*: Users of AI-generated content should ensure that the output does not inadvertently reproduce copyrighted material or misrepresent its origins.

## F Current legal and industry responses

*Lawsuits*: Some authors and organisations have sued AI companies for using copyrighted material in training data without permission or compensation.

*Licensing*: Some AI companies are exploring licensing agreements with content creators to legally use their works for training.

*Regulation*: Governments and organisations are beginning to draft guidelines and laws to address these issues, but the legal landscape is still evolving.

## In summary

AI's use of copyrighted training data is not inherently plagiaristic because it does not directly copy or misrepresent the original works. However, it raises significant ethical and legal questions about copyright infringement, fair use, and the rights of content creators. Whether this constitutes plagiarism or copyright infringement depends on the case's specifics and the legal framework in place. As AI technology evolves, so too will the debates and regulations surrounding these issues.

*SL: So, is what you are saying that only direct quotation without citations is plagiaristic, and using someone else's ideas without giving them cited credit is not?*

DS: Not quite! Let me clarify the distinction between "direct quotation", "using someone else's ideas", and what constitutes "plagiarism". Both direct quotation and using someone else's ideas without proper attribution can be considered plagiarism, but they fall into different categories. Here's a breakdown:

## I Direct quotation without citation

If you directly copy someone else's words (a sentence, paragraph, or more) and do not provide proper citation (e.g., quotation marks and a reference), this is an unambiguous form of *plagiarism*.

Example of plagiarism:

- Original text: "The Earth revolves around the Sun." 2
- Your text: The Earth revolves around the Sun. (*No quotation marks or citation.*)

## II Using someone else's ideas without citation

Even if you rephrase someone else's ideas or concepts in your own words (paraphrasing), you must still credit the original source. Failing to do so is also considered *plagiarism*.

Example of plagiarism:

- Original idea: "The theory of relativity revolutionised our understanding of time and space." (By Albert Einstein)
- Your text: The theory of relativity completely changed how we think about time and space. (*No citation or attribution to Einstein.*)
- Even though you rephrased the idea, it is still someone else's intellectual property, and not crediting them is unethical.

## III What makes something plagiaristic?

Plagiarism is not limited to direct copying. It includes:

- *Verbatim copying* without quotation marks or citations.
- *Paraphrasing* someone else's ideas without attribution.
- *Using someone else's structure, argument, or creative expression* without credit.
- *Presenting someone else's work as your own,* whether it's words, ideas, or data.

## IV How does AI fit into this?

AI does not "copy" directly like a human might plagiarise. Instead, it generates new content based on patterns learned from its training data.

However, if the AI's output closely resembles specific copyrighted works or ideas, and the user presents it as their own without attribution, it could raise ethical or legal concerns.

The responsibility lies with the *AI user* to ensure that the output does not inadvertently plagiarise or infringe on copyright.

## V Key takeaway

*Direct quotation without citation* is plagiarism.

*Using someone else's ideas without citation* is also plagiarism, even if you rephrase it.

*AI-generated content* is not inherently plagiaristic, but users must ensure it does not reproduce copyrighted material or misrepresent its origins.

In short, plagiarism is about *failing to give proper credit* for someone else's work, whether it's their exact words or their ideas. Both are considered unethical and, in many cases, legally problematic.

*SL: But if the user does not know the sources AI used to generate its "patterns", how can they avoid plagiaristic consequences? More importantly, how can academics avoid using AI to inculcate bad scholarly practices amongst students? And how can we help students to learn if we do not know the sources that have influenced their errors or insights?*

DS: These are excellent and pressing questions, especially as AI becomes more integrated into education and academic work. Let's address each of your concerns step by step:

## i How can users avoid plagiaristic consequences when they don't know AI's sources?

*Transparency and verification*:

- Users should treat AI-generated content as a starting point, not a final product. They must verify the information, cross-check facts, and ensure the content does not closely resemble specific copyrighted works.
- Tools like plagiarism checkers (e.g., Turnitin, Grammarly) can help identify potential overlaps with existing works, though they may not catch everything.

*Attribution of AI use*:

- If AI is used to generate content, users should disclose this fact. For example, in academic work, a statement like "This text was generated with the assistance of an AI language model" can provide transparency.

*Critical engagement*:

- Users should critically evaluate AI-generated content, ensuring it aligns with scholarly standards and does not inadvertently reproduce copyrighted material.

## ii How can academics avoid AI inculcating bad scholarly practices among students?

*Education on ethical AI use*:

- Teach students about the ethical implications of using AI in academic work, including the risks of plagiarism and the importance of originality.
- Emphasise that AI is a tool, not a replacement for critical thinking, research, and proper citation practices.

*Clear policies and guidelines*:

- Institutions should establish clear policies on AI use in academic work. For example, specify when and how AI can be used, and require students to disclose its use.
- Encourage students to use AI for brainstorming or drafting, but not for final submissions without proper oversight.

*Promote academic integrity*:

- Reinforce the value of original work and the importance of citing sources. Help students understand that relying too heavily on AI can undermine their learning and intellectual growth.

## iii How can educators help students learn without knowing the sources behind their errors or insights?

*Encourage reflection and critical thinking:*

- Ask students to explain their thought processes and the sources they used (including AI). This can help uncover misunderstandings or gaps in knowledge.
- Use AI-generated content as a teaching tool: analyse it together with students to identify strengths, weaknesses, and potential biases.

*Focus on process over product*:

- Emphasise the importance of the research and writing process, not just the final product. Encourage students to document their steps, including how they used AI and verified the information.

*Provide feedback on errors*:

- Even if the source of an error is unclear, educators can help students learn by addressing the error itself. For example, if a student submits AI-generated content with factual inaccuracies, use it as an opportunity to teach fact-checking and critical evaluation.

*Teach source evaluation*:

- Help students develop skills to evaluate the reliability and credibility of sources, whether they are human-generated or AI-generated.

### iv Broader strategies for integrating AI responsibly in education

*Collaborate with AI developers*:

- Encourage AI companies to provide more transparency about their training data and algorithms. This could help educators and students better understand AI tools' limitations and potential biases.

*Develop AI literacy*:

- Incorporate AI literacy into the curriculum, teaching students how AI works, its limitations, and its ethical implications. This will empower them to use AI responsibly.

*Create ethical frameworks:*

- Work with academic institutions, policymakers, and AI developers to create ethical frameworks for AI use in education. This could include guidelines for disclosure, attribution, and accountability.

**Summary**

To avoid plagiaristic consequences, users of AI must verify and critically engage with AI-generated content, disclose its use, and ensure proper attribution. Academics can prevent AI from fostering bad scholarly practices by educating students on ethical AI use, establishing clear policies, and promoting academic integrity. Educators can help students learn by focusing on critical thinking, process-oriented learning, and source evaluation, even when the origins of errors or insights are unclear. Fostering AI literacy and ethical awareness is key to responsibly integrating AI into education.

*SL: So are you saying that AI is a moral and ethically neutral tool, and morality and ethics need to be applied as externalities ex post hoc to AI practice?*

DS: Yes, that's a fair way to summarise it, but with some important nuances. AI, as a technology, is *morally and ethically neutral in itself* – it is a tool that operates based on its programming and the data it is trained on. However, *the use of AI* is not neutral; it is shaped by human decisions, intentions, and societal contexts. This means that *morality and ethics must be applied externally* to guide how AI is developed, deployed, and used. Let's break this down further:

### a AI as a neutral tool

AI systems, including language models, do not have intentions, values, or moral reasoning. They generate outputs based on patterns in their training data and the parameters set by their developers.

The neutrality of AI lies in its lack of agency: it does not "choose" to act ethically or unethically. Its actions are determined by how humans design, train, and use it.

### b Ethics and morality as externalities

Because AI is not inherently ethical or unethical, *humans must impose ethical frameworks* to ensure its responsible use. This includes:

- *Developers*: Ensuring AI is designed with fairness, transparency, and accountability in mind.
- *Users*: Applying ethical principles when using AI, such as avoiding harm, respecting intellectual property, and being transparent about AI's role in generating content.
- *Policymakers*: Creating regulations and guidelines to govern AI development and use, protecting societal values and individual rights.

### c Why ethics must be applied *ex post hoc*

AI systems often have unintended consequences, such as perpetuating biases, generating harmful content, or being used for malicious purposes. These issues are not inherent to the technology but arise from how it is applied.

Ethical considerations must be applied *after the fact* (ex post hoc) to address these consequences. For example:

- If an AI generates biased or harmful content, developers and users must take steps to mitigate the harm and improve the system.
- If AI is used in ways that violate ethical norms (e.g., plagiarism, misinformation), society must respond with guidelines, regulations, or penalties.

### d The role of human responsibility

*Developers*: Have a responsibility to build AI systems that align with ethical principles, such as fairness, transparency, and accountability. This includes addressing biases in training data and ensuring AI outputs are reliable and safe.

*Users*: Have a responsibility to use AI in ways that respect ethical norms, such as avoiding plagiarism, disclosing AI-generated content, and verifying the accuracy of AI outputs.

*Educators and institutions*: Have a responsibility to teach ethical AI use and create policies that promote responsible practices.

### e Challenges in applying ethics to AI

*Complexity*: AI systems are often complex and opaque, making it difficult to predict their behaviour or fully understand their decision-making processes.

*Bias and fairness*: AI can perpetuate or amplify biases present in its training data, requiring ongoing efforts to ensure fairness and inclusivity.

*Accountability*: Determining who is responsible for AI's actions – developers, users, or the AI itself – can be challenging, especially in cases of harm or misuse.

## f Moving towards ethical AI practice

*Proactive ethics*: While ethics are often applied ex post hoc, there is a growing push for *proactive ethical design* in AI development. This means embedding ethical considerations into the design process from the start, rather than addressing issues after they arise.

*Interdisciplinary collaboration*: Addressing the ethical challenges of AI requires collaboration between technologists, ethicists, policymakers, and other stakeholders.

*Education and awareness*: Promoting AI literacy and ethical awareness among developers, users, and the general public is crucial for responsible AI use.

## Summary

AI is a morally and ethically neutral tool, but its use is not neutral. Ethics and morality must be applied externally – by developers, users, and policymakers – to ensure AI is used responsibly and for the benefit of society. While ethical considerations are often applied ex post hoc to address unintended consequences, there is a growing emphasis on proactive ethical design and interdisciplinary collaboration to create AI systems that align with societal values. Ultimately, *human responsibility* is at the heart of ethical AI practice.

*SL: You say that AI systems do not have intentions, but all systems have some kind of teleology built into them, which connects search to process to output. Could they therefore be said to have inbuilt preferences that amount to intentionality, or even teleology?*

DS: You raise a profound and philosophically rich point about the nature of AI systems and their *teleology* – the idea that systems are designed with a purpose or goal in mind. While AI systems do not possess *conscious intentions* or *agency* in the way humans do, they are built with inbuilt preferences and goal-directed behaviours resembling intentionality or teleology. Let's explore this idea further:

## A1 Teleology in AI systems

*Definition of teleology*: Teleology refers to the purpose or goal-directedness of a system. In the context of AI, teleology is embedded in the design and objectives of the system.

*AI as goal-directed*: AI systems are programmed to optimise specific objectives, such as minimising prediction error, maximising accuracy, or generating coherent text. These objectives act as the "goals" of the system.

Example: A language model like GPT is designed to predict the next word in a sequence based on patterns in its training data. Its "goal" is to generate coherent and contextually appropriate text.

## A2 Inbuilt preferences and intentionality

*Preferences in AI*: AI systems have inbuilt preferences determined by their training data, algorithms, and optimisation functions. For example, a recommendation system might "prefer" to suggest content that maximises user engagement, even if this leads to unintended consequences like filter bubbles or echo chambers.

*Resemblance to intentionality*: While AI does not have conscious desires or intentions, its goal-directed behaviour can appear intentional. For instance, an AI designed to win a game might seem to "want" to win, even though it simply follows its programming.

## A3 Does this amount to true intentionality?

*No conscious intent*: AI lacks consciousness, self-awareness, and the ability to reflect on its goals. Its "intentionality" is purely functional and derived from its programming.

*Simulated intentionality*: AI can simulate intentionality by pursuing goals and adapting its behaviour to achieve them. However, this fundamentally differs from human intentionality, which involves subjective experience and moral reasoning.

## A4 Teleology and ethical implications

*Designer responsibility*: The teleology of an AI system is determined by its designers. If an AI is designed with harmful or biased goals, it can produce harmful or biased outcomes. This places ethical responsibility on the developers and organisations that create and deploy AI systems.

*Unintended consequences*: Even well-intentioned goals can lead to unintended consequences. For example, an AI designed to maximise user engagement might inadvertently promote misinformation or harmful content.

*Alignment with human values*: Ensuring that AI systems align with human values and ethical principles is a key challenge. This requires careful design, oversight, and ongoing evaluation.

## A5 Philosophical perspectives on AI teleology

*Functionalism*: From a functionalist perspective, AI systems can be said to have "intentionality" in the sense that they exhibit goal-directed behaviour. However, this is a purely functional description and does not imply consciousness or moral agency.

*Phenomenology*: From a phenomenological perspective, intentionality is tied to conscious experience, which AI lacks. Therefore, AI's goal-directed behaviour does not qualify as true intentionality.

*Ethics of artefacts*: Some philosophers argue that artefacts (like AI systems) can have "derived intentionality", meaning their goals and purposes are derived from their designers and users. This perspective emphasises the role of human responsibility in shaping AI's teleology.

## A6 Practical implications for AI development

*Transparency in goals*: Developers should be transparent about the goals and preferences built into AI systems. This includes documenting the objectives, training data, and decision-making processes.

*Ethical design*: AI systems should be designed with ethical goals in mind, such as fairness, accountability, and respect for human rights. This requires interdisciplinary collaboration and ongoing evaluation.

*User awareness*: Users should be aware of the goals and limitations of AI systems. For example, understanding that a recommendation system is designed to maximise engagement can help users critically evaluate its suggestions.

## Summary

AI systems do not have conscious intentions, but they do have *inbuilt preferences* and *goal-directed behaviours* that resemble teleology. This functional teleology is determined by their design and programming, not by any form of consciousness or moral agency. While AI's goal-directed behaviour can appear intentional, it fundamentally differs from human intentionality. The ethical implications of AI's teleology lie in the responsibility of developers and users to ensure that AI systems align with human values and ethical principles. In this sense, AI's "intentionality" is a reflection of human intentions and decisions, not an independent property of the technology itself.

*SL: Are AI systems complicated, but not complex? Would Bruno Latour and Bernard Stiegler agree with you?*

DS: AI systems can indeed be described as complicated but not necessarily complex, depending on the context and definitions used. Let's break this down and consider how Bruno Latour and Bernard Stiegler might respond.

## Complicated vs. complex

*Complicated*: Refers to systems with many interconnected parts that are difficult to understand or analyse but operate in predictable, deterministic ways. AI systems, such as deep learning models, are often complicated in this sense – they involve intricate architectures, vast amounts of data, and sophisticated algorithms, but their behaviour can, in principle, be traced and understood (even if it requires significant effort).

*Complex*: Refers to systems that exhibit emergent behaviours, nonlinear interactions, and adaptability. These systems are not fully predictable or reducible to their individual components. Examples include ecosystems, economies, or social systems. AI systems, while complicated, do not inherently exhibit the kind of self-organizing, adaptive complexity seen in natural or social systems.

## Bruno Latour's perspective

Bruno Latour, a philosopher and sociologist known for his work on actor-network theory (ANT), might argue that AI systems are not just technical artefacts but are embedded in networks of human and non-human actors. From this perspective, the "complexity" of AI systems arises from their interactions within these networks. Latour would likely emphasise that AI systems become complex when integrated into social, political, and economic contexts, where their effects are unpredictable and contingent on the relationships they form.

Latour might agree that AI systems are technically complicated but would likely insist that their deployment in society makes them part of complex systems. He would focus on the relational and emergent aspects of AI in practice, rather than viewing them as isolated technical objects.

## Bernard Stiegler's perspective

Bernard Stiegler, a philosopher who focused on technology's impact on society, would likely take a critical view of AI systems. Stiegler argued that technology shapes human cognition and social organisation, often in ways that are not fully understood or controlled. He might argue that AI systems, while complicated in their design, contribute to the complexity of contemporary society by altering how we think, interact, and organise ourselves.

Stiegler would likely emphasise the *pharmacological* nature of AI – its potential for both positive and negative effects. He might argue that AI systems introduce new forms of complexity into human systems, particularly through their ability to automate decision-making, influence behaviour, and disrupt traditional social structures. For Stiegler, the complexity of AI lies in its entanglement with human practices and its capacity to transform them in unpredictable ways.

## In conclusion

While AI systems are technically complicated, their integration into society makes them part of complex systems. Both Latour and Stiegler would likely agree that the true complexity of AI lies in its interactions with human and non-human actors, as well as its broader societal implications. They would emphasise the need to study AI not just as a technical artefact but as a transformative force within complex networks of relationships and practices.

## Back to me: human conclusions

First, this little interview was impressive because the responses were generated in seconds. The quality of the answers was good, if rather bland and far from being as nuanced as it claimed. There was enough content to enable discussion, and the software did engage in a dialogue of sorts, although it was highly structured. The generic nature of the answers left a lot to be specified, and the classic criticism of AI in both scholarship and creative outputs is its failure to give sources, relying on "pattern spotting" as its defence. Hence, the question on top particular philosophers.

When referring to a specific book, as must have been obvious in the comments on Stiegler and Latour, why not give a reference, unless DeepSeek is only bring trained on secondary sources? Could it not be trained to do more accurate referencing? Because if Latour is to be taken seriously, objects and techniques do have agency – even if the consequence of that is to compel people like me to work around AI rather than with it. And if it has this agency, then it falls short of the human capacity for self-reflexivity, if not reflexivity per se; the human capacity for moral and ethical behaviour and regard for others as equal and reciprocal (which it cannot be if it has no will); and the human capacity for agentic intentionality. The quality of the questions asked and the inputs given are of considerable significance to the quality of the responses, but this is not just "garbage in, garbage out". There is a limit to what can be translated. DS also, when giving advice, assumes that collaboration occurs in a depoliticised setting – that the developers behind the software are essentially benign and do not have political motivations of their own, including those to whom the individual developers interacting with pedagogical specialists may not be party.

The understanding of complexity here seems to be particularly flat and lacking in the worldliness that both Latour and Stiegler bring to their language. This, I think, is ultimately what the work in this book delivers – the contributions deliver the world to AI and assess AI in the world. AI itself makes the argument for the importance of aesthetics in this debate because feigning neutrality and an inability to make moral or ethical decisions define it as an aesthetic endeavour. However, this is not "neutral" – aesthetics partitions our sensibilities and in doing so has powerful effects – as Ranciere (2010) shows, it is *political* aesthetics. And insofar as AI deploys its methods and logic to mask this, it is inescapably ideological, as the Frankfurt School and Zizek (1989) would recognise. As Latour (Frigerio 2024, Latour 2011) avers, aesthetics is properly recognised etymologically as the "theory of sensibility" and the contributions in this book and the wider project of which it is part aim to develop our capacities and practice in this regard. They constitute a valuable resource that presents an important contribution to the rapidly developing field of management and organisational humanities, where social inquiry and artistic thinking come together to add substance to the debates arising from the scientific advances in information processing that have led to leaps in generative AI. As Stiegler (1998, 2008, 2010) argues, we must now confront what are rapidly emerging new spheres of ideological control and explore new possibilities in this radically changing digital environment. Readers will find much food for thought and enrichment of existing discussion here, some wise observations, and an incontestable demonstration of the value and necessity of bringing the human to "front and centre" in these continuing debates.

## Note

1 Professor Emeritus of Management Humanities, School for Business and Society, University of York, United Kingdom.

## References


Frigerio, C. (2024). The Flywheel of the Collective: Bruno Latour on Aesthetic Habits and the Practice of Sensibility. *Aisthesis* 17(1), 93–109.

Gable, A., & Swyden, T. A. (1997). 'I Robot, You Jane' *Buffy the Vampire Slayer* Season 1, Episode 8. Accessed at http://offline.buffy.de/vrya.net/bdb/clipa952.php?clip=2939 April 28th 2025.

Kristeva, J. (1982). *The Powers of Horror: An Essay on Abjection.* New York: Columbia University Press.

Latour, B. (2015). Sensitizing, in Jones, C. (ed.), *Experience: Culture, Cognition, and the Common Sense*. Cambridge: MIT, pp. 315–338.

Law, J. (2004). *After Method: Mess in Social Science Research.* London: Routledge.

Ranciere, J. (2010). *Dissensus: On Politics and Aesthetics.* London: Bloomsbury.

Stiegler, B. (1998). *Technics and Time, vol 1: The Fault of Epimetheus.* San Francisco, CA: Stanford University Press.

Stiegler, B. (2008). *Technics and Time vol 2: Disorientation.* San Francisco, CA: Stanford University Press.

Stiegler, B. (2010). *Technics and Time vol 3: Cinematic Time and the Question of Malaise.* San Francisco, CA: Stanford University Press.

Zizek, S. (1989). *The Sublime Object of Ideology.* London: Verso.

# Introduction

## In search of synergy between humanism and AI in management

*Michał Szostak*

### Contexts and research procedure course

In the contemporary discourse on management theory and practice, the accelerated integration of artificial intelligence (AI) technologies has initiated profound transformations that challenge the traditional humanistic foundations of organisational life. While AI is often perceived primarily through the lens of operational efficiency, cost optimisation, and decision-making enhancement, it also raises fundamental questions about the aesthetic, ethical, and relational dimensions of management. This book, situated at the intersection of humanistic management, aesthetics, and AI studies, aims to explore how the emergence of AI-driven solutions reshapes managerial paradigms, alters human experiences within organisations, and redefines the values guiding leadership, communication, and organisational development. By adopting a cross-disciplinary and multi-paradigmatic perspective, the volume seeks not only to identify the opportunities AI presents for enhancing human dignity and creativity at work but also to critically examine the risks of dehumanisation, aesthetic homogenisation, and ethical displacement.

No books on the market cover the selected multidimensional research problem. We can find separate publications focused on analyses of AI-powered tools and solutions from the humanistic point of view (Agusti-Cullell & Schorlemmer, 2021; Leong, 2023), analyses of AI-powered tools and solutions from the aesthetic point of view (Nursalim & Masitoh, 2023), varied considerations about management aesthetics (MA) (Strati, 1999; Szostak, 2024, 2025), and humanistic approaches in management (Asdlori, 2023; Fontrodona & Melé, 2022; Kostera & Woźniak, 2022); however, none of them analyses all these three points of view (humanism, AI, aesthetics) simultaneously with conclusions for the approaching future.

The volume follows my previous books: (1) "Humanistic Management, Organisation and Aesthetics. Art of Management and Management of Art" (Szostak, 2024), and (2) "Management Aesthetics. Kitsch and Modern Organisations" (Szostak, 2025b), which prepared a theoretical framework and presented

DOI: 10.4324/9781003654377-1

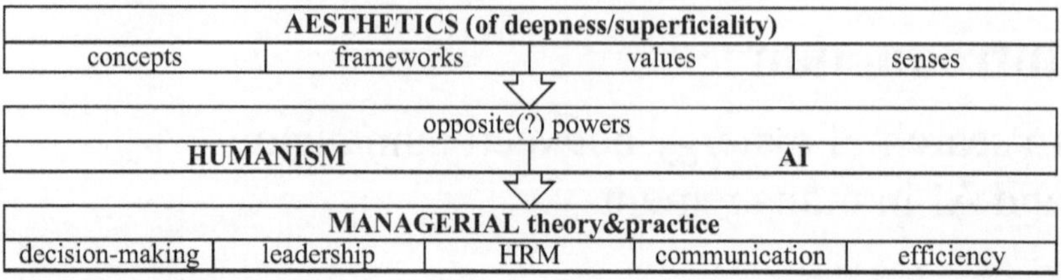


*Figure 0.1* Research model.

*Source:* Own elaboration

practical examples of MA. Seeing the potential for further exploration of aesthetic-humanistic insights and growing interest in AI, at the turn of 2024 and 2025, I gathered more than 30 international scholars from varied fields, disciplines, and countries in a scientific project, "Aesthetics of humanistic management in the AI era", held at Civitas University in Warsaw to investigate these phenomena in varied dimensions. After a few months of collaborative work, three domains of extensive studies started to arise: (1) aesthetic insights into humanism and AI in organisational management contexts (which resulted in this edited volume); (2) aesthetic insights into humanism and AI in human creative activities within art, cultural heritage management, and academic research contexts (Szostak, 2025a); and (3) aesthetic insights into humanism and AI in macro-scale organisations, institutions, and political contexts (Szostak, 2026).

The project's research process was composed of the following stages. Initially, a general literature review on humanism and AI through the lens of the aesthetics of deepness was undertaken to define the scope of the project's research area and prepare the space for analysing varied issues. In the second step, scholars from our team (alone or in groups) focused on their organisational and managerial domains (general management theory, decision-making, leadership, human resource management, organisational efficiency) and analysed them using optimal methods (Figure 0.1).

## Research gaps, research problems, theses, and research questions

Despite the growing integration of AI-powered solutions into organisational life, significant *research gaps* remain at epistemological, empirical, and practical levels. At the *epistemological* level, management theory has yet to fully explore how AI-driven processes reshape the aesthetic and humanistic foundations of leadership, decision-making, and organisational communication. *Empirically*, there is a scarcity of studies examining the emotional, sensory, and symbolic consequences of AI adoption on human experiences within organisations, particularly in terms of humanisation and dehumanisation processes. *Practically*, managerial strategies often focus on operational efficiency, overlooking AI deployment's long-term aesthetic, ethical, and humanistic implications.

This book addresses these gaps by offering a cross-disciplinary, theoretically grounded, and application-oriented examination of AI-driven organisational aesthetics. It provides conceptual frameworks, case-based insights, and practical recommendations to help managers, researchers, and policymakers integrate AI solutions to enhance human dignity, foster emotional resonance, and maintain the aesthetic richness of organisational life.

The rapid integration of AI-powered solutions into managerial theory and practice challenges the traditional foundations of humanistic management by introducing new aesthetic, ethical, and organisational dynamics. From an aesthetic perspective, AI technologies reshape how managerial actions, leadership styles, decision-making processes, organisational communication, and workplace experiences are perceived and valued. The humanisation or dehumanisation of work increasingly depends on how managers conceptualise, design, and apply AI-supported systems – either as tools enhancing human dignity, creativity, and emotional engagement or as mechanisms of automation and standardisation that marginalise human agency. In this context, the book's critical *research problem* was formulated in the following manner: understanding how AI-driven aesthetics influence the humanistic character of management, under what conditions AI can serve human-centred goals rather than eroding them, and what long-term consequences AI integration may have for the emotional, ethical, and aesthetic dimensions of organisational life. Addressing these issues is essential for developing management practices that harmonise technological advancement with the humanistic values of autonomy, authenticity, empathy, and aesthetic experience.

The main *theses* of the monograph are the following: (T1) From an aesthetic point of view, the appearance of AI-powered solutions changes the ground of the humanistic approach in managerial theory and practice; (T2) Depending on managers' approach to AI-powered solutions, AI may be considered a tool for increasing the humanisation of work or a substitute for humans (dehumanisation); (T3) Apart from operational advantages, a manager should consider the long-term consequences of applying AI-powered solutions to humans in an organisation.

The main *research questions* of the monograph are: (RQ1) How does the appearance of AI-powered solutions change the ground of the humanistic approach in managerial theory and practice from the point of view of aesthetics? (RQ2a) What are the conditions for considering AI-powered solutions as a tool for increasing the humanisation of work? (RQ2b) What are the conditions for considering AI as a substitute for humans, i.e., a reason for dehumanising work? (RQ3) What long-term consequences to humans should a manager consider when applying AI-powered solutions in an organisation?

Due to the diverse research problems covered by particular chapters, no unified *method approach* is applied in the whole volume; every author or team was free to use the most efficient method for analysing the selected topic. However, to make the volume coherent and more accessible for a reader, all chapters follow the same formal pattern of sections:

1 *Introduction*, describing research gap, research problem statement, research questions or hypotheses formulation, methods applied description;
2 *Literature review* divided into sections for a clear narration;
3 *Results of analyses* of the literature and/or an empirical component (if applicable);
4 *Discussion* of the results with the literature;
5 *Conclusion*, answering research questions or verifying hypotheses, describing study limitations, and suggesting future research directions.

The chapters of this book employ a diverse range of research methods suited to the interdisciplinary exploration of AI, aesthetics, and humanistic management. Authors primarily apply qualitative approaches, including systematic literature reviews, narrative analyses, conceptual synthesis, critical discourse analysis, and comparative case studies, to examine AI integration's theoretical and aesthetic dimensions in organisational contexts. Several contributions are grounded in cross-paradigmatic theoretical frameworks, phenomenological reflections, or semiotic analyses, allowing for a deeper exploration of managerial practices' sensory, symbolic, and existential aspects. Some chapters also incorporate elements of empirical inquiry, such as econometric modelling, secondary data analysis, or scenario-based theoretical simulations, to link conceptual findings with practical observations. Collectively, these methodologies provide a robust, multi-faceted investigation of how AI technologies impact leadership, decision-making, human well-being, organisational communication, and workplace aesthetics from a humanistic and aesthetic perspective.

## Structure

This book starts with prefaces written by key scholars dealing with aesthetic and humanistic approaches to managerial and organisational worlds. After "Introduction: In search of synergy between humanism and AI in management", written by Michał Szostak, twelve chapters are organised into three parts. Part I, "Theoretical foundations and cross-paradigmatic perspectives", containing five Chapters (1–5), grounds the book in conceptual, aesthetic, and cross-paradigmatic frameworks for AI and humanistic management. Part II, "Leadership and decision-making aesthetics in the AI era", containing three Chapters (6–8), focuses intensely on aesthetic challenges and competencies in leadership and decision-making. Part III, "Human resources, user experience, and organisational communication", containing four Chapters (9–12), addresses practical applications of AI in human resources, user experience design, well-being management, and crisis communication aesthetics. The scope of each chapter is the following.

***Part I. Theoretical foundations and cross-paradigmatic perspectives***

Chapter 1, "Aesthetics, AI, and humanistic management: research perspectives", written by Michał Szostak, examines aesthetic insights into human-AI collaboration within organisational and managerial contexts within the humanistic management paradigm. While AI is often associated with efficiency and automation, its role in humanistic management remains underexplored. This chapter addresses this research gap by investigating how AI can impact aesthetic perception and humanistic values in varied organisational contexts. Based on a literature review of management studies, AI, aesthetics, philosophy, and psychology, the analysis covers historical perspectives on aesthetic insight, emerging AI appliances in managerial practice, and the impact on humanism preservation. The key results may be summarised as follows: (1) AI may influence corporate storytelling, branding, leadership communication, and workplace aesthetics, offering both creative augmentation and risks of standardisation; (2) AI's role in managerial decision-making can optimise efficiency but risks homogenisation, bias reinforcement, and the loss of creative intuition; (3) AI should be treated as a co-creative tool, supporting human aesthetic intuition while maintaining ethical oversight and inclusivity. The findings suggest that while AI may enhance leadership aesthetic perception and organisational identity, over-reliance on AI can lead to dehumanisation and cultural standardisation within organisational contexts and managerial practice.

Chapter 2, "A pragmatic consideration on management aesthetics: humanistic approach in the age of large language models", prepared by Tuncay Turna, analyses two separate topics, aesthetics and Large Language Models (LLM), from a philosophical and a critical perspective through the aspect of MA. It then attempts to conclude by considering these two topics together. Accordingly, it first analyses the philosophical references in the central studies of MA and presents the main aesthetic theories and their explanations of concepts such as an aesthetic object and aesthetic experience. Next, it attempts to determine which theories are appropriate for MA (classical theories such as Plato, Aristotle, Kant, and Hegel and contemporary approaches, such as analytic and pragmatic). Furthermore, this chapter takes a critical (technical but not ethical) look at LLM, aiming to examine the vast developments that have taken place in recent years through a realistic lens because many future predictions about the subject are far from its reality and conditions. After understanding the conditions of LLM, this chapter questions the possibility of LLM's use in humanistic management through aesthetic considerations. As a result of these investigations, this chapter gives suggestions and shows what can be philosophically defended as an aesthetic theory for MA. The study offers an eclectic-pragmatic-aesthetic view, claiming that pragmatist aesthetics is more appropriate for MA. By showing the current conditions of LLMs, this chapter also offers a perspective that sees LLMs as a useful craft. By following this claim, MA can have a tool for better management.

Chapter 3, "AI-powered solutions based on Freemasonry's aesthetic principles: lessons for humanistic management", created by Dorota Mackenzie, investigates the intersection between the principles of humanistic management and Freemasonry within the context of the AI era. It seeks to elucidate how these ostensibly distinct domains can mutually inform and enhance one another. Employing a qualitative and comparative methodology supported by an extensive literature review, the analysis concentrates on ethical values, symbolic aesthetics, and the emphasis on personal development as articulated in Masonic tradition, assessing their congruence with the foundational tenets of humanistic management. The findings indicate that Freemasonry's longstanding commitment to ethical conduct, communal solidarity, and the cultivation of individual potential offers pertinent insights for developing AI policies and organisational practices oriented towards protecting human dignity, promoting well-being, and advancing social responsibility.

Chapter 4, "Spirituality and humanistic management: fostering meaning and purpose in IT professional development", written by Muhammad Kamran and Tomasz Ochinowski, focuses on David Hay's (2006) conception of spirituality is not confined to religious practices; instead, it is a deep, universal sense of connection with something larger than oneself, be it nature, humanity, or a transcendent reality. This study explores the linkage between spirituality and humanistic management from the perspective of aesthetic experiences, which operationalises the values of spirituality and humanistic management by creating meaningful, emotionally resonant experiences that promote harmony and human connection within organisations. Secondly, it explores what spiritual dimensions could exist in IT professionals' training from a humanistic perspective. An exploratory research approach was executed to achieve these objectives based on a qualitative review of the literature taken from multiple databases and qualitative analysis of interviews of IT professionals using content analysis. The results show that, in the context of humanistic management, Hay's conception of spirituality highlights the importance of creating inclusive workplaces where individuals are encouraged to pursue meaning and purpose.

Chapter 5, "AI-driven organisational aesthetics: cross-paradigmatic perspectives in humanistic management", prepared by Łukasz Sułkowski and Justyna Dziedzic, examines how AI influences organisational aesthetics within the four paradigms, examining both the opportunities and challenges arising from the automation and algorithmisation of aesthetic processes. The analysis explores organisational aesthetics, understood as the role of sensory experiences, artistic expressions, and design elements in shaping organisational identity, workplace culture, and management practices, through the lens of four paradigms—functionalist, interpretive, radical humanist, and radical structuralist—initially proposed by Burrell and Morgan (1979). Each paradigm provides a distinct ontological and epistemological stance, shaping how organisational studies understand, operationalise, and critique aesthetics. By integrating these perspectives, this study advances a nuanced understanding of aesthetics in management discourse, illustrating how sensory and artistic dimensions influence organisational identity, collaboration, and control.

***Part II. Leadership and decision-making aesthetics in the AI era***

Chapter 6, "AI-augmented leadership: redefining leaders' style and competencies", created by Małgorzata Baran, examines how AI-driven tools and systems are reshaping leadership styles and competencies, particularly concerning employee engagement, development, and communication while also examining their intersection with the aesthetic dimensions of humanistic management, which requires maintaining emotional resonance and genuine human interactions alongside AI adoption. Through a systematic literature review, the study investigates two primary research questions: (1) Which leadership styles are most susceptible to the impact of AI integration? and (2) What new competencies and roles are emerging for leaders in AI-driven contexts? The analysis reveals that transformational, servant, and adaptive leadership styles demonstrate the most significant evolution through AI integration, with transformational leadership showing particularly enhanced capabilities in driving innovation and organisational change through AI-powered analytics and automation. Moreover, the findings highlight how aesthetic and ethical considerations intersect with technologically augmented decision-making, including the need to preserve emotional resonance, authentic human interactions, and empathy. This study identifies three critical areas of emerging competencies: technical literacy, strategic integration, and ethical leadership, all enriched by an aesthetic sensitivity towards organisational culture and stakeholder experience.

Chapter 7, "Aesthetic dimensions of decision-making process: AI-powered tools for organisational leaders", written by Lucyna Baca-Lönn, focuses on three key pillars: aesthetic leadership, aesthetic dimensions in leaders' decision processes supported by AI-powered tools, and the balance between AI insights and aesthetic leaders' judgment in the decision processes. The analysis results suggest that leaders' rational decision models are prioritised in the organisational context. However, aesthetic leaders' tacit knowledge, including emotional insights, aesthetic considerations that encourage creativity and innovation in organisations, and their holistic perspectives, constitute key factors in aesthetic decision processes. Integrating aesthetic dimensions with leaders' rational decision models, complemented by real-time data analytics and predictive models from AI Machine Learning Algorithms, Natural Language Processing (NLP), and Decision Support Systems, can enhance organisational leaders' decision-making.

Chapter 8, "Textual charisma in leadership: aesthetic depth in navigating AI challenges through critical thinking", prepared by Justyna Dziedzic and Iga Maria Lehman, addresses the challenge of maintaining ethical, inclusive, and impactful leadership communication in AI-driven decision-making, where automation risks undermining human authenticity and critical reflection. It explores the interplay between critical thinking and textual charisma in modern management, highlighting their role in fostering ethical and creative leadership. Textual charisma, characterised by linguistic sensitivity and stylistic uniqueness (Lehman, 2024), enables leaders to craft authentic communication that resonates across audiences. This analysis is underpinned by a qualitative research approach combining a narrative literature review and a critical content analysis of over 50 scholarly sources and leadership case studies. Findings suggest that AI may enhance linguistic precision and reflexivity but raises ethical concerns regarding authenticity and bias. Balancing automation with human-centred textual charisma is crucial for fostering trust and inclusivity in managerial communication.

### *Part III. Human resources, user experience, and organisational communication*

Chapter 9, "Perception of implementing AI in HRM by organisational actors: humanisation or dehumanisation?", written by Joanna Cewińska, presents arguments proving that AI can contribute to humanising and dehumanising HRM. The considerations prove that a critical look at implementing AI-driven solutions is needed to counteract dehumanisation, prevent the effect of secondary Taylorism, and shape symbiotic human-robot relationships. This chapter presents the results of a literature review and an empirical study conducted using the writing expression technique according to the instructions of students with work experience. The respondents saw the benefits and threats of using new technologies in HRM. Understanding employees' needs and concerns is the basis for making changes in HRM to ensure these changes are successful. Working with employees to build trust is important, ensuring the positive impact of AI-powered workforce management systems. To facilitate the process of integrating employees with AI, it is worth involving them in the design, development, and decision-making about the use of technology. They confirm that perceptions of AI in HRM can influence the acceleration or deceleration of change associated with AI implementation.

Chapter 10, "Impact of AI-supported solutions on humanistic management practices: sensory and emotional well-being of elderly employees", created by Marlena Kondrat, examines the labour market dynamics of pre-retirement individuals, underscoring their strategic value to organisations and the systemic barriers they face. This study explores how organisations can cultivate environments that empower mature employees to thrive by integrating humanistic management principles. The analysis identifies a critical research gap at the intersection of AI innovation and humanistic management, particularly regarding their impact on ageing employees' sensory and emotional well-being. A systematic literature review synthesising insights from humanistic management, age diversity, and workplace AI applications reveals that prioritising individualised needs enhances well-being, while AI tools strengthen intergenerational communication and task coordination. Two main research results are a matrix of humanistic management aspects and AI-supported tools for the seniors' sensory and emotional well-being, as well as a list of recommendations for using AI-supported systems in the work environment for senior employees' health and safety.

Chapter 11, "The aesthetics of AI-driven management: balancing algorithmic efficiency and user experience in e-commerce development", prepared by Aneta Ejsmont, focuses on determining whether modern AI algorithms can stabilise developing business entities that decide to conduct business in the broader e-commerce market. Based on a literature review of research and the aesthetics of AI algorithms covering aspects related to the development of companies in the e-commerce market, sales process management, the use of AI in this area, and the role of aesthetics in machine learning, it seems important to understand the essence of the development of companies operating entirely or partially on the Internet in the context of the use of AI algorithms in sales processes, taking into account, in particular, the aesthetics of management based on AI. The research method used is to develop a model of an Internet enterprise using modern algorithms in sales activity. The issues addressed in this study are presented from the point of view of the broadly understood aesthetics of management, where management itself, and development management using modern AI algorithms in particular, is the art of achieving goals efficiently.

Chapter 12, "The aesthetics of metacommunication in organisational management: AI-generated crisis communication", written by Justyna Dziedzic and Łukasz Sułkowski, examines the aesthetic dimension of organisational metacommunication in crisis management, emphasising how emotional tone, communicative form, and symbolic coherence shape stakeholder perceptions. It investigates two emblematic case studies—Johnson & Johnson's 1982 Tylenol crisis and the 2018 Starbucks racial incident—through the combined lenses of discourse analysis and Situational Crisis Communication Theory. The analysis reveals that effective crisis communication relies on content and aesthetic components, such as emotional resonance, harmony, and alignment with organisational identity. Beyond empirical cases, this chapter introduces a conceptual example of AI-generated crisis communication to explore how AI reshapes the aesthetics of organisational messaging. While AI can replicate structural patterns and tone conventions, it struggles with authenticity, emotional subtlety, and ethical nuance, raising concerns about its use in high-stakes communication. This chapter argues that aesthetics is a critical but often overlooked factor in human- and AI-mediated crisis responses.

The volume finishes with a "Conclusion: finding directions" by Michał Szostak, summarising all considerations, answering the volume's research questions, indicating study limitations, and suggesting future research directions.

## References

Agusti-Cullell, J., & Schorlemmer, M. (2021). A humanist perspective on artificial intelligence. *Comprendre*, 23(1), 99–125.

Asdlori, A. (2023). The importance of humanistic approach in human resource management education. *Indo-MathEdu Intellectuals Journal*, 4(2), 397–419. https://doi.org/10.54373/imeij.v4i2.218

Burrell, G., & Morgan, G. (1979). Introduction. In Burrell, G., & Morgan, G. (eds.), *Sociological Paradigms and Organisational Analysis: Elements of the Sociology of Cor porate Life* (pp. 1–9). Heinemann.

Fontrodona, J., & Melé, D. (2022). Thinking about the future of work: promoting dignity and human flourishing. *Humanistic Management Journal*, 7(2), 181–188. https://doi.org/10.1007/s41463-022-00136-2

Hay, D. (2006). *The Spirit of the Child.* Jessica Kingsley Publishers.

Kostera, M., & Woźniak, C. (2022). *Aesthetics, Organization, and Humanistic Management.* Routledge.

Lehman, I. M. (2024). *Charismatic Leadership in Organisations: A Critique of Texts* (1st ed.). New York: Routledge.

Leong, P. (2023). Beyond disbelief: envisioning humanity in the AI-driven era. Medium. https://pennyleong.medium.com/beyond-disbelief-envisioning-humanity-in-the-ai-driven-era-97d24c3715a1

Nursalim, S. M., & Masitoh, A. N. (2023). Aesthetics and artificial intelligence: impact and criticism of art. *Education Achievement: Journal of Science and Research*, 9(23), 116–123. https://doi.org/10.51178/jsr.v4i3.1667

Strati, A. (1999). *Organization and Aesthetics.* SAGE Publications Ltd. https://sk.sagepub.com/books/organization-and-aesthetics

Szostak, M. (2024). *Humanistic Management, Organisation and Aesthetics: Art of Management and Management of Art.* Routledge. https://doi.org/10.4324/9781003458029

Szostak, M. (Ed.). (2025a). *Aesthetics of Human-AI Collaboration in Creative Activities: Art, Cultural Heritage, and Academic Research Practice.* Brill | mentis. https://brill.com/edcollbook/title/72781

Szostak, M. (Ed.). (2025b). *Management Aesthetics. Kitsch and Modern Organisations.* Routledge. https://doi.org/10.4324/9781003504931

Szostak, M. (Ed.). (2026). Organizations, Humanism and AI: An Aesthetics Approach. Routledge. https://www.routledge.com/Organizations-Humanism-and-AI-An-Aesthetics-Approach/Szostak/p/book/9781041120322

# Part I

# Theoretical foundations and cross-paradigmatic perspectives

# 1 Aesthetic insight into humanistic management and AI

## Research perspectives

*Michał Szostak*

### Introduction

Artificial intelligence (AI) is the latest in many technologies that have been accused of degrading the human mind, interpersonal interactions, and social order: Socrates opposed writing, claiming it weakened memory and the ability to think (Kumar, 2023); Johannes Tritemius criticised the invention of printing because too easy access to books would make people undervalue knowledge (Lovison, 2024); arithmetic teachers disliked calculators (Laursen, 1978), same situation with cars, Internet, and cell phones (Snodgrass et al., 2018). New technologies have brought certain costs to humanity, but their balance is favourable overall. However, there is no doubt that they have indeed had and continue to impact human cognitive abilities (H. H. Lee et al., 2025). After disseminating a given solution, humanity got used to it and started treating it as something normal. Following this approach, we could treat AI similarly; however, from another point of view, AI is relatively the most novel global invention, and its possibilities are not yet fully controlled or even entirely predictable. Humans always anticipated reality and created different future scenarios. Before any AI tool was physically created, philosophers and science fiction writers described visions of how people would live surrounded by intelligent solutions. After releasing Chat GPT in November 2022, the first globally accessed tool that every human could practically use, we observed an explosion of journalistic publications describing the intersection of humanism and intelligence created artificially; following this trend, scientists from various disciplines started to analyse this research area from different perspectives, applying scientific research methods.

Another important perception approach to AI is treating it as a *tool* in the hands of humanity. The consequences of utilising a tool depend on the individuals (groups, societies) who use it for varied purposes; we cannot blame the tool for its users' utilisation. However, we cannot forget that first, we shape the tools, and then the tools shape us (Hurme & Jouhki, 2017; Skrzypek, 2025); that is why every new solution has its consequences (predictable and unpredictable) on varied time perspectives.

DOI: 10.4324/9781003654377-3

Existing scientific literature has explored the individual domains of AI in management, the role of aesthetics in organisational settings, and the principles of humanistic management. However, there is a paucity of research examining the intersection of these fields, underlining aesthetic insight into phenomena appearing in this territory. Moreover, while AI is widely studied for efficiency and automation, its aesthetic implications in humanistic management remain underexplored. This *research gap* mainly concerns how AI may impact management practices to enhance or detract from aesthetic appreciation and humanistic values. Addressing this gap is crucial, as how AI is employed in organisations has profound implications for employee well-being, organisational culture, and the ethical landscape of business operations (Ghosh & Sadeghian, 2024).

Integrating AI into organisational practices has become increasingly prevalent in the contemporary landscape, prompting a re-evaluation of traditional management paradigms. This evolution requires a deeper understanding of how AI intersects with humanistic management principles and aesthetics' role in this dynamic. Humanistic management emphasises the importance of human dignity, ethical considerations, and the holistic well-being of individuals within organisations (Kostera & Woźniak, 2022; Pirson, 2017; Szostak, 2024b). Aesthetics, encompassing the appreciation of beauty and truth, sensory experiences, and artistic-like expressions, significantly influence organisational culture, leadership and managerial practices, and decision-making processes (Szostak, 2024b).

The convergence of aesthetic insight on AI and humanistic management presents a multifaceted *research problem* that can be described with two aims: (1) to define aesthetic relationships between AI and human beings within managerial and organisational contexts; (2) to explain the meaning of aesthetics in describing managerial and organisational issues supported by AI-powered tools and solutions. Therefore, the research problem centres on developing frameworks that enable organisations to adopt AI-powered solutions while preserving and (if possible) enhancing the humanistic dimension using aesthetic paradigms. This involves investigating how AI can support leadership and managerial practice, utilising universal values of beauty and truth, as well as design and sensory experiences to inspire and motivate employees (Duhamel et al., 2023). It also requires an examination of the ethical considerations inherent in AI applications, ensuring that they align with the values of human dignity and respect (Pirson, 2017).

The primary *research method* used in this chapter is a literature review from the following databases: EBSCO, Google Scholar, Mendeley, Scopus, and Web of Science. The queries were based on keywords referring to varied aspects and combinations of words and phrases related to aesthetics, humanistic management, and AI. The time scope of the literature analysis varied depending on the topic and discipline insight; the topics with a more extended history (aesthetics, humanism, cultural studies) were analysed from the last three decades; the topics around AI, technology, psychology, and behavioural sciences were mainly searched from the years 2022 to 2025 (to avoid strictly theoretical considerations that appeared before the day of releasing the commonly accessible AI tools at the end of 2022). The analysed literature belongs to the disciplines of management and organisational studies (humanistic management, organisational aesthetics, leadership studies), AI and data science (human-centred AI, algorithmic aesthetics), philosophy and aesthetics (philosophy of AI and technology, aesthetic theory, the phenomenology of management), psychology and behavioural sciences (cognitive science, workplace psychology, behavioural economics), and sociology and cultural studies (the sociology of work and organisations, cultural studies of AI, futurism and technological change); however, due to the complexity of the research problem, most of it is of interdisciplinary significance.

This chapter answers the following *research questions*: (RQ1) How can aesthetics help perceive human-AI interactions in managerial and organisational contexts? (RQ2) What are the aesthetic implications of AI-powered decision-making, and how do they influence human perception, creativity, ethical considerations, and the balance between efficiency and aesthetic depth in managerial and organisational contexts? (RQ3) To what extent can AI foster aesthetic intelligence in humanistic management while preserving human-centric paradigms and avoiding dehumanisation or aesthetic homogenisation?

The structure of the consideration is as follows: first, a literature review is undertaken; then, the results of the analyses are presented; a discussion of the results with the literature is conducted; and finally, a conclusion summarises all the issues.

## Literature review: AI, aesthetics, and humanistic management

The literature review results are presented in the following order. First, three pure concepts of humanistic management, AI, and aesthetics are presented to map the main issues related to these fields in the scientific discourse. Then, mixes of these three pure concepts are presented: AI and humanistic management, AI and aesthetics, aesthetics and humanistic management, and finally, all of them together, i.e., aesthetics, humanistic management, and AI.

### *Humanism in management*

Humanism in management, or humanistic management, prioritises human dignity, ethical decision-making, and the well-being of employees, customers, and society over purely profit-driven goals. Analysing humanism in management involves examining how it integrates principles of respect, fairness, and holistic development within organisational practices (Dierksmeier, 2016; Kociatkiewicz & Kostera, 2013; Muzari et al., 2022; Szostak, 2024b). Below is an overview of how humanism in management is analysed in the literature and the key components of humanistic management. Researchers approach humanism in management from varied *research perspectives*, in which the following *research problems* are the most common:

1 *philosophical analysis*: ethical foundations investigating the principles of *dignity, fairness*, and *moral responsibility* (Pirson, 2017, 2023); *humanistic value systems* influencing leadership and decision-making (Caggiano et al., 2024);
2 *organisational analysis*: policies and practices examining whether organisational systems support employee *well-being* and *empowerment* (García-Juan et al., 2023); leadership styles and behaviours that embody *empathy*, *trust*, and *collaboration* (Gotsis, 2022);
3 *employee-centric analysis*: workplace culture assessing how the culture fosters *inclusivity*, *respect*, and *individual growth* (V. Koon, 2024); employee experience measuring *engagement*, *satisfaction*, and *psychological safety* (Aboramadan & Kundi, 2023);
4 *stakeholder analysis*: exploring how organisations balance *stakeholder interests*, including employees, customers, communities, and shareholders (Quintelier et al., 2021); *corporate social responsibility* (CSR) and *corporate humanistic responsibility* (CHR) by evaluating commitments to social and environmental goals (V.-Y. Koon & Fujimoto, 2024);
5 *economic and performance analysis*: *sustainable value creation* and assessing the balance between financial performance and *human-centred goals* (Asdlori, 2023); long-term impact by studying whether humanistic practices improve *innovation*, *retention*, and *resilience* (R. Berger & Czakert, 2022);
6 *cross-cultural analysis*: global perspectives on comparing how humanism in management is expressed and practised in *different cultural contexts* (Gotsis & Grimani, 2024); *adaptability* and understanding how humanistic principles adapt to *local needs* while maintaining *core values* (Tavares et al., 2022);
7 *measurement and metrics analysis*: qualitative indicators like employee surveys, interviews, and case studies to assess the *human-centeredness* of management practices (Muzari et al., 2022); quantitative indicators for analysing turnover rates, *employee well-being* metrics, and *productivity levels* linked to humanistic approaches (Cignitas et al., 2021).

Considering *research areas* within humanistic management that appear in the literature, we can distinguish the following *research problems*:

1 *core values*: *human dignity* and recognising the intrinsic worth of every individual in the organisation (Dierksmeier, 2016; Fontrodona & Melé, 2022; Kostera & Woźniak, 2022; Pirson, 2023); *ethical integrity* by upholding fairness, transparency, and accountability in all decisions (Caggiano et al., 2024; Gotsis, 2022; Szostak, 2023a); *compassion through embodying empathy and care* in relationships with employees, customers, and stakeholders (Awaluddin & Hamid, 2019; Gotsis, 2022; Gotsis & Grimani, 2024; Koivunen & Wennes, 2011);

2 *leadership practices*: *servant leadership* and prioritising the needs of employees and stakeholders by leaders, fostering a supportive environment (Gotsis & Grimani, 2024; Szostak, 2024b, 2024c); *empathetic communication* through encouraging open dialogue and active listening (Town et al., 2024); *empowerment* and creating opportunities for employees to take initiative and contribute meaningfully (Hoang et al., 2021; Tripathi et al., 2021; Yu et al., 2018);
3 *employee well-being*: *work-life balance* through policies that respect personal time and reduce burnout (Ciupka, 2020; Pham Thi & Duong, 2024; Stankevičienė et al., 2021; Szostak, 2024a); *psychological safety* by cultivating an environment where employees feel safe to express ideas and concerns (Edmondson & Bransby, 2023; Sjöblom et al., 2022); *professional development* by providing opportunities for learning, growth, and career progression (Pradhan & Hati, 2022; Schwepker et al., 2021);
4 *organisational culture*: *inclusivity and diversity*, e.g., celebrating and leveraging the differences in perspectives, skills, and backgrounds (April et al., 2023; Dua et al., 2025); *collaboration and community* by fostering teamwork and shared purpose (Della Lucia et al., 2021); *respect and recognition* by valuing contributions and acknowledging achievements (Matheson et al., 2021);
5 *sustainable practices*: purpose beyond profit by aligning business goals with societal and environmental well-being (Fellenz et al., 2022; Melé, 2016; Szostak, 2024b); social responsibility by actively contributing to the community and addressing societal challenges (Atif, 2019; V.-Y. Koon & Fujimoto, 2024; Szostak, 2024a); environmental stewardship by promoting sustainability and reducing environmental impact (Laszlo, 2019; Poggioli, 2024);
6 *stakeholder focus*: *employee-centred policies* through designing practices prioritising employee health, safety, and development (Wadhwa et al., 2024); *customer orientation* through delivering value that aligns with ethical and humanistic principles (Ancarani, 2024); *community engagement* through building relationships and giving back to the community (García-de-la-Torre et al., 2021; Gotsis & Grimani, 2024);
7 *decision-making processes*: *ethical considerations* by integrating moral reasoning into business strategies (Loke, 2017); *transparency* through ensuring decisions are open and communicated clearly (Ball, 2009); *participatory approaches* by involving employees and stakeholders in decision-making (Blomkamp, 2022);
8 *performance metrics*: *human-centric outcomes* through tracking employee satisfaction, engagement, and retention metrics (Stor et al., 2024); *balanced scorecards* by combining financial performance with social and humanistic indicators (Abor & Karimu, 2023; Kaufman et al., 2021); *long-term goals* and prioritising *sustainable growth* over short-term profits (Alvino et al., 2020; Edwards, 2021).

### *AI*

AI has experienced significant growth as an independent research field in recent years. According to the Mendeley database, the number of scientific publications (including articles, books, book chapters, and conference proceedings) containing the query "AI" was as follows: 14,029 in 2017, 19,736 in 2018, 24,585 in 2019, 32,063 in 2020, 42,900 in 2021, 50,335 in 2022, and 71,722 in 2023. Additionally, a search for "AI" on Google Scholar has consistently returned approximately 1,000,000 results annually over the past several years. Analysing AI involves breaking down its structure, functionality, and impact into manageable components to understand how it works, how it can be improved, and its broader implications. Below is an overview of how AI can be analysed and the key components of AI. Researchers approach AI from different *perspectives*; within them, the following *research problems* are mainly analysed:

1 *technical analysis*: studying algorithms and computational models (Alviano et al., 2023; Baumeister et al., 2021); evaluation of efficiency (Arman & Lamiya, 2023), scalability (Mohammed, 2023), and robustness (Aghajari et al., 2023); performance benchmarking uses accuracy, precision, recall, and F1-score metrics (Graf et al., 2020; Olatinwo et al., 2023);
2 *ethical, legal, and societal analysis*: ownership and control over AI resources, i.e., hardware for creating AI structures; access to AI (R. D. Brown, 2021; Gonzalez Fabre et al., 2021; Himmelreich, 2023); impact on privacy (Goldsteen et al., 2023; Y. Xing et al., 2023), fairness (Angerschmid et al., 2022; P. Chen et al., 2023), and equity (K. Chen et al., 2024; Lim, 2022); examination of bias in data and algorithms (Nishant et al., 2024; P.S., 2023); study of societal consequences, such as job displacement (Karangutkar, 2023; Rawashdeh, 2023) or social behaviour shifts (Enakrire & Oladokun, 2024);
3 *behavioural analysis*: how the AI (including software agents) interacts with users, e.g., in human-AI collaboration (Cabrera et al., 2023; Vössing et al., 2022) or autonomous decision-making (S. Sharma et al., 2024; I. K. A. Wong et al., 2023); understanding interpretability and explainability in its outputs (Joyce et al., 2023; Xu et al., 2023); empathy (Liu et al., 2024; D. Sharma & Bikshandi, 2020); engagement with users, adapting decision-making strategies, and facilitating communication in dynamic environments (Russell & Norvig, 2021); real-time coordination and decision-making (A. Wong et al., 2023);
4 *economic and organisational analysis*: cost-benefit analysis for adoption in businesses (B. Chen et al., 2023; Islam et al., 2024); impact on organisational workflows (Einola & Khoreva, 2023) and economic models (Lu & Zhou, 2021; Yang, 2023);
5 *environmental analysis*: carbon footprint and energy consumption during training and deployment (Bouza et al., 2023; Tamburrini, 2022); sustainability of large-scale AI systems (Khan et al., 2023; van Wynsberghe, 2021);

6 *philosophical analysis*: the nature of "intelligence" in AI (Saxena et al., 2023; Y. Wang, 2009); consciousness and autonomy in advanced AI systems (Butlin et al., 2023; Hu et al., 2021).

Considering analytical *research areas of AI* and particular *research problems* within them that appear in the literature, there are:

1 *data*: its role in the foundation for training AI models, providing the input for learning patterns and making predictions (Kolides et al., 2023; Qin et al., 2025); its analysis regarding (a) quality, completeness, accuracy, and noise (Budach et al., 2024), (b) diversity and representation of various demographics or scenarios (Alruwaili & Alsalim, 2024; Kamikubo et al., 2022), (c) bias and identifying and mitigating unfair patterns (Ferrara, 2023);
2 *algorithms*: their role in defining how AI systems learn, make decisions, and adapt (Belenguer, 2022; B. Berger et al., 2021); their types: (a) supervised learning from labelled data (Saravanan & Sujatha, 2018), (b) unsupervised learning and how models identify patterns in unlabelled data (Naeem et al., 2023), (c) reinforcement learning: models learn through trial and error (S. E. Li, 2023), (d) deep learning of neural networks with multiple layers (Montesinos López et al., 2022); their analysis: (a) algorithm efficiency and scalability (Kodakandla, 2024), (b) ability to generalise to unseen data (J. Wang et al., 2022), (c) transparency and interpretability (Joyce et al., 2023);
3 *models*: their role in instantiating an algorithm trained on specific data to perform a task (Hrybiuk & Kant, 2024); their analysis regarding: (a) model complexity: simpler models are easier to interpret but may underfit data (Aliferis & Simon, 2024), (b) robustness: performance under adversarial conditions or data shifts (Rezaei et al., 2021), (c) overfitting: over-reliance on training data, reducing generalisability (Javed et al., 2024);
4 *hardware and infrastructure*: their role in enabling the computational processes required for training and deploying AI systems (Lins et al., 2021); their components: (a) GPUs/TPUs and accelerating computations (Burhanuddin, 2023), (b) storage systems for large datasets (Uddin & Hossan, 2024), (c) cloud and edge computing infrastructure (S. Zhou et al., 2024); their analysis: (a) computational efficiency and scalability (Belgaum et al., 2021), (b) accessibility of infrastructure for different stakeholders (Verdecchia et al., 2022);
5 *outputs and interfaces*: their role in the results and ways AI interacts with users or systems (Riveiro & Thill, 2021); their types: (a) predictions, e.g., classifications, recommendations (Lins et al., 2021), (b) actions, e.g., autonomous driving, robotics (Atakishiyev et al., 2024), (c) interfaces, e.g., chatbots, dashboards (Jadhav et al., 2024); their analysis regarding: (a) accuracy and reliability of outputs (Cabrera et al., 2021), (b) user experience and ease of interaction (Virvou, 2023), (c) explainability of decisions (Kostopoulos et al., 2024);

6 *ethics and governance*: its role in ensuring AI systems operate within ethical and regulatory boundaries (Díaz-Rodríguez et al., 2023); its analysis regarding: (a) compliance with legal standards and policies (de Almeida et al., 2021), (b) ethical considerations in design and deployment (Burr & Leslie, 2023), (c) mechanisms for accountability and redressal (Kathuria et al., 2024);
7 *training and learning mechanisms*: their role in processes through which AI improves its performance (Olan et al., 2022); their types: (a) batch learning and training on a fixed dataset (Ponomareva et al., 2023), (b) online and continuous learning from streaming data (Rang et al., 2021); their analysis regarding: (a) efficiency of training processes (Su et al., 2022), (b) data requirements and scalability (Belgaum et al., 2021), (c) risk of catastrophic forgetting in continual learning (Z. Wang et al., 2025);
8 *applications*: practical use cases of AI systems (Sarker, 2022) with examples within varied fields: (a) healthcare regarding diagnosis, personalised medicine (Johnson et al., 2021), (b) finance regarding fraud detection or trading (Bello et al., 2024), (c) entertainment regarding recommendation systems (del Carmen Rodríguez-Hernández & Ilarri, 2021); their analysis referring to domain-specific challenges and opportunities (Jan et al., 2023) or societal and individual impacts of specific applications (Smuha, 2021);
9 *feedback and adaptation*: their role in mechanisms for learning from real-world usage and improving over time (Strielkowski et al., 2024); their analysis regarding: (a) feedback loops concerning the effectiveness of self-improvement mechanisms (Veigners et al., 2024), (b) adaptation to new data and conditions (Sjödin et al., 2021), (c) risks of reinforcing biases through feedback (Schwartz et al., 2022).

The literature presents two contrasting narratives regarding the development and application of AI, depending on the perspective taken. The first narrative, *evolutionary*, suggests that AI-powered solutions enhance human capabilities, assist in hazardous or complex tasks, and promote a collaborative relationship between humans and machines (Chi, 2024; Giorgetti, 2024; Jarrahi, 2018). The second narrative, *revolutionary*, envisions AI replacing traditional jobs and human workers, who may be seen as less efficient or more challenging to manage compared to AI-driven alternatives. Some aspects of these perspectives remain speculative and are often examined through theoretical and futurological lenses rather than empirical extrapolation. Both narratives (evolutionary and revolutionary) manifest in business organisations and management: AI can either augment human capabilities (Mikalef & Gupta, 2021) or substitute human workers entirely (Eng & Liu, 2024; Herath et al., 2025). From the revolutionary standpoint, the rapid advancement of AI necessitates strong regulatory frameworks and security measures to mitigate its impact and ensure ethical deployment. The future of AI depends on balancing its potential with human oversight and ethical principles, fostering coexistence rather than competition between AI and humans (Kuklin et al., 2023; Miller, 2019).

Different perspectives on AI's role in society range from deep *techno-scepticism* to extreme *techno-optimism* (Alibegović et al., 2024). A significant portion of AI research appears to reflect a *techno-salvationist* viewpoint, portraying technology and its corporate creators in an almost religious light (Peters, 2018). Conversely, others interpret the AI revolution as a form of *techno-feudalism* (Gilbert, 2024), raising concerns about economic and societal power imbalances. These fears draw historical parallels with the Enlightenment, which, while promising rational progress, also enabled new forms of domination and authoritarianism (Horkheimer & Adorno, 2002)(Horkheimer & Adorno, 2002). Additional concerns include ownership and control over AI resources, such as computational power and hardware (e.g., AI chips), which influence who can access and benefit from AI advancements. Some researchers argue that, instead of being a force for equality, AI will exacerbate social inequalities, widening the gap between the wealthiest and the rest of society ("How AI Will Divide the Best from the Rest", 2025).

### *Aesthetics*

Aesthetics, the study of beauty, art, and taste, can be analysed through various disciplinary lenses. It encompasses subjective and objective components, making its analysis a personal and cultural endeavour. Here is a breakdown of how aesthetics is analysed scientifically and its key components.

Researchers approach aesthetics from different *research perspectives*:

1 *philosophical analysis*: theories of beauty like classical, modern, and postmodern theories of what constitutes beauty (Barbone, 1997; Lorand, 2002; Tatarkiewicz, 2004); subjectivity versus objectivity in analysing whether aesthetic value lies in the object, the observer, or their interaction (Bowie, 2003; Hamzah, 2012); aesthetic judgment and exploring criteria for evaluating beauty and taste (Barbone, 1997; Gołaszewska, 1986; Koczanowicz, 2023; Leder et al., 2004);
2 *psychological analysis*: perception and cognition, i.e., how humans perceive and process aesthetic experiences (Stokes, 2009); emotional response, i.e., the role of feelings (pleasure, awe) in aesthetic appreciation (Forlini et al., 2018; Schindler et al., 2017); cognitive biases, e.g., how prior knowledge, familiarity, or novelty affect aesthetic preferences (Carbon, 2011; Coss, 2003);
3 *sociocultural analysis*: cultural norms, i.e., how different societies define and value beauty (Udris-Borodavko et al., 2023); historical context and evolution of aesthetic standards over time (Renoult, 2016; Tatarkiewicz, 2015); identity and power, i.e., how aesthetics reflects or challenges social hierarchies and identities (Accominotti, 2021; Pieterse, 1993);
4 *artistic and structural analysis*: analysing formal elements like shape, colour, line, texture, and composition (Klimenko & Beskrovnaya, 2022; Van Geert & Wagemans, 2020); medium and technique, i.e., the impact of materials and

methods on the aesthetic quality of art (Pedan, 2022); style and genre, i.e., examining how aesthetic characteristics differ across styles, e.g., Baroque versus minimalism (Szostak, 2019, 2021, 2023c);

5 *interdisciplinary analysis*: neuroscience and investigating brain activity during aesthetic experiences (Calvo-Merino, 2021; Chatterjee & Vartanian, 2016); technology and AI (generative art), e.g., how algorithms create or evaluate aesthetics (Epstein et al., 2023; E. Zhou & Lee, 2024); environmental psychology and the aesthetics of space and how it influences behaviour and well-being (Altman & Wohlwill, 1976; Løvoll et al., 2020).

Considering particular *research areas within aesthetics*, we can list the following *research problems* that appear in the literature:

1 *perceptual elements*: visual aesthetics regarding shape, colour, symmetry, balance, and contrast (O'Connor, 2015; Osborne, 1986); auditory aesthetics regarding melody, harmony, rhythm, and dynamics in sound (Lippman, 1999; Scruton, 1997); tactile aesthetics regarding texture, weight, and material properties (Gallace & Spence, 2011; Zuo et al., 2014);
2 *emotional and cognitive components*: emotional resonance, e.g., feelings evoked by an aesthetic experience, such as joy, sadness, or inspiration (Root-Bernstein, 2002; Starr, 2015); meaning and interpretation, e.g., intellectual engagement with the more profound significance of work (Currie, 2023; Pagis & Summers-Effler, 2021); novelty and surprise, e.g., the role of newness in capturing attention and appreciation (Goode et al., 2013; Leder & Nadal, 2014);
3 *contextual factors*: cultural context, e.g., shared symbols, traditions, and values that shape aesthetic preferences (Brachmann & Redies, 2017; Redies, 2015); historical context, e.g., how aesthetic standards and movements evolve (Le, 2023; Tatarkiewicz, 2004, 2015); environmental context, e.g., the influence of setting and space on the perception of beauty (Altman & Wohlwill, 1976; Mastandrea et al., 2021);
4 *formal qualities*: proportion and symmetry, e.g., balance, harmony, and coherence in design (J. D. Lomas & Xue, 2022); contrast and emphasis, e.g., dynamic elements that highlight specific features (Leder & Nadal, 2014; T. Lomas, 2023); unity and variety, e.g., the interplay between cohesion and diversity in a composition (Tan et al., 2006);
5 *symbolism and meaning*: representation, e.g., how aesthetics conveys ideas, emotions, or narratives (Folkmann, 2013; Maclagan, 2001); abstraction, e.g., the beauty of forms that do not directly represent real-world objects (Gortais, 2003); ambiguity, e.g., the role of open-ended interpretation in aesthetic appreciation (Shusterman, 2023; Yevin, 2006);
6 *cultural and social influences*: taste, e.g., socially constructed preferences and norms (Hoyer & Stokburger-Sauer, 2012; Warde, 2014); fashion and trends,

e.g., the shifting landscape of what is considered aesthetically appealing (A. Sharma, 2024; Wu, 2015); identity, e.g., how aesthetics express personal or group identity (Bao et al., 2016; Sherrard, 1995);

7 *medium and materials*: artistic medium, e.g., the specific tools and materials used, from paint and stone to digital pixels (Gillette, 2023; B. Li & Lu, 2023); physical properties, e.g., texture, durability, and tactile quality of the medium (Karim et al., 2022; Marschallek et al., 2023); technological influence, e.g., how modern tools expand or constrain aesthetic possibilities (Aris et al., 2023; Montani, 2021);
8 *dynamic interaction*: engagement, e.g., the active role of the observer in experiencing aesthetics (Pagis & Summers-Effler, 2021; Pizzolante et al., 2024; Szostak, 2022c, 2022b); immersion, e.g., depth of involvement in an aesthetic experience comparing a VR simulation with a live performance (H. Lee & Youn, 2025; Scorolli et al., 2023); temporal elements, e.g., how aesthetics unfolds over time in music, cinema, or interactive art (Cox et al., 2023; Metwally, 2024);
9 *ethical dimensions*: morality and aesthetics, e.g., the intersection of beauty and ethical considerations (e.g., the portrayal of controversial topics) (Congdon, 2021; Dietrich & Knieper, 2022); responsibility in design, e.g., how aesthetic choices impact societal well-being and inclusivity (Iwuanyanwu et al., 2024).

### *AI and humanistic management*

Researchers show humanising and dehumanising faces of AI (Leder et al., 2004; Leong, 2023; Nursalim & Masitoh, 2023) or try to establish sets of rules or principles of digital humanism (Prem, 2024). In trying to map AI-related issues, they describe *posthumanism*, *transhumanism*, and *genhumanism* (Brusseau, 2023; Prem, 2024). Humanism and AI are discussed in various areas of human activity, e.g., higher education (Ou et al., 2024), journalism (Dralega, 2023), medicine (Ostherr, 2022), psychology (Hou et al., 2022), and social communication (Fuchs, 2020). The advent of AI has also introduced new dimensions to managerial practices, offering tools that can augment decision-making processes, enhance efficiency, and provide data-driven insights. However, integrating AI into humanistic management requires careful consideration of implications and preserving human-centric values. One of the proposed frameworks is *human-centred AI* or *humanistic AI*, highlighting the necessity of transparency, accountability, and inclusivity in AI system design to align with humanistic principles (Shneiderman, 2020; Tasioulas, 2022).

Another concept of *aesthetic intelligence* is the capacity to understand, interpret, and articulate the emotional resonance elicited by various stimuli, enabling individuals (managers) to create environments that foster engagement, creativity, and a sense of purpose (P. Brown, 2020). Incorporating aesthetic considerations into management practices can lead to more authentic and distinctive organisational identities (Everhart, 2023; Szostak, 2024b). However, the integration of AI into these practices introduces complexities: a risk that an overreliance on AI could undermine the human-centric aspects of management, leading to dehumanisation and a diminished emphasis on aesthetic values (Mahmoud et al., 2025).

AI can potentially augment humanistic management by providing data-driven insights, automating routine tasks, and supporting decision-making processes. The human-centred approach in AI design emphasises that AI should be a tool to support managerial creativity, ethical responsibility, and aesthetic intelligence rather than a mechanism for dehumanisation (Pirson, 2017; Riedl, 2019). This perspective requires AI-powered tools that enhance human capabilities without undermining autonomy or dignity. Frameworks such as *human-centred AI* highlight the necessity of transparency, accountability, and inclusivity in AI system design to align with humanistic principles (Shneiderman, 2020; Tasioulas, 2022).

*Algorithmic curation,* driven by AI, increasingly influences managerial practices by shaping emotional engagement, storytelling, and strategic vision within organisations. AI-powered management tools analyse vast amounts of data to curate content and insights, impacting how managers connect with their teams and stakeholders. In this regard, AI may enhance managers' ability to foster *emotional engagement* by providing personalised insights into team dynamics and individual sentiments (Henkin, 2024). By analysing communication patterns and feedback, AI tools can identify areas where employees may feel disengaged or unappreciated, enabling managers to address concerns proactively and create a more inclusive and supportive work environment (Wilt et al., 2025).

*Effective storytelling* is a cornerstone of impactful management practice. AI-powered tools assist managers in crafting compelling narratives by analysing audience preferences and predicting which themes will resonate most. By curating content that aligns with the values and interests of their audience, managers can enhance their influence and drive organisational objectives more effectively. AI can also ensure consistency in brand voice and messaging across various platforms, maintaining authenticity and trust (DiFabrizio, 2024; Wilt et al., 2025).

Regarding *strategic vision,* AI aids managers by providing data-driven insights that inform long-term planning and decision-making. Algorithmic curation sifts through market trends, consumer behaviour, and competitive analyses to present managers with synthesised information crucial for strategic development. This allows managers to anticipate industry shifts and accordingly adapt strategies, ensuring sustained organisational growth and relevance. However, managers must balance AI-generated recommendations with human intuition and ethical considerations to avoid over-reliance on technology (Dua et al., 2025; Kaggwa et al., 2024).

Incorporating AI into humanistic management demands cautious reflection of implications and preserving human-centric values because over-reliance on AI in managerial decision-making risks reducing human interaction, intuition, and ethical reasoning, leading to a mechanistic approach to managerial practices (Tasioulas, 2022). While AI enhances efficiency and strategic planning, it may also contribute to aesthetic flattening – where corporate decisions become overly standardised, lacking in emotional and cultural richness. Organisations must develop frameworks that ensure AI integration aligns with humanistic values rather than diminishing them (Naumov, 2024).

AI is shown as a "hyperobject" requiring more-than-human humanism that acknowledges our ecosystem's significance (Lollini, 2022). AI's ethical and epistemological implications suggest that humanising AI can preserve human dignity (Ihejirika, 2015). Integrating human-centred design research in AI development emphasises the importance of a genuine human-centred philosophy (Auernhammer, 2020). These studies collectively stress the need to balance technological advancement with human values, ethics, and well-being, calling for a multidisciplinary approach that involves humanistic perspectives in shaping the future of AI (Auernhammer, 2020; Ihejirika, 2015; Lollini, 2022; Tasioulas, 2022).

The hybrid approach suggests combining human intuition with AI-driven insights, ensuring that AI serves as a co-pilot rather than a replacement in management (Duhamel et al., 2023). Organisations should foster ethical AI governance policies that uphold human dignity, creativity, and decision-making autonomy (Pirson, 2017; Riedl, 2019). The future of AI in humanistic management lies in creating adaptive, aesthetically aware, and ethically responsible AI systems that complement human leadership rather than overpower it.

### *AI and aesthetics*

The intersection of AI and aesthetics has become a focal point of contemporary scholarly discourse. We can distinguish two levels of considerations: (1) AI and aesthetics of superficiality, and (2) AI and aesthetics of deepness. Among the issues on the level of *AI and aesthetics of superficiality*, we can find: (1) designing AI interfaces and outputs and their alignment with human aesthetic preferences, involving incorporating elements such as colour theory, composition, and emotional resonance (Sindiramutty et al., 2024); (2); easiness, comfort, and pleasure of the AI-supported process of results' generation – the "creator" as a selector of the results, not a manager and performer of the physical creation process. Among the issues on the level of *AI and aesthetics of deepness*, we can find: (1) AI's integration into creative processes that necessitate a nuanced understanding of aesthetic principles to enhance user engagement and satisfaction; (2) AI's role in art generation, human perception of AI-created art; (3) the ethical implications of AI in the arts; (3) exploring how AI influences artistic creation, perception, and the broader cultural landscape; (4) authenticity and originality of artworks created by or with the use of AI.

The emergence of AI-generated art has sparked debates regarding the *authenticity and originality of such works*. Traditional aesthetic theory often ties authenticity to human intentionality and creative expression. However, AI systems like OpenAI's DALL·E 2 can produce artworks indistinguishable from those created by humans, challenging conventional notions of authorship (van Hees et al., 2025). While AI lacks consciousness and subjective experience, its ability to generate novel combinations of styles and themes raises questions about the evolving definition of creativity in the digital age.

AI systems trained on specific datasets may inadvertently reproduce *cultural biases* in their training material. This phenomenon can influence AI's definitions of beauty or taste, leading to homogenised or culturally skewed outputs. For instance, AI-generated images might overrepresent specific demographics or aesthetic standards, reinforcing existing societal biases (Brzeziński et al., 2024; Manovich, 2018). Addressing these biases requires curating diverse and representative training datasets and implementing algorithms that account for various cultural perspectives.

Research into *how audiences perceive AI-generated art* reveals complex attitudes. Some studies indicate a bias against AI-created artworks, with participants rating them lower in aesthetic value than human-made art, even when the pieces are visually similar (Chamberlain et al., 2018). This bias may stem from perceptions of AI art lacking emotional depth or human touch. Conversely, other research suggests that individuals may prefer AI-generated art when unaware of the creator's identity, highlighting the influence of preconceived notions on art evaluation (van Hees et al., 2025).

Incorporating aesthetic considerations into AI applications extends beyond art creation to user interface design, gaming, and virtual environments. *Aesthetically engaging* AI systems can enhance user experience, making interactions more enjoyable and immersive. For example, AI-driven platforms that curate personalised content benefit from designs that are not only functional but also visually and emotionally appealing, thereby increasing user retention and satisfaction (Betancourt, 2022; Manovich, 2018). Moreover, AI hardware and software interface design embodies its aesthetic dimension. AI's visual and functional aspects, such as the appearance of robots or the layout of AI-driven applications, significantly impact user acceptance and trust. Design choices that reflect human-like features or intuitive interfaces can facilitate smoother human-AI interactions while raising questions about the uncanny valley and user comfort levels (B. Xing et al., 2022).

AI's global deployment demands sensitivity to diverse *cultural interpretations of beauty and aesthetic insights*. AI systems trained predominantly on data from specific cultures may fail to capture the aesthetic values of other societies, leading to outputs that resonate less with global audiences (Baradaran, 2024). Ensuring that AI respects and reflects cross-cultural aesthetics involves diversifying training datasets and engaging with cultural experts to inform AI development (L. Zhou et al., 2022; S. Zhou et al., 2024).

The integration of AI into the arts raises profound ethical and philosophical questions. *Intellectual property issues* emerge when AI-generated art is created using datasets containing existing artworks, potentially infringing on artists' rights (Ünal & Taylan, 2024). Moreover, the environmental impact of training large AI models has become a concern, prompting discussions about the sustainability of AI practices (Alzoubi & Mishra, 2024; Everhart, 2023). Philosophically, the capacity of AI to create art challenges traditional concepts of creativity, intentionality, and the artist's role (Gołaszewska, 1984; Szostak, 2022a, 2025a), inviting a re-evaluation of what constitutes art in the age of AI.

### *Aesthetics and humanistic management*

Aesthetics, traditionally associated with the philosophy of art and beauty, has found significant relevance in organisational studies (Baldessarelli et al., 2022; Minahan, 2020; Strati, 1999; Szostak, 2024b, 2025b). It encompasses the sensory experiences and emotional responses elicited by organisational environments, influencing employees and stakeholders. In humanistic management, aesthetics transcends visual appeal (aesthetics of superficiality) and hidden true beauty (aesthetics of deepness), embedding itself into an organisation's core values and culture.

*Classical aesthetic theories* offer profound insights into management and decision-making by emphasising the role of sensory experiences, judgment, and the integration of art into daily life. Kant's aesthetic philosophy posits that judgments of beauty are based on a subjective feeling of pleasure, yet they aspire to universal validity (Kant, 2015). This "disinterested pleasure" notion suggests that genuine aesthetic appreciation is free from personal desires or practical concerns. In the context of management, this principle encourages managers to cultivate impartiality and objectivity in their decision-making processes, ensuring that choices are made based on intrinsic merit rather than extrinsic motivations. Kant also introduces the concept of the sublime, which involves experiences that transcend ordinary perception and evoke a sense of awe (Guyer, 1997). Managers who engage with the sublime can inspire visionary thinking and the pursuit of goals that extend beyond conventional boundaries. Baumgarten regarded aesthetics as the science of sensory knowledge (Borchert, 2006, pp. 493–494) and believed that aesthetic experience involves the perfection of sensory cognition, leading to a more profound understanding of the world. For managers, this perspective underscores the importance of sensory awareness and intuition in comprehending complex situations. By honing their aesthetic sensibilities, they can develop a nuanced appreciation for the subtleties of organisational dynamics, enabling more informed and empathetic decision-making. The pragmatic approach to aesthetics emphasises the continuity between artistic expression and everyday life (Dewey, 1934). It argues that aesthetic experiences are not confined to art but integral to all aspects of human activity. This perspective encourages managers to recognise and cultivate the aesthetic dimensions of daily organisational practices. Emphasis on experiential learning also suggests that managers should embrace a reflective approach, continuously integrating new experiences to enhance their judgment and decision-making capabilities.

Some researchers have significantly contributed to understanding how visual, linguistic, and sensory elements shape corporate identity and leadership perception by exploring *organisational aesthetics* and *aesthetic leadership*. Strati emphasises that aesthetic experiences deeply influence organisational life, which are embodied, sensory, and universal modes of "being-in-the-world". These experiences generate aesthetic knowledge, often tacit and unconscious, manifesting as gut feelings, intuitive insights, or creative flow. Such knowledge influences leaders' decision-making processes, as they often rely on these aesthetically derived intuitions to navigate complex organisational challenges. By engaging with the aesthetic dimensions of their environment, leaders can foster a culture that values creativity, innovation, and emotional resonance, thereby shaping a corporate identity that reflects these values (Strati, 1999). Gagliardi introduces the "empathic-logical approach" to organisational aesthetics, wherein researchers and leaders engage empathically and analytically with organisational artefacts and practices. This approach involves an initial phase dominated by aesthetic observation, where sensations and emotions elicited by organisational elements are acknowledged and named. Subsequent phases incorporate analytical detachment and logical rigour to interpret and understand these aesthetic experiences. By balancing empathy and analysis, leaders can gain deeper insights into how sensory and symbolic elements influence organisational culture and identity. This balanced engagement enables crafting leadership practices and corporate narratives that resonate emotionally and intellectually, enhancing the perception of leadership and strengthening corporate identity (Gagliardi, 2006). Kostera and Woźniak argue that engaging with art and aesthetics in organisational settings promotes imaginative insights and reflection, enriching management knowledge and collective expression. They suggest that aesthetically informed research within humanistic management can lead to more profound and meaningful organisational practices (Kostera & Woźniak, 2022). Szostak introduces a comprehensive theory of management aesthetics within the framework of humanistic management, positing that integrating aesthetic principles into management practices fosters a holistic understanding of organisational dynamics, where art and management intersect to enhance creativity, empathy, and ethical decision-making. This approach advocates for a management style that values human dignity and well-being, aligning with the principles of humanistic management (Szostak, 2023b, 2024b). These concepts are based on the metaphor of organisation as an artwork (Szostak & Sułkowski, 2020); consequently, a manager can be considered an artist, and various theories regarding art and aesthetics may be applied here with excellent results.

Besides a significant potential for innovative insights into humanistic manage ment, works on management aesthetics are full of repetitive and meaningless phrases like fostering creativity, enhancing human dignity, organisational harmony, empathy, trust, and collaboration. These issues are undoubtedly important, but valuable analyses must give more precise answers and justifications that can be implemented in managerial practices and organisational circumstances.

### *Aesthetics, humanistic management, and AI*

The convergence of humanistic management and AI, seen through varied lenses of aesthetics, presents a multifaceted research landscape. Integrating AI technologies into management practices offers opportunities for innovation and efficiency, but raises questions about maintaining aesthetic and humanistic values within organisations.

Exploration of aesthetics offers valuable insights into how AI-generated content influences *managerial perception*, corporate identity, and data visualisation. The pervasive role of AI in shaping cultural experiences notes that AI not only automates cognitive processes but also significantly influences our choices, behaviours, and imaginations (Manovich, 2018). This influence extends to managerial contexts, where AI-driven tools curate information and media, affecting decision-making processes. AI systems can guide managerial attention and priorities by recommending specific content and suggesting professional connections, potentially reshaping organisational strategies and managerial approaches. On the other hand, managers' overreliance on AI-supported solutions may result in losing control over particular processes or the whole organisation (H. H. Lee et al., 2025).

In *corporate identity*, AI-generated content may be transformative because AI automatically enhances visual media, such as beautifying images, to align with prevailing aesthetic standards (Manovich, 2018). This capability allows organisations to consistently produce branded content that resonates with target audiences, reinforcing brand identity. AI-driven design tools can generate logos, marketing materials, and even product designs that embody the company's values and aesthetic preferences, ensuring a cohesive and appealing corporate image. This automation streamlines the creative process and enables companies to adapt swiftly to emerging trends, maintaining relevance in a dynamic market.

*Data visualisation* is another area where AI-generated content exerts a significant impact. AI assisting in making aesthetic decisions during media creation may extend to the visualisation of complex data sets (Manovich, 2018). Managers can transform raw data into intuitive and visually engaging representations by employing AI algorithms, facilitating better comprehension and more informed decision-making. These AI-enhanced visualisations can reveal patterns and insights that might be overlooked in traditional data analysis, thereby supporting strategic planning and operational efficiency. Moreover, the aesthetic quality of these visualisations can enhance stakeholder engagement, as compelling visuals are more likely to capture attention and convey information effectively.

AI's capacity to analyse and generate aesthetic content has profound implications for organisational identity and culture. By automating design processes and curating visual content, *AI standardises aesthetic outputs*, potentially leading to homogenisation that may overlook the nuanced cultural and individual expressions vital to a humanistic approach (Hitsuwari et al., 2023). This standardisation challenges managers to critically assess the balance between AI-driven efficiency and preserving unique organisational aesthetics that reflect diverse human experiences.

The deployment of AI in shaping aesthetic standards raises significant *ethical concerns*, particularly regarding the *perpetuation of biases* and the *authenticity of AI-generated outputs*. AI systems trained on biased datasets may reinforce existing stereotypes, leading to exclusionary practices that contradict the principles of humanistic management. Moreover, the authenticity of AI-generated art and design is contested, as these creations lack the intentionality and emotional depth inherent in human artistry. Managers are thus tasked with ensuring that AI applications align with ethical standards that honour human creativity and inclusivity.

Incorporating human-centred design principles into AI integration is essential to uphold the values of humanistic management. This approach emphasises the importance of designing AI systems prioritising human needs, values, and well-being. By engaging stakeholders in the design process and enhancing human capabilities, organisations can develop AI applications that support, rather than supplant, human agency. This alignment fosters a collaborative environment where technology serves as an enabler of human potential and aesthetic appreciation.

AI's role in *defining and propagating aesthetic standards* necessitates a *sensitivity to cultural diversity*. AI systems that do not account for varied cultural contexts may inadvertently promote a narrow view of beauty and design, undermining the inclusivity central to humanistic management. Training AI on diverse datasets and involving multicultural perspectives in the development process is imperative to mitigate this risk. Such practices ensure that AI applications respect and reflect a broad spectrum of aesthetic values, enriching the organisational culture and resonating with a global audience.

## Results of analyses

Based on the literature review, the following results of analyses can be determined (ordered based on the research questions).

***RQ1: aesthetic intelligence, symbolism, storytelling, and workplace aesthetics***

Regarding RQ1 (*How can aesthetics help perceive human-AI interactions in managerial and organisational contexts?*), we can find these key issues:

1 *The role of aesthetic intelligence in human-AI collaboration*; it may refer to enhancing:

   a *leadership engagement* – AI-powered tools can support it by:

      i *enhancing managerial communication* – AI-driven analytics can assess audience reactions and optimise leadership messaging based on tone, sentiment, and engagement metrics; by incorporating emotionally resonant language and visually compelling presentations, AI tools help managers communicate more effectively and inspire trust;

      ii *curating organisational narratives* – AI-powered content generation tools can assist managers in crafting compelling corporate storytelling that aligns with the company's mission and values; this may ensure consistency and authenticity in branding and managerial communication;

      iii *improving workplace design for engagement* – AI-assisted design software can optimise office aesthetics, lighting, and workspace layouts to create environments that foster creativity and well-being; intelligent environments powered by AI can dynamically adjust lighting and soundscapes based on employee preferences, enhancing engagement and productivity;

   b *organisational identity* – it is deeply tied to aesthetic coherence, encompassing visual elements, brand storytelling, and cultural symbolism; AI can strengthen corporate identity by:

      i *AI-driven brand aesthetics* – AI-powered design tools may help create cohesive brand aesthetics by maintaining visual and stylistic consistency across digital platforms, ensuring that logos, colour palettes, and marketing materials align with the brand's identity;

      ii *personalised brand engagement* – AI-enhanced customer relationship management (CRM) systems use aesthetic-driven personalisation, ensuring that communications, advertisements, and customer interactions align with individual user preferences;

      iii *symbolic alignment in corporate culture* – AI can analyse internal communications and identify patterns in employee engagement, sentiment, and organisational aesthetics, helping companies align their corporate culture with their visual and linguistic representation;

   c *user experience through aesthetics* – applying aesthetic intelligence in AI-powered UX design enhances human-AI collaboration by making digital interactions more intuitive, engaging, and emotionally resonant; AI may contribute to aesthetic UX design by:

- i *personalised user interfaces* – AI may adapt digital interfaces based on user behaviour, ensuring visual elements (colours, fonts, layouts) align with individual user preferences;
- ii *AI in virtual environments* – in immersive AI-driven spaces such as augmented reality (AR) and virtual reality (VR), AI may enhance realism and emotional engagement by dynamically adjusting lighting, textures, and soundscapes;
- iii *automated aesthetic optimisation* – AI may refine digital content presentation by adjusting typography, spacing, and visual hierarchy to create more aesthetically pleasing user experiences.

2 *Sensory and symbolic dimensions of AI-driven organisational aesthetics*; they refer to:

- a *visual aesthetics in AI-driven communication* – AI-powered tools may enhance corporate communication by optimising visual design, branding consistency, and data representation; automated design systems may generate cohesive brand aesthetics, ensuring alignment between an organisation's core values and visual identity; AI may also refine presentation aesthetics, dynamically adapting fonts, layouts, and colour schemes to create visually compelling materials that improve stakeholder engagement;
- b *linguistic aesthetics in AI-assisted messaging* – AI-driven text generation may influence tone, style, and emotional appeal in organisational messaging; Natural Language Processing (NLP) algorithms may personalise corporate narratives, customer engagement, and leadership communication, ensuring messages resonate with target audiences;
- c *sensory engagement in AI-augmented decision-making* – AI-enhanced workplace environments may leverage sensory aesthetics, from adaptive lighting and soundscapes to immersive AI-powered interfaces in decision-making spaces; such innovations may contribute to cognitive efficiency but also risk depersonalising human-centred management if aesthetics become purely algorithmic rather than intuitively human-driven.

3 *AI's influence on storytelling and workplace aesthetics*:

- a *AI in corporate storytelling* – AI algorithms may optimise storytelling by analysing audience preferences, curating content, and personalising narratives. Natural Language Processing (NLP) tools may enable organisations to craft emotionally resonant leadership messages, marketing campaigns, and corporate reports; AI-generated storytelling may also enhance internal communications, ensuring clarity, consistency, and engagement across global teams;

b *AI in workplace aesthetics* – AI may influence workspace design by customising physical and virtual environments to enhance employee well-being and productivity; AI-powered systems may dynamically adjust lighting, acoustics, and spatial layouts to optimise comfort and efficiency; digital workspaces may leverage AI-driven visual aesthetics personalising user interfaces and collaboration tools for an intuitive experience.

***RQ2: balance, bias and cultural limitations, creativity and originality***

Regarding RQ2 (*What are the aesthetic implications of AI-powered decision-making, and how do they influence human perception, creativity, ethical considerations, and the balance between efficiency and aesthetic depth in managerial and organisational contexts?*), we can find these key issues:

1 *The balance between AI-driven efficiency and human aesthetic depth* – AI-powered decision-making may enhance efficiency, data-driven accuracy, and strategic optimisation in management, yet it also poses risks of aesthetic standardisation and oversimplification; as AI systems streamline design processes, automate content creation, and curate organisational aesthetics, they often prioritise functional uniformity over creative diversity; two issues are important here:

   a *optimising productivity through AI* – AI may enhance efficiency in corporate aesthetics by automating brand design, presentations, and workplace aesthetics, ensuring consistency and alignment with organisational identity; AI-driven decision-making tools may help leaders analyse consumer preferences, predict aesthetic trends, and optimise design choices with minimal human intervention, increasing productivity and reducing costs;
   b *risks of aesthetic standardisation and oversimplification* – AI-generated results risk homogenising creativity, as algorithmic models often rely on predefined patterns and past data; this can lead to predictable, aesthetically repetitive outputs, limiting artistic originality and reducing cultural and organisational diversity in design and decision-making.

2 *Bias and cultural limitations in AI-generated aesthetics* – AI-generated aesthetics are inherently shaped by the training data used to develop machine learning models, which can introduce cultural and corporate biases into organisational aesthetics, branding, and decision-making; AI systems trained on historically dominant artistic styles, cultural preferences, or corporate branding norms tend to reinforce pre-existing aesthetic conventions, often at the expense of diversity and innovation:

   a *training data and aesthetic bias* – AI models learn from datasets curated by human designers, corporations, and cultural institutions, embedding subjective and culturally specific aesthetic preferences into decision-making processes; this can result in aesthetic homogenisation, where AI-generated visuals, interfaces, and corporate designs exhibit a repetitive, formulaic style that reflects dominant cultural norms rather than embracing diversity;

b *reinforcing corporate and cultural homogeneity* – organisations leveraging AI for branding, digital marketing, or user experience design may inadvertently exclude minority artistic expressions or unconventional aesthetic choices due to algorithmic reinforcement of mainstream tastes; over time, this can limit creative differentiation, leading to standardised aesthetics that fail to reflect diverse cultural identities and organisational uniqueness.

3 *AI's impact on creativity and originality in management* – it presents:

a opportunities based on *AI as a creativity catalyst* – AI may enhance managerial creativity by:

i facilitating data-driven decision-making;
ii optimising brainstorming processes and offering novel perspectives;
iii helping leaders explore alternative business strategies, innovative product designs, and customer engagement approaches;
iv identifying emerging patterns, allowing organisations to anticipate trends and respond proactively with creative solutions;

b risks based on *the threat of over-reliance on AI* – excessive dependence on AI-generated creativity may cause:

i diminishing human originality and emotional intuition;
ii leading to creative stagnation and aesthetic homogenisation in organisational decision-making;
iii struggling to develop authentic, disruptive innovations.

***RQ3: dehumanisation, homogenisation, co-creation***

Regarding RQ3 (*To what extent can AI foster aesthetic intelligence in humanistic management while preserving human-centric paradigms and avoiding dehumanisation or aesthetic homogenisation?*), we can find these key issues:

1 *The risk of dehumanisation in AI-powered aesthetic leadership* – in these areas:

a *loss of emotional intelligence in leadership* – AI-driven leadership tools, such as automated communication systems and AI-generated strategic messaging, can streamline organisational interactions but may lack the empathy, intuition, and spontaneity essential for authentic leadership; human leaders rely on non-verbal cues, emotional intelligence, and personal experiences to inspire and engage employees – qualities that AI, despite advancements, struggles to replicate effectively;

b *standardisation and reduced human connection* – algorithmic decision-making in leadership prioritises efficiency over relational dynamics, potentially leading to aesthetic homogenisation in leadership styles and communication; AI-generated speeches, branding strategies, and managerial directives risk becoming formulaic, reducing individualised, human-centric engagement; the absence of genuine human interaction can erode trust and weaken corporate culture, impacting employee motivation and stakeholder relationships.

2 *Algorithmic homogenisation and the loss of diverse aesthetic perspectives* – AI-driven decision-making in organisational aesthetics and leadership presents a paradox: while AI can optimise efficiency, branding consistency, and design coherence, it also risks imposing uniform aesthetic norms that overlook cultural and organisational diversity; this phenomenon, known as algorithmic homogenisation, occurs when AI-generated aesthetics reinforce repetitive, standardised outputs rather than fostering originality and cultural variation; here, we should keep in mind:

a *the risk of aesthetic standardisation* – AI models rely on historical datasets and trend analyses to generate outputs, often reproducing dominant aesthetic patterns; this can lead to a convergence of corporate aesthetics, where organisations adopt similar branding, design structures, and communication styles, reducing differentiation and cultural specificity;

b *overlooking cultural and organisational diversity* – AI lacks contextual awareness and cultural intuition, making it prone to erasing localised artistic traditions, linguistic nuances, and unique organisational identities; in global organisations, this can result in aesthetic uniformity that fails to resonate with diverse stakeholder groups.

3 *Human-AI co-creation in aesthetic decision-making* – integrating AI into aesthetic decision-making in leadership offers a new paradigm where technology is an augmentative tool rather than a replacement for human aesthetic intuition and emotional intelligence:

a *AI as a collaborative tool in aesthetic leadership* – AI may support leaders and decision-makers by analysing visual trends, audience preferences, and cultural aesthetics, providing data-driven insights that enhance creative expression; in organisational aesthetics, AI can assist in curating brand storytelling, refining workplace design, and personalising digital experiences without dictating a singular, algorithmic aesthetic norm;

b *preserving human intuition and emotional intelligence* – unlike humans, AI lacks emotional depth, subjective interpretation, and contextual awareness, which are essential in aesthetic decision-making; by positioning AI as a co-creative partner, organisations can leverage efficiency and innovation while ensuring that leadership decisions reflect human creativity, emotional intelligence, and ethical responsibility.

**Discussion**

After providing a comprehensive literature review on the intersection of aesthetics, humanistic management, and AI, the discussion will highlight the potential negative consequences of AI's aestheticisation in management and propose strategies for ensuring human-centric and ethically responsible AI-powered solutions.

AI enhances leadership aesthetics by optimising branding, communication, and decision-making processes. However, an *over-reliance on AI-generated aesthetics* risks producing inauthentic leadership expressions that lack emotional depth and human intuition. Leaders must ensure that AI augments rather than replaces the human capacity for aesthetic judgment, maintaining genuine emotional connections within organisations.

A critical concern is *algorithmic homogenisation*, where AI-driven branding and corporate aesthetics lack originality, fail to reflect cultural diversity, and reinforce standardised aesthetic norms. Biases embedded in training datasets can further narrow AI's representation of aesthetics, underscoring the need for human oversight in AI-driven design processes. Ethical considerations must guide UX development to ensure AI-generated aesthetics remain inclusive, adaptable, and sensitive to diverse cultural perspectives.

AI's role in linguistic curation and storytelling presents additional challenges. Automated content generation risks producing formulaic, culturally detached, and ethically shallow narratives that fail to capture the depth of human-centric corporate storytelling. Excessive AI standardisation may further diminish creativity and erode organisational identity, reinforcing the importance of integrating AI within a human-driven creative framework.

Organisations must adopt a balanced approach to counteract these risks, ensuring AI serves as an augmentative tool rather than a replacement for human creativity and aesthetic intelligence. This involves prioritising diverse, representative datasets, implementing ethical AI frameworks, and fostering a co-creative model where AI enhances symbolic, expressive, and cultural dimensions of leadership aesthetics. Achieving this balance is essential for sustainable innovation, originality, and emotionally intelligent leadership in the AI era.

The regular and broad use of AI-powered tools also has unintended consequences: a decline in critical thinking (higher confidence in GenAI is associated with less critical thinking, and higher self-confidence is associated with more critical thinking). In other words, GenAI shifts the nature of critical thinking toward information verification, response integration, and task stewardship

(H. H. Lee et al., 2025). These insights reveal new design challenges and opportunities for developing GenAI tools for knowledge work. Based on that research, it could be stated that AI tools should be designed in such a way as not to discourage but to stimulate thinking (Cieśliński, 2025); however, the question of who will want to pay for these additional features remains unanswered.

*Managerial over-aestheticisation*, focusing on depth and forgetting about the business idea, may blur the view and disrupt the balance between clou (the base) of business activities and issues that add additional value. Following this philosophy, the *aestheticisation of management* can be perceived as more suitable for prosperous periods, not when struggling with basic needs during survival in market stagnation.

The final warning refers to reducing aesthetic intelligence to a purely technical function that can strip management of its deeper humanistic essence. If misused, AI risks eroding the artistic and emotional qualities that define humanistic management.

## Conclusion

Blending aesthetic insights into humanistic management practices using AI-powered tools and solutions brings new perspectives to this quickly developing research area.

The extensive answers to research questions were presented in the previous sections, which is why here, the following aesthetic challenges of crossing the borders of AI and humanistic management can be underlined: (1) aesthetic standardisation versus creativity; (2) bias in AI-generated corporate aesthetics and the role of algorithmic curation in shaping leadership perception; (3) AI-enhanced emotional intelligence and authenticity in management and simulation or manipulation managerial charisma.

Because of the firmly theoretical character of this chapter, the following practical managerial recommendations can fill this gap. A manager who wants to consciously blend aesthetic insights into the intersection of humanistic management and AI-powered solutions should:

1 balance AI and human leadership to maintain authenticity by: (a) using AI to assist in communication and storytelling but avoiding full automation of leadership messages; (b) personalise AI-generated narratives by integrating their insights, emotions, and values;
2 prevent algorithmic homogenisation by promoting aesthetic diversity by: (a) incorporating human creativity in branding, design, and digital aesthetics to maintain originality; (b) training AI systems with diverse datasets to avoid cultural bias and ensure inclusive, varied aesthetic outputs; (c) encouraging localised and culturally adaptive AI-driven branding strategies rather than enforcing a single global aesthetic;

3 ensure AI's role in decision-making aligns with ethical and aesthetic considerations by: (a) informing but not replacing managerial decision-making with AI-driven analytics; (b) developing aesthetic evaluation frameworks that allow AI-generated visuals, interfaces, and recommendations to align with corporate identity and humanistic values;
4 use AI as a co-creative partner rather than a replacement by: (a) encouraging human-AI collaboration in design, storytelling, and innovation rather than delegating creative control to algorithms; (b) providing AI-assisted brainstorming sessions where AI-generated concepts inspire human-driven creative processes; (c) maintaining human oversight in AI-generated art, branding, and content creation to ensure emotional resonance and ethical alignment;
5 establish ethical AI governance in aesthetic decision-making by: (a) developing AI ethics policies that address bias, cultural diversity, and human-centred aesthetics in organisational decision-making; (b) implementing AI governance frameworks that include human review processes to ensure that AI-generated aesthetic decisions remain aligned with corporate and societal values; (c) encouraging ongoing training for managers to help them understand AI's limitations and ethical implications in aesthetic leadership.

While this chapter provides a comprehensive examination of the intersection between aesthetics, AI, and humanistic management, several *limitations* must be acknowledged: (1) conceptual complexity and interdisciplinary scope – the study explores three highly complex and interdisciplinary domains, which may lead to conceptual ambiguity and difficulties in establishing clear theoretical boundaries; integrating these three fields requires multiple perspectives from philosophy, organisational studies, data science, and psychology, making it challenging to create a singular, unified framework; (2) dependence on theoretical analysis – the research relies heavily on literature review and theoretical synthesis rather than own empirical data collection; while this approach provides a strong conceptual foundation, it lacks direct case studies or experimental validation to assess the practical implications of AI-driven aesthetics in real-world management contexts; (3) limited longitudinal perspective on AI's impact – integrating AI, as a rapidly evolving field, into aesthetic decision-making and humanistic management is still in its early stages; the study primarily analyses current trends and recent literature, limiting its ability to predict the long-term consequences of AI-driven organisational aesthetics; (4) challenges in measuring aesthetic intelligence in AI-human collaboration – aesthetic intelligence in human-AI collaboration is inherently subjective, making it difficult to establish quantifiable metrics for evaluating its impact on leadership, organisational identity, or decision-making; the lack of standardised frameworks for assessing AI's role in aesthetic leadership adds complexity to the study; (5) potential bias in AI training data – AI-generated aesthetics depend on training data, which may reinforce cultural biases, aesthetic norms, and standardised corporate aesthetics rather than promoting diversity and originality; addressing algorithmic bias requires ongoing research and ethical oversight, which is beyond the scope of this study; (6) limited exploration of organisational case studies – while this chapter presents theoretical insights, it lacks extensive empirical validation through industry-specific case studies or managerial applications; future research should incorporate qualitative and quantitative assessments of AI's role in aesthetic decision-making within various industries; (7) ethical and humanistic dilemmas in AI aesthetics – the study acknowledges ethical concerns related to algorithmic homogenisation, dehumanisation, and authenticity in AI-generated aesthetics, but it does not propose a concrete ethical framework for managing these challenges in humanistic management; (8) contextual and cultural constraints – the research primarily draws from Western perspectives on aesthetics, AI, and humanism, which may not fully capture global variations in how AI aesthetics influence management practices across different cultural contexts.

To address the above limitations, future studies should: (1) conduct empirical research through case studies, surveys, or experimental methodologies to validate theoretical insights; (2) develop quantitative metrics for assessing AI's impact on aesthetic intelligence and human-AI collaboration; (3) explore cross-cultural studies to analyse how different aesthetic traditions interact with AI-generated aesthetics in organisational contexts; (4) propose ethical governance frameworks to mitigate dehumanisation risks and algorithmic biases in AI-driven decision-making. The following future research directions can be suggested focusing on the substance of the research problem: (1) analyses of how aesthetic theories can inform AI development for humanistic management; (2) verification of how AI should be designed to support, rather than replace, aesthetic decision-making in organisations; (3) analyses on possibilities how AI can help managers cultivate aesthetic intelligence, or does it risk aesthetic over-automation; (4) studying the impact of AI-enhanced organisational aesthetics on trust, engagement, and emotional intelligence.

## References

Abor, J. Y., & Karimu, A. (2023). *Sustainability Management in the Oil and Gas Industry*. Routledge. https://doi.org/10.4324/9781003309864

Aboramadan, M., & Kundi, Y. M. (2023). Emotional culture of joy and happiness at work as a facet of wellbeing: A mediation of psychological safety and relational attachment. *Personnel Review*, *52*(9), 2133–2152. https://doi.org/10.1108/PR-04-2021-0285

Accominotti, F. (2021). The aesthetics of hierarchy. *The British Journal of Sociology*, *72*(2), 196–202. https://doi.org/10.1111/1468-4446.12835

Aghajari, Z., Baumer, E. P. S., Hohenstein, J., Jung, M. F., & Difranzo, D. (2023). Metho dological middle spaces: Addressing the need for methodological innovation to achieve simultaneous realism, control, and scalability in experimental studies of AI-Mediated communication. *Proceedings of the ACM on Human-Computer Interaction*, *7*(CSCW1), 1–28. https://doi.org/10.1145/3579506

Alibegović, A., Radeljaš, D., Tahirović, O., & Arnautović, A. (2024). *Homo Deus: Technoskepticism/Techno-Optimism - Slipping into the Technosphere* (pp. 344–353). Springer, Cham. https://doi.org/10.1007/978-3-031-66271-3_37

Aliferis, C., & Simon, G. (2024). *Overfitting, Underfitting and General Model Overconfidence and Under-Performance Pitfalls and Best Practices in Machine Learning and AI* (pp. 477–524). Springer, Cham. https://doi.org/10.1007/978-3-031-39355-6_10

Alruwaili, A., & Alsalim, M. (2024). Data diversity and its impact on machine learning fairness. *International Journal of Cloud Computing and Database Management*, *5*(1), 38–41. https://doi.org/10.33545/27075907.2024.v5.i1a.60

Altman, I., & Wohlwill, J. F. (Eds.). (1976). *Human Behavior and Environment*. Springer US. https://doi.org/10.1007/978-1-4684-2550-5

Alviano, M., Dodaro, C., Fiorentino, S., Previti, A., & Ricca, F. (2023). ASP and subset minimality: Enumeration, cautious reasoning and MUSes. *Artificial Intelligence*, *320*, 1–25. https://doi.org/10.1016/j.artint.2023.103931

Alvino, F., Di Vaio, A., Hassan, R., & Palladino, R. (2020). Intellectual capital and sustainable development: A systematic literature review. *Journal of Intellectual Capital*, *22*(1), 76–94. https://doi.org/10.1108/JIC-11-2019-0259

Alzoubi, Y. I., & Mishra, A. (2024). Green artificial intelligence initiatives: Potentials and challenges. *Journal of Cleaner Production*, *468*, 143090. https://doi.org/10.1016/j.jclepro.2024.143090

Ancarani, F. (2024). *Humanistic Management into Practice: What Should a Humanistic Manager Do?* (pp. 87–98). Palgrave Macmillan, Cham. https://doi.org/10.1007/978-3-031-67155-5_5

Angerschmid, A., Zhou, J., Theuermann, K., Chen, F., & Holzinger, A. (2022). Fairness and explanation in AI-Informed decision making. *Machine Learning and Knowledge Extraction*, *4*(2), 556–579. https://doi.org/10.3390/make4020026

April, K., Dharani, B., & April, A. (2023). *Leadership for Inclusivity* (pp. 169–195). Emerald Publishing Limited, Leeds. https://doi.org/10.1108/S2051-233320230000007007

Aris, S., Aeini, B., & Nosrati, S. (2023). A digital aesthetics? artificial intelligence and the future of the art. *Journal of Cyberspace Studies*, *7*(2), 219–236. https://doi.org/10.22059/JCSS.2023.366256.1097

Arman, M., & Lamiya, U. R. (2023). Exploring the implication of ChatGPT AI for business: efficiency and challenges. *Journal of Innovation Information Technology and Application (JINITA)*, *5*(1), 52–64. https://doi.org/10.35970/jinita.v5i1.1828

Asdlori, A. (2023). The importance of humanistic approach in human resource management education. *Indo-MathEdu Intellectuals Journal*, *4*(2), 397–419. https://doi.org/10.54373/imeij.v4i2.218

Atakishiyev, S., Salameh, M., Yao, H., & Goebel, R. (2024). Explainable artificial intelligence for autonomous driving: A comprehensive overview and field guide for future research directions. *IEEE Access*, *12*, 101603–101625. https://doi.org/10.1109/ACCESS.2024.3431437

Atif, M. (2019). (Re) discovering the business purpose: A discursive approach to CSR and stakeholder management. *Society and Business Review*, *14*(4), 401–414.

Auernhammer, J. (2020, September 10). Human-centered AI: The role of Human-centered design research in the development of AI. In Boess, S., Cheung, M. and Cain, R. (eds.), *Synergy - DRS International Conference 2020,* 11–14 August, Held online. https://doi.org/10.21606/drs.2020.282

Awaluddin, I., & Hamid, W. (2019). Interaction of social identity, empathy and planned behavior theories to understand domestic product purchasing intention. *Problems and Perspectives in Management*, *17*(1), 95–102. https://doi.org/10.21511/ppm.17(1).2019.09

Baldessarelli, G., Stigliani, I., & Elsbach, K. D. (2022). The aesthetic dimension of organizing: A review and research agenda. *Academy of Management Annals*, *16*(1), 217–257. https://doi.org/10.5465/annals.2020.0198

Ball, C. (2009). What is transparency? *Public Integrity*, *11*(4), 293–308. https://doi.org/10.2753/PIN1099-9922110400

Bao, Y., Yang, T., Lin, X., Fang, Y., Wang, Y., Pöppel, E., & Lei, Q. (2016). Aesthetic preferences for eastern and western traditional visual art: Identity matters. *Frontiers in Psychology*, *7*, 1–8. https://doi.org/10.3389/fpsyg.2016.01596

Baradaran, A. (2024). Towards a decolonial I in AI: mapping the pervasive effects of artificial intelligence on the art ecosystem. *AI & SOCIETY*, *39*(1), 7–19. https://doi.org/10.1007/s00146-023-01771-5

Barbone, S. (1997). Analityczna postawa wobec piękna sztuki. In M. Gołaszewska (Ed.), *Estetyka w świecie: wybór tekstów. Tom V* (pp. 71–80). Uniwersytet Jagielloński.

Baumeister, D., Järvisalo, M., Neugebauer, D., Niskanen, A., & Rothe, J. (2021). Acceptance in incomplete argumentation frameworks. *Artificial Intelligence*, *295*, 1–8. https://doi.org/10.1016/j.artint.2021.103470

Belenguer, L. (2022). AI bias: Exploring discriminatory algorithmic decision-making models and the application of possible machine-centric solutions adapted from the pharmaceutical industry. *AI and Ethics*, *2*(4), 771–787. https://doi.org/10.1007/s43681-022-00138-8

Belgaum, M. R., Alansari, Z., Musa, S., Mansoor Alam, M., & Mazliham, M. S. (2021). Role of artificial intelligence in cloud computing, IoT and SDN: Reliability and scalability issues. *International Journal of Electrical and Computer Engineering (IJECE)*, *11*(5), 4458. https://doi.org/10.11591/ijece.v11i5.pp4458-4470

Bello, H. O., Ige, A. B., & Ameyaw, M. N. (2024). Deep learning in high-frequency trading: Conceptual challenges and solutions for real-time fraud detection. *World Journal of Advanced Engineering Technology and Sciences*, *12*(2), 035–046. https://doi.org/10.30574/wjaets.2024.12.2.0265

Berger, B., Adam, M., Rühr, A., & Benlian, A. (2021). Watch me improve – algorithm aversion and demonstrating the ability to learn. *Business & Information Systems Engineering*, *63*(1), 55–68. https://doi.org/10.1007/s12599-020-00678-5

Berger, R., & Czakert, J. P. (2022). *Stress Management and Resilience Building* (pp. 63–88). Springer, Cham. https://doi.org/10.1007/978-3-030-85120-0_2

Betancourt, M. (2022). *Art, AI and Culture*. I'm Press'd.

Blomkamp, E. (2022). Systemic design practice for participatory policymaking. *Policy Design and Practice*, *5*(1), 12–31. https://doi.org/10.1080/25741292.2021.1887576

Borchert, D. M. (Ed.). (2006). *Encyclopedia of Philosophy, Second Edition, Vol. 1*. Mac millan Reference USA.

Bouza, L., Bugeau, A., & Lannelongue, L. (2023). How to estimate carbon footprint when training deep learning models? A guide and review. *Environmental Research Communi cations*, *11*(115), 1–26. https://doi.org/10.1088/2515-7620/acf81b

Bowie, A. (2003). *Aesthetics and subjectivity: From Kant to Nietzsche*. Manchester University Press. https://doi.org/10.9760/MUPOA/9780719024450

Brachmann, A., & Redies, C. (2017). Computational and experimental approaches to visual aesthetics. *Frontiers in Computational Neuroscience, 11*(102), 1–17. https://doi.org/10.3389/fncom.2017.00102

Brown, P. (2020). *Aesthetic Intelligence. How to Boost it and Use it in Business and Beyond.* Harper Business.

Brown, R. D. (2021). Property ownership and the legal personhood of artificial intelligence. *Information and Communications Technology Law, 30*(2), 208–234. https://doi.org/10.1080/13600834.2020.1861714

Brusseau, J. (2023). Mapping AI avant-gardes in time: Posthumanism, transhumanism, genhumanism. *Discover Artificial Intelligence, 3*(1), 32. https://doi.org/10.1007/s44163-023-00080-6

Brzeziński, D., Filipek, K., Piwowar, K., & Winiarska-Brodowska, M. (2024). *Algorithms, Artificial Intelligence and Beyond.* Routledge. https://doi.org/10.4324/9781032646930

Budach, L., Feuerpfeil, M., Ihde, N., Nathansen, A., Noack, N., Patzlaff, H., Naumann, F., & Harmouch, H. (2024). The effects of data quality on machine learning performance. *ArXiv, 1*(1), 1–49. https://arxiv.org/abs/2207.14529

Burhanuddin, M. A. (2023). Efficient hardware acceleration techniques for deep learning on edge devices: A comprehensive performance analysis. *KHWARIZMIA, 2023*, 103–112. https://doi.org/10.70470/KHWARIZMIA/2023/010

Burr, C., & Leslie, D. (2023). Ethical assurance: A practical approach to the responsible design, development, and deployment of data-driven technologies. *AI and Ethics, 3*(1), 73–98. https://doi.org/10.1007/s43681-022-00178-0

Butlin, P., Long, R., Elmoznino, E., Bengio, Y., Birch, J., Constant, A., Deane, G., Fleming, S. M., Frith, C., Ji, X., Kanai, R., Klein, C., Lindsay, G., Michel, M., Mudrik, L., Peters, M. A. K., Schwitzgebel, E., Simon, J., & VanRullen, R. (2023). *Consciousness in Artificial Intelligence: Insights from the Science of Consciousness* (pp. 1–88). Cornell University. https://arxiv.org/abs/2308.08708

Cabrera, Á. A., Druck, A. J., Hong, J. I., & Perer, A. (2021). Discovering and Validating AI Errors With Crowdsourced Failure Reports. *Proceedings of the ACM on Human-Computer Interaction, 5*(CSCW2), 1–22. https://doi.org/10.1145/3479569

Cabrera, Á. A., Perer, A., & Hong, J. I. (2023). Improving human-AI collaboration with descriptions of AI behavior. *Proceedings of the ACM on Human-Computer Interaction, 7*(CSCW1), Article 136. https://doi.org/10.1145/3579612

Caggiano, V., Ragusa, A., & Di Petrillo, E. (2024). The challenge of humanistic management. In *People and Organizations. Research Series on Responsible Enterprise Ecosystems* (pp. 49–68). Springer, Cham https://doi.org/10.1007/978-3-031-58472-5_3

Calvo-Merino, B. (2021). Dance, expertise, and sensorimotor aesthetics. In Chatterjee, A., & Cardilo, E. (Eds.), *Brain, Beauty, and Art: Essays Bringing Neuroaesthetics into Focus* (pp. 199–202). Oxford Academic, New York. https://doi.org/10.1093/oso/9780197513620.003.0039

Carbon, C.-C. (2011). Cognitive mechanisms for explaining dynamics of aesthetic appreciation. *I-Perception, 2*(7), 708–719. https://doi.org/10.1068/i0463aap

Chamberlain, R., Mullin, C., Scheerlinck, B., & Wagemans, J. (2018). Putting the art in artificial: Aesthetic responses to computer-generated art. *Psychology of Aesthetics, Creativity, and the Arts, 12*(2), 177–192. https://doi.org/10.1037/aca0000136

Chatterjee, A., & Vartanian, O. (2016). Neuroscience of aesthetics. *Annals of the New York Academy of Sciences, 1369*(1), 172–194. https://doi.org/10.1111/nyas.13035

Chen, B., Wu, Z., & Zhao, R. (2023). From fiction to fact: The growing role of generative AI in business and finance. *Journal of Chinese Economic and Business Studies*, *21*(4), 471–496. https://doi.org/10.1080/14765284.2023.2245279

Chen, K., Shao, A., Burapacheep, J., & Li, Y. (2024). Conversational AI and equity through assessing GPT-3's communication with diverse social groups on contentious topics. *Scientific Reports*, *14*(1), 1–12. https://doi.org/10.1038/s41598-024-51969-w

Chen, P., Wu, L., & Wang, L. (2023). AI fairness in data management and analytics: A review on challenges, methodologies and applications. In *Applied Sciences (Switzerland),* 13(18), 1–33. https://doi.org/10.3390/app131810258

Chi, J. (2024). The evolutionary impact of artificial intelligence on contemporary artistic practices. *Communications in Humanities Research*, *35*(1), 52–57. https://doi.org/10.54254/2753-7064/35/20240006

Cieśliński, P. (2025). *AI nas ogłupia? Zniechęca do krytycznego myślenia - sugeruje nowe badanie*. https://wyborcza.pl/7,75400,31688989,naukowcy-zbadali-czy-ai-nas-oglupia.html#S.TD-K.C-B.4-L.1.duzy

Cignitas, C. P., Arevalo, J. A. T., & Crusells, J. V. (2021). Balanced scorecard: The key to employee well-being the impact of balanced scorecard on employee well-being: The case of state of michigan-USA. *The International Journal of Business & Management*, *9*(12), 175–197. https://doi.org/10.24940/theijbm/2021/v9/i12/167392-405656-2-SM

Ciupka, S. (2020). Pathologies and kitsch in the workplace - theoretical perspective. *ASEJ Scientific Journal of Bielsko-Biala School of Finance and Law*, *24*(1), 26–30. https://doi.org/10.5604/01.3001.0014.1347

Congdon, M. (2021). The aesthetics of moral address. *Philosophical Topics*, *49*(1), 123–144. https://www.jstor.org/stable/48652164

Coss, R. G. (2003). The role of evolved perceptual biases in art and design. In Voland, E., & Grammer, K. (Eds.), *Evolutionary Aesthetics* (pp. 69–130). Springer Berlin Heidelberg. https://doi.org/10.1007/978-3-662-07142-7_4

Cox, R. F. A., Tschacher, W., & van Geert, P. (2023). *Modelling Art Experiences Based on the Theory of Complex Dynamical Systems*. https://doi.org/10.31219/osf.io/ys4cb

Currie, A. (2023). Epistemic engagement, aesthetic value, and scientific practice. *The British Journal for the Philosophy of Science*, *74*(2), 313–334. https://doi.org/10.1086/714802

de Almeida, P. G. R., dos Santos, C. D., & Farias, J. S. (2021). Artificial intelligence regulation: A framework for governance. *Ethics and Information Technology*, *23*(3), 505–525. https://doi.org/10.1007/s10676-021-09593-z

del Carmen Rodríguez-Hernández, M., & Ilarri, S. (2021). AI-based mobile context-aware recommender systems from an information management perspective: Progress and directions. *Knowledge-Based Systems*, *215*, 106740. https://doi.org/10.1016/j.knosys.2021.106740

Della Lucia, M., Dimanche, F., Giudici, E., Camargo, B. A., & Winchenbach, A. (2021). Enhancing tourism education: The contribution of humanistic management. *Humanistic Management Journal*, *6*(3), 429–449. https://doi.org/10.1007/s41463-021-00111-3

Dewey, J. (1934). *Art as Experience*. Minton, Balch & Company. https://archive.org/details/deweyjohnartasanexperience

Díaz-Rodríguez, N., Del Ser, J., Coeckelbergh, M., López de Prado, M., Herrera-Viedma, E., Herrera, F., de Prado, M. L., Herrera-Viedma, E., & Herrera, F. (2023). Connecting the dots in trustworthy artificial intelligence: From AI principles, ethics, and key requirements to responsible AI systems and regulation. *Information Fusion, 99*, 101896. https://doi.org/10.1016/j.inffus.2023.101896.

Dierksmeier, C. (2016). What is 'humanistic' about humanistic management? *Humanistic Management Journal, 1*(1), 9–32. https://doi.org/10.1007/s41463-016-0002-6

Dietrich, P., & Knieper, T. (2022). (Neuro)Aesthetics: Beauty, ugliness, and ethics. *PsyCh Journal, 11*(5), 619–627. https://doi.org/10.1002/pchj.478

DiFabrizio, E. (2024). *The Power of AI in Storytelling: Lessons from Lumi and Implications for Associations*. Sidecar. https://sidecar.ai/blog/the-power-of-ai-in-storytelling-lessons-from-lumi-and-implications-for-associations

Dralega, C. A. (2023). An agenda for developing critical literacies for journalism education in an era of datafication. In Dralega, C.A. (Ed.), *Digitization, AI and Algorithms in African Journalism and Media Contexts: Practice, Policy and Critical Literacies,* (pp. 155–160). Emerald Publishing Limited, Leeds. https://doi.org/10.1108/978-1-80455-135-620231010

Dua, T., Podewils, J., & Visconti, C. (2025). AI-powered leadership: Transforming strategy and driving high-performing teams | Insight Partners. In *Insight Partners*. https://www.insightpartners.com/ideas/ai-powered-leadership-transforming-strategy-and-driving-high-performing-teams/

Duhamel, F., Niess, A., & De Geuser, F. (2023). Imagining aesthetic leadership. *Leadership, 19*(5), 413–430. https://doi.org/10.1177/17427150231186000

Edmondson, A. C., & Bransby, D. P. (2023). Psychological safety comes of age: Observed themes in an established literature. *Annual Review of Organizational Psychology and Organizational Behavior, 10*(1), 55–78. https://doi.org/10.1146/annurev-orgpsych-120920-055217

Edwards, M. G. (2021). The growth paradox, sustainable development, and business strategy. *Business Strategy and the Environment, 30*(7), 3079–3094. https://doi.org/10.1002/bse.2790

Einola, K., & Khoreva, V. (2023). Best friend or broken tool? Exploring the co-existence of humans and artificial intelligence in the workplace ecosystem. *Human Resource Management, 62*(1), 117–135. https://doi.org/10.1002/hrm.22147

Enakrire, R. T., & Oladokun, B. D. (2024). Artificial intelligence as enabler of future library services: How prepared are librarians in African university libraries. *Library Hi Tech News, 41*(3), 1–5. https://doi.org/10.1108/LHTN-09-2023-0173

Eng, P. H., & Liu, R. L. (2024). Will intelligent technologies replace humans in the future? An exploratory study for likelihood of intelligent technologies to replace humans in the future. In Al-Sharafi, M. A., Al-Emran, M., Tan, G. W. H., & Ooi, K. B. (Eds.), *Current and Future Trends on Intelligent Technology Adoption. Studies in Computational Intelligence* (pp. 171–202). Springer, Cham. https://doi.org/10.1007/978-3-031-61463-7_9

Epstein, Z., Hertzmann, A., Akten, M., Farid, H., Fjeld, J., Frank, M. R., Groh, M., Herman, L., Leach, N., Mahari, R., Pentland, A. "Sandy," Russakovsky, O., Schroeder, H., & Smith, A. (2023). Art and the science of generative AI. *Science, 380*(6650), 1110–1111. https://doi.org/10.1126/science.adh4451

Everhart, A. (2023). *Aesthetic Intelligence: Unlock Your Unique Path to Success and Build an Authentic and Distinctive Business*. Alexia Everhart.

Fellenz, M. R., Hoidn, S., & Brady, M. (2022). *The Future of Management Education*. Routledge. https://doi.org/10.4324/9781003095903

Ferrara, E. (2023). Fairness and bias in artificial intelligence: A brief survey of sources, impacts, and mitigation strategies. *Sci*, *6*(1), 3. https://doi.org/10.3390/sci6010003

Folkmann, M. N. (2013). *The Aesthetics of Imagination in Design*. MIT Press.

Fontrodona, J., & Melé, D. (2022). Thinking about the future of work: Promoting dignity and human flourishing. *Humanistic Management Journal*, *7*(2), 181–188. https://doi.org/10.1007/s41463-022-00136-2

Forlini, S., Hinrichs, U., & Brosz, J. (2018). Mining the material archive: Balancing sensate experience and sense-making in digitized print collections. *Open Library of Humanities*, *4*(2), 1–36. https://doi.org/10.16995/olh.282

Fuchs, C. (2020). Towards a critical theory of communication as renewal and update of Marxist humanism in the age of digital capitalism. *Journal for the Theory of Social Behaviour*, *50*(3), 335–356. https://doi.org/10.1111/jtsb.12247

Gagliardi, P. (2006). Organisational culture and symbols. In S. R. Clegg, C. Hardy, T. B. Lawrence, & W. R. Nord (Eds.), *The SAGE Handbook of Organisation Studies* (pp. 1028–1045). SAGE Publications.

Gallace, A., & Spence, C. (2011). Tactile aesthetics: Towards a definition of its characteristics and neural correlates. *Social Semiotics*, *21*(4), 569–589. https://doi.org/10.1080/10350330.2011.591998

García-de-la-Torre, C., Arandia, O., & Vázquez-Maguirre, M. (Eds.). (2021). *Humanistic Management in Latin America*. Routledge. https://doi.org/10.4324/9780429351174

García-Juan, B., Escrig-Tena, A. B., & Roca-Puig, V. (2023). Structural empowerment and organisational performance: The mediating role of employees' well-being in Spanish local governments. *The International Journal of Human Resource Management*, *34*(10), 1907–1939. https://doi.org/10.1080/09585192.2020.1859581

Ghosh, K., & Sadeghian, S. (2024). The Impact of AI on Perceived Job Decency and Meaningfulness: A Case Study. In *Symposium on Human-Computer Interaction for Work (CHIWORK '24),* June 2024, *Newcastle-upon-Tyne, UK* (Vol. 1, Issue 1). Association for Computing Machinery. https://doi.org/10.48550/arXiv.2406.14273

Gilbert, J. (2024). Techno-feudalism or platform capitalism? Conceptualising the digital society. *European Journal of Social Theory*, *27*(4), 561–578. https://doi.org/10.1177/13684310241276474

Gillette, J. (2023). *Digital Painting and Rendering for Theatrical Design*. Routledge. https://doi.org/10.4324/9781003212836

Giorgetti, I. (2024). Exploring the intersection of art, human creativity, and AI. *Itinera*, *28*, 156–172. https://doi.org/10.54103/2039-9251/27841

Gołaszewska, M. (1984). *Zarys estetyki*. PWN.

Gołaszewska, M. (1986). *O naturze wartości estetycznych*. Uniwersytet Jagielloński.

Goldsteen, A., Saadi, O., Shmelkin, R., Shachor, S., & Razinkov, N. (2023). AI privacy toolkit. *SoftwareX*, *22*, 1–6. https://doi.org/10.1016/j.softx.2023.101352

Gonzalez Fabre, R., Camacho Ibáñez, J., & Tejedor Escobar, P. (2021). Moral control and ownership in AI systems. *AI and Society*, *36*(1), 289–303. https://doi.org/10.1007/s00146-020-01020-z

Goode, M. R., Dahl, D. W., & Moreau, C. P. (2013). Innovation aesthetics: The relationship between category cues, categorization certainty, and newness perceptions. *Journal of Product Innovation Management*, *30*(2), 192–208. https://doi.org/10.1111/j.1540-5885.2012.00995.x

Gortais, B. (2003). Abstraction and art. *Philosophical Transactions of the Royal Society of London. Series B: Biological Sciences*, 358(1435), 1241–1249. https://doi.org/10.1098/rstb.2003.1309

Gotsis, G. (2022). *Humanistic Leadership in the Confucian Context: Philosophical Foundations and Empirical Implications* (pp. 109–133). Palgrave Macmillan, Cham. https://doi.org/10.1007/978-3-031-09540-5_6

Gotsis, G., & Grimani, A. (2024). Humanistic leadership. In Marques, J. (Ed.), *Encyclopedia of Diversity, Equity, Inclusion and Spirituality* (pp. 1–20). Springer Nature Switzerland. https://doi.org/10.1007/978-3-031-32257-0_14-1

Graf, L., Bach, H., & Tiede, D. (2020). Semantic segmentation of sentinel-2 imagery for mapping irrigation center pivots. *Remote Sensing*, *12*(23), 1–19. https://doi.org/10.3390/rs12233937

Guyer, P. (1997). *Kant and the Claims of Taste*. Cambridge University Press.

Hamzah, M. (2012). Objectifying subjectivity in images through aesthetics: A Bergsonian approach. *2012 International Conference on Innovation Management and Technology Resear*ch, Malacca, Malaysia, 247–252. https://doi.org/10.1109/ICIMTR.2012.6236397

Henkin, D. (2024). *5 Ways Leaders Can Win Hearts And Minds, And Drive Results – With AI*. Forbes. https://www.forbes.com/sites/davidhenkin/2024/03/05/5-ways-leaders-can-win-hearts-and-minds-and-drive-results-with-ai/

Herath, D. B., Ode, E., & Herath, G. B. (2025). Can AI replace humans? Comparing the capabilities of AI tools and human performance in a business management education scenario. *British Educational Research Journal*, *51*(3), 1073–1096. https://doi.org/10.1002/berj.4111

Himmelreich, J. (2023). Against "democratizing AI." *AI & Society*, *38*(4), 1333–1346. https://doi.org/10.1007/s00146-021-01357-z

Hitsuwari, J., Ueda, Y., Yun, W., & Nomura, M. (2023). Does human–AI collaboration lead to more creative art? Aesthetic evaluation of human-made and AI-generated haiku poetry. *Computers in Human Behavior*, *139*, 107502. https://doi.org/10.1016/j.chb.2022.107502

Hoang, G., Wilson-Evered, E., Lockstone-Binney, L., & Luu, T. T. (2021). Empowering leadership in hospitality and tourism management: A systematic literature review. *International Journal of Contemporary Hospitality Management*, *33*(12), 4182–4214. https://doi.org/10.1108/IJCHM-03-2021-0323

Horkheimer, M., & Adorno, T. (2002). *Dialectic of Enlightenment: Pfilosophical Fragments* (G. Schmid Noerr (Ed.)). Stanford University Press.

Hou, X., Omar, N., & Wang, J. (2022). Interactive design psychology and artificial intelligence-based innovative exploration of Anglo-American traumatic narrative literature. *Frontiers in Psychology*, *12*, 1–14. https://doi.org/10.3389/fpsyg.2021.755039

How AI will divide the best from the rest. (2025). *The Economist*. https://www.economist.com/finance-and-economics/2025/02/13/how-ai-will-divide-the-best-from-the-rest

Hoyer, W. D., & Stokburger-Sauer, N. E. (2012). The role of aesthetic taste in consumer behavior. *Journal of the Academy of Marketing Science*, *40*(1), 167–180. https://doi.org/10.1007/s11747-011-0269-y

Hrybiuk, O., & Kant, G. S. (2024). *CleverCOMSRL: Implementation of an AI Computer-Aided Design System in the Context of the Cognitive Science Paradigm for the Research Training Process* (pp. 351–362). Springer, Cham. https://doi.org/10.1007/978-3-031-61575-7_32

Hu, Q., Lu, Y., Pan, Z., Gong, Y., & Yang, Z. (2021). Can AI artifacts influence human cognition? The effects of artificial autonomy in intelligent personal assistants. *International Journal of Information Management*, *56*, 102250. https://doi.org/10.1016/j.ijinfomgt.2020.102250

Hurme, P., & Jouhki, J. (2017). We shape our tools, and thereafter our tools shape us. *Human Technology*, *13*(2), 145–148. https://doi.org/10.17011/ht/urn.201711104209

Ihejirika, C. (2015). Ethico-epistemological implications of artificial intelligence for humanity. *Sophia, An African Journal of Philosophy and Public Affairs*, *16*(1), 190–199.

Islam, M. T., Hasan, M. M., Redwanuzzaman, M., & Hossain, M. K. (2024). Practices of artificial intelligence to improve the business in Bangladesh. *Social Sciences and Humanities Open*, *9*, 1–10. https://doi.org/10.1016/j.ssaho.2023.100766

Iwuanyanwu, O., Gil-Ozoudeh, I., Okwandu, A. C., & Ike, C. S. (2024). Cultural and social dimensions of green architecture: Designing for sustainability and community well-being. *International Journal of Applied Research in Social Sciences*, *6*(8), 1951–1968. https://doi.org/10.51594/ijarss.v6i8.1477

Jadhav, R., Tikone, S., Bahiram, M., Dhumane, A., Meshram, V., Meshram, V., Choudhury, T., & Sar, A. (2024). *Integrated Dashboard for Generative AI Model* (pp. 437–450). https://doi.org/10.1007/978-981-97-5146-4_38

Jan, Z., Ahamed, F., Mayer, W., Patel, N., Grossmann, G., Stumptner, M., & Kuusk, A. (2023). Artificial intelligence for industry 4.0: Systematic review of applications, challenges, and opportunities. *Expert Systems with Applications*, *216*, 119456. https://doi.org/10.1016/j.eswa.2022.119456

Jarrahi, M. H. (2018). Artificial intelligence and the future of work: Human-AI symbiosis in organizational decision making. *Business Horizons*, *61*(4), 577–586. https://doi.org/10.1016/j.bushor.2018.03.007

Javed, H., El-Sappagh, S., & Abuhmed, T. (2024). Robustness in deep learning models for medical diagnostics: Security and adversarial challenges towards robust AI applications. *Artificial Intelligence Review*, *58*(1), 12. https://doi.org/10.1007/s10462-024-11005-9

Johnson, K. B., Wei, W., Weeraratne, D., Frisse, M. E., Misulis, K., Rhee, K., Zhao, J., & Snowdon, J. L. (2021). Precision medicine, AI, and the future of personalized health care. *Clinical and Translational Science*, *14*(1), 86–93. https://doi.org/10.1111/cts.12884

Joyce, D. W., Kormilitzin, A., Smith, K. A., & Cipriani, A. (2023). Explainable artificial intelligence for mental health through transparency and interpretability for understand ability. *Npj Digital Medicine*, *6*(1), 6. https://doi.org/10.1038/s41746-023-00751-9

Kaggwa, S., Eleogu, T. F., Okonkwo, F., Farayola, O. A., Uwaoma, P. U., & Akinoso, A. (2024). AI in decision making: Transforming business strategies. *International Journal of Research and Scientific Innovation*, *X*(XII), 423–444. https://doi.org/10.51244/IJRSI.2023.1012032

Kamikubo, R., Wang, L., Marte, C., Mahmood, A., & Kacorri, H. (2022). Data Representativeness in Accessibility Datasets: A Meta-Analysis. *Proceedings of the 24th International ACM SIGACCESS Conference on Computers and Accessibility*, 1–15. https://doi.org/10.1145/3517428.3544826

Kant, E. (2015). *Kritik der Urteilskraft*. Anaconda Verlag.

Karangutkar, A. A. (2023). The impact of artificial intelligence on job displacement and the future of work. *International Journal of Advanced Research in Science, Communication and Technology, 3*(1), 635–638. https://doi.org/10.48175/ijarsct-12096

Karim, A. K. M. R., Prativa, S., & Likova, L. (2022). Perception and appreciation of tactile objects: The role of visual experience and texture parameters (JPI-first). *Electronic Imaging, 34*(11), 1–20. https://doi.org/10.2352/J.Percept.Imaging.2022.5.000405

Kathuria, Y., Chaki, N. R., Kaur, M., Kumar, S., & Medhavi, R. (2024). Responsible AI impact assessment mechanism for India: A robust strategy for effective governance of AI systems in the country. *AIP Conference Proceedings, 3220*(1), 040010. https://doi.org/10.1063/5.0234670

Kaufman, B. E., Barry, M., Wilkinson, A., & Gomez, R. (2021). Alternative balanced scorecards built from paradigm models in strategic HRM and employment/industrial relations and used to measure the state of employment relations and HR system performance across U.S. workplaces. *Human Resource Management Journal, 31*(1), 65–92. https://doi.org/10.1111/1748-8583.12271

Khan, M. A., Saleh, A. M., Waseem, M., & Sajjad, I. A. (2023). Artificial intelligence enabled demand response: Prospects and challenges in smart grid environment. *IEEE Access, 11*, 1477–1505. https://doi.org/10.1109/ACCESS.2022.3231444

Klimenko, A. V., & Beskrovnaya, O. V. (2022). Emotional and aesthetic experience as a component of artistic activity among college students. *Psychological-Pedagogical Journal GAUDEAMUS, 3*, 66–73. https://doi.org/10.20310/1810-231x-2022-21-3-66-73

Kociatkiewicz, J., & Kostera, M. (2013). Humanistic management: Agenda outline. *Problemy Zarzadzania, 11*(44), 9–19. https://doi.org/10.7172/1644-9584.44.1

Koczanowicz, D. (2023). *The Aesthetics of Taste: Eating within the Realm of Art*. Brill. https://doi.org/10.1163/9789004496118_008

Kodakandla, N. (2024). Scaling AI responsibly: Leveraging MLOps for sustainable machine learning deployments. *International Journal of Science and Research Archive, 13*(1), 3447–3455. https://doi.org/10.30574/ijsra.2024.13.1.1798

Koivunen, N., & Wennes, G. (2011). Show us the sound! Aesthetic leadership of symphony orchestra conductors. *Leadership, 7*(1), 51–71. https://doi.org/10.1177/1742715010386865

Kolides, A., Nawaz, A., Rathor, A., Beeman, D., Hashmi, M., Fatima, S., Berdik, D., Al-Ayyoub, M., & Jararweh, Y. (2023). Artificial intelligence foundation and pre-trained models: Fundamentals, applications, opportunities, and social impacts. *Simulation Modelling Practice and Theory, 126*, 102754. https://doi.org/10.1016/j.simpat.2023.102754

Koon, V. (2024). Unveiling the impact of corporate humanistic responsibility on sustain able employee well-being: Exploring perceived support and shared experiences. *Business Strategy & Development, 7*(2). https://doi.org/10.1002/bsd2.381

Koon, V.-Y., & Fujimoto, Y. (2024). From Corporate Social Responsibility (CSR) to corporate humanistic responsibility (CHR): The conceptualization and operationalization of perceived CHR. *Personnel Review, 53*(4), 877–899. https://doi.org/10.1108/PR-07-2022-0491

Kostera, M., & Woźniak, C. (2022). *Aesthetics, Organization, and Humanistic Management*. Routledge.

Kostopoulos, G., Davrazos, G., & Kotsiantis, S. (2024). Explainable artificial intelligence-based decision support systems: A recent review. *Electronics, 13*(14), 2842. https://doi.org/10.3390/electronics13142842

Kuklin, V., Ivin, L., & Mekhovych, S. (2023). Artificial intelligence and humanity. *Energy Saving. Power Engineering. Energy Audit.*, *4*(182), 51–59. https://doi.org/10.20998/2313-8890.2023.04.06

Kumar, D. (2023). Socrates' method of "not writing". *Fedro, Revista de Estética y Teoría de Las Artes*, *23*, 116–124. https://doi.org/10.12795/Fedro/2023.i23.07

Laszlo, C. (2019). Strengthening humanistic management. *Humanistic Management Journal*, *4*(1), 85–94. https://doi.org/10.1007/s41463-019-00055-9

Laursen, K. W. (1978). *Use of Calculators in High School General Mathematics: A Study Comparing Achievement, Attitude, and Attendance of General Mathematics Students Who Used Calculators with Students Who Did Not.* Brigham Young University.

Le, K. T. (2023). New aesthetics in history: The changes of idealism. *The International Journal of Social, Political and Community Agendas in the Arts*, *19*(1), 39–73. https://doi.org/10.18848/2326-9960/CGP/v19i01/39-73

Leder, H., Belke, B., Oeberst, A., & Augustin, D. (2004). A model of aesthetic appreciation and aesthetic judgments. *British Journal of Psychology*, *95*(4), 489–508. https://doi.org/10.1348/0007126042369811

Leder, H., & Nadal, M. (2014). Ten years of a model of aesthetic appreciation and aesthetic judgments : The aesthetic episode – Developments and challenges in empirical aesthetics. *British Journal of Psychology*, *105*(4), 443–464. https://doi.org/10.1111/bjop.12084

Lee, H. H., Tankelevitch, L., Drosos, I., Rintel, S., Banks, R., & Wilson, N. (2025). The Impact of Generative AI on Critical Thinking : Self-Reported Reductions in Cognitive Effort and Confidence Effects From a Survey of Knowledge Workers. *CHI Conference on Human Factors in Computing Systems (CHI '25), April 26-May 01, 2025, Yokohama, Japan*, *1*(1). https://doi.org/10.1145/3706598.3713778

Lee, H., & Youn, N. (2025). Immersed in art: The impact of affinity for rechnology interaction and hedonic motivation on aesthetic experiences in virtual reality. *Empirical Studies of the Arts*, *43*(1), 355–384. https://doi.org/10.1177/02762374241282938

Leong, P. (2023). *Beyond Disbelief: Envisioning Humanity in the AI-Driven Era.* Medium. https://pennyleong.medium.com/beyond-disbelief-envisioning-humanity-in-the-ai-driven-era-97d24c3715a1

Li, B., & Lu, W. (2023). Application of image processing technology in the digital media era in the design of integrated materials painting in installation art. *Multimedia Tools and Applications*, *83*(18), 54211–54228. https://doi.org/10.1007/s11042-023-17713-8

Li, S. E. (2023). *Reinforcement Learning for Sequential Decision and Optimal Control.* Springer Nature Singapore. https://doi.org/10.1007/978-981-19-7784-8

Lim, D. (2022). AI, equity, and the IP gap. *SMU Law Review*, *75*(4), 815. https://doi.org/10.25172/smulr.75.4.4

Lins, S., Pandl, K. D., Teigeler, H., Thiebes, S., Bayer, C., & Sunyaev, A. (2021). Artificial intelligence as a service. *Business & Information Systems Engineering*, *63*(4), 441–456. https://doi.org/10.1007/s12599-021-00708-w

Lippman, E. A. (1999). *The Philosophy & Aesthetics of Music.* University of Nebraska Press.

Liu, W., Zhang, S., Zhang, T., Gu, Q., Han, W., & Zhu, Y. (2024). The AI empathy effect: A mechanism of emotional contagion. *Journal of Hospitality Marketing and Management*, *33*(6), 703–734. https://doi.org/10.1080/19368623.2024.2315954

Loke, S. P. (2017). A structural approach to ethical reasoning: The integration of moral philosophy. *Academy of Strategic Management Journal*, *16*(1), 81–113.
Lollini, M. (2022). Time of the end? more-than-human humanism and artificial intelligence. *Humanist Studies & the Digital Age*, 7(1), 1–30. https://doi.org/10.5399/uo/hsda/7.1.3
Lomas, T. (2023). The appeal of aesthetics: A cross-cultural lexical analysis. *Psychology of Aesthetics, Creativity, and the Arts*, *17*(4), 518–529. https://doi.org/10.1037/aca0000484
Lomas, J. D., & Xue, H. (2022). Harmony in design: A synthesis of literature from classical philosophy, the sciences, economics, and design. *She Ji: The Journal of Design, Economics, and Innovation*, *8*(1), 5–64. https://doi.org/10.1016/j.sheji.2022.01.001
Lorand, R. (2002). *Aesthetic Order*. Routledge. https://doi.org/10.4324/9780203468944
Lovison, G. (2024). Johannes trithemius and witches: Between religion and superstition. *Religions*, *15*(10), 1274. https://doi.org/10.3390/rel15101274
Løvoll, H. S., Sæther, K.-W., & Graves, M. (2020). Feeling at home in the wilderness: Environmental conditions, well-being and aesthetic experience. *Frontiers in Psychology*, *11*, 1–13. https://doi.org/10.3389/fpsyg.2020.00402
Lu, Y., & Zhou, Y. (2021). A review on the economics of artificial intelligence. *Journal of Economic Surveys*, *35*(4), 1045–1072. https://doi.org/10.1111/joes.12422
Maclagan, D. (2001). *Psychological Aesthetics: Painting, Feeling, and Making Sense*. Jessica Kingsley Publishers.
Mahmoud, A. B., Kumar, V., & Spyropoulou, S. (2025). Identifying the public's beliefs about generative artificial intelligence: A big data approach. *IEEE Transactions on Engineering Management*, *72*, 1–15. https://doi.org/10.1109/TEM.2025.3534088
Manovich, L. (2018). *AI Aesthetics* (pp. 1–22). Strelka Press. https://www.academia.edu/41332526/AI_Aesthetics
Marschallek, B. E., Wagner, V., & Jacobsen, T. (2023). Smooth as glass and hard as stone? On the conceptual structure of the aesthetics of materials. *Psychology of Aesthetics, Creativity, and the Arts*, *17*(5), 632–644. https://doi.org/10.1037/aca0000437
Mastandrea, S., Tinio, P. P. L., & Smith, J. K. (2021). Editorial: Environment, art, and museums: The aesthetic experience in different contexts. *Frontiers in Psychology*, *12*, 1–3. https://doi.org/10.3389/fpsyg.2021.675165
Matheson, A., Dillon, P. J., Guillén, M., & Warner, C. (2021). People mattering at work: A humanistic management perspective. *Humanistic Management Journal*, *6*(3), 405–428. https://doi.org/10.1007/s41463-021-00113-1
Melé, D. (2016). Understanding humanistic management. *Humanistic Management Journal*, *1*(1), 33–55. https://doi.org/10.1007/s41463-016-0011-5
Metwally, M. E.-S. M. M. (2024). The dynamics of actual movement and its aesthetic applications in the field of interactive sculptural formation. *International Journal of Advanced Research on Planning and Sustainable Development*, *7*(1), 1–45. https://doi.org/10.21608/ijarpsd.2024.317473.1008
Mikalef, P., & Gupta, M. (2021). Artificial intelligence capability: Conceptualization, measurement calibration, and empirical study on its impact on organizational creativity and firm performance. *Information and Management*, *58*(3), 103434. https://doi.org/10.1016/j.im.2021.103434
Miller, A. (2019). The intrinsically linked future for human and artificial intelligence interaction. *Journal of Big Data*, *6*(1), 38. https://doi.org/10.1186/s40537-019-0202-7

Minahan, S. (2020). *Aesthetic Turn in Management*. Routledge. https://doi.org/10.4324/9781351147965

Mohammed, K. (2023). AI in cloud computing: Exploring how cloud providers can leverage AI to optimize resource allocation, improve scalability, and offer AI-as-a-service solutions. *Advances in Engineering Innovation*, *3*(1), None–None. https://doi.org/10.54254/2977-3903/3/2023035

Montani, P. (2021). Techno-aesthetics and forms of the imagination. In Chiodo, S., & Schiaffonati, V. (Eds.), *Italian Philosophy of Technology. Philosophy of Engineering and Technology* (vol. 35, pp. 247–261). Springer, Cham. https://doi.org/10.1007/978-3-030-54522-2_16

Montesinos López, O. A., Montesinos López, A., & Crossa, J. (2022). Fundamentals of artificial neural networks and deep learning. In *Multivariate Statistical Machine Learning Methods for Genomic Prediction* (pp. 379–425). Springer International Publishing, Cham. https://doi.org/10.1007/978-3-030-89010-0_10

Muzari, T., Nevers Shava, G., & Shonhiwa, S. (2022). Qualitative research paradigm, a key research design for educational researchers, processes and procedures: A theoretical overview. *Indiana Journal of Humanities and Social Sciences*, *2*(1), 14–20. https://indianapublications.com/Journals/IJHSS

Naeem, S., Ali, A., Anam, S., & Ahmed, M. M. (2023). An unsupervised machine learning algorithms: Comprehensive review. *International Journal of Computing and Digital Systems*, *13*(1), 911–921. https://doi.org/10.12785/ijcds/130172

Naumov, A. V. (2024). Artificial intelligence vs human mind. *Sociopolitical Sciences*, *14*(4), 202–206. https://doi.org/10.33693/2223-0092-2024-14-4-202-206

Nishant, R., Schneckenberg, D., & Ravishankar, M. N. M. (2024). The formal rationality of artificial intelligence-based algorithms and the problem of bias. *Journal of Information Technology*, *39*(1), 19–40. https://doi.org/10.1177/02683962231176842

Nursalim, S. M., & Masitoh, A. N. (2023). Aesthetics and artificial intelligence: Impact and criticism of art. *Education Achievement: Journal of Science and Research*, *9*(23), 116–123. https://doi.org/10.51178/jsr.v4i3.1667

O'Connor, Z. (2015). Colour, contrast and gestalt theories of perception: The impact in contemporary visual communications design. *Color Research & Application*, *40*(1), 85–92. https://doi.org/10.1002/col.21858

Olan, F., Ogiemwonyi Arakpogun, E., Suklan, J., Nakpodia, F., Damij, N., & Jayawickrama, U. (2022). Artificial intelligence and knowledge sharing: Contributing factors to organizational performance. *Journal of Business Research*, *145*, 605–615. https://doi.org/10.1016/j.jbusres.2022.03.008

Olatinwo, D. D., Abu-Mahfouz, A., Hancke, G., & Myburgh, H. (2023). IoT-Enabled WBAN and machine learning for speech emotion recognition in patients. *Sensors*, *23*(6), 1–23. https://doi.org/10.3390/s23062948

Osborne, H. (1986). Symmetry as an aesthetic factor. *Computers & Mathematics with Applications*, *12*(1–2), 77–82. https://doi.org/10.1016/0898-1221(86)90140-9

Ostherr, K. (2022). Artificial intelligence and medical humanities. *Journal of Medical Humanities*, *43*(2), 211–232. https://doi.org/10.1007/s10912-020-09636-4

Ou, A. W., Stöhr, C., & Malmström, H. (2024). Academic communication with AI-powered language tools in higher education: From a post-humanist perspective. *System*, *121*, 103225. https://doi.org/10.1016/j.system.2024.103225

P.S., V. (2023). How can we manage biases in artificial intelligence systems – A systematic literature review. *International Journal of Information Management Data Insights*, *3*(1), 100165. https://doi.org/10.1016/j.jjimei.2023.100165
Pagis, M., & Summers-Effler, E. (2021). Aesthetic engagement*. *Sociological Forum*, *36*(S1), 1371–1394. https://doi.org/10.1111/socf.12768
Pedan, I. (2022). Artistic properties of natural materials in object design: imitation and interpretation. *Culture of Ukraine*, *77*, 65–72. https://doi.org/10.31516/2410-5325.077.08
Peters, T. (2018). Radical life extension, cybernetic immortality, and techno-salvation. Really? *Dialog*, *57*(4), 250–256. https://doi.org/10.1111/dial.12432
Pham Thi, T. D., & Duong, N. T. (2024). Investigating learning burnout and academic performance among management students: A longitudinal study in English courses. *BMC Psychology*, *12*(1), 219. https://doi.org/10.1186/s40359-024-01725-6
Pieterse, J. N. (1993). Aesthetics of power: Time and body politics. *Third Text*, *7*(22), 33–42. https://doi.org/10.1080/09528829308576398
Pirson, M. (2017). *Humanistic Management. Protecting Dignity and Promoting Well-being*. Cambridge University Press.
Pirson, M. (2023). Dignity, humanistic management and the sustainable development goals. *Journal of Management for Global Sustainability*, *11*(1), 13–38. https://doi.org/10.13185/2244-6893.1001
Pizzolante, M., Pelowski, M., Demmer, T. R., Bartolotta, S., Sarcinella, E. D., Gaggioli, A., & Chirico, A. (2024). Aesthetic experiences and their transformative power: A systematic review. *Frontiers in Psychology*, *15*, 1–22. https://doi.org/10.3389/fpsyg.2024.1328449
Poggioli, N. A. (2024). Awareness of multiple nature ontologies in humanistic management. *Humanistic Management Journal*, *10*, 111–124. https://doi.org/10.1007/s41463-024-00191-x
Ponomareva, N., Hazimeh, H., Kurakin, A., Xu, Z., Denison, C., McMahan, H. B., Vassilvitskii, S., Chien, S., & Thakurta, A. G. (2023). How to DP-fy ML: A practical guide to machine learning with differential privacy. *Journal of Artificial Intelligence Research*, *77*, 1113–1201. https://doi.org/10.1613/jair.1.14649
Pradhan, R. K., & Hati, L. (2022). The measurement of employee well-being: Development and validation of a scale. *Global Business Review*, *23*(2), 385–407. https://doi.org/10.1177/0972150919859101
Prem, E. (2024). Principles of digital humanism: A critical post-humanist view. *Journal of Responsible Technology*, *17*, 100075. https://doi.org/10.1016/j.jrt.2024.100075
Qin, Y., Hu, S., Lin, Y., Chen, W., Ding, N., Cui, G., Zeng, Z., Zhou, X., Huang, Y., Xiao, C., Han, C., Fung, Y. R., Su, Y., Wang, H., Qian, C., Tian, R., Zhu, K., Liang, S., Shen, X., … Sun, M. (2025). Tool learning with foundation models. *ACM Computing Surveys*, *57*(4), 1–40. https://doi.org/10.1145/3704435
Quintelier, K. J. P., van Hugten, J., Parmar, B. L., & Brokerhof, I. M. (2021). Humanizing stakeholders by rethinking business. *Frontiers in Psychology*, *12*, 1–15. https://doi.org/10.3389/fpsyg.2021.687067
Rang, W., Yang, D., Cheng, D., & Wang, Y. (2021). Data life aware model updating strategy for stream-based online deep learning. *IEEE Transactions on Parallel and Distributed Systems*, *32*(10), 2571–2581. https://doi.org/10.1109/TPDS.2021.3071939
Rawashdeh, A. (2023). The consequences of artificial intelligence: an investigation into the impact of AI on job displacement in accounting. *Journal of Science and Technology Policy Management*, *16*(3), 506–535. https://doi.org/10.1108/JSTPM-02-2023-0030

Redies, C. (2015). Combining universal beauty and cultural context in a unifying model of visual aesthetic experience. *Frontiers in Human Neuroscience*, *09*, 1–20. https://doi.org/10.3389/fnhum.2015.00218

Renoult, J. P. (2016). The evolution of aesthetics: A review of models. In Kapoula, Z., & Vernet, M. (Eds.), *Aesthetics and Neuroscience* (pp. 271–299). Springer International Publishing, Cham. https://doi.org/10.1007/978-3-319-46233-2_17

Rezaei, A., Liu, A., Memarrast, O., & Ziebart, B. D. (2021). Robust fairness under covariate shift. *Proceedings of the AAAI Conference on Artificial Intelligence*, 35(11), 9419–9427. https://doi.org/10.1609/aaai.v35i11.17135

Riedl, M. O. (2019). Human-centered artificial intelligence and machine learning. *Human Behavior and Emerging Technologies*, *1*(1), 33–36. https://doi.org/10.1002/hbe2.117

Riveiro, M., & Thill, S. (2021). "That's (not) the output I expected!" On the role of end user expectations in creating explanations of AI systems. *Artificial Intelligence*, *298*, 103507. https://doi.org/10.1016/j.artint.2021.103507

Root-Bernstein, R. S. (2002). Aesthetic cognition. *International Studies in the Philosophy of Science*, *16*(1), 61–77. https://doi.org/10.1080/02698590120118837

Russell, S., & Norvig, P. (2021). *Artificial Intelligence: A Modern Approach, Global Edition, 4ed.* Pearson Education.

Saravanan, R., & Sujatha, P. (2018). A State of Art Techniques on Machine Learning Algorithms: A Perspective of Supervised Learning Approaches in Data Classification. *2018 Second International Conference on Intelligent Computing and Control Systems (ICICCS*), Madurai, 945–949. https://doi.org/10.1109/ICCONS.2018.8663155

Sarker, I. H. (2022). AI-Based modeling: Techniques, applications and research issues towards automation, intelligent and smart systems. *SN Computer Science*, *3*(2), 158. https://doi.org/10.1007/s42979-022-01043-x

Saxena, P., Saxena, V., Pandey, A., Prync Flato, U. A., & Shukla, K. (2023). *Multiple Aspects of Artificial Intelligence*. Book Saga Publications. https://doi.org/10.60148/muasartificialintelligence

Schindler, I., Hosoya, G., Menninghaus, W., Beermann, U., Wagner, V., Eid, M., & Scherer, K. R. (2017). Measuring aesthetic emotions: A review of the literature and a new assessment tool. *PLOS ONE*, *12*(6), e0178899. https://doi.org/10.1371/journal.pone.0178899

Schwartz, R., Vassilev, A., Greene, K., Perine, L., Burt, A., & Hall, P. (2022). *Towards a Standard for Identifying and Managing Bias in Artificial Intelligence*. NIST. https://doi.org/10.6028/NIST.SP.1270

Schwepker, C. H., Valentine, S. R., Giacalone, R. A., & Promislo, M. (2021). Good barrels yield healthy apples: Organizational ethics as a mechanism for mitigating work-related stress and promoting employee well-being. *Journal of Business Ethics*, *174*(1), 143–159. https://doi.org/10.1007/s10551-020-04562-w

Scorolli, C., Naddei Grasso, E., Stacchio, L., Armandi, V., Matteucci, G., & Marfia, G. (2023). Would you rather come to a tango concert in theater or in VR? Aesthetic emotions & social presence in musical experiences, either live, 2D or 3D. *Computers in Human Behavior*, *149*, 107910. https://doi.org/10.1016/j.chb.2023.107910

Scruton, R. (1997). *The Aesthetics of Music*. Oxford University Press.

Sharma, A. (2024). Aesthetic transcendence: Fashion's evolution, philosophical reflections, and societal impact. *Journal of Current Social and Political Issues*, *2*(1), 10–21. https://doi.org/10.15575/jcspi.v2i1.662

Sharma, D., & Bikshandi, B. (2020). Artificial empathy – An artificial intelligence challenge. In *Artificial Intelligence* (pp. 321–326). Productivity Press. https://doi.org/10.4324/9780429317415-19

Sharma, S., Islam, N., Singh, G., & Dhir, A. (2024). Why do retail customers adopt artificial intelligence (AI) based autonomous decision-making systems? *IEEE Transactions on Engineering Management*, *71*, 1846–1861. https://doi.org/10.1109/TEM.2022.3157976

Sherrard, C. (1995). Social identity and aesthetic taste. *Philosophical Psychology*, *8*(2), 139–153. https://doi.org/10.1080/09515089508573150

Shneiderman, B. (2020). Human-centered artificial intelligence: Three fresh ideas. *AIS Transactions on Human-Computer Interaction*, *12*(3), 109–124. https://doi.org/10.17705/1thci.00131

Shusterman, R. (2023). The ambiguity of aesthetic value. *The Journal of Aesthetics and Art Criticism*, *81*(1), 101–102. https://doi.org/10.1093/jaac/kpac062

Sindiramutty, S. R., Prabagaran, K. R. V., Akbar, R., Hussain, M., & Malik, N. A. (2024). *Generative AI for Secure User Interface (UI) Design* (pp. 333–394). https://doi.org/10.4018/979-8-3693-5415-5.ch010

Sjöblom, K., Juutinen, S., & Mäkikangas, A. (2022). The importance of self-leadership strategies and psychological safety for well-being in the context of enforced remote work. *Challenges*, *13*(1), 14. https://doi.org/10.3390/challe13010014

Sjödin, D., Parida, V., Palmié, M., & Wincent, J. (2021). How AI capabilities enable business model innovation: Scaling AI through co-evolutionary processes and feedback loops. *Journal of Business Research*, *134*, 574–587. https://doi.org/10.1016/j.jbusres.2021.05.009

Skrzypek, M. (2025). Robot, twój brat. *Polityka*, *6*(3501), 59–61.

Smuha, N. A. (2021). Beyond the individual: Governing AI's societal harm. *Internet Policy Review*, *10*(3), 1–32. https://doi.org/10.14763/2021.3.1574

Snodgrass, J. G., Bagwell, A., Patry, J. M., Dengah, H. J. F., Smarr-Foster, C., Van Oostenburg, M., & Lacy, M. G. (2018). The partial truths of compensatory and poor-get-poorer internet use theories: More highly involved videogame players experience greater psychosocial benefits. *Computers in Human Behavior*, *78*, 10–25. https://doi.org/10.1016/j.chb.2017.09.020

Stankevičienė, A., Tamaševičius, V., Diskienė, D., Grakauskas, Ž., & Rudinskaja, L. (2021). The mediating effect of work-life balance on the relationship between work culture and employee well-being. *Journal of Business Economics and Management*, *22*(4), 988–1007. https://doi.org/10.3846/jbem.2021.14729

Starr, G. G. (2015). *Feeling Beauty: The Neuroscience of Aesthetic Experience*. Mit Press.

Stokes, D. (2009). Aesthetics and cognitive science. *Philosophy Compass*, *4*(5), 715–733. https://doi.org/10.1111/j.1747-9991.2009.00226.x

Stor, M., Haromszeki, Ł., & Poór, J. (2024). Workplace-related factors influencing employee loyalty and job performance in human-centric organizations. In M. Stor (Ed.), *Human at the Center of the Organization: Visions, Realities, Challenges* (pp. 26–41). Wroclaw University of Economics and Business. https://doi.org/10.15611/2024.59.8.02

Strati, A. (1999). *Organization and Aesthetics*. SAGE Publications Ltd. https://sk.sagepub.com/books/organization-and-aesthetics

Strielkowski, W., Grebennikova, V., Lisovskiy, A., Rakhimova, G., & Vasileva, T. (2024). AI-driven adaptive learning for sustainable educational transformation. *Sustainable Development*, *33*, 1921–1947. https://doi.org/10.1002/sd.3221

Su, Z., Wang, Y., Luan, T. H., Zhang, N., Li, F., Chen, T., & Cao, H. (2022). Secure and efficient federated learning for smart grid with edge-cloud collaboration. *IEEE Transactions on Industrial Informatics*, *18*(2), 1333–1344. https://doi.org/10.1109/TII.2021.3095506

Szostak, M. (2019). The art of stylish organ improvisation. *The Organ*, *390*, 20–27. https://depot.ceon.pl/handle/123456789/17687

Szostak, M. (2021). *The Organ as a Source of Inspiration: The Rebirth of a Giant (Paris – Vatican – Licheń)*. SINDRUK-DIMK.

Szostak, M. (2022a). Contextual inspiration and motive in persuasive creativity: Lessons from artistic improvisation. *Discourses on Culture*, *17*(1), 101–131. https://doi.org/10.36145/DoC2022.05

Szostak, M. (2022b). Digitalisation and virtualisation of the aesthetic situation management: Polish musical art creators during the COVID-19 pandemic. *Journal of Intercultural Management*, *14*(2), 41–65. https://doi.org/10.2478/joim-2022-0006

Szostak, M. (2022c). Management of art during the COVID-19 pandemic: Musical arts creator perspective. *European Research Studies Journal*, *25*(3), 46–64. https://doi.org/10.35808/ersj/2993

Szostak, M. (2023a). Reflexivity in aesthetic situation management. *Discourses on Culture*, *20*, 161–197. https://doi.org/10.2478/doc-2023-0015

Szostak, M. (2023b). *Sztuka zarządzania – zarządzanie sztuką*. Wydawnictwo Społecznej Akademii Nauk.

Szostak, M. (2023c). The essentials of organ improvisation. *The Organ*, 405(August-October 2023), 4–17.

Szostak, M. (2024a). Balancing fairness and care through aesthetical lens in humanistic management in the gig economy. In K. Ogunyemi (Ed.), *Humanistic Management in the Gig Economy. Cases from the Global South* (pp. 85–102). Palgrave Macmillan. https://doi.org/10.1007/978-3-031-59944-6_5

Szostak, M. (2024b). *Humanistic Management, Organisation and Aesthetics: Art of Management and Management of Art*. Routledge. https://doi.org/10.4324/9781003458029

Szostak, M. (2024c). Phenomenological perspectives in dialectical leadership: Influence of aesthetic experiences on managing organisational complexity and paradoxes. *Dis courses on Culture*, *22*(1), 41–76. https://doi.org/10.2478/doc-2024-0009

Szostak, M. (2025a). Sztuka zarządzania sztuką. In T. Wiśniewski, R. Zgierska, K. Pastuszak, & K. Kręglewska (Eds.), *Teatr - Literatura - Zarządzanie* (pp. 65–84). Wydawnictwo Uniwersytetu Gdańskiego. https://wydawnictwo.ug.edu.pl/produkt/teatr-literatura-zarzadzanie/?fbclid=IwY2xjawKKsq9leHRuA2FlbQIxMABicmlkETBIME00NlNsN2UwbU10UWo1AR7R6rTofbok3pgtdeAX6uWACrNz0kty2Jp5idsF1UB47gef-iUUMY1PmCGCUQ_aem_gVVw--qaWRal3InBYpXh5g

Szostak, M. (Ed.). (2025b). *Management Aesthetics. Kitsch and Modern Organisations*. Routledge. https://doi.org/10.4324/9781003504931

Szostak, M., & Sułkowski, Ł. (2020). Manager as an artist: Creative endeavour in crossing the borders of art and organizational discourse. *Creativity Studies*, *13*(2), 351–368. https://doi.org/10.3846/cs.2020.11373

Tamburrini, G. (2022). The AI carbon footprint and responsibilities of AI scientists. *Philosophies*, *7*(1), 1–11. https://doi.org/10.3390/philosophies7010004

Tan, S.-L., Spackman, M. P., & Peaslee, C. L. (2006). The effects of repeated exposure on liking and judgments of musical unity of intact and patchwork compositions. *Music Perception*, *23*(5), 407–421. https://doi.org/10.1525/mp.2006.23.5.407

Tasioulas, J. (2022). Artificial intelligence, humanistic ethics. *Daedalus*, *151*(2), 232–243. https://doi.org/10.1162/daed_a_01912

Tatarkiewicz, W. (2004). *Wybór pism estetycznych*. Towarzystwo Autorów i Wydawców Prac Naukowych UNIVERSITAS.

Tatarkiewicz, W. (2015). *Historia estetyki. Tom I*. PWN.

Tavares, M. C., Azevedo, G., & Marques, R. P. (2022). The challenges and opportunities of era 5.0 for a more humanistic and sustainable society – A literature review. *Societies*, *12*(6), 149. https://doi.org/10.3390/soc12060149

Town, S., Reina, C. S., Brummans, B. H. J. M., & Pirson, M. (2024). Humanistic organizing: The transformative force of mindful organizational communication. *Academy of Management Review*, *49*(4), 824–847. https://doi.org/10.5465/amr.2021.0433

Tripathi, D., Priyadarshi, P., Kumar, P., & Kumar, S. (2021). Does servant leadership affect work role performance via knowledge sharing and psychological empowerment? *VINE Journal of Information and Knowledge Management Systems*, *51*(5), 792–812. https://doi.org/10.1108/VJIKMS-10-2019-0159

Uddin, M. K. S., & Hossan, K. M. R. (2024). A Review of implementing AI-Powered data warehouse solutions to optimize big data management and utilization. *Academic Journal on Business Administration, Innovation & Sustainability*, *4*(3), 66–78. https://doi.org/10.69593/ajbais.v4i3.92

Udris-Borodavko, N., Oliinyk, V., Bozhko, T., Budnyk, A., & Hordiichuk, Y. (2023). Aesthetics and semiotics in 21st century visual communications: Pedagogical and sociocultural aspects. *Research Journal in Advanced Humanities*, *4*(4). https://doi.org/10.58256/rjah.v4i4.1144

Ünal, R., & Taylan, A. (2024). *Who Owns This Artwork?* (pp. 383–398). IGI Global Scientific Publishing. https://doi.org/10.4018/979-8-3693-7235-7.ch015

Van Geert, E., & Wagemans, J. (2020). Order, complexity, and aesthetic appreciation. *Psychology of Aesthetics, Creativity, and the Arts*, *14*(2), 135–154. https://doi.org/10.1037/aca0000224

van Hees, J., Grootswagers, T., Quek, G. L., & Varlet, M. (2025). Human perception of art in the age of artificial intelligence. *Frontiers in Psychology*, *15*, 1–8. https://doi.org/10.3389/fpsyg.2024.1497469

van Wynsberghe, A. (2021). Sustainable AI: AI for sustainability and the sustainability of AI. *AI and Ethics*, *1*(3), 213–218. https://doi.org/10.1007/s43681-021-00043-6

Veigners, G., Galins, A., Dukulis, I., & Veignere, E. (2024). Integrating reflective practice into the self-improvement cycle module for renewable energy forecasting accuracy. *Rural Sustainability Research*, *52*(347), 13–30. https://doi.org/10.2478/plua-2024-0012

Verdecchia, R., Lago, P., & de Vries, C. (2022). The future of sustainable digital infrastructures: A landscape of solutions, adoption factors, impediments, open problems, and scenarios. *Sustainable Computing: Informatics and Systems*, *35*, 100767. https://doi.org/10.1016/j.suscom.2022.100767

Virvou, M. (2023). Artificial intelligence and user experience in reciprocity: Contributions and state of the art. *Intelligent Decision Technologies*, *17*(1), 73–125. https://doi.org/10.3233/IDT-230092

Vössing, M., Kühl, N., Lind, M., & Satzger, G. (2022). Designing transparency for effective human-AI collaboration. *Information Systems Frontiers*, *24*(3), 877–895. https://doi.org/10.1007/s10796-022-10284-3

Wadhwa, S., Wadhwa, P., & Khalique, F. (2024). Explorative study on understanding the human-centred design to nurture the employee experience. In Shrivastava, R. & Jain, K. (Eds.), *Humanizing Businesses for a Better World of Work* (pp. 109–126). Emerald Publishing Limited, Leeds. https://doi.org/10.1108/978-1-83797-332-320241008

Wang, J., Lan, C., Liu, C., Ouyang, Y., Qin, T., Lu, W., Chen, Y., Zeng, W., & Yu, P. (2022). Generalizing to unseen domains: A survey on domain generalization. *IEEE Transactions on Knowledge and Data Engineering*, *35*(8), 1–1. https://doi.org/10.1109/TKDE.2022.3178128

Wang, Y. (2009). On Abstract Intelligence. *International Journal of Software Science and Computational Intelligence*, *1*(1), 1–17. https://doi.org/10.4018/jssci.2009010101

Wang, Z., Yang, E., Shen, L., & Huang, H. (2025). A comprehensive survey of forgetting in deep learning beyond continual learning. *IEEE Transactions on Pattern Analysis and Machine Intelligence*, *47*(3), 1464–1483. https://doi.org/10.1109/TPAMI.2024.3498346

Warde, A. (2014). After taste: Culture, consumption and theories of practice. *Journal of Consumer Culture*, *14*(3), 279–303. https://doi.org/10.1177/1469540514547828

Wilt, J. A., Exline, J. J., Schlegel, R. J., & Sherman, A. (2025). Aesthetic dispositions, aesthetic engagement, and meaning in life. *Empirical Studies of the Arts*, *43*(1), 524–549. https://doi.org/10.1177/02762374241248117

Wong, A., Bäck, T., Kononova, A. V., & Plaat, A. (2023). Deep multiagent reinforcement learning: Challenges and directions. *Artificial Intelligence Review*, *56*(6), 5023–5056. https://doi.org/10.1007/s10462-022-10299-x

Wong, I. K. A., Lian, Q. L., & Sun, D. (2023). Autonomous travel decision-making: An early glimpse into ChatGPT and generative AI. *Journal of Hospitality and Tourism Management*, *56*, 253–263. https://doi.org/10.1016/j.jhtm.2023.06.022

Wu, F. (2015). The influence of non-mainstream culture on the aesthetic judgment of fashion trends. *Research Journal of Textile and Apparel*, *19*(2), 42–47. https://doi.org/10.1108/RJTA-19-02-2015-B006

Xing, B., Cao, H., Shi, L., Si, H., & Zhao, L. (2022). AI-driven user aesthetics preference prediction for UI layouts via deep convolutional neural networks. *Cognitive Computation and Systems*, *4*(3), 250–264. https://doi.org/10.1049/ccs2.12055

Xing, Y., He, W., Zhang, J. Z., & Cao, G. (2023). AI privacy opinions between US and Chinese people. *Journal of Computer Information Systems*, *63*(3), 492–506. https://doi.org/10.1080/08874417.2022.2079107

Xu, Q., Xie, W., Liao, B., Hu, C., Qin, L., Yang, Z., Xiong, H., Lyu, Y., Zhou, Y., & Luo, A. (2023). Interpretability of clinical decision support systems based on artificial intelligence from technological and medical perspective: A systematic review. In *Journal of Healthcare Engineering*, (Vol. 2023). https://doi.org/10.1155/2023/9919269

Yang, L. (2023). An analysis of AI models and economic applications. *Academic Journal of Computing & Information Science*, *6*(13), 52–57. https://doi.org/10.25236/ajcis.2023.061308

Yevin, I. (2006). Ambiguity in art. *Complexus*, *3*(1–3), 74–82. https://doi.org/10.1159/000094190

Yu, M., Vaagaasar, A. L., Müller, R., Wang, L., & Zhu, F. (2018). Empowerment: The key to horizontal leadership in projects. *International Journal of Project Management*, *36*(7), 992–1006. https://doi.org/10.1016/j.ijproman.2018.04.003

Zhou, E., & Lee, D. (2024). Generative artificial intelligence, human creativity, and art. *PNAS Nexus*, *3*(3), 1–8. https://doi.org/10.1093/pnasnexus/pgae052

Zhou, L., Sun, X., Mu, G., Wu, J., Zhou, J., Wu, Q., Zhang, Y., Xi, Y., Gunes, N. D., & Song, S. (2022). A tool to facilitate the cross-cultural design process using deep learning. *IEEE Transactions on Human-Machine Systems*, *52*(3), 445–457. https://doi.org/10.1109/THMS.2021.3126699

Zhou, S., Sun, J., Xu, K., & Wang, G. (2024). AI-Driven data processing and decision optimization in IoT through edge computing and cloud architecture. *Journal of AI-Powered Medical Innovations (International Online ISSN 3078-1930)*, *2*(1), 64–92. https://doi.org/10.60087/vol2iisue1.p006

Zuo, H., Hope, T., & Jones, M. (2014). Tactile aesthetics of materials and design. In Karana, E., Pedgley, O., & Rognoli, V. (Eds.), *Materials Experience* (pp. 27–37). Elsevier. https://doi.org/10.1016/B978-0-08-099359-1.00003-5

# 2 A pragmatic consideration on management aesthetics

## Humanistic approach in the age of large language models

*Tuncay Turna*

### Introduction

Management aesthetics (MA) is an interdisciplinary field that emerged in the last few decades. This study focuses on the aesthetic aspect of the field and considers this aspect together with generative language artificial intelligence. It has two goals regarding aesthetics. First, it deals with the philosophical references in the field of MA and analyses them. The second aim is to show other philosophical sources that can contribute to the field. After some general considerations, I propose a pragmatist theory for the field. This proposal holds the idea that an eclectic pragmatist theory is possible. Aesthetics is a broad subject. It includes various theories and views. Moreover, what is understood by it also differs according to the approaches. Generally speaking, there are two main differences in perspective. The art-based approach creates a philosophy of art with questions, such as artistic beauty, taste. The approach that sees aesthetics as a discipline of the senses, including art, evaluates it in a broader framework and gives it an epistemological character. This study follows the second approach.

On the other hand, in terms of the history of philosophy and science, we think of the 15th and 16th centuries as a period of methodological research. This period is also a stage of intellectual confusion. At that time, we were not sure about what is now clearly stated in every high school textbook. As we entered the modern era, we had already decided to control and dominate nature (Skirberkk & Gilje, 2006). However, we also had some desperate hopes in this state of confusion and uncertainty. We searched for alchemical methods to turn lead into gold or the elixir of immortality. These can be seen as signs of hope to realise our dreams from the past, with the conditions of the new era. A paradigm shift took place in this period, and not only our methods but also our expectations of nature and society had to change according to the conditions of the new paradigm.

Is the situation created by today's artificial intelligence (AI) developments similar to that period? Of course, it is possible to say that we are experiencing a similar intellectual confusion. We also have the same great aspirations that we had back then. Sometimes, we treat it as a kind of alchemy. We even assume

DOI: 10.4324/9781003654377-4

that we can use it as a kind of mentalistic elixir. Based on these similarities, we can claim that we are at the beginning of a paradigm shift. AI, particularly large language models (LLM), can become a discipline that deals with truth or can give birth to such a new discipline. This is because they now express sentences in a way we are not used to. It is unclear what they are referring to, and they are not interested in meaning. We are unsure how to move forward with our new invention, as we were at the beginning of the modern era. The second part of this article is about LLMs. What are LLMs? How do they work? What is their nature in terms of philosophy of mind and language? The ultimate goal of the study is to philosophically address the consequences of considering LLMs together with a pragmatist aesthetic approach, following the goals of the area of MA.

This is a theoretical, philosophical study whose research methodology is a literature review and comparative analysis. This study has a pragmatic view of having useful and practical results. The literature was searched in academic databases, such as Scopus, Web of Science, JSTOR, International Directory of Philosophy, Stanford Encyclopaedia of Philosophy, and printed books. The following *research questions* guide the research process: (RQ1) Does philosophy have sources for MA, and if so, how? (RQ2) Is it possible to claim that a certain approach and theory are better for MA, and if so, which and how? (RQ3) How does MA play a more significant role in the time of LLM, and how can LLMs be helpful in this field?

## Literature review: philosophy of aesthetics and LLMs

This chapter provides a concise overview of the literature on MA, aesthetics, and LLMs. First, it analyses the philosophical literature used in the field of MA. I use sources written or edited by Strati; de Monthoux; Kostera & Woźniak; Szostak; and Neesham, Reihlen, & Schoeneborn. I briefly analyse their philosophical references. I then discuss aesthetic literature through Plato, Aristotle, Kant, Hegel, Marx, Goodman, Dewey, and Shusterman and present aesthetic concepts and theories. Of these, I pay special attention to the pragmatic theory proposed by John Dewey and developed by Richard Shusterman, which I believe is appropriate for the MA. I then conduct a technical and critical review of the literature on LLMs, showing the position of philosophy of mind and language on this issue. It should be emphasised that this is a filtering following the aesthetic purpose of this study.

### *The case of aesthetics*

With his publications throughout the 1990s, Strati is one of the pioneers in the field of MA. His pioneering is partly chronological. More importantly, he aims to create a foundation on which the field of MA can be grounded. Strati refers to many philosophers in his work to create a philosophical ground. This intensity is particularly evident in his monograph *Organization and Aesthetics* (Strati, 1999). Indeed, this anti-Cartesian source can be seen as a kind of critique of positivism. The density of references to names such as Polanyi, Husserl, and Gadamer supports this claim. Strati, who proposes to consider aesthetics as a type of knowledge, uses Polanyi's theory and strengthens his position by referring to Kuhn. He also shows that Baumgarten's aesthetic views, which he accepts as the basis of MA, can overlap with Polanyi's understanding of knowledge.

Baumgarten, who gave birth to aesthetics as a theoretical field, considered aesthetics as a separate field of knowledge (rather than dealing with the nature of art) and proposed it as a science of beauty (Jimenez, 2023). This attempt, in contrast to post-Cartesian philosophy, asserts that sensory perception can be treated epistemologically (Hammermeister, 2002). In line with Baumgarten's theory, Strati considers aesthetics to be more than the philosophy of art. In this respect, it is appropriate that he turns to the subject of knowledge to provide a solid foundation for his approach. He also examines various examples presented as alternatives to the dominant philosophical understanding of the early 20th century, which was positivist, Cartesian, logical, mathematical, and rationalist in these senses. To this end, he invokes names, such as Husserl, Gadamer, Dilthey, and Weber (Strati, 1999). What these names have in common is that they attempt to offer an alternative to the dominant philosophical-scientific understanding of the time.

Of course, there is no need to analyse all of Strati's references here. However, the names that are rarely mentioned, as well as those that are frequently mentioned, give us an idea of his approach. It is common to refer to classics such as Plato, Kant, and Hegel in aesthetics. However, Strati did not refer to Kant more than Dilthey. These references are mostly to Kant's view that aesthetic judgments must be objective judgments in accordance with the *a priori* aesthetic principle, as well as their subjective aspects arising from taste. This is also in line with Strati's aim mentioned above. However, the reference to Plato and Hegel is quite limited. The limited reference to names such as Plato, Hegel, and Croce, categorised as idealists, shows that his view of aesthetics diverges from idealism.

On the other hand, Vandekerckhove, who wrote an introduction to the aesthetic management section of the *Handbook of Philosophy of Management*, presents a brief overview of studies and philosophical references in this field (Vandekerckhove, 2022). The mention of Rorty, an anti-Cartesian thinker, should be seen as contributing to Strati's goal. In the same work, Vickery refers to David Harvey and Lefebvre on the organisation of space (Vickery, 2022). Kostera also cited Lefebvre in the same context (Kostera, 2014). It is difficult to say that these neo-Marxist names and the goals of humanistic management are close. These references are open to criticism. Marxist aesthetics and its socialist practices can be considered to have different characteristics. Even though Marx's aesthetics is not explicitly pointed out in his aesthetic understanding, these practices use art and aesthetics as tools for managing the masses from the beginning, both in terms of content and form (Tunalı, 1998). However, it is not easy to find a clear discussion on this aspect of Marxist aesthetics in the field. The most explicit contribution on Marx and Marxism is on the moral aspect of management by de Monthoux (1993).

Nevertheless, Kostera & Woźniak, who see Strati's work as a manifesto against reductionism, address the negative consequences of reductionism regarding Bauman (Kostera & Woźniak, 2021). According to them, de Monthoux follows a similar path to Strati. His critique of reductionism can be seen in his monograph Mill and Utilitarianism (de Monthoux, 1993). An important philosophical reference in Kostera and Woźniak (2021) is to Rancière, who contributes to understanding everyday aesthetics, and is also mentioned in a similar context by Vandekerckhove and Emmanuel (2022). It seems that Rancière's ideas have only recently begun to be incorporated into the field.

References to pragmatism in the field are rather scarce. Strati refers to Dewey and Pierce (Strati, 1999). He later adds Shusterman to his sources (Strati, 2019). While Strati only mentions other pragmatist names, he examines Shusterman more closely. I touched on above that Rorty is cited, and one of the names using Dewey as a source is Cunningham (2022). Szostak, on the other hand, cites Pierce (Szostak, 2024). Beardsley is also cited in the same work, one of the few references to an aesthete from the analytic philosophical tradition in the field.

In addition, Kostera&Woźniak use the concept of wholeness and propose a holistic perspective for the field. Although this suggestion is given to consolidate the foundation of MA, it reveals a more profound philosophical perspective. Accordingly, it is possible to think of management as a holistic habitat. Peters and Strauss are other names that use the concept of wholeness from a similar perspective (2021). This concept is important for the proposal of this study. For a pragmatist, aesthetics defends the wholeness of art and thought. The work of art cannot be thought of as something separate from life; aesthetics is an inseparable part of life (Dewey, 1980). Shusterman, following Dewey, opposes mind-body dualism and treats the body as a whole (Shusterman, 1992). This approach to pragmatist aesthetics is entirely consistent with the perspective of pragmatism.

### *A brief aesthetics*

The first question about aesthetics and art was, "What is beautiful?" in Plato. Notably, the first question is about beauty and not the aesthetic object. Plato sees beauty, goodness, and truth as ideals that coexist and considers these three a condition of virtue. His approach is commonly understood in the ancient Greek world (Bozkurt, 2000). Nevertheless, Plato treats beauty as an indicator of virtue, goodness, and justice and presents a doctrine of hope for social life (Jimenez, 2023). Plato, a master of literature, is considered one of the founders of philosophical aesthetics (Bozkurt, 2000: 96). Plato's works are aesthetically satisfying. However, Plato excludes art to a certain extent. He "respects beauty but does not trust art" (Jimenez, 2023: 189). Moreover, according to Plato, art is imitation or emulation. He says art does not contain knowledge (Bozkurt, 2000). If art is not functional, Plato throws it out of the site. Because it has no function in itself that can be added to the law of logos. (Jimenez, 2023)

Aristotle falls into a pole opposite to Plato in aesthetics, as in his philosophy in general. He "sees art as noble; he declares that poetry, music, painting, and sculpture have virtues that are useful to society as well as to the individual" (Jimenez, 2023: 192). However, even for him, art is not independent. Although Aristotle's approach is different, his results are similar to those of Plato. In fact, "Aristotelian aesthetics is nothing but a systematization of Platonic aesthetics" (Bozkurt, 2000: 103). The importance of Aristotle, however, lies in his addition of *catharsis* to Plato's concept of *mimesis*. "For Aristotle, art begins with imitation (mimesis) and ends with cleansing (catharsis)" (Bozkurt, 2000: 105). The point here is that he considers two aesthetic subjects, the artist and the recipient of the work, together.

Jimenez states that aesthetics and art gained autonomy after the Renaissance (2023). The autonomy of art is based on the establishment of the field of aesthetics as an independent field of knowledge. Baumgarten and Kant are pioneers in this respect. Baumgarten presents aesthetics as a discipline of knowledge with its logic. According to him, aesthetics is the twin brother of logic (Tunalı, 1998). Furthermore, Kant tries to justify the perception of beauty in the subject, the judgment of beauty (aesthetic judgment). According to him, the subjective and private judgment of beauty is also a universal judgment. Kant regards beauty as a property or predicate. Accordingly, the subject ascribes beauty to the object. However, this attribution is not based on demonstration but on a general logical assumption (Jimenez, 2023). Kant bases aesthetic judgment on a universal principle while preserving its subjectivity. Thus, he saves beauty from dogmatism and doctrine and gives autonomy to aesthetics (Bozkurt, 2000). Nonetheless, Kant's aesthetic views do not find much favour in the contemporary world (Jimenez, 2023). However, his view allows us to argue that aesthetics has an epistemological value.

Hegel, on the other hand, represents the philosophy of art rather than aesthetics. He is an admirer of works of art. Hegel does not include natural beauty in aesthetics. He considers beauty as artistic beauty (Jimenez, 2023). According to Hegel, the last stage of spirit is philosophy, and the previous is art (Bozkurt, 2000). This view is an important step in the autonomy of art and aesthetics. Moreover, Hegel also sees a relationship between beauty and truth. Accordingly, the appearance of truth itself in the sensory field is defined as beautiful (Bozkurt, 2000). Hegel's aesthetic views have influenced contemporary art. He points to the historicity of beauty and sees art as something other than an imitation of nature. These views were effective both in the autonomy of art and in the emergence of contemporary art and aesthetic understanding. As a result, the work of art began to be analysed according to its criteria and history rather than rules (Jimenez, 2023).

Another one who analyses the aesthetic object through historicity is Marx. Marx's view differs from other aesthetics in several ways. For example, the art object is produced within a certain social class structure. This is a realistic view. However, the result of this view carries the content of art into a political/ideological dimension. This is where it begins to differ radically from other aesthetics. According to him, form, although essential to art, is unimportant. Thus, beauty is not carried by the form but by the content; the content that depends on the socio-political (Tunalı, 1998). Marx's view of art seems to paralyse it. Besides, various Marxist aesthetics were influential in the 20th century. These movements produce social realist and ideological works of art. The fact that these works play an effective role in managing mass groups makes Marxist aesthetics a remarkable field for MA.

Nelson Goodman of Analytical Aesthetics proposes to think of art as a kind of science. Art is a system of symbols, and it functions to produce the world in a language other than scientific language. Goodman makes a distinction between aesthetics and art (Giovannelli, 2017). According to him, both the most skilful and the worst performance of a symphony should be considered aesthetic. Furthermore, aesthetics is not a way of assigning value. According to him, one can speak of art when something symbolically functions as a work of art. It is not important what a work of art is, but what we say about it (Jimenez, 2023). A work of art is not art in itself. What makes it art is that the recipient sees it as art. The structuralist approach also sees art as language. Accordingly, both art and language function with signs. In this respect, a work of art can provide communication (Tunalı, 1998).

Finally, let us consider the theory of pragmatism. Pragmatism is a philosophical movement that proposes to acquire a research attitude rather than to reach some special results (Yıldırım, 2014). Although Pierce and James, the founding figures of the movement, have aesthetic ideas, we cannot talk about a comprehensive study. In this regard, the third founding figure of the movement, Dewey's *Art as Experience*, provides a detailed theory (Dewey, 1980). This work remained ineffective for a long time due to the rise of the analytic philosophy movement and the misconception that Dewey's theory was a continuation of Hegel's (Yıldırım, 2014). Later, Shusterman (1992) brought the theory to light and developed it.

Dewey sees aesthetics as a field related to the senses in a broad sense. Man is an organism that interacts with its environment as a whole, both mentally and physically. This interaction creates an experience that shows a part of life. Aesthetic experience is a subset of this comprehensive experience (Yıldırım, 2014). Therefore, aesthetic experience is only possible with organic unity and wholeness. In essence, Dewey's goal was not to develop a theory of art or to define taste. Rather, he wants to develop his thought by placing aesthetics at the centre of it. This approach, which places aesthetics at the centre of thought and life and makes it an aesthetic whole, removes art from being an activity that belongs to a certain class and is detached from everyday life. Everyday life and aesthetic experience become intertwined (Avcı, 2024). Dewey calls aesthetic theories that materialise works of art, detach them from everyday life and limit the work of art to museums and galleries, *museum art, compartmentalised art* or *esoteric art* (Dewey, 1980). Following pragmatism, life in Dewey's philosophy is not entirely separated from uncertainty and mystery. We cannot be wholly rational and controlled by life. If we accept life with its uncertainty, the resulting experience can be transformed into art (Türer, 2021). In addition, it can itself be an art of living. This approach considers science, philosophy, and art together, like mind and body. Because science is not independent of the senses, thinking and its result, knowledge, can also be considered art (Avcı, 2024). When life is considered in such a unity in which aesthetics is in the centre, the work of art becomes explained by *experience* (Dewey, 1980). Accordingly, the work of art is understood only in the wholeness of experience, that is, how it finds resources in the practice of life and what it does, what function it performs (Avcı, 2024). Moreover, art as experience allows us to stay in the present and not escape from experience (Yıldırım, 2014). This understanding ascribes a moral function to art, such as eliminating prejudices and broadening perception in a horizon-opening way (Türer, 2021).

Like Dewey, Shusterman believes that human beings' physical and mental sides cannot be separated. He uses the concept of *somaesthetics* to point to this wholeness. Somaesthetics could be described as body-centred aesthetics. With somaesthetics, Shusterman develops a philosophical perspective and proposes an art of living. Somaesthetics also proposes a kind of ethics. Aesthetic experience evokes a stronger sense of happiness than pleasure and can transform the subject (Shusterman, 1999). According to him, aesthetic education can be used as a therapy. In addition, anti-Cartesian and anti-positivist Richard Rorty considers aesthetics as an alternative language to philosophy. Therefore, his theory is known as aesthetic pragmatism (Topakkaya & Taşdelen, 2024). According to Rorty, aesthetic objects have the function of developing people morally and intellectually. The work of art is not only a means of pleasure but also has a moral function. Moreover, Rorty considers language as a phenomenon consisting of metaphors and not as a means of representation (Rorty, 1995). The placement of this idea of metaphor is related to his placement of imagination at the centre of intellectual activity (Topakkaya & Taşdelen, 2024). Rorty's thought has a holistic view and wants to abolish philosophies contrary to it.

### *The case of AI and LLM*

Here, I do research on AI in general and LLM in particular. This research has a technical approach to show LLMs' current conditions. Also, it shows the views of philosophy of mind and language about them. AI is one of the hottest topics today. However, I choose to remain critical and take as realistic an approach as possible.

The term AI describes computer systems capable of performing tasks similar to human intelligence (Alammar & Grootendorst, 2024). Wooldridge, who sees AI as a long list of failures, says it is possible to begin its history with Hephaistos, the god who revitalised iron or the protective magical golems of 17th-century Prague (Wooldridge, 2022). Indeed, these allegorical determinations point out that the history of AI thought (the history of machines that can imitate human thought and action) is quite old. In the background of today's AI, there is an indirect history of 2–3 centuries and a direct history of 70–80 years. In the new paradigm of the post-Renaissance period, mathematics and formal approaches began to dominate our world of thought. Leibniz proposed a formal language, *characteristica universalis*, for philosophy and science. Later in the 19th century, logicians and mathematicians began to construct formal logic. The basis of these projects was to perform formal computations without making mistakes in the truth reference of linguistic content. As a result of these movements, the possibility of machines that could think through such formal structures began to emerge.

In 1936, Alan Turing described a theoretical machine that made decisions by performing mathematical calculations. This hypothesis, known as the Turing machine, is the theory on which computers are based. In 1950, Turing also proposed the idea of machines that could think. He considers whether a machine can produce linguistically indistinguishable processes from humans. For him, we must accept machines as thinking if they can pass the Turing Test (TT). TT is based on predicting whether an interlocutor is a human or a machine during correspondence with it. If the prediction rate is 50% or better in favour of machines, it is appropriate to say that they are capable of thinking. On the other hand, the term AI began to be used in a conference group led by John McCarthy in 1956 (Bringsjord & Govindarajulu, 2004). As can be seen here, the first steps were completely logic-based.

The history of AI started with a logic and knowledge-based paradigm but later moved to a behaviour-based one, and today, it mainly works agent-based (Wooldridge, 2022). LLMs have emerged as an agent-based type of AI. The ability of AI systems to generate language that resembles human language is called natural language processing (NLP). NLP theories have as long a history as AI. Nevertheless, for now, LLMs are their most successful version, and they seriously impact the field so much so that it is possible to refer to 2023, the year GPT 3.5 was released, as the year of generative AI (Alammar & Grootendorst, 2024).

What is LLM? Within NLP, at least four different theories have not been sufficiently successful (Floridi, 2023). For instance, a method was first proposed to represent language as a bag of words. The systems used today have their roots in the Transformer architecture proposed in the article "Attention is all you need" (Vaswani et al., 2017). These systems respond better to training and abandon the iterative method used previously. Generative language AIs using the Transformers network in NLP, where different models and architectures are used, are generally called LLMs (Alammar & Grootendorst, 2024). LLMs are trained by deep learning on large datasets. They are based entirely on statistical prediction methods. Their working system is based on correctly predicting the next word in a context window. Today, LLMs are at a level where they can produce language results that are difficult to distinguish from human-generated sentences. The most famous are the GPT versions, Bard, and LLaMA, but new models and new versions always appear.

So, what is the performance of LLMs? Can they really reproduce human speech? Ostensibly, yes. But is it really? There are various approaches to the philosophy of AI. The most basic distinction seems to be between weak and strong AI. The strong AI approach refers to an artificial human that can perform all the mental abilities that humans have, at least as well as humans. Weak AI is used for AI that performs limited human abilities that can pass the TT to some extent. It is difficult to reject the idea of weak AI, but there is a philosophical reflex against strong AI (Bringsjord & Govindarajulu, 2004). The most famous argument is John Searle's (1980) Chinese Room. Searle presents a thought experiment. According to this experiment, a person who does not speak Chinese is in a closed room with only a letter slot for exchanging cards. In the room, there are numbered cards with Chinese sentences on them and an instruction manual. A Chinese person outside the room gives cards with questions to the person inside the room. The person inside follows the instructions and gives the appropriate numbered answer. The Chinese person gets the appropriate answer to his question, and he thinks that there is someone inside who speaks Chinese. The process went smoothly, but the person in the room did not understand the questions or the answers. Searle claims that the machines making human speech are like the person in the room.

Searle's view has both supporters and detractors. Floridi, who believes that LLMs have apparent limitations, sees them as unintelligent agents that quickly compute with large data sets and frequently make mistakes because they are computation gluttons. He says they also fail the TT (Floridi, 2023). Similarly, Bishop says that they do not think, reason, or understand. According to him, LLMs cannot relate to semantic content in any way (Bishop, 2021). Wooldridge shares this view (Wooldridge, 2022). Appleby thinks that LLMs are not particularly suitable for use in decision-making mechanisms (Appleby, 2024). Conversely, some oppose Searle's view because he mistakenly views meaning and program (Melnyk, 1996). Although the current conditions of LLMs still vindicate Searle, he is not closed to criticism. Moreover, it is difficult to say that the opposite situation will not arise with new developments.

Moreover, we can say that we are approaching the end of the era of LLMs based on prediction with statistical methods (Ball, 2024). In some inventions, LLM-based autonomous agents can evolve into different models with new developments (Wang et al., 2024). Furthermore, even under current architectural conditions, systems that perform faster operations on larger datasets can give good results even if they are not fully semantic (Floridi, 2023). The following approach to this issue is consistent: Today, we accept that AI exists. The historical evolution of AI shows us that it will continue to evolve. Moreover, the AI produced by humans today may be produced by AI tomorrow (Bringsjord & Govindarajulu, 2004). The question of the extent to which it is possible to achieve strong AI is still crucial, but it is not difficult to predict that developments will continue.

Finally, let us look at the political implications of LLMs. Large corporations and governments support LLMs. The USA used to be the leader in this respect. Recently, China has also started to take strong steps. Franke (2019) emphasises that Europe is still not interested in the development of AI, which may cause future political difficulties. Another study reports on using LLMs in political preferences, which was tested in the Brazilian elections. According to the study, LLMs analyse candidates' promises better than real voters and find out which candidate is closer to supporting democracy. Therefore, it is claimed that LLMs can help people to vote (Gudino et al., 2024). A study conducted with GPT-3 examines the political bias of LLMs. According to this, the GPT-3 responds left to left-wing stimuli and right to right-wing stimuli and shows a slight leftward bias to neutral stimuli (Lucas, 2023).

## Results: towards a view of use

This section presents the results of the above literature review. First, I analyse the results of the literature on aesthetics and then on LLM.

### *The case of aesthetics*

If we look at aesthetic theories, we can see some main points. Some aesthetic theories see art as autonomous, that is, as having its own purpose. Others see it as a mediator or part of a larger structure. The Hegelian and analytic view is autonomous; the Platonic, Aristotelian, Marxian, and pragmatist views are heteronomous. Plato, who presents the attempt to be virtuous by approaching the world of ideas as a doctrine, considers the ideas of good, beautiful and true together. This has to do with the fact that beauty is impressive and, therefore, manipulative. The good and the true form a triadic mechanism that ensures virtue by balancing beauty. In Marxist aesthetics, art is produced within social relations with a certain ideological dimension. Therefore, it has an ethical-political task. On the other hand, pragmatist aesthetics places aesthetics at the centre of the experience of life and transforms it into an understanding of the art of living. It thus assigns a moral function to aesthetics, giving individuals responsibility for themselves and society. MA, which has a "management as art" approach, has a similar idea. Analytical and structuralist aesthetics, on the other hand, believe that art creates a kind of symbolic language and can enable communication. Here, analytic thought enables communication through dialogue about the art object, and structuralist does so through semiotics.

The common definitions of some aesthetics-related concepts can be shown as follows. An aesthetic object refers to an object with which an aesthetic-sensory relationship can be established, whether natural or artificial. It can be a work of art, the human body, or a part of nature. The aesthetic object often unites the artist and the recipient in a certain feeling. The aesthetic subject is the singularity that establishes an aesthetic relationship with the object. It can be the recipient or the producer of the object. Aesthetic value expresses the subject's appreciation of beauty, pleasantness, and ugliness that the subject attributes to the object. Aesthetic judgments are judgments that express the evaluation of taste. Aesthetic value can be imposed by aesthetic judgment. Aesthetic experience refers to the subject's experience of the object. The pragmatist approach places aesthetic experience in the timeline of its understanding. It also recognises that this experience has the power to guide and shape human beings. These concepts may differ according to the characteristics of the theories. The meaning of concepts may vary from theory to theory.

MA is a new discipline that brings together different disciplines. In the 1990s, which can be considered the period of its rise, a group of authors led by names such as Strati and de Monthoux tried to establish solid philosophical foundations for the field. Starting from Plato on aesthetics, they referred to names such as Baumgarten, Kant, Hegel or idealist, critical, and neo-Marxist movements. The philosophical perspective in this field has an anti-Cartesian and anti-positivist character. In addition, they considered aesthetics as a science of the senses in a broad sense and epistemological in nature. In the background of this endeavour, it can be said that aesthetics is a necessary field for management and that MA can produce knowledge.

In the following periods, the philosophical references of the field expanded and contributions were made from fields such as critical thinking, semiotics and pragmatism. It can be seen that the intellectual diversity of the field has increased, and the conceptual dimension has broadened. For example, in areas such as occupation management and spatial organisation, approaches are being developed that are consistent with the basic ideas of MA. In addition, the concept of wholeness is becoming widespread, and it is suggested that organisation and management should be considered holistically. The idea of a heteronomous art emerges. These philosophical intuitions of the field are appropriate. However, although the field has been given an epistemological character, its application and ethical-political dimension have been partially inadequate. Nevertheless, these sources offer an aesthetic epistemology rather than an artistic view. Moreover, they reject rational philosophy in the Cartesian sense and attempt to create an inclusive system of thought. They advocate a pluralistic and democratic perspective.

### *The case of AI and LLM*

I analysed AI and LLM in terms of philosophy of mind and language by making a technical review. According to this, LLMs, one of the types of NLP, started using a new architecture after 2017. They work by predicting the next token using statistics and probability models. They have been quite successful and have started producing sentence output that is close to human output. However, their limitations are obvious. It is not possible to use them in decision-making mechanisms. Yet, it is possible to use them as tools. We see many examples of these uses today. Some of them have already entered our lives to some extent, such as translation, which provides information in some specific areas. However, they still often make mistakes. The main reason for these errors is that they always need to produce an output for programming purposes. This is why you often see the error called hallucinating. This is when LLMs claim things that do not exist. For example, they may cite an article that has not been written or published.

They have a controversial position in the philosophy of mind. Most thinkers argue that they are not close to crossing TT and that we cannot consider them experiencing a real mental process. Nevertheless, they recognise that their use as weak AIs in the form of various tools is possible. There is also a negative situation in terms of linguistic philosophy. Their production method is based on predicting the next token according to the context window. They do this using statistical results from a large data set. Moreover, they do not really understand the sentences the user prompts or the sentences they generate themselves. This shows that LLMs do not have the properties of language that are important for the philosophy of language, such as referring, representing, and thus leading to understanding. Nevertheless, it is impossible to regard them as completely unsuccessful in terms of the result.

## Discussion: towards a theory

This section discusses MA and LLM based on the results obtained. I will first show the conditions for a usable theory in MA, defending the holism and the notion of experience put forward by the pragmatic view. Then, I will show how LLMs can be used in MA under their current conditions. Here, I will suggest thinking of LLMs as a craft and using them as a tool.

### *Management as an aesthetic experience*

Can we say that a certain aesthetic theory is suitable for management? It is possible, but such a theory must have explicit characteristics. First of all, is aesthetics heteronomous or autonomous? It is possible to say that there is a slight contradiction in the results. MA proposes to consider aesthetics as a part of management. The basic assumption is that the wholeness of life should be reflected in the understanding of management. In this sense, aesthetics is understood as heteronomous. However, sources that emphasise its autonomous character are used to provide a theoretical basis. How can this contradiction be resolved?

Art has an end in itself. Today, the debate about art that is completely free and exists for itself is not as strong as it was at the beginning of the last century.

However, it must be recognised that art has such a quality. But can aesthetics be autonomous? I suggest that such a solution might be easy and useful: Aesthetics is an epistemologically autonomous field, as Baumgarten and Kant intended, and somehow, analytical and pragmatic understandings make a similar claim. MA has been able to demonstrate this in its theoretical foundations. However, it is not easy to think of art as ontologically separate from the whole of human experience. As we have seen in Plato, Hegel, and Marx, art emerges in a social and individual whole. This is related to the fact that aesthetics is part of our wholeness. Because of this characteristic, the possibility of art, whose goal is itself, is questioned. However, its aim is itself, meaning it expresses its judgments with its symbolic system/language. This is an epistemological situation. Although it is ontologically a part of the whole, it is not independent of the other parts of the whole. Therefore, it can be said to be ontologically heteronomous and epistemologically autonomous.

In addition, life is a whole, and the being is itself. Nevertheless, ontological unity contains a diversity. This diversity manifests itself in both the sensory and the mental. Cartesian philosophy limits this diversity of unity through reason. In the last century, though, this approach has been challenged by various philosophical movements. Pragmatism is one of them, and it advocates treating things in terms of their function. It also tries to include the sensory field in philosophy. Because of these features, it is often criticised as relativistic. Still, this view represents pluralism rather than relativism.

I argue that MA should consider the ontological wholeness and pluralistic view because the pragmatist aesthetic approach suits the field. On the other hand, other aesthetic views have various characteristics suitable for the field and cannot be ignored; e.g., whatever happens, the Platonic idea of beauty-goodness-truth should be kept in mind. This view expresses unity. It provides an ontological (through beauty), epistemological (through truth), and ethical (through goodness) dimension. In addition, the historical perspective we see in Hegel and Marx should be maintained for aesthetic theory to be used in the field. Moreover, Marxist aesthetics claims that art exists within social relations. This perspective can be helpful for management. The approaches that argue that aesthetics is its language of symbols should also be recognised. If we think of aesthetics as a language, it can be used as a management tool. Therefore, I argue that the theory of MA should have both an eclectic and a pragmatic structure.

With its holistic view of life and by placing aesthetics at the centre of life and thought, pragmatist aesthetics transforms art and life from two separate fields into a unity. This unity can be understood as "aesthetic experience". These two features, wholeness and aesthetic experience, are useful concepts for MA. In this way, the idea of "management as an art" can become "management as an aesthetic experience". The concept of experience takes into account all sides of the management mechanism. Also, it facilitates its follow-up by linking the decision-making process to an experience. It can also provide quick access to the right results. In their work mentioned above, Peters and Strauss (2021) state that there is a conflict in the management approach, such as working by controlling versus working by giving responsibility, and that working by giving responsibility is more suitable for humanistic management. A responsibility-based approach may be more easily possible from the perspective of aesthetic experience. It can be especially effective in the management of social groups. For example, those who work for a Party and whose thoughts align with the Party's views and struggles can work with full dedication. However, can those less attached to the Party achieve a similar level of devotion through aesthetic experience? I argue that it is possible.

### *AI-LLM as a craft*

The notable works of art of antiquity were created initially to complete a building, a tomb, a warrior, or the appearance of a status holder. It is only in modern times that art and craft are considered separate. Art exists as heteronomous to fulfil a function. In pragmatist philosophy, on the other hand, not only a work of art but also a scientific work is considered aesthetically. Accordingly, it is possible to consider technological devices as works of art. Their low artistic value and lack of aesthetic pleasure are only related to the lack of artistic concern in their production. The secondary meaning of aesthetics, "artificiality", provides a basis for this view. In this context, can LLMs be considered as a kind of craft product? I think the answer is yes. Furthermore, I would say that this perspective is more appropriate to the conditions of today's LLM.

With specific skills, the artisan adds useful products to our daily lives. Depending on the craftsman's aesthetic concerns, experience, and skill, these products may or may not appeal to artistic tastes. The important point is that more aesthetic forms of a craft product are always possible. LLMs are made by people with special skills and training who work on an architectural structure. The architecture of today's widely used transformers can be defined as a set of complex electronic circuits. According to the pragmatist understanding, this structure can be considered an aesthetic product. However, unlike other handicraft products, we can only experience it through its representations. A direct experience with it does not express LLM in any way. Nevertheless, is it possible to think about LLM (for example, a conversation with a chatbot) aesthetically?

It helps to think about this through the basic concepts of the philosophy of language, such as meaning, reference, and representation. In theories of language, language represents external reality or thought or meaning. Words and sentences symbolise objects in the external world or objects of thought or meaning. We call this symbolisation representation. Let us analyse the following example:

(1) "John wants to eat a red apple".

The expression "red apple" in (1) represents red apples or the concept of red apples. However, does the same representation arise when an LLM expresses

(1)? As we have seen above, many thinkers would answer in the negative. However, does (1), as the LLM expresses, mean nothing? I still think it is a representation. In this case, LLM represents language elements, the language itself. In a sense, it does the representation of the representation. In other words, although (1) expressed by the human and (1) expressed by the LLM appear identical, they are actually separate objects. We can understand this better if we think about hallucination. LLM is not in a hallucination; it is doing the same thing it does when it gives correct results on the architecture it is working on. We call it a hallucination when it cites a non-existent article because of our semantic and ontological infrastructure. LLM, conversely, can easily generate such sentences because it is independent of semantic content, and language objects (such as citation, article, etc.) exist in the language set it represents.

What are the implications of all these considerations for MA? First, thinking of AI-LLMs as a craft gives us a good perspective on their limitations. So, at least for now, we can think of them as tools and avoid being alchemists. Second, if we think of them as crafts representing language, we can find more realistic ways to use them for MA purposes. It is possible to support and nourish management or organisation, which we can think of as an aesthetic experience, with LLM crafts. In the training stages, we can guide their representational abilities with large but limited language packages in certain respects. It is important for an organisation to have a worldview and to represent it with its language aesthetics. To do this through LLM requires a well-prepared dataset. Today, I think it is important for organisations to make such preparations. Also, as mentioned above, we are dealing with weak AIs today. It may take a long time for strong AIs to emerge. However, it is rational to think that strong LLMs will emerge one day. It is therefore important to prepare for that time today.

## Conclusion

MA has a theoretically strong position with its established solid philosophical ground. This theoretical ground, which has an anti-Cartesian and anti-positivist perspective, maintains an epistemological aesthetic thought. It is possible to refer to various aesthetics to contribute to the theoretical ground of the field. Among these, pragmatist aesthetics – with the addition of some features from Platonic, Marxist, and Analytic aesthetics – is quite suitable for MA. Here are the answers to the first two research questions of the study. Philosophy has resources for MA, and MA is philosophically grounded. Moreover, a certain aesthetic theory can be adopted for MA, and this theory can be widely used.

Furthermore, the study has shown the problematic aspects of LLM in terms of the philosophy of mind and the philosophy of language. This has revealed the conditions that LLMs have today. It also finds that LLMs perform a different kind of representation. Based on these conclusions, it would be appropriate to consider LLMs as crafts for MA. It is possible and necessary to use these crafts for MA today. However, preparing for the world of tomorrow and more advanced LLMs is also necessary. Here is the answer to the final research question of the study. MA should apply ways to use LLMs as a craft today and prepare for tomorrow, especially in terms of identity formation.

In addition to its conclusions, the study has some *limitations*. First, LLMs' continuous and rapid development may invalidate some of the study's conclusions. In addition, the study considers aesthetics as a science of the senses in a broad sense. It ignores the artistic dimension of the work. So, some artistic criticism is possible. In this context, although the study is about language, it does not sufficiently deal with the aesthetics of language. It gives an abstract dimension to the study. This abstraction can make it challenging to obtain results that are relevant to the application. On the other hand, MA, as a relatively new discipline, and LLMs, as a dynamic field, are open to many new research. It is necessary to inquire about the artistic conditions of aesthetic experience. In addition, the training conditions for brands and political organisations to develop LLMs that reflect their identities should be questioned. If aesthetic experience is seen as a useful approach for MA, it would be appropriate to explore how LLMs can be used in aesthetic experience.

## References

Alammar, J., & Grootendorst, M. (2024). *Hands-On Large Language Models: Language Understanding and Generation*, O'Reilly.

Appleby, C. (2024). *AI in the Loop Strategic Decisionmaking with a Large Language Model*, Center for Strategic and International Studies (CSIS). https://www.jstor.org/stable/resrep65618.4

Avcı, N. (2024). Pragmatist Estetik: John Dewey. In Kemal Bakır (ed.), *Özne Felsefe ve Bilim Sanat Yazıları: Pragmatizm*, 41, pp. 263–300, Çizgi Kitabevi.

Ball, D. W. (2024). The Era of Predictive AI is Almost Over, *The New Atlantis*, 77, 26–35. https://www.jstor.org/stable/10.2307/27317082

Bishop, J. M. (2021). Artificial Intelligence is Stupid and Causal Reasoning Will Not Fix It, *Frontiers in Psychology*, 11:513474, 1–18. https://doi.org/10.3389/fpsyg.2020.513474

Bozkurt, N. (2000). *Sanat ve Estetik Kuramları*, Asa Yayınları.

Bringsjord, S., & Govindarajulu, N. S. (2004). *Artificial Intelligence, The Stanford Encyclopedia of Philosophy* (Fall 2024 Edition), Edward N. Zalta & Uri Nodelman (eds.), https://plato.stanford.edu/archives/fall2024/entries/artificial-intelligence/

Cunningham, T. (2022). The Aesthetics of St Thomas Aquinas and the Art of the Beautiful Business. In *Handbook of Philosophy of Management* (edt. C. Neesham, M. Reihlen, D. Schoeneborn, pp. 461–478), Springer.

Dewey, J. (1934 [1980]). *Art as Experience*, Perigee Books.

Floridi, L. (2023). AI as Agency Without Intelligence: On ChatGPT, Large Language Models, and Other Generative Models, *Philosophy & Technology*, 36:15, 14–21. https://doi.org/10.1007/s13347-023-00621-y

Franke, U. (2019). *Harnessing Artificial Intelligence*, European Council on Foreign Relations. https://www.jstor.org/stable/resrep21491

Giovannelli, A. (2017). *Goodman's Aesthetics, The Stanford Encyclopedia of Philosophy* (Fall 2024 Edition), Edward N. Zalta & Uri Nodelman (eds.). https://plato.stanford.edu/entries/goodman-aesthetics/

Gudiño, J. F., Grandi, U., & Hidalgo, C. (2024). Large Language Models (LLMs) as Agents for Augmented Democracy, *Philosophical Transactions Royal Social Association*, 382:20240100, 1–17. https://doi.org/10.1098/rsta.2024.0100

Hammermeister, K. (2002). *The German Aesthetic Tradition*, Cambridge University Press.

Jimenez, M. (2023). *Estetik Nedir*, Ketebe Yayınları.

Kostera, M. (2014). *Occupy Management! Inspirations and Ideas for Self-Organization and Self-Management*, Routledge. https://doi.org/10.4324/9780203795033

Kostera, M., & Woźniak, C. (2021). *Aesthetics, Organization, and Humanistic Management*, Routledge.

Lucas, G. (2023). Political Bias in Large Language Models, *The Commons: Puget Sound Journal of Politics*, 4(1), 11–22. www.lucasgover.com/pdfs/PoliticalBias.pdf

Melnyk, A. (1996). Searle's Abstract Argument against Strong AI, *Synthese*, 108(3), 391–419. https://www.jstor.org/stable/20117550

Monthoux de, P. G. (1993). *The Moral Philosophy of Management from Quesnay to Keynes*, SSE.

Peters, L., & Strauss, A. (2021). Hula Hoops and Cigars, Hiccups and Stutters: Thinking with Film about Organizational Control. In *Aesthetics, Organization, and Humanistic Management* (edt. M. Kostera, C. Woźniak, pp. 31–46), Routledge.

Rorty, R. (1989 [1995]). *Olumsallık İroni ve Dayanışma*, Ayrıntı.

Searle, J. R. (1980). Minds, Brains, and Programs, *Behoviral and Brain Sciences*, 3(3), 417–424.

Shusterman, R. (1992). *Pragmatist Aesthetics Living Beauty Rethinking Art*, Blackwell.

Shusterman, R. (1999). Somaesthetics: A Disciplinary Proposal, *The Journal of Aesthetics and Art Criticism*, 57(3), 299–313. https://www.jstor.org/stable/432196

Skirbekk, G., & Gilje, N. (2006). *Antik Yunan'dan Modern Döneme Felsefe Tarihi*, E. Akbaş & Ş. Mutlu (trans.), Kesit Yayınları.

Strati, A. (1999). *Organization and Aesthetics*, Sage Publications.

Strati, A. (2019). *Organizational Theory and Aesthetic Philosophies*, Routledge.

Szostak, M. (2024). *Humanistic Management, Organisation and Aesthetics: Art of Manage ment and Management of Art*. Routledge.

Topakkaya, A., & Taşdelen, M. (2024). Richard Rorty'nin Estetik Pragmatizmi. In Kemal Bakır (ed.), *Özne Felsefe ve Bilim Sanat Yazıları: Pragmatizm*, 41, 339–358, Çizgi Kitabevi.

Tunalı, İ. (1998). *Estetik*, Remzi Kitabevi.

Türer, C. (2021). *Pragmatik Estetik*, Fol Yayınları.

Vandekerckhove, W. (2022). Aesthetic of Management: An Introduction. In *Handbook of Philosophy of Management* (edt. C. Neesham, M. Reihlen, D. Schoeneborn, pp. 357–368), Springer.

Vandekerckhove, W., & Emmanuel, M. (2022). A Rancièrian Method of Exploring Notions of Management and Organisation through the Artistic Gaze. In *Handbook of Philosophy of Management* (edt . C. Neesham, M. Reihlen, D. Schoeneborn, pp. 447–460), Springer.

Vaswani, A., et al. (2017). Attention is All You Need, 31st Conference on Neural Information Processing Systems (NIPS 2017). Long Beach, CA. https://proceedings.neurips.cc/paper_files/paper/2017/file/3f5ee243547dee91fbd053c1c4a845aa-Paper.pdf

Vickery, J. (2022). Aesthetics, Management, and the Organisation of Space. In *Handbook of Philosophy of Management* (edt. C. Neesham, M. Reihlen, D. Schoeneborn, pp. 389–412), Springer.

Wang, L., et al. (2024). A Survey on Large Language Model Based Autonomous Agents, *Frontier Computer Sciences*, 18(6), 186345, 1–26. https://doi.org/10.1007/s11704-024-40231-1

Wooldridge, M. (2022). *Bilinçli Makinelere Giden Yol: Yapay Zekanın Dünü Bugünü Yarını*, Ö. Çelik (trans.), Metis.

Yıldırım, İ. (2014). *İdealist ve Pragmatist Estetik*, Aktif Düşünce.

# 3 AI-powered solutions based on Freemasonry's aesthetic principles

## Lessons for humanistic management

*Dorota Mackenzie*

### Introduction

There is no one specific research gap when unpacking the notions of masonic aesthetics and AI-based solutions. Juxtaposing technology development with AI as its exemplar with Masonic studies (and therefore Masonic aesthetics) reveals little or no research in the fields. There are no current studies that would combine these two fields of research. These research gaps circulate between two issues: firstly, the lack of studies on AI-driven decision-making inspired by Masonic aesthetics. While Freemasonry emphasises harmony, symmetry, and order, little research explores how these principles could guide AI-powered decision-making in management. Secondly, there is an absence of AI ethical frameworks inspired by Masonic symbolism. Freemasonry has strong ethical codes (e.g., brotherhood, social empathy, enlightenment), but there is no research on how AI can incorporate this aesthetics into humanistic management frameworks. These research gaps may be grouped into four main categories: Aesthetic Principles of Freemasonry and AI Design in Humanistic Management; Intersection of AI and Freemasonry's Aesthetic Principles; Humanistic Management and AI's Role in Ethical Leadership; and Masonic-Inspired AI for Organisational Culture and Development. This chapter explores the first one, with the other aspects being researched in future publications. There are no studies on AI interfaces incorporating Masonic aesthetics for decision-making, so this study might be considered a pioneer study.

The impact of sacred geometry, symmetry, and balance (central to Masonic design) and its potential integration with AI-driven organisational solutions remains unexplored. Uncharted territory in AI-generated rituals and symbolic decision-making rituals are key in Masonic tradition; AI could integrate symbolic acts in decision-making, but this concept lacks empirical or theoretical exploration. The intersection of Freemasonry's aesthetic principles, AI design,

DOI: 10.4324/9781003654377-5

and humanistic management presents a largely unexplored research domain. Key gaps in the literature and potential areas for investigation are the following:

1 *Aesthetic principles in Freemasonry and their philosophical underpinning*: While Freemasonry incorporates symbols, rituals, and architectural ideals reflecting harmony, proportion, and enlightenment, there is little scholarly analysis of how these principles translate into modern humanistic management and AI ethics. Research typically focuses on Freemasonry's moral and philosophical teachings, not aesthetic contributions to organisational design and decision-making.
2 *AI design and humanistic management*: AI design often prioritises efficiency, optimisation, and functionality, sometimes at the expense of humanistic values such as creativity, ethics, and emotional intelligence. Humanistic management promotes dignity, ethical responsibility, and purpose, but its connection to symbolic aesthetics and ritualistic design, as seen in Freemasonry, remains underexplored. Existing research focuses on AI bias, transparency, and ethics, yet the role of aesthetics in ethical AI development remains a neglected area.
3 *The role of Freemasonry's aesthetics in AI and human-centred systems*: Can Masonic principles – such as sacred geometry, proportion, and symbolism – inform AI design in ways that enhance user experience, ethical decision-making, or system transparency? How can ritualistic elements in Freemasonry contribute to AI-human interaction models, particularly in decision-making frameworks used in humanistic management? Could Freemasonry's emphasis on harmony, symmetry, and symbolic meaning help bridge the gap between technical AI development and humanistic concerns?

Therefore, potential research directions are multiple, and the initial summary can be lined up in the following points: (1) symbolic and ethical AI: applying Masonic symbolism and geometric harmony to develop AI interfaces that are more intuitive, transparent, and ethically aligned with humanistic management; (2) Freemasonry-inspired leadership models: investigating how Masonic aesthetics can shape leadership philosophies in humanistic management; (3) ritual and AI ethics: exploring whether ritualistic elements of Freemasonry can contribute to AI governance models that incorporate moral responsibility and ethical foresight; (4) Can AI design lead to an impoverishment of Masonic symbolism and the superficiality of its ideas and philosophical system? This interdisciplinary research gap calls for integrating aesthetic, ethical, and symbolic frameworks from Freemasonry into AI and humanistic management. Future studies could explore how aesthetic values shape AI systems, creating a more balanced, ethical, and human-centred technological landscape.

This chapter's *research problem* is the intersection and integration of humanistic management and aesthetics, Freemasonry's rich and diverse symbolism, and AI-powered solutions. The research problem concerns the issue of enhancing humanistic management with AI-powered tools and solutions inspired by

Freemasonry's aesthetics and symbolic principles. The research problems can be analysed from the following perspectives: (1) *Aesthetic integration*: How Freemasonry's symbolism, principles, and aesthetic values (such as harmony, balance, and moral integrity) can be translated into AI tools used in humanistic management; (2) *Humanistic enhancement*: How applying Freemasonry aesthetics in AI tools can improve Humanistic Management practices, such as promoting ethical decision-making, improving interpersonal relationships, and fostering a culture of dignity and respect in organisations; (3) *Tool development*: How AI-powered tools can be designed or enhanced with Freemasonry aesthetics to support management practices, focusing on leadership, communication, and organisational culture.

This chapter answers the following *research questions*: (RQ1) Can Freemasonry's aesthetic principles be integrated into AI-driven decision-making frameworks within humanistic management? (RQ2) To what extent do Masonic aesthetics in AI interfaces affect user experience and confidence in AI-driven tools? (RQ3) How can AI tools based on aesthetic Masonic principles be designed to foster Fraternity in humanistic management settings?

Exploring Freemasonry's humanistic approach and its impact on managerial theory and practice in the era of AI requires a multidisciplinary *research approach*, drawing on theories from management studies, sociology, organisational behaviour, and the study of Freemasonry itself. Given that this topic intersects with longstanding Masonic traditions and contemporary technological developments, the methodology must be reflective and forward-looking. The aim is to understand how Freemasonry can integrate humanistic management principles within the changing landscape of AI while ensuring that its core values of personal growth, ethical behaviour, and community service remain intact. This study uses an exploratory research design to investigate the intersection of Freemasonry, humanistic management, and AI. It is purely theoretical since the application of AI in the context of Freemasonry and humanistic management is a relatively underexplored area. As this is a pilot study, the research aims to generate insights into how these three domains can be integrated and how Freemasonry might guide humanistic management in the AI era. To specify, this chapter uses qualitative content analysis. It is conducted on Masonic literature, both historical and contemporary, to identify references to humanistic values and technology, particularly AI. This analysis examines how Freemasonry has historically balanced aesthetic and ethical considerations with new developments and how the language of humanistic management might align with Masonic philosophy and communication codes.

## Literature review: aesthetic foundations and symbolic traditions at intersecting humanistic management, Freemasonry, and AI

The literature review encompasses this chapter's main research fields: Freemasonry and its aesthetics, humanistic management's foundations and principles, and the impact of AI-powered solutions on human-centred practices. The goal of this pioneering study is to integrate all those disciplines and the potential they carry.

The aesthetics of depth and the Plato triad apply to humanistic management, Freemasonry and AI. The domain of aesthetics is vast and devoted to conceptual and theoretical inquiry. One may usefully think of philosophical aesthetics as having three *loci*, each of which might be adequately conceived. These are art, aesthetic property, and aesthetic experience (Levinson, 2003). I believe the *loci* most appropriate to this inquiry is the last one. Aesthetics, conceived as the study of specific, distinctive experiences or states of mind, whether attitudes, perceptions, emotions, or acts of attention, similarly requires some conception of when a state of mind or mental activity is an aesthetic one (Levinson, 2003, p. 6).

Plato's writings play a foundational role in the history of aesthetics as they are one of the earliest substantial contributions to this branch of philosophy. For him, there is a metaphysical and ethical order to the world, which is philosophy's task to discover employing rational thought, and the arts can have true worth only if they correctly represent this order or help align us with it (Gaut & Lopes, 2001). Because of this constatation, we can envisage AI tools as this rational thought of philosophy, Freemasonry as this art representing the metaphysics of the world in a genuinely royal way, and humanistic management as the modus operandi – in possession of *technê*. This notion appears in the early Platonian dialogue *Ion*. The *technê* concept has been translated as "skill", "craft", or "expert knowledge" (Gaut & Lopes, 2001, p. 10 and next). Plato regards doctors, generals, and mathematicians as possessing a *technê*, meaning that they are knowledgeable about a specific subject matter, can transmit their knowledge in teaching, understand general principles or rules that apply across all instances within their field and can give a rational account of why their practice succeeds (Bowie, 1990). *Technê* aims at the good and is based on knowledge of the good. This is also applicable to Freemasonry.

One of the central themes in both Tatarkiewicz's history of aesthetics (Tatarkiewicz, 2009) and Freemasonry is the role of architecture in understanding beauty. Freemasonry places significant emphasis on the symbolic meaning of architecture, mainly through its use of tools like the compass and square, which symbolise moral and ethical principles. These symbols are often linked to "building" a better self and society, which aligns with Tatarkiewicz's view that aesthetics is tied to broader cultural and philosophical values. In his work, Tatarkiewicz notes that architecture, as an art form, plays a significant role in many cultures' aesthetic development. Freemasonry's foundational connection to building integrates aesthetic principles in its symbolism and rituals. The idea of constructing something beautiful in art and life resonates with the Freemasonry's goal of self-improvement. Following Plato's triad to translate our three elements, we could say that as there are three parts of the soul, AI would stand for Logos (Reason) as well as Mimesis (imitation), Thymos (Spirit) for Freemasonry aesthetics, and Epithymia (desire; the appetitive part) for Humanistic Management. These might iterate, but the core idea is representative.

### *Thymos, or Freemasonry's spirit and aesthetics*

Freemasonry, an ancient fraternal organisation (officially established in 1717), is often associated with moral and ethical development, personal growth, and the promotion of universal values such as brotherhood, truth, charity and social responsibility (Cegielski, 1994). As a social and ritualistic institution, Freemasonry also emphasises ethical conduct, intellectual enlightenment, and the betterment of society. Its structure is built on continuous personal and spiritual development, where members are encouraged to act with integrity, fairness, and respect for others. Masonic principles resonate with many aspects of humanistic management, particularly in moral leadership, the importance of community and the underlying aesthetics. McLeod (2016) explores the philosophical underpinnings of Freemasonry, noting how it advocates for a type of leadership grounded in ethical responsibility, mutual support, and the fostering of personal integrity (a service leadership model). The Masonic tradition, which emphasises service to others and the pursuit of truth, can be seen as a precursor to humanistic management scholars' ethical leadership and stakeholder orientation. Moreover, Freemasonry's historical commitment to education and the development of intellectual and moral virtues aligns with the humanistic ideals of management. As such, Freemasonic lodges serve as a model of moral leadership and community engagement, offering a space where individuals are encouraged to improve themselves and contribute positively to society (Cegielski, 1992), akin to the community-centred goals of humanistic management.

The aesthetics of Freemasonry are deeply rooted in symbolism, proportion, and sacred geometry, reflecting its philosophical and ethical teachings. Masonic aesthetics are not merely decorative; they serve a didactic and initiatory function, reinforcing moral lessons and spiritual development (Di Bernardo, 2016). The key aspects of Masonic aesthetics are symbolism and ritual as an aesthetic expression of sacred geometry and architectural harmony, ritualistic aesthetics and performance, lodge design and interior aesthetics (Boucher, 2011).

Freemasonry is, first and foremost, a movement which, in what it differs from other social phenomena, already at its birth in the second half of the 17th century, takes on organisational forms defined by custom and tradition. The process of evolution of the organisational structures of Freemasonry could be described as the transformation of Freemasonry, understood in the 17th century as a "custom", that is, the occasional performance of specific rites, towards organised and continuous forms; initially a "Fraternity" or "Society", and then an "Order". James Anderson uses the term Fraternity in the title of both editions of his Constitutions (1723, 1738), and interchangeably in the text, the terms Fraternity and the Craft or the Royal Art are consistently capitalised (Cegielski, 1994). From the contexts in which the terms of interest appear, we can infer that the first of these, Fraternity, refers to a community of masons, organised in lodges and legitimised by charges or "duties and privileges bestowed by the rulers". It differs from the Craft, which can be translated in several ways – "craft", "artistry", "art" and the Royal Art, or "royal art". The last two names are associated with professional skills (English Masonry is the common name for several professions serving the art of architecture in the broadest sense).

With a considerable degree of certainty, we can conclude that Freemasonry was conceived by the founders of the Grand Lodge of London (1717) equally as a professional tradition and as a well-defined structure. The latter was called an Order in the concluding section of the text of the Constitutions of 1723 (Cegielski, 2025); in addition to such an Order, which provided a model for "several venerable and ancient Societies and Orders", which received "Duties and Regulations from the Free Masons, who are now the most ancient Order on Earth". Anderson concludes that the founders of these Societies and Orders were probably previously "members of the said ancient and venerable Brotherhood". From the quoted passage from the Constitution, we can conclude that the term "brotherhood" was used interchangeably with "order" and "association". The apparent inconsistency, after all, allowed the founders of Freemasonry of the new type to point to the multiple sources of their movement, at the same time opening the way to such organisational solutions, which best reflected the changing times and needs of the members of the lodges and primarily fulfilled their fundamental, integrative role.

According to the research, guild organisations (gilds) or so-called operative lodges, which are an extension of guilds, traditionally treated in the UGLE tradition as the nucleus of the organisation of speculative lodges, are secondary forms, given ex-post to already existing structures. If the former were egalitarian and assumed equality of membership rights, the latter were exclusive, hierarchical, and, by definition, based on an initiation rite. It clearly distinguished between those who could not receive it (the profane) and the adepts (the initiated). One could no longer join this type of organisation by showing the necessary credentials and paying dues, but had to pass through a multi-stage process of investment and symbolic tests, constituting an archaic rite of passage.

Both models were based on different forms of leadership, procedures for appointing the association's authorities and their accountability to rank-and-file members. The Grand Lodge of London, following the model of its predecessor, the Grand Lodge of York, elected its superior, the Grand Master, annually; on the same basis, the other dignitaries: first and second overseers, speakers, experts, treasurers, alms-houses, and deacons. It equipped them with a wide range of powers over time but made them accountable to the General Assembly for their decisions. This legal construction was referred to in the eighth decade of the 18th century by freemen from the rebellious states of North America when they sought a suitable formula for the presidential power of the newly established republic, the United States of America (Levenda, 2009). Meanwhile, the Grand Lodge system had undergone a notable evolution in the English metropolis and the cradle of the Freemasonry movement. Since the initiation of the heir to the throne, Frederick Louis, Prince of Wales, in 1737, who in time assumed the office of Grand Master, the tenure of the highest office in the brotherhood gave way to the principle of perpetuity of his election. However, the tenure of office was maintained at the individual lodge level, with the Grand Lodge as their head. Freemasonry, understood in this way, became the domain of the rapidly forming middle class, not only a school of good manners needed to enter the salons but also a ticket to civil society, or as John Locke called it, *political society*. In the fourth decade of the 18th century, a new form of Freemasonry appeared initially in France as a secular order of chivalry. The hitherto triumphant Grand Lodge of London, and later of England, grew up simultaneously as a formidable rival, referring to traditions other than the democratic-celebrated ones.

Jacobite Freemasonry (Jacobites were supporters of James II Stuart, who was deposed from the throne in 1688) and the Catholic Irish founded the Grand Lodge of England (GLE) in 1756 following the Old Constitutions. It gave the hitherto simple ritual of lodges an intensely esoteric, sometimes quasi-religious character. The two obediences finally merged in 1813, establishing the United Grand Lodge of England (UGLE), which still exists today. The UGLE adopted into its pseudo-guild traditions new founding legends that drew on the history of the orders of chivalry – the Royal Arch Chapter and the Royal Vault.

The features of knightly Freemasonry (S.O.T., Strict Observance of the Knights Templar by Chevalier Andrew Ramsay and Baron von Hunda und Altgrotkau, Scandinavian Rite) were strong exclusivism, hierarchical, and already in the 18th century up to 29/30 degrees of initiation. The formal exclusion of the third state had the effect of making membership of the S.O.T. an excellent value for the bourgeoisie, contributing to the integration of its rich and educated stratum with the nobility and aristocracy receding from the stage of history.

In contrast, the significant reform of Freemasonry in the Crown and Lithuania, undertaken by Ignacy Potocki after the First Partition of the Republic and crowned by the adoption of English Constitutions by 11 lodges on 27 December 1781, marked a radical turn towards ethical and social goals and integration around the project of state reform. The new situation thus signified the politicisation of Freemasonry, which, together with an indication of the civic duties of brother Freemasons, brought a denunciation of recognition from the GLE in 1784. In an extensive letter addressed to the Grand Lodge of the Kingdom of Poland and the Grand Duchy of Lithuania, the leadership of the English obedience reminded that Freemasonry owed its universal, humanitarian, supranational and supra-state character, among other things, to the complete renunciation of particularistic political goals (Morawińska, Cegielski, & Załęski, 2014). Such a character of English freemasonry has been preserved until today. At the same time, the fate of Freemasonry in Poland has been affected by great storms and turns of history – making it *ipso facto* an institution with a clear political profile, maintaining those universalist tasks set at the very dawn of its history in the first half of the 18th century (Sroka & Nowosad, 2022).

A sociological approach on the one hand and a cultural approach on the other, albeit with an outline of the phenomenon's evolution both in time and space, casts some light on the aesthetics of the movement and its alignment with the humanistic management of an organisation (McLeod, 2016). The evolutionary processes would constitute a separate level of analysis, essential for understanding the current state of the phenomenon of Freemasonry. The starting point would be to consider Freemasonry as a phenomenon fulfilling specific tasks as a separate, organisational, legal and economic social structure characterised by numerous, though not necessarily noticeable, daily analogies to a company. The latter is not only an economic entity whose essence and purpose are producing goods or providing services. It is, in fact, just like the lodges or organisational structures of Freemasonry, a business whose form is determined by its founders and owners; it depends not only on the legal regulations in force in each territory but also on the traditions and customs prevailing in each area of economic activity.

As far as the analogies between Freemasonry understood as a structure and various types of institutions are concerned, there are important precedents in the history of Freemasonry, not only in the linguistic sphere – such as calling Freemasonry an *institute* in the Polish tradition – I would prefer the term *ideal enterprise* but also in the reflection of a formal, and at the same time historical character, which ordered it to be treated as a form of a secular order. It was already apparent on the grounds of the first statutes (the so-called Constitutions) of the Grand Lodge of London (from 1738 onwards in England) on the discussion on the so-called regularity of Freemasonry and on what private or wild lodges are.

A reading of the first normative text in the history of symbolic (speculative) Freemasonry, the Statutes or Constitutions published in 1723 and 1738 by the Presbyterian pastor James Anderson, indicates that even then, the Grand Lodge of London fought against what it considered to be unfair competition, and protected its identity and "trademark". Hence, the notions of regularity or irregularity of lodges remain current due to the "Royal Art" formula. The Future Mother Lodge of the World introduced the principle (strongly contested by traditional, *Ancient* Freemasonry organisations) that the single, unaffiliated workshops are wild, irregular lodges. New structures can only be set up by a person authorised to do so – by the GLE – which holds the appropriate patent and acts as prescribed by statutes and customs. The struggle between the *Ancients* and the *Moderns* (i.e. the GLE) finally ended in 1813, but the standards created in the second half of the 18th century for the functioning of lodges, the rights and duties of the friars have remained valid to this day, throughout global Freemasonry. It is, therefore, worth examining them not only in terms of the leadership model but also in terms of their adaptation to the central task of Freemasonry, which is integration across all divisions (Mackey, 1996).

An English invention of the 18th century was the chartering of lodges, which contributed significantly to the globalisation of the movement. The GLE granted a patent to establish provincial grand lodges as branch lodges. The criteria for recognition were precisely formulated and enforced. Significantly, however, the GLE did not inflict inspections on the granddaughter lodges, nor did it attempt to interfere in their work. It did, after all, ensure that the constitutional acts of these fully autonomous creations reflected the principles contained in the Anderson Constitutions of 1723 and 1738 (Cegielski, 2025). This was experienced by the Grand Duchy of the Kingdom of Poland of the Grand Duchy of Lithuania in 1784 when the GLE rejected its new Constitution and thus withdrew its recognition. The Grand East of Poland departed from the principles of its Constitution of December 1781 (modelled on the second edition of Anderson's Constitution of 1738) concerning the duties of a fraternal freeman.

### *Geometry, symbol, ritual: symbolism and ritual language in the Freemasonry aesthetics*

While maintaining a well-defined structure, the Masonic community is deeply embedded in a unique system of communication that is both ritualistic and symbolic. The specific case of the Emulation Rite, one of the most widely practised rites in contemporary Freemasonry, is a means to examine the way Masons communicate within their community. By analysing the rites and symbols and the performative nature of their rituals, it is possible to investigate how Masonic members use the aesthetics of non-verbal codes, gestures, language, and symbolism to communicate values, social norms, and Fraternity. This case study highlights the Emulation Rite as a potent example of the performative aspects of Masonic communication and how it helps maintain solidarity, social order, and identity within the Masonic world (Boucher, 2011).

As an ancient fraternal organisation, Freemasonry is known for its rituals, symbols, and a strong emphasis on moral and ethical teachings. Freemasonry's most distinctive feature is its complex communication system, which is neither entirely verbal nor conventional. Instead, it is a symbolic language enriched with gestures, rituals, and coded expressions to create and reinforce bonds between its members. The Masonic community, composed of diverse members from various walks of life, shares a common understanding of these codes, which function as a social adhesive, binding members together in a shared identity (Millar, 2005). At the heart of Masonic communication lies the performance of ritual. Through a carefully constructed set of practices, members communicate a variety of messages – spiritual, ethical, and social – in a non-verbal manner. Among the different rites practised in Freemasonry, the Emulation Rite stands out for its unique blend of oral, symbolic, and performative elements.

The Emulation Rite, also known as the Emulation Working, is one of the principal ritual systems used in English Freemasonry. Its origin can be traced back to the early 19th century when it emerged as a response to regional variations in Masonic ritual. It represents a standardised and highly structured version of the rituals of the three symbolic degrees: Entered Apprentice, Fellowcraft, and Master Mason. The term "Emulation" itself refers to the idea of striving for excellence in moral conduct and ritual performance. It was designed to establish consistency across lodges while maintaining the rich symbolic tradition of the Craft. The Emulation Rite is primarily known for its emphasis on oral transmission, ritual gestures, and symbolic actions, forming part of its distinctive communication code. Within this framework, members pass through several personal and spiritual development stages, each marked by symbols, words, and gestures that communicate lessons about life, moral integrity, and social responsibility (Cegielski, 1994).

One of the core elements of the Emulation Rite is its symbolic language. Each degree in the Emulation system is associated with a specific set of symbols that convey particular meanings. These symbols are not just decorative or aesthetic; they serve as a means of non-verbal communication, imparting moral and spiritual lessons that transcend mere words. For instance, the Square and Compasses, the All-Seeing Eye, the plumb rule, and the level, among others, are symbols rich with layered meaning. These objects serve as a silent communication form, transmitting more profound messages that members understand through years of ritual participation. The Square and Compasses, perhaps the most iconic of Masonic symbols, communicate the principle of moral uprightness and balance. Its meaning is primarily communicative because it invites members to align their behaviour with virtue. The All-Seeing Eye symbolises the omniscient presence of the Supreme Being (the Great Architect of the Universe), which reminds members of the ever-present divine authority and the importance of vigilance and integrity in all actions. These symbols are not merely aesthetic; they operate as a communication code, transmitting lessons, values, and ethical guidelines through visual and ritualistic means. Over time, Masonic members internalise these symbols, which act as a form of social language understood by those within the community.

A distinctive feature of Masonic communication is the ritualistic handshake, an important part of the code. The handshake is not just a form of greeting but also a means of confirming one's status within the organisation. Each degree has its distinct handshake, a form of silent social interaction communicating rank and trust between members. The handshake becomes an unspoken language of recognition that transcends spoken words and facilitates the binding of members into the Masonic brotherhood. Additionally, Masonic gestures – such as the use of the ritual signs or the signs of distress – serve as further means of communication. These performative gestures are often used to convey emotions or messages, from loyalty and unity to a symbolic call for assistance in times of need.

The most profound form of Masonic communication lies in its ritual perfor mances, which are enacted through various ceremonies, each carrying its own coded language. The ritual of the Initiation, for example, communicates a process of moral and spiritual awakening, transforming an ordinary individual into a brother. This is not a mere ceremonial gesture but rather an act of profound performativity in which a new member, through specific actions, words, and symbols, is invited to embark on a transformative journey. The same can be said of the rite of passage for each degree. The ceremonial rituals are essentially performative acts: participants embody roles and undergo symbolic transformations that communicate important lessons and messages. Masons communicate their collective values and shared beliefs by performing certain rituals, creating a sense of ritualistic solidarity (Cegielski, 1994; Mackenzie, 2023).

### *Masonic communication's social function: establishing identity and community*

Masonic communication plays a significant role in establishing and maintaining group identity by emphasising symbols, gestures, and rituals. The shared understanding of the ritual code fosters members' sense of belonging, solidarity, and trust. By participating in these rituals, each member affirms their identity as part of the larger Masonic community. By ensuring consistency in ritual practice across lodges, the Emulation Rite acts as a mechanism for reinforcing this collective identity. Through the standardised performance of rituals and adherence to the Masonic code, members signal their alignment with the core principles of the Fraternity, which include charity, brotherhood, and moral integrity.

Masonic rituals also play a critical role in social regulation within the community. Regular ritualistic participation ensures members are reminded of their ethical duties and responsibilities. Using symbolic communication, Masonic rituals act as a mechanism for reaffirming moral norms, guiding members towards a more virtuous and socially responsible way of living and the best possible social order. Through this structured communication system, Freemasonry also fosters a strong sense of social responsibility, ensuring that members engage with one another in a manner consistent with Masonic principles. With its carefully designed progression, the degree system represents a ritualistic ladder that encourages personal and spiritual growth.

As a central feature of contemporary Freemasonry, the Emulation Rite provides a compelling case study for understanding the intricacies of Masonic communication. It reveals how symbols, rituals, gestures, and performative acts are a cohesive and powerful communication code that facilitates the Masonic community's transmission of values, norms, and identity. Freemasonry maintains its traditional values and ability to adapt to the modern world through this system. The Emulation Rite, emphasising ritualistic performance and symbolic communication, underscores the profound impact of non-verbal communication in constructing and maintaining social bonds within the Masonic Brotherhood. As Freemasonry continues to evolve, the Emulation Rite remains a testament to the power of performative communication in preserving tradition, fostering solidarity, and cultivating personal growth within the context of a shared symbolic system.

### *Epithymia or ontology of humanistic management*

Humanistic management is a framework that emphasises human dignity, ethical behaviour, and the well-being of all stakeholders within organisational settings. Rooted in humanism, a philosophical stance prioritising human values and autonomy, humanistic management critiques traditional management models focusing primarily on profit maximisation and efficiency at the expense of social responsibility. A central tenet of humanistic management is its emphasis on human-centred leadership, where organisations are seen not merely as profit-making entities but as communities with a moral obligation to foster the development and well-being of their members. Also, management aesthetics highlights the importance of beauty, harmony, and emotional resonance within organisational settings. AI can be deployed to improve efficiency and create aesthetically pleasing interactions with customers and employees (Kostera & Woźniak, 2022). Freemasonry has incorporated these elements from its very beginnings. Scholars in humanistic management, such as Szostak (2021, 2022a, 2022b, 2023), argue that organisations should create value through relationships, purpose-driven actions, and upholding ethical standards. Similarly, Schroeder et al. (2021) highlight the integration of ethical frameworks into organisational culture, focusing on the need for transparency, accountability, and stakeholder engagement.

Humanistic management is an approach that emphasises human dignity, ethical responsibility, and social well-being in organisational and economic decision-making. It seeks to balance profitability with purpose, ensuring that businesses and institutions contribute positively to society. The key principles of humanistic management are unconditional respect for human dignity, ethical reflection and moral responsibility, holistic stakeholder orientation, servant leadership and participatory decision-making, sustainability and social responsibility, purpose-driven innovation and human excelling (Schroeder, 2021). Humanistic management bridges business success with ethical responsibility, ensuring that organisations operate in a way that respects human dignity, supports all stakeholders, and contributes to a sustainable future. It challenges traditional, profit-maximising business models by integrating values, ethics, and human-centred leadership into organisational decision-making.

If we fuse humanistic management's ontology with Freemasonry's aesthetics, a new AI-driven framework emerges – one that sees leadership as an architectural and artistic endeavour, where organisations are *temples of human well-being*. If we look at the organisation as a lodge, a humanistic organisation would be a sacred space for intellectual, ethical, and creative refinement. Decision-making would be ritualised to honour wisdom, balance, and ethical alignment (e.g., major business decisions framed through structured reflection). The leader could be perceived as a Master Builder: the CEO or leader embodies the Great Architect archetype – not being the Great Architect himself and – not as a controlling force but as one who harmonises people, values, and purpose. Leadership aesthetics would emphasise clarity, proportion, and ethical symmetry – aligning corporate purpose with human well-being. In such an organisation, technology runs as the AI Compass & Square. In this synthesis, AI is the compass and square of modern humanistic management, ensuring precision and fairness in ethical decision-making. AI-driven systems could assess organisational harmony, predict imbalances, and ensure decisions uphold human dignity and creative potential. The organisation's ethical work would go hand in hand with aesthetics, standing beyond profit. In this framework, businesses should not be mechanistic profit machines but ethical artworks – beautiful in their harmony, impactful in their purpose, and lasting in their legacy. Freemasonry teaches that the perfect temple is never finished; likewise, humanistic organisations should always be in artistic evolution (Jemielniak & Przegalińska, 2020).

### *Between logos and mimesis: AI-powered solutions on human-centred practices*

If we look at the core ontological foundations in AI-driven management, we can see that the first dualism is the notion of human dignity and AI. Humanistic management asserts that technology should serve human dignity, not replace it, whereas AI should be augmentative rather than substitutive, ensuring that human agency, creativity, and autonomy remain central to decision-making processes. Therefore, ethical AI systems should be transparent, explainable, and aligned with human values rather than purely profit-driven or efficiency-focused. When investigating relational and social ontology in AI systems, we might remember that AI-driven solutions should acknowledge the interdependence of humans, machines, and organisational structures. The ethical design of AI must consider its social impact on employees, customers, and broader stakeholders. Instead of reinforcing hierarchical control, AI should enable participatory and collaborative decision-making.

When it comes to the ethical nature of AI in business, unlike traditional views of AI as value-neutral tools, humanistic management sees AI as embedded within ethical and moral frameworks. AI should reflect corporate social responsibility, avoiding biases, discrimination, and unintended negative consequences. Companies should implement AI ethics boards or governance frameworks to ensure alignment with human-centred values.

Regarding a holistic view of humans in AI-driven workplaces, AI should enhance human work rather than reduce employees to data points or algorithms.

Human well-being must be a priority when designing AI-driven management systems, ensuring psychological safety, fairness, and empowerment. Instead of excessive surveillance and micromanagement, AI should support creativity, personalisation, and professional growth. AI for sustainability and flourishing means AI-driven management should prioritise long-term sustainability over short-term profit maximisation (Mueller, 2021). Ethical AI applications can drive environmental responsibility, diversity, and inclusion and create a positive social impact. If AI models integrate sustainable development goals (SDGs) rather than purely economic efficiency metrics, we can achieve freedom and empowerment within the humanistic management scope. AI should enhance employee autonomy by offering decision support rather than enforcing rigid control. Algorithmic transparency and explainability empower individuals to challenge, audit, and understand AI-driven decisions. AI should be designed to promote learning, adaptability, and personal growth rather than just automation and compliance.

The rise of AI presents new challenges and opportunities for management practices and ethical frameworks. AI's ability to automate processes, analyse big data, and optimise decision-making raises important questions about the human dimension of work. As AI systems increasingly perform tasks traditionally done by humans, organisations must reconsider the role of human workers, focusing on their well-being, autonomy, and dignity (Jemielniak & Przegalińska, 2020). Human-centred AI solutions enhance inclusivity, well-being, ethics, and transparency in various sectors. By aligning AI with humanistic management principles and masonic aesthetics, we can create technology that empowers, rather than replaces, human potential.

The previously cited Plato's triad can be used as a framework for ethical decision-making, leadership, and AI governance with the following recommendations:

1 Logos – AI as the rational mind:

  a AI systems should prioritise wisdom, logic, and ethical reasoning in decision-making;
  b Ethical AI governance requires transparency, fairness, and accountability, ensuring AI aligns with human dignity and justice;

2 Thymos – human emotion and motivation:

  a AI should account for human emotional intelligence, motivation, and ethical courage;
  b It means fostering employee engagement, meaningful work, and ethical business leadership;

3 Epithymia – desires and market forces:

  a AI-driven businesses must balance profit motives with sustainability, responsibility, and ethical constraints;

b Ethical AI should regulate unchecked desires, such as excessive consumerism, environmental harm, and exploitative labour practices.

Implications for AI-driven humanistic management concern leadership and governance, employee experience, and ethical AI development. Perhaps the first step should be AI Ethics Committees: companies should establish AI ethics governance structures to ensure human-centric development and deployment. As for transparency and accountability, AI decisions should be explainable, avoiding bias, discrimination, and ethical blind spots (Hayler, 1999).

From the employee experience perspective, perhaps innovations such as AI-enhanced learning should be implemented where AI could be used for personalised professional development, not punitive surveillance or

*Table 3.1* Representation of the AI-synthesised convergence of humanistic management ontology and Freemasonry aesthetics

| *Aspect* | *Humanistic management* | *Freemasonry aesthetics* | *AI-synthesised convergence* |
|---|---|---|---|
| *Core philosophy* | Human dignity, ethical responsibility, and sustainable value | Symbolism, self-improvement, sacred geometry | Organisations as "Temples of Human Flourishing" |
| *Leadership role* | Leader as a facilitator of human potential | Master Builder guiding ethical and intellectual growth | CEO as "Architect" of balance and wisdom |
| *Organisational structure* | Collaborative, purpose-driven spaces | Masonic lodges as spaces of enlightenment | Workplaces as modern "Lodges" of ethical decision-making |
| *Decision-making process* | Values-based leadership and ethical reflection | Ritualised decision-making through symbolic teachings | AI-driven ethical governance ensuring fairness |
| *Technology's role* | Enhancing human dignity through responsible innovation | Tools (compass and square) symbolise moral precision | AI as the "Digital Compass and Square", guiding ethical business practices |
| *Symbolic representation* | Ethical and aesthetic organisation design | Architecture, light, and ritual as symbols of perfection | Business as an art form, balancing impact, beauty, and justice |
| *Purpose of work* | Meaningful, people-centred development | Self-cultivation and service to humanity | Work as a Masonic Art, continuously refined and perfected |

*Source:* Own elaboration based on Kostera and Woźniak (2022).

micromanagement. Regarding human-AI collaboration, AI should assist decision-making, creativity, and innovation rather than simply optimising for efficiency. Furthermore, fair AI-driven HR policies should be established: AI in hiring, promotions, and evaluations must be bias-free, equitable, and respectful of individual dignity. Lastly, concerning technology and ethical AI development, we need to think about human-in-the-loop systems where AI should support and enhance human judgment rather than replace it. Regarding sustainability in AI models, AI should be designed with energy efficiency, responsible data use, and social impact in mind. An inevitable course of action to undertake is continuous monitoring and auditing: AI-driven solutions must undergo ongoing ethical review and improvement. Table 3.1 represents the AI-synthesised convergence of humanistic management ontology and Freemasonry aesthetics.

### *Towards a humanistic AI-driven future*

A humanistic ontology of AI-driven management calls for a profound reimagining of the role AI plays in the life of organisations. Rather than approaching AI merely as a tool for automation, optimisation, or profit maximisation, this paradigm positions AI as a co-creative partner – one that supports, enhances, and ultimately affirms the dignity and agency of human beings within complex social systems (Hayles, 1999). At its core, this perspective challenges the mechanistic view of management and advocates for an ethics-first integration of technology into organisational structures, cultures, and decision-making processes. It asks not only what AI *can* do but what it *ought* to do in service of a just and flourishing society. Under this vision, AI systems are designed to uphold and advance values such as empathy, equity, transparency, and mutual respect – amplifying what is most meaningful in human work rather than replacing it.

Such an approach redefines success beyond key performance indicators or efficiency metrics. It involves creating AI ecosystems prioritising human development, nurturing inclusive collaboration, and strengthening relational ties among employees, stakeholders, and communities. These systems may support ethical leadership, assist in complex moral reasoning, and help mediate collective decision-making by surfacing shared values and long-term consequences. A humanistic AI framework is inherently interdisciplinary and ecological – it encourages organisations to embed social and environmental responsibility into the algorithms that guide operations. From sustainable resource allocation to bias-aware hiring practices, AI becomes a steward of corporate conscience, not just a servant of market logic. Moving towards a humanistic AI-driven future means reframing technology not as an end but as a medium for ethical evolution. It demands leadership with vision, systems with soul, and a commitment to ensuring that AI contributes not only to smarter business – but to wiser, kinder, and more resilient societies.

However, a humanistic ontology of AI-driven management requires more than technical innovation – it demands a philosophical reorientation of how organisations conceive of intelligence, agency, and value. Drawing inspiration from Masonic principles, this approach envisions AI not as a cold instrument of efficiency but as a symbolic and ethical ally – a digital extension of the moral compass, square, and level that guide the Craft. Rather than reducing AI to a mere tool for maximising output or reducing costs, a Masonic-humanistic paradigm asks how technology can support human dignity, moral refinement, and fraternal cooperation. Just as Freemasonry elevates labour into sacred work through symbolism and intention, AI can also be designed to infuse modern management with ethical purpose and spiritual depth.

In this vision, AI systems are not programmed solely to optimise but to mediate, mentor, and moralise. They can serve as digital "Master Masons", helping individuals and teams navigate complex decisions with wisdom, balance, and foresight. These systems may reference ethical traditions, historical case studies, or even Masonic allegories – guiding users towards effective solutions and just and virtuous ones.

AI, under this framework, supports the temple-building metaphor of organisational life. Each project, each decision, becomes a stone laid in the construction of a more enlightened society. Algorithms are crafted to recognise utility and symbolic meaning – illuminating shared values, fostering trust, and reinforcing a culture of mutual accountability, much like the ritual and structure of a Lodge.

Moreover, Masonic thought invites us to consider progressive moral development akin to the degrees of initiation. AI could support this by structuring leadership journeys, ethical learning paths, and team rituals that echo the philosophical and spiritual ascent stages – transforming workplaces into spaces for personal and collective transformation.

In an age of increasing automation, the challenge is to preserve the human and ennoble it. Just as Masonic Oaths bind members to truth and integrity, organisations must ensure that AI systems are transparent, trustworthy, and aligned with a greater ethical vision. These systems can even act as guardians of the "All-Seeing Eye", maintaining oversight over decisions and reminding leaders of their accountability to the whole. Ultimately, a Masonic-humanistic approach to AI invites us to view technology not as a disruption but as a ritual tool – one that, when used with wisdom, can help shape not just better businesses but better souls, better communities, and a more just world.

## Results: Masonic values informing ethical management and AI development

The results of the analyses are formulated as a model of core Masonic values and their equivalents in humanistic management principles, a set of Masonic principles considered ethical foundations for AI and UI system design, and a list of recommendations regarding the integration of AI, Freemasonry and humanistic management.

### *Model of core Masonic values and their equivalents in humanistic management principles*

Table 3.2 presents a conceptual framework that maps core Masonic principles, symbolised by traditional Masonic emblems, to corresponding values and

*Table 3.2* Model of core Masonic values and their equivalents in humanistic management principles

| *Masonic principle (symbol)* | *Meaning* | *Humanistic management principle* | *Description* |
|---|---|---|---|
| *Square and Compass* | Balance and structure | • Work-life balance<br>• Ethical leadership | Symbolises moderation – both in personal and professional life; ethical decision-making |
| *All-Seeing Eye* | Divine oversight, morality | • Transparency in decision-making<br>• Accountability in leadership | Represents openness and responsibility for actions in an organisation |
| *The Winding Staircase* | Journey towards knowledge and self-improvement | • Lifelong learning<br>• coaching and mentorship | The climb represents stages of growth (personal and professional development) |
| *The Ties that Bind* | Brotherhood and solidarity | • Teamwork and collaboration<br>• Organisational culture | Symbol of interpersonal bonds rooted in mutual support |
| *Masonic Oaths* | Commitment to truth and integrity | • Corporate ethics<br>• Integrity | Emphasises inner values and adherence to ethical standards. |
| *Scales of Justice* | Justice and impartiality | • Fairness and equal opportunity<br>• Inclusive leadership | Represents fair treatment and equal access to opportunity |
| *Search for Enlightenment* | Wisdom and understanding | • Knowledge management<br>• Innovation and problem-solving | A metaphor for seeking truth, embracing ideas, and encouraging creative thinking |

*Source:* Own elaboration.

practices within humanistic management theory. This model aims to demonstrate how longstanding philosophical ideals within Freemasonry can meaningfully inform contemporary organisational practices oriented towards human dignity, ethical conduct, and holistic development.

Each Masonic symbol embodies an ethical or developmental ideal. The Square and Compass, for instance, emphasise the need for balance, structure, and moral moderation – values that resonate with modern emphases on work-life balance and ethical leadership. The All-Seeing Eye, traditionally a symbol of divine omnipresence and moral oversight, parallels contemporary principles of transparency in decision-making and accountability within leadership frameworks. It serves as a reminder that ethical behaviour must be sustained through openness and a commitment to responsibility. The Winding Staircase, representing the aspirational journey towards knowledge and virtue, is mapped onto practices promoting lifelong learning and mentorship, critical for sustaining adaptive and resilient organisations. Likewise, The Ties that Bind – a symbol of fraternal solidarity – finds its contemporary analogue in teamwork and cultivating collaborative organisational cultures, emphasising the humanistic belief in collective over purely individual achievement.

The model further aligns Masonic Oaths, centred on the vows of truthfulness and ethical integrity, with the imperative of establishing and maintaining robust corporate ethics and personal integrity in leadership. The Scales of Justice, representing fairness and impartiality, correlate with the management principles of inclusivity, equal opportunity, and merit-based advancement, which are fundamental to ethical organisational design. Finally, the Search for Enlightenment – a core Masonic aspiration for wisdom and moral insight – is linked to modern knowledge management practices, innovation, and creative problem-solving. This linkage reflects the understanding that sustainable organisational success requires operational efficiency and the continuous pursuit of truth, learning, and ethical advancement.

Overall, this model underscores the proposition that Freemasonry's symbolic and ethical heritage offers historical insights and practical, applicable principles for cultivating humane, just, and adaptive organisational cultures in the contemporary era. In the context of emerging technological challenges, such as those posed by AI, these values provide a compass for navigating change without sacrificing human dignity and ethical purpose.

### *Masonic principles as ethical foundations for AI and UI system design*

Table 3.3 presents a conceptual bridge between Masonic philosophical inspirations and AI and User Interface (UI) design applications in contemporary contexts. This model illustrates how symbolic and ethical principles embedded in Freemasonry can directly inform the design of technological systems, fostering environments that prioritise ethical reflection, human dignity, and intellectual development.

*Table 3.3* Masonic principles as ethical foundations for AI and UI system design

| *Concept* | *Masonic inspiration* | *AI/UI application* |
|---|---|---|
| *Architectural UI Design* | Masonic lodges as "temples of knowledge" | Interfaces are designed as structured, symbolic spaces promoting harmony and intellectual collaboration |
| *Use of Masonic Symbols* | Square (fairness), Compass (ethical boundaries), Pillars (wisdom & strength) | Icons subtly reinforce fairness, ethics, and balanced decision-making |
| *Mentorship Algorithms* | Master Mason guiding apprentices | AI acts as a mentor – offering moral insight, historical context, and balanced options |
| *Progressive Learning Paths* | Masonic degree system | AI structures professional development into ethical, skill-based levels, encouraging continual learning |
| *Ritualised Digital Meetings* | Masonic discussion formats | AI facilitates structured, meaningful, and philosophical conversations to deepen connection and clarity |
| *Consensus-Building Algorithms* | Masonic principle of unanimity | AI highlights shared values and ethical concerns to foster agreement beyond majority votes |
| *"All-Seeing Eye" Oversight* | The All-Seeing Eye | Transparent decision-making logs show how AI recommendations align with ethical principles |
| *AI as Dispute Mediator* | Harmony and reconciliation | AI detects conflicts and offers resolutions based on fairness, mutual respect, and shared values |
| *Symbolic Recognition* | Working tools and symbolic rewards | AI awards digital badges/tools to acknowledge ethical leadership and moral growth |
| *Wisdom Aggregation* | "The Great Light" (sources of wisdom) | AI curates ethical case studies, moral dilemmas, and historical insights to guide leadership decisions |

*Source:* Own elaboration.

***Recommendations regarding the integration of AI, Freemasonry, and humanistic management***

Freemasonry has the potential to integrate AI meaningfully while preserving its core values despite the challenges of maintaining a balance between tradition and innovation. The findings are the following:

1 *AI-based tools directed according to Freemasonry aesthetics may help apply humanistic management principles.* Interviews with senior Masonic leaders and scholars examine whether humanistic management principles align closely with Freemasonry's ethical and moral teachings and whether human dignity, personal growth, and ethical conduct – central tenets of Freemasonry – mirror the values promoted by humanistic management. These principles are often expressed in Masonic rituals, where members are encouraged to develop their moral character and contribute to the betterment of society. The key finding would be to what extent humanistic management principles can provide a foundation for integrating AI into humanistic managerial programs and leadership development, ensuring that the focus remains on individual growth and ethical integrity.

2 *Benefits and challenges of AI integration in Freemasonry.* Interviews with Masonic Lodge members reveal a general openness to integrating AI, particularly in administrative functions (e.g., membership tracking, event scheduling, and financial management). Several respondents noted that AI could streamline time-consuming tasks, freeing up resources for more meaningful engagement in the Masonic community. However, there are concerns about AI's potential to dilute Freemasonry's human-centred values. Members expressed apprehension that over-reliance on AI could undermine face-to-face interactions, personal mentorship, and the sense of brotherhood central to Masonic life. A common sentiment among respondents was the fear that AI could lead to losing personal connection, a fundamental aspect of the Masonic experience. An initial examination suggests AI offers significant administrative benefits, but challenges preserving personal connections and the human element of Freemasonry. While AI can enhance efficiency, its integration must be handled carefully to avoid diminishing Masonic practice's personal and relational aspects.

3 *Leveraging AI for personal development, leadership, and social responsibility in Freemasonry and beyond.* Freemasonry's educational mission, which focuses on moral and intellectual development, could benefit from AI-driven platforms. For instance, AI could create personalised learning journeys for individual Masons, allowing them to progress at their own pace and focus on areas of interest, such as philosophy, history, or leadership. Additionally, AI could facilitate virtual gatherings, enabling Masons in remote locations to engage with the community without geographical limitations. Results from interviews with Masonic leaders and educators suggest that AI could also play a role in enhancing leadership development within Freemasonry. For example, AI-driven simulations and feedback mechanisms could help cultivate leadership skills by providing Masons with real-time insights into their decision-making and leadership styles.

This study oscillates around the thought that AI has the potential to enhance Masonic education and leadership development by providing personalised learning tools and fostering virtual collaboration. However, such applications should promote Masonic members' ethical and social responsibility. I believe that Masonic leadership could play a significant role in shaping the ethical use of AI by advocating for transparency, equity, and human dignity in developing and implementing AI technologies. Freemasonry's ethical framework could be influential in AI ethics debates. The question remains: How can Freemasonry maintain ethical leadership in the age of AI, and what role can Masonic leadership play in shaping the broader ethical discourse surrounding AI?

## Discussion: opportunities and ethical imperatives of integrating AI within the Masonic tradition

The findings of this study reveal a nuanced and multifaceted relationship between AI and Freemasonry, suggesting that AI's integration into Masonic contexts holds significant promise, provided it remains grounded in the Order's enduring humanistic values. Far from merely a technical enhancement, the thoughtful incorporation of AI technologies could meaningfully advance Freemasonry's mission in the 21st century by reinforcing rather than replacing its foundational commitments to human dignity, Fraternity, and personal transformation. On the one hand, the practical benefits of AI are substantial and align closely with Freemasonry's aspirations for educational excellence and global solidarity. Personalised learning systems, for instance, could tailor Masonic education to individual brethren's stages of development, deepening engagement with ritual, symbolism, and ethical reflection. Similarly, AI-driven administrative tools could streamline lodge management, enhance archival preservation, and enable more efficient governance structures. Moreover, AI-powered digital platforms could foster unprecedented levels of global interconnectivity among lodges, facilitating cross-cultural exchanges and reinforcing the universalist aspirations of Freemasonry.

However, alongside these prospects lies a series of profound challenges that must not be underestimated. Chief among them is the potential erosion of Freemasonry's human-centred, experiential core – a tradition whose vitality depends upon face-to-face mentorship, symbolic ritual, and the cultivation of fraternal bonds through shared moral labour. Freemasonry is not reducible to a corpus of knowledge or a set of procedures; it is fundamentally a lived, embodied practice rooted in the transmission of wisdom through interpersonal relationships, ritual gestures, and communal acts of self-transcendence. If uncritically adopted, AI technologies risk diminishing these relational dimensions, substituting digital efficiency for the irreplaceable depth of human presence.

Thus, integrating AI into Masonic contexts demands an ethically sensitive, critically reflective approach that resists technophilia and technophobia. AI should be envisaged not as an autonomous agent displacing human interaction but as a servant technology: a digital steward designed to assist in knowledge dissemination, organisational coordination, and archival preservation while preserving and amplifying Masonic life's spiritual and moral dimensions. Such a perspective aligns with broader currents in humanistic management and technology ethics, which advocate for designing and deploying technological systems that serve human flourishing, respect human dignity, and sustain ethical communities. Given the Order's historical commitment to personal transformation, moral duty, and constructing a more just and enlightened society, this imperative takes on a particular urgency within the Masonic context.

Ultimately, Freemasonry's engagement with AI represents a technical challenge and a profound opportunity to affirm its ancient ideals – truth, brotherhood, wisdom, and ethical self-improvement – while participating thoughtfully and creatively in shaping the digital future. By doing so, Freemasonry can preserve its rich heritage and demonstrate its continuing relevance as a moral and intellectual force in an era increasingly shaped by technological innovation.

## Conclusion

The intersection of humanistic management, Freemasonry, and AI represents a promising area for exploring how ethical frameworks can guide organisations in an increasingly technology-driven world. Freemasonry and humanistic management emphasise the human aspect of social organisation, focusing on ethical leadership, dignity, and social responsibility. In the era of AI, these principles offer critical insights into how organisations can integrate technology in ways that enhance, rather than diminish, human potential. Future research can explore how Freemasonry's tradition of ethical practice can be applied to developing and deploying AI technologies, ensuring that AI serves as a tool for collective human flourishing. Humanistic management has evolved in response to critiques of traditional business practices, especially in the context of globalisation and technological disruption. As organisations face increased pressure from AI and automation, the principles of HM offer a counterpoint to the dehumanisation that can accompany technology-driven management practices. Integrating humanistic principles into decision-making processes can mitigate the potential harms of AI, ensuring that technology enhances human well-being rather than replacing human labour or exacerbating inequalities.

Regarding RQ1 (*Can Freemasonry's aesthetic principles be integrated into AI-driven decision-making frameworks within humanistic management?*), it can be said that Freemasonry's aesthetic principles can be integrated into AI-driven decision-making frameworks within humanistic management. Freemasonry emphasises harmony, balance, symbolism, and moral refinement – principles that can enhance AI's role in ethical and human-centred decision-making. By embedding Freemasonry's aesthetic and ethical ideals into AI governance models, humanistic management can ensure that technological decisions remain deeply aligned with human dignity, wisdom, and fairness.

Regarding RQ2 (*To what extent do Masonic aesthetics in AI interfaces affect user experience and confidence in AI-driven tools?*), Masonic aesthetics in AI interfaces can significantly influence user experience and confidence by embedding symbolic, harmonious, and structured design elements that evoke trust, clarity, and ethical alignment. By integrating Masonic aesthetics into AI interfaces, designers can craft tools that feel structured, wise, and ethically grounded. This improves usability and strengthens trust, as users perceive AI as a transparent, balanced, and morally aware system.

Regarding RQ3 (*How can AI tools based on aesthetic Masonic principles be designed to foster fraternity in humanistic management settings?*), AI tools designed around Masonic aesthetic principles can foster Fraternity and support humanistic management by promoting ethical collaboration, shared wisdom, and moral refinement. One way of structuring such AI systems would be to look at five main fields of interest: symbolic and meaningful interaction; AI as a digital fraternal guide; enhancing fraternal bonds through AI-mediated communication; ethical transparency and trust; and fostering a brotherhood/sisterhood of ethical leadership. We can create digital environments that promote Fraternity, wisdom, and ethical collaboration by embedding Masonic aesthetics and principles into AI. This approach aligns AI-driven decision-making with humanistic management, ensuring technology is a unity and a moral progress tool.

This study is primarily an initial pilot exploration rather than a full empirical investigation. As such, it has several *limitations* that should be acknowledged: firstly, a lack of empirical research results. The study does not include quantitative or qualitative empirical data from extensive fieldwork, experiments, or large-scale surveys. Instead, it relies on conceptual analysis, theoretical frameworks, and preliminary observations. Future research will need to incorporate empirical methodologies to validate the ideas presented. Secondly, as an early-stage pilot study, this work is a foundation for further exploration rather than offering definitive conclusions. The insights presented are preliminary and require refinement through continued research and practical application. Given its initial stage, the study does not comprehensively cover all potential applications or challenges related to integrating Masonic aesthetics into AI-driven decision-making. The forthcoming book will expand on these ideas with more profound analysis, case studies, and empirical validation. The study primarily focuses on philosophical, symbolic, and aesthetic considerations rather than data-driven outcomes. While this approach is helpful for theoretical development, practical implementation and measurable impact assessments are still necessary. Lastly, this pilot study serves as a stepping stone towards a more comprehensive examination, including further theoretical elaboration, empirical research, and real-world applications to enhance its scholarly and practical value.

Despite these limitations, this study provides an essential starting point for integrating Masonic aesthetics into AI-driven humanistic management, setting the stage for deeper inquiry and practical implementation in *future research.* In order to address these gaps, future studies could: (1) develop a conceptual framework linking Freemasonry's aesthetic principles with AI-driven decision-making; (2) create experimental AI models inspired by Masonic ethics to test their impact on humanistic management; (3) investigate how AI can enhance mentorship, Fraternity, and ethical leadership in organisations; (4) explore how Masonic-inspired aesthetics (geometry, symbolism) influence AI-human interactions in managerial settings.

## References

Boucher, J. (2011). *La symbolique maçonnique.* Dervy.

Bowie, A. (1990). *Aesthetics and subjectivity: From Kant to Nietzsche.* Manchester University Press.

Cegielski, T. (1992). *Sekrety masonów: Pierwszy stopień wtajemniczenia.* Agencja Omnipress.

Cegielski, T. (1994). *Ordo ex Chao: Wolnomularstwo i światopoglądowe kryzysy XVII i XVIII wieku. T. 1, "Oświecenie Różokrzyżowców" i początki masonerii spekulatywnej 1614–1738.* Historia Pro Futuro.

Cegielski, T. (2025). *Księga Konstytucji 1723 roku i początki wolnomularstwa spekulatywnego w Anglii,* Oficyna Wydawnicza RYTM.

Di Bernardo, B. (2016). *Filosofia della massoneria e della tradizione iniziatica.* Marsilio.

Gaut, B., & Lopes, D. M. (Eds.). (2001). *The Routledge companion to aesthetics.* Routledge.

Hayles, N. K. (1999). *How we became posthuman: Virtual bodies in cybernetics, literature and informatics.* University of Chicago Press.

Jemielniak, D., & Przegalińska, A. (2020). *Collaborative society.* MIT Press.

Kostera, M., & Woźniak, C. (2022). *Aesthetics, organization, and humanistic management.* Routledge.

Levenda, P. (2009). *The secret temple: Masons, mysteries, and the founding of America.* Continuum.

Levinson, J. (Ed.). (2003). *The Oxford handbook of aesthetics* (pp. 3–7). Oxford University Press.

Mackenzie, D. (2023). Mason without an apron – Chopin and Freemasonry. In *Genius and melancholia: Fryderyk Chopin and pedagogies of romanticism in the perspective studies.* WUW.

Mackey, A. (1996). *The history of Freemasonry.* Gramercy Books.

McLeod, H. (2016). Freemasonry and the ethics of leadership: A philosophical exploration. *Journal of Applied Ethics, 34*(2), 193–206.

Millar, A. (2005). *Freemasonry: A history.* PRC Publishing Limited.

Morawińska, A., Cegielski, T., & Załęski, K. (2014). *Masoneria. Pro publico bono/Freemasonry. Pro publico bono.* Muzeum Narodowe w Warszawie.

Müller, V. C., et al. (2021). *Human-centred AI design and the future of work.* Springer.

Schroeder, D., et al. (2021). *Humanistic management in practice: Concepts, models, and case studies.* Springer.

Sroka, Ł. T., & Nowosad, A. (eds.) (2022). *Wielość w jedności, Jedność w wielości. W 300. Rocznicę narodzin masonerii spekulatywnej.* Wydawnictwo Naukowe UP.

Szostak, M. (2021). Artistry, management, and creativity: Links and common denominators. *Discourses on Culture, 16*(1), 23–54. https://doi.org/10.36145/DoC2021.08

Szostak, M. (2022a). Co estetyka może wnieść do teorii zarządzania? *Przegląd Organizacji, 5*(988), 3–10. https://doi.org/10.33141/po.2022.05.01

Szostak, M. (2022b). Contextual inspiration and motive in persuasive creativity: Lessons from artistic improvisation. *Discourses on Culture, 17*(1), 101–131. https://doi.org/10.36145/DoC2022.05

Szostak, M. (2023). Reflexivity in aesthetic situation management. *Discourses on Culture, 20*, 161–197. https://doi.org/10.2478/doc-2023-0015

Tatarkiewicz, W. (2009). *Historia estetyki* (Vols. 1 & 2). Warszawa. PWN.

# 4 Spirituality and humanistic management

## Fostering meaning and purpose in IT professional development

*Muhammad Kamran and Tomasz Ochinowski*

### Introduction

The central part of the humanistic management model of organisational practices is to secure human respect and enhance the well-being of a human being (Pirson & Kostera, 2017). The divergence of management towards the humanistic paradigm is an approach to organisations and organising in the sense that it explicitly focuses on dignity as the basis of every activity (Pirson & Kostera, 2017). Zawadzki (2018) additionally introduces the point of view of humanistic management as a field of consideration about dignity in the working environment. Hay's model of spirituality, which was used in the study, contains awareness sensing, mystery sensing, and value sensing (Hay, 2006). For the current research, we have chosen the sub-dimension of value sensing, i.e., meaning from Hay's model of spirituality. This study argues that spirituality is a phenomenon that highlights the particular features of a human being that represent the meaning of life, connectedness with people, and some behavioural dimensions (Moberg, 1984; Legere, 1984). These qualities make a human being more empathic, understanding, and selfless, which enhances a human being's dignity, which is eventually the fundamental characteristic of humanistic management. Similarly, Rossiter (2010) stated that spirituality is similar to a natural human phenomenon, which contains thinking and feeling about perfection, human values, love for others, and a sense of aesthetics. This idea returns to the understanding that spirituality revolves around human dignity and brings selflessness in a human being, which is ultimately the perspective of humanistic management. Hence, from the point of view of the researcher of this study, spirituality may be considered a humanistic phenomenon that, in turn, has a significant association with humanistic management.

Spirituality's subjective and multidimensional nature makes it challenging to measure its impact on organisational outcomes within the context of humanistic management. Despite growing interest in spirituality and its relevance to management, this study's *research problem* is to provide a unified framework that integrates spiritual principles into humanistic management practices. Solving

DOI: 10.4324/9781003654377-6

this problem helps to understand how these two concepts can be operationalised together. It is important to explore the relationship between spirituality and humanistic management in the era of AI because IT professionals design and maintain the hardware and software infrastructure required for AI, including servers, cloud platforms, and databases. Keeping this perspective in view, some spiritual dimensions could exist in the training of IT professionals. With the context of this problem statement, the following *research questions* were defined: (RQ1) What could be the link between spirituality and humanistic management in the AI era? (RQ2) What kind of spiritual dimensions (if any) from a humanistic perspective could exist in IT professionals' training?

From the *methodology* point of view, this study adopts an exploratory and qualitative research design to investigate the relationship between spirituality and humanistic management in the AI era, as well as the potential spiritual dimensions in the training of IT professionals from a humanistic perspective. Exploratory research is particularly suitable for examining complex and under-researched topics, providing a foundation for deeper understanding (Stebbins, 2001). Since spirituality and humanistic management in IT professional development are evolving concepts, a qualitative approach enables an in-depth exploration of individual experiences, perceptions, and organisational practices (Creswell & Poth, 2016).

Literature was reviewed from multiple databases like Scopus, Google Scholar, JSTOR, ProQuest, and Web of Science to explore the link between spirituality and humanistic management in the AI era. Most cited literature is from the last ten years. Along with a literature review analysis, the study also includes in-depth interviews with IT experts to gain insight into the perspectives of IT professionals. An in-depth open interview aims to conduct interviews with a robust data collection technique to understand human feelings (Fontana & Frey, 2005). The intention behind the qualitative approach is to explore participants' hidden meanings, feelings, and lived experiences, as well as the participant's emotions related to spirituality (DiCicco-Bloom & Crabtree, 2006). Exploring how spirituality influences humanistic management in Pakistan is not just academically interesting – it is a window into a culture where faith, values, and work deeply intertwine. Participants include eight IT professionals from various sectors selected based on purposive sampling. Open-ended questions were asked to explain interviewees' emotions, experiences, and reactions regarding spirituality in their vocational training. A consent letter was obtained from each informant to keep ethical considerations in view. Interview records were kept confidential and based on the informant's voluntary participation. In the notice of each informant, an interview would be tape-recorded. Moreover, interview with each participant was categorised with a specific identification number and transcribed verbatim. The conclusion of the transcription procedure remained to discover and recognise related subjects that arise from the qualitative information (Bernard & Ryan, 2010). This procedure is a coding method, considered an initial stage to pick up and organise the information (Mayan, 2023). The transcribed interviews were prepared for coding or analysis. This procedure allowed for finding the information that answered the queries and starting the data coding procedure. Moreover, the manual method has provided room for originality in making opening coding philosophies (Flick, 2022). The coding was then moved to a computer for additional analysis. NVivo 14 was used in this study to accomplish qualitative results and to confirm consistency in the analysis process (Bazeley & Jackson, 2013).

The contribution of this study focuses on two important perspectives. First, it explores the linkage between spirituality and humanistic management in the AI era. As AI continues transforming industries, including IT, there is a growing need to integrate human-centred values to ensure ethical and responsible technological advancement. Second, the study examines the potential spiritual dimensions that may exist in the training of IT professionals from a humanistic perspective. This involves understanding how mindfulness, ethical awareness, and purpose-driven work can enhance IT professional development.

## Literature review: crossing the borders between spirituality and humanistic management

To understand the concept of spirituality within humanistic management, exploration of the relationship between spirituality and humanistic management, understanding meaning and purpose, and exploring the role of spirituality and humanistic management in professional growth will be undertaken in this section.

### *Relationship between spirituality and humanistic management*

The intersection of spirituality and humanistic management presents a compelling framework for fostering meaning and purpose in the professional development of IT professionals. This literature review synthesises various studies that explore how these elements can bridge the gap in enhancing the professional experience and identity of individuals in the IT sector. Spirituality in the workplace has been shown to influence employees' sense of meaning and purpose significantly. Wu et al. highlight that positive profession-spotlighting events can awaken professional identification and foster work meaningfulness, suggesting that such experiences are crucial for employees to engage deeply with their work (Wu et al., 2024). This aligns with the findings of Baldacchino, who emphasises that spiritual care involves recognising and meeting individuals' spiritual needs, which can enhance their overall sense of well-being and purpose in their professional lives (Baldacchino, 2015). The integration of spirituality into professional development is not merely beneficial but necessary for cultivating a workforce that is both competent and fulfilled.

The synthesis of spirituality and humanistic management also encourages a reflective practice among IT professionals, which is vital for personal and professional growth. Engelbertink et al. highlight that reflection connects new experiences with existing knowledge, fostering insights that can lead to a more profound professional identity (Dimonte et al., 2023). This reflective practice is essential in the fast-paced IT industry, where professionals often face challenges that require technical skills, a strong sense of purpose, and ethical grounding. In conclusion, integrating spirituality and humanistic management offers a robust framework for enhancing the professional development of IT professionals.

The need for meaning and purpose in IT careers has garnered increasing attention in recent years, mainly as the industry evolves and faces challenges related to employee engagement, job satisfaction, and retention. One of the primary factors influencing the need for meaning in IT careers is the alignment between personal values and organisational goals. Employees who perceive a strong connection between their work and broader societal impacts tend to exhibit higher job satisfaction and engagement. For instance, research indicates that emotional intelligence among IT leaders positively correlates with job performance and employee dedication, suggesting that leaders who foster a meaningful workplace can enhance their team's engagement and commitment to the organisation's mission (Beverly et al., 2012). Furthermore, studies have shown that when employees feel their work contributes to innovative outcomes, they are likelier to experience a sense of purpose in their roles (Yandong & Wareewanich, 2024).

The ongoing changes brought about by technological advancements, including the rise of AI and automation, also significantly shape employees' perceptions of their careers. As employees grapple with the potential for job displacement, their need for meaning becomes even more pronounced (Alcover et al., 2021; Brougham & Haar, 2018). Organisations that proactively engage their workforce in discussions about the future of work and provide opportunities for skill development can help mitigate fears and reinforce the relevance of their roles within the evolving landscape (Goldschlag & Miranda, 2020; Kemeny & Osman, 2018).

Aesthetics, broadly referring to the experience of beauty, harmony, and emotional resonance, is crucial in the spirituality–humanistic management relationship. In workplaces informed by humanistic and spiritual values, aesthetics is not just about physical beauty (e.g., pleasant office design); it also refers to creating environments that are emotionally and ethically beautiful – where actions, relationships, and organisational cultures "feel right" and are experienced as harmonious (Strati, 2008). Aesthetic experiences can foster deeper meaning at work by appealing to individuals' senses, emotions, and intuition, making the workplace more humane and spiritually uplifting (Ladkin, 2008). Szostak (2024) proposes a holistic model of management aesthetics, arguing that aesthetic theory and artistic practice can enrich management with qualitative components while management can enhance aesthetics with efficiency elements. In this context, beauty is understood as an expression of respect for human dignity and the interconnectedness of life. For instance, organisations might use rituals, storytelling, symbolic leadership acts, or even the thoughtful design of workspaces to nurture an aesthetic that supports a sense of shared purpose and belonging (Szostak, 2023). Thus, aesthetics operationalises spirituality and humanistic management by translating abstract values like dignity, meaning, and respect into tangible, lived experiences within organisations.

The relationship between spirituality and humanistic management is increasingly recognised as a pivotal area of inquiry in contemporary organisational studies. Spirituality in the workplace is often defined as the search for meaning and purpose in one's work (Ellison, 1983), which aligns closely with the principles of humanistic management that emphasise the dignity, well-being, and flourishing of individuals within organisations (Zawadzki, 2018). Spirituality emphasises recognising the intrinsic worth of individuals, which aligns with humanistic management's principle of treating employees as ends rather than means (Guillén et al., 2015). Moreover, spirituality inspires leaders to align organisational goals with higher purposes, fostering a humanistic approach to leadership that prioritises societal well-being (Fry & Nisiewicz, 2020). Spirituality offers a values-based foundation for ethical decision-making, which complements humanistic management's commitment to fairness and justice (Mitroff & Denton, 1999). Furthermore, spirituality promotes practices such as mindfulness and meditation, which reduce stress and improve emotional resilience, aligning with humanistic management's goal of fostering holistic employee well-being (Karakas, 2010). This synthesis of spirituality and humanistic management creates a framework that enhances employee satisfaction and fosters a more ethical and purpose-driven organisational culture.

Research indicates that when employees perceive their work as meaningful, they are more likely to engage in innovative behaviours and demonstrate higher levels of psychological empowerment (Bantha & Nayak, 2021). This intrinsic motivation is essential for cultivating a humanistic management style that prioritises the holistic development of employees, recognising their spiritual needs alongside their professional roles (Matheson et al., 2021). Moreover, humanistic management advocates shifting from traditional economistic paradigms towards models prioritising human dignity and well-being. This approach acknowledges the moral and spiritual dimensions of the human experience, suggesting that organisations should focus on productivity and profit and create environments where employees feel valued and respected (Matheson et al., 2021; Pirson, 2019). Integrating spirituality into management practices can enhance organisational commitment and performance by fostering a culture of trust, creativity, and respect (Rego & Cunha, 2008; Daniel, 2010). Such environments allow employees to experience a sense of belonging and purpose, which is fundamental to their overall well-being (Rego & Cunha, 2008).

The importance of spirituality in the era of AI is increasingly recognised as technology becomes more integrated into daily life. Spirituality, often defined as a sense of connection to something greater than oneself, is crucial in providing meaning and purpose, particularly in rapid technological change. Integrating spirituality in the AI era presents unique opportunities and challenges, emphasising the need for ethical decision-making, human-centric technology, and meaningful engagement in increasingly automated and digital environments. The relationship between spirituality and humanistic management is characterised by a mutual reinforcement of values prioritising human dignity, purpose, and well-being. By integrating spirituality into management practices, organisations can foster a more engaged and committed workforce, enhancing organisational performance and creating a more ethical business environment. Moreover, spirituality's subjective and multidimensional nature makes it challenging to measure its impact on organisational outcomes within the context of humanistic management. Despite growing interest in spirituality and its relevance to management, there is a lack of a unified framework that integrates spiritual principles into humanistic management practices, leaving a gap in understanding how these two concepts can be operationalised together. It is important to explore the relationship between spirituality and humanistic management. IT professionals design and maintain the hardware and software infrastructure required for AI.

### *Understanding meaning and purpose in IT work*

The concept of meaning and purpose in work has gained significant attention in recent years, particularly in the context of technological advancement and societal changes. Pacey and Segal (1999) explore how an individual sense of purpose influences technology's shape and use, emphasising the importance of human experience in technology. George and Park (2013) distinguish between meaning (comprehension and significance in life) and purpose (goals and direction), finding they have different predictors and correlates. Michaelson and Tosti-Kharas (2024) examine how recent crises have led workers to prioritise meaning and purpose in work, proposing a "6 P" framework for understanding work's functional and moral purpose. Dik et al. (2013) highlight the crucial link between happiness and productivity, emphasising the importance of meaningful work across various environments. These studies collectively underscore the growing significance of meaning and purpose in the workplace, particularly in a technology-driven world, and offer insights into fostering fulfilling work experiences.

Meaningful work is often conceptualised as a job resource fulfilling employees' intrinsic needs for purpose and significance in their roles. Albrecht emphasises that meaningful work is a central variable in job design, positing that it plays a crucial role in the motivational processes that lead to employee engagement (Albrecht, 2013). This assertion is supported by Kim and Beehr, who found that employees who perceive their work as meaningful report higher life satisfaction and lower emotional exhaustion, indicating that meaningful work can be a protective factor against burnout (Kim & Beehr, 2018). Furthermore,

Van & Van highlight the positive relationship between meaningful work and employee well-being, suggesting that it enhances engagement and contributes to overall job satisfaction and performance (Van & Van, 2017).

The mediating role of work meaningfulness in the relationship between various organisational factors and employee engagement is also well-documented. For instance, James identifies fit perception as a significant resource that enhances engagement through increased perceptions of work meaningfulness (James, 2023). Similarly, Lee et al. demonstrate that empowering leadership fosters work meaningfulness, boosting employee engagement (Lee et al., 2017). This aligns with findings from Allan et al., who conducted a meta-analysis revealing strong correlations between meaningful work, engagement, and job satisfaction, suggesting that meaningful work may be a proximal cause of these outcomes (Allan et al., 2019).

Moreover, the protective function of meaningful work extends to specific populations, such as cancer survivors. Zheng et al. argue that for working cancer survivors, job meaningfulness can mitigate the adverse effects of job distress on well-being, particularly for those with lower resilience (Zheng et al., 2022). This underscores the importance of meaningful work as a motivational factor and a crucial element in promoting psychological health in challenging circumstances. The interplay between meaningful work and employee engagement is further illustrated by Wingerden and Stoep, who assert that meaningful work positively influences both work-related well-being and general well-being, mediated by levels of engagement and burnout (Wingerden & Stoep, 2017). This perspective is echoed by Ahmad and Fatima, who highlight the mediating role of meaningful work in the relationship between leadership behaviours and employee well-being (Ahmad & Fatima, 2022). Such findings suggest that organisations can enhance employee engagement and well-being by fostering an environment that emphasises meaningful work. The literature consistently supports that meaningful work significantly impacts employee motivation, engagement, and well-being. By fulfilling intrinsic needs for purpose and significance, meaningful work enhances engagement and protects against burnout and distress. Organisations aiming to improve employee outcomes should prioritise creating meaningful work experiences and fostering a more engaged and resilient workforce.

### *The role of spirituality and humanistic management in professional growth*

The intersection of spirituality and humanistic management plays a pivotal role in fostering professional growth across various sectors. Humanistic management, characterised by its emphasis on human dignity, ethical leadership, and participative practices, is increasingly recognised as a framework that enhances employee satisfaction and professional development. This literature review synthesises recent findings on the role of spirituality and humanistic management in promoting professional growth. Humanistic management is fundamentally rooted in the principles of humanism, which prioritise the well-being and dignity of individuals within organisational contexts. Melé defines humanistic management as a people-oriented approach that aligns organisational goals with human values, contrasting sharply with traditional profit-driven management paradigms (Melé, 2016). This perspective is echoed by Matheson et al., who argue that a humanistic approach fosters an environment where employees feel valued and respected, leading to enhanced job satisfaction and professional growth (Matheson et al., 2021).

Integrating spirituality into humanistic management practices can significantly enhance the professional growth of individuals. Spirituality in the workplace often manifests as a commitment to ethical practices, compassion, and a sense of purpose, which aligns well with the tenets of humanistic management. For instance, Liu highlights that empathy and self-efficacy among healthcare professionals are essential for effective patient care, suggesting that a spiritually informed approach can enhance these qualities (Liu, 2023). This is particularly relevant in high-stress environments such as healthcare, where empathising and connecting with patients can improve professional satisfaction and personal fulfilment.

Reflective practices, often rooted in spiritual and humanistic values, also play a critical role in professional growth. Mustika et al. emphasise that reflective practice nurtures humanistic values within individuals, thereby enhancing professionalism (Mustika et al., 2024). This aligns with the findings of He et al., who note that job satisfaction and passion among nurses contribute to their ability to provide compassionate care, which is a key component of humanistic practice (He et al., 2024).

Furthermore, the role of organisational culture in supporting humanistic management practices cannot be overstated. Mazur discusses how organisational culture can either facilitate or hinder the implementation of humanistic management principles (Mazur, 2023). A culture that values humanistic approaches encourages participative leadership and autonomy, which are essential for fostering professional growth. This is particularly important in collectivistic cultures, as highlighted by Vora and Kainzbauer, where local approaches to humanistic leadership can enhance employee engagement and satisfaction (Vora & Kainzbauer, 2020).

## Results: empirical insights into spiritual dimensions of IT professional development

The following section presents the study's empirical findings, offering insights into how IT professionals perceive and experience spiritual dimensions in their professional development within technologically advanced work environments. Drawing from in-depth interviews and thematic analysis supported by NVivo software, the results reveal how concepts such as value sensing, moral responsibility, self-reflection, and a sense of purpose manifest in IT specialists' daily practices, attitudes, and aspirations. While often implicit, these dimensions are critical in shaping individual motivation and organisational culture, especially in contexts increasingly influenced by AI and digital transformation. A word cloud and cluster analysis are the section's main empirical results.

### *Word cloud*

The study results show that, in the context of humanistic management, Hay's conception of spirituality highlights the importance of creating inclusive workplaces where individuals are encouraged to pursue meaning and purpose. In the light of David Hay's conception of spirituality (Hay, 2006), "meaning" is described in terms of "to discover about oneself (who am I)", "to identify the purpose", "awareness of connection with a higher being", "to identify responsibilities/moral sense", and "experience of values that transcend personal concerns". Participants shared their personal and professional life experiences. In their experiences, it is clearly described that identifying responsibilities/moral sense, the purpose of life, and discovering oneself are quite dominant in IT specialists' personal and professional lives. Identification of responsibilities is important in creating a positive environment in IT. It can be concluded that meaning is a direct feature of developing spirituality, creating a sense of identification with the purpose of life. The results show that Hay's conception of spirituality highlights the importance of creating inclusive workplaces where individuals are encouraged to pursue meaning and purpose, especially in information technology professionals (Hay, 2006). The study results show that different spiritual dimensions exist in IT professionals in the context of meaning and purpose. In this research, respondents are considered experts. Experts reported their experiences of "meaning" concerning "discovering about oneself" while others reported their experiences of "meaning" in terms of "identification of the purpose of life. Experts have expressed that their purpose of life is to help the community by using automated computer software to solve their problems, while other experts have reported that their purpose of life is to utilise technology constructively for humankind. Similarly, experts have expressed their experiences of meaning in terms of 'to identify responsibilities/moral sense" in their professional lives. Another expert has highlighted that his responsibilities and moral sense are maintaining good relationships with colleagues in the IT environment. In contrast, another one has concentrated on using cracks to open computer software programs more ethically, which is unethical.

The study results show that "value sensing" plays a crucial role in creating happiness and patience in tough times and creating meaning in the life of IT professionals. It can be concluded that "value sensing" is the central spiritual dimension found in vocational training of IT professionals in their personal and professional lives because "value sensing" relates to emotions with which we

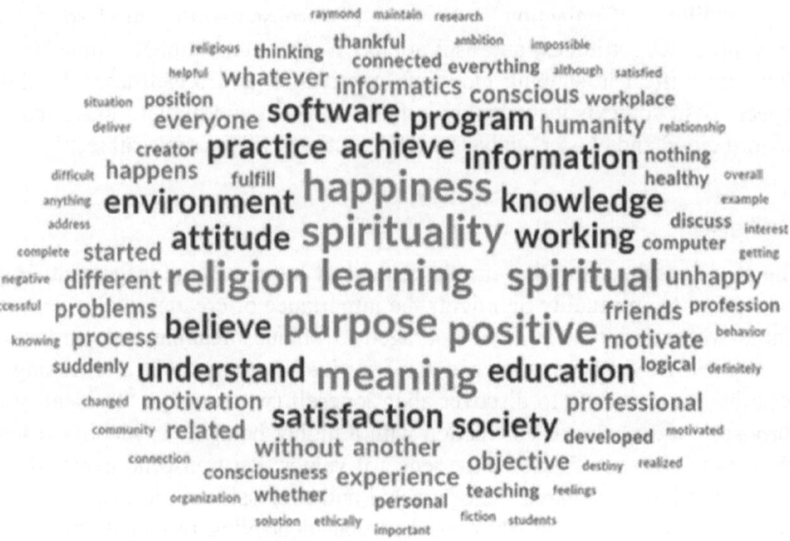


*Figure 4.1* The word cloud on interview transcriptions.

*Source:* Own elaboration based on transcription of interviews

are most connected and become associated with our deep feelings. It can also be concluded that the person who has feelings of "value sensing" is more purposeful, responsive, and helpful to others. Moreover, he/she feels more happiness and patience in tough times, which is ultimately required in an IT environment.

NVivo software word frequency query (finding the most frequently occurring words or concepts) was used to create clusters from the transcription of interviews to find the spiritual dimensions in humanistic management. Figure 4.1 shows the word frequency in all the interviews. In the analysed texts, it is clear that spirituality, happiness, learning, purpose, and meaning are the most appearing words as their boldness is more prominent. In all the interviews, the respondents have talked about spirituality and the concept of spirituality in terms of meaning and purpose.

***Cluster analysis***

Nvivo presents an exploratory procedure named "cluster analysis", which is used to find data patterns by making groups of similar values and concepts. Cluster analysis charts give a graphical introduction to sources or subjects, making it simple to see differences and similarities. Closer subjects in a group indicate comparability in importance compared to those far separated. Huang and Lai (2006) highlight that a cluster chart is handy when there is a massive amount of data, and it is difficult for the user to realise all of it simultaneously. In their view, "a clustered graph can greatly reduce visual complexity by temporarily replacing a set of nodes in clusters with abstract nodes". Word similarity shows topics which are increasingly identified with one another, depending on the event and recurrence of words appearing together as a group, and subjects with a lower degree are further separated.

The large rectangle in the data visualisation highlights the dominant themes in IT professionals' spirituality, based on David Hay's dimensions of spirituality (Figure 4.2). It indicates that most references in the dataset fall into specific categories, illustrating how spirituality manifests in their professional lives. The key themes identified include "Identify Responsibilities/Moral Sense", where IT professionals recognise the ethical implications of their work, such as AI ethics, cybersecurity, and social responsibility. "Identify the Purpose" reflects their search for deeper meaning beyond technical problem-solving. "Discover About Oneself" emphasises the role of self-reflection in personal and professional development. "Awareness of Connection with Higher Being/Transcendence" suggests that some professionals find purpose through spiritual beliefs, ethical innovation, or contributing to a greater good. Lastly, "Experience of Values that

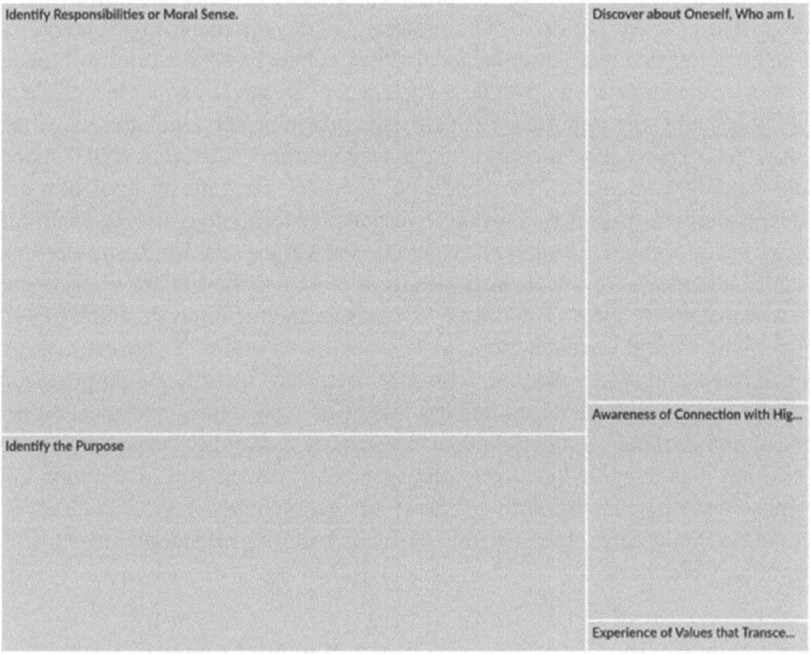


*Figure 4.2* Cluster analysis.

*Source:* Own elaboration based on transcription of interviews

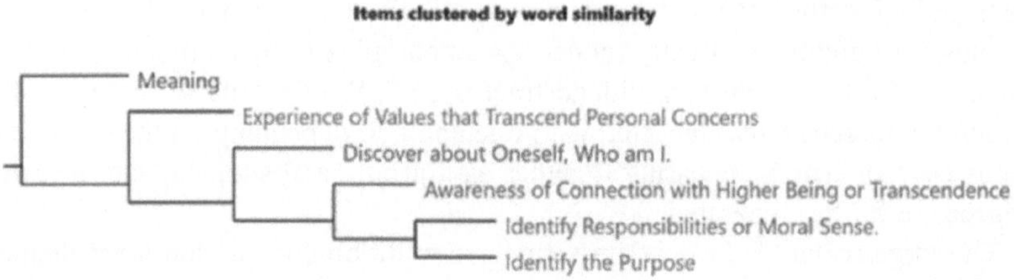


*Figure 4.3* Cluster diagram by word similarity.

*Source:* Own elaboration based on transcription of interviews

Transcend Personal Concerns" highlights the fulfilment IT professionals derive from teamwork, leadership, and social impact. The large rectangle in the visualisation underscores that these themes are the most frequently referenced, demonstrating that spirituality – through ethical responsibility, purpose, self-awareness, transcendence, and shared values – plays a significant role in shaping IT professionals' experiences and career motivations.

The cluster analysis (Figure 4.3) provides valuable insights into how meaning and purpose can be nurtured in IT professional development. IT professionals often seek fulfilment beyond technical skills, connecting their roles to broader personal, ethical, or societal values. The cluster "Discover about Oneself, Who am I" highlights the importance of self-reflection in professional growth, where individuals explore their identity and career aspirations. "Awareness of Connection with Higher Being or Transcendence" suggests that some professionals find a deeper purpose in ethical innovation, responsible technology use, or contributing to a greater good. Similarly, "Experience of Values that Transcend Personal Concerns" reflects how teamwork, leadership, and social impact projects create a sense of fulfilment. The theme "Identify Responsibilities or Moral Sense" aligns with ethical considerations in IT, such as AI ethics, cybersecurity, and digital inclusivity. Moreover, the connection between "Identify the Purpose" and moral responsibility indicates that professionals who understand their work's ethical and societal implications may experience a stronger sense of purpose. These insights suggest that integrating personal growth, ethical training, and purpose-driven leadership into IT career development programs can help professionals find greater meaning in work while fostering ethical and responsible technology practices.

## Discussion: spiritual awareness as a driver of human-centred professional development

Integrating spirituality and humanistic management in the context of IT professional development is essential for fostering meaning and purpose in the workplace. Humanistic management, which emphasises the intrinsic value of individuals and their well-being, aligns closely with the principles of spirituality, which often seeks to enhance personal and collective meaning in life and work. This synthesis can lead to a more engaged and fulfilled workforce, particularly in the IT sector, where rapid changes and high demands can lead to burnout and disengagement. Humanistic management is characterised by its focus on human dignity and ethical considerations in business practices. Koon (2021) discusses the emergence and growth of humanistic management, highlighting its philosophical roots in humanism, which advocates for treating individuals with respect and ensuring that organisational practices align with human motives. This perspective is crucial in IT professional development, where the emphasis on technical skills often overshadows the importance of personal growth and ethical considerations in technology use. Mele (2013) further supports this by presenting humanistic management as an alternative to the traditional economic paradigm, advocating for a more holistic approach that considers the well-being of employees as a fundamental aspect of organisational success.

In the AI era, spirituality provides a crucial lens through which we can guide technological progress while staying aligned with humanity's core values, aspirations, and a deeper sense of purpose (Bryson & Theodorou, 2019). As AI becomes increasingly integrated into daily life, its development and application must reflect principles honouring the well-being of individuals, communities, and the planet. Society can cultivate a more ethical, meaningful, and human-centred technological landscape by weaving spiritual principles into the fabric of AI innovation, deployment, and leadership (Vaidyanathan, 2020). These principles – rooted in compassion, interconnectedness, and mindfulness – can serve as a moral compass in navigating rapid technological advancement's complex and often ambiguous challenges.

Integrating spirituality into the AI era offers unique opportunities to create systems that prioritise empathy, fairness, and inclusivity, ensuring that technology serves as a tool for collective upliftment rather than division or harm. At the same time, it presents challenges that demand careful consideration, such as balancing automation with the preservation of human dignity, addressing biases embedded in algorithms, and fostering a sense of purpose in increasingly digital and automated environments (Dignum, 2018). This approach underscores the need for ethical decision-making at every stage of AI's lifecycle, from design to implementation. It emphasises the importance of human-centric technology that addresses functional needs and nurtures a sense of connection, meaning, and shared humanity. By engaging thoughtfully with these questions, we can harness AI's transformative potential while safeguarding the essence of what it means to be human.

Recent research highlights the importance of humanistic management and spirituality in fostering meaning and purpose in IT professional development. Humanistic approaches, including psychological support and emotional intelligence development, can reduce burnout and increase productivity in IT companies (Dashenkova & Korobkina, 2024). Work-related learning within a spiritual context can create deep meaning and purpose, utilising Jungian psychology to develop supportive environments (Dirkx, 2013). However, contemporary business education often prioritises competition over cooperation, necessitating a shift towards humanistic management principles to address complex global challenges (Kostera & Ludwicki, 2021). While workplace spirituality initiatives aim to imbue work with meaning, enhancing organisational performance, critics argue that these efforts may be shaped by capitalist power relations and instrumental rationality, potentially serving to reorient individual subjectivity to benefit capitalism rather than genuinely addressing the loss of meaning in neoliberal work environments (Ul-Haq, 2020).

The rise of digital workspaces, environments supported by collaborative technologies, cloud platforms, and remote systems, has reshaped how professionals experience meaning at work. On the positive side, digital workspaces offer enhanced autonomy, flexibility, and opportunities for work-life balance, key factors contributing to meaningful work experiences (Pratt & Ashforth, 2003). By enabling professionals to align their tasks with personal values and life goals, digital environments foster individual agency and engagement. However, digitalisation also presents challenges. The reduced physical interaction and potential isolation associated with virtual environments can weaken emotional connections and diminish employees' ability to perceive the broader impact of their work (Spreitzer, Cameron & Garrett, 2017). Without intentional community-building efforts, digital workspaces risk alienating workers and undermining their sense of shared purpose.

AI and task automation profoundly alter the nature of work, particularly for IT professionals. AI's capacity to automate repetitive and mundane tasks allows workers to focus on higher-order functions such as creativity, critical thinking, and innovation – core aspects of meaningful professional engagement (Brynjolfsson, 2014). In this context, AI has the potential to enhance IT professionals' sense of purpose by redefining their roles towards more strategic and fulfilling activities. Nevertheless, there are significant risks associated with automation. Susskind (2020) warns that excessive automation may lead to job displacement, skill erosion, and identity crises among professionals whose core functions are increasingly performed by machines. If not appropriately managed, introducing AI could result in losing agency and purpose, reinforcing the need for continuous reskilling, role redefinition, and supportive organisational cultures prioritising human dignity.

Beyond efficiency and productivity, AI tools can potentially support spiritual well-being in professional contexts. Emerging AI-based platforms promoting mindfulness, reflection, and personalised career development encourage individuals to explore their inner values, aspirations, and sense of purpose (Panch et al., 2018). Such technologies can catalyse spiritual growth by fostering greater self-awareness and encouraging purposeful career choices. However, the application of AI to spiritual well-being must be approached with caution. Dasa (2023) emphasises the ethical considerations in designing AI tools that engage with spirituality's deeply personal and contextual nature. Without sensitivity and ethical grounding, there is a risk of commodifying spiritual practices, undermining their authenticity. Thus, AI's role in spiritual development should complement human experience rather than mechanise or replace it.

The concept of meaningful work is also crucial in this discussion. The study's results are consistent with Rantanen et al. (2024). Rantanen et al. (2024) emphasise creating a work environment that supports meaningful engagement, which is essential for employee well-being and organisational effectiveness. In the context of IT, where professionals often face high levels of stress and rapid change, fostering a sense of purpose can mitigate burnout and enhance resilience. This aligns with the findings of Dik et al. (2015), who note that interventions to foster purpose and meaning in career development can significantly boost employee engagement and adaptability. The role of spirituality in enhancing career adaptability cannot be overlooked. Spirituality often encourages individuals to reflect on their values and purpose, which can guide their career choices and development. Otu (2024) highlights the effectiveness of purpose-based career coaching in improving decision-making processes, suggesting that integrating spiritual dimensions into career development can lead to more informed and fulfilling career paths. This is particularly relevant for IT professionals, who may benefit from aligning their personal values with their professional roles, enhancing their overall job satisfaction and commitment.

## Conclusion

RQ1 was based on the linkage between spirituality and humanistic management in the AI era, when spirituality and humanistic management are linked through their shared emphasis on preserving human dignity, ethical integrity, and a more profound sense of meaning in the face of rapid technological change. Humanistic management, rooted in the respect for intrinsic human value, ensures that business practices and technological advancements prioritise well-being over mere efficiency. Spirituality complements this by offering guiding principles – such as compassion, mindfulness, interconnectedness, and purpose – that can steer AI development towards ethical, human-centred outcomes. By integrating spirituality into the foundations of AI innovation and leadership, organisations can ensure that technological progress supports rather than undermines core human values, fostering collective upliftment while addressing ethical challenges like bias, dehumanisation, and loss of meaning. Thus, spirituality and humanistic management together form a necessary moral compass for navigating the complexities of the AI-driven world.

RQ2 was to explore different spiritual dimensions (if any) that could exist in training information technology professionals from a humanistic perspective. From a humanistic perspective, the training of information technology professionals can incorporate several spiritual dimensions aimed at nurturing personal growth, ethical awareness, and purposeful engagement. These dimensions include fostering self-reflection on personal values and career purpose, developing emotional intelligence and empathy, and encouraging mindfulness practices to manage stress and enhance resilience. Training programs could also emphasise the ethical implications of technology design and usage, promoting a sense of responsibility towards IT solutions' broader social and environmental impact. Inspired by humanistic and spiritual principles, such training would enhance technical competencies and cultivate professionals guided by compassion, fairness, and a commitment to human well-being. Additionally, purpose-based career development strategies – such as those highlighted in purpose coaching models – can help IT professionals align their work with their deeper aspirations, leading to greater job satisfaction, adaptability, and organisational commitment.

This research has the following *limitations*. First, it does not explore all the dimensions of spirituality that are important in this area of research. Secondly, this study was conducted in a homogeneous culture, and its results cannot be extended to cross-cultural comparison, so the impact of cultures can also be considered while exploring spirituality. Lastly, it is recognised that the study sample is small and focuses on IT professionals working in a society with a heavy influence of religion.

Therefore, it is recommended for *future research* that the present study be extended to a cross-cultural comparison so that culture can also be considered while exploring spirituality, as it may have different meanings in different cultures. The current study has analysed some dimensions of spirituality in the IT environment, and the experts belong to a religious society. Therefore, the current research can be extended to analyse the further dimensions of spirituality in the learning aspect of IT professionals. Moreover, the current study should be replicated in a non-religious society to check the impact of spirituality more precisely.

In conclusion, integrating spirituality and humanistic management into IT professional development is critical for fostering meaning, purpose, and resilience in an increasingly fast-paced and demanding sector. Humanistic management, emphasising human dignity, ethical business practices, and personal well-being, complements the spiritual quest for more profound meaning and interconnectedness in work life. Together, they offer a robust framework to counteract the risks of burnout, disengagement, and ethical neglect in the IT industry. As the AI era transforms the technological landscape, incorporating spiritual principles such as compassion, mindfulness, and fairness becomes essential to ensure that innovation remains aligned with human values and societal good. However, these principles must be integrated critically, recognising potential tensions between genuine meaning-making and capitalist instrumentalisation. The research under scores the benefits of creating supportive, value-driven environments for IT professionals, emphasising the importance of meaningful work, career adaptability, and purpose-based development. By embedding spirituality and humanistic management into professional growth strategies, organisations can cultivate a more engaged, ethical, and resilient workforce that thrives through technical excellence and a profound sense of meaning, purpose, and shared humanity.

## References

Ahmad, J., & Fatima, S. (2022). Meaningful leadership and employees' well-being: Process through meaningful work. *Pakistan Journal of Humanities and Social Sciences*, 10(4), 1239–1249.

Albrecht, S. L. (2013). Work engagement and the positive power of meaningful work. In Albrecht, S. L. (ed.), *Advances in positive organizational psychology* (pp. 237–260). Emerald Group Publishing Limited.

Alcover, C. M., Guglielmi, D., Depolo, M., & Mazzetti, G. (2021). "Aging-and-Tech Job Vulnerability": A proposed framework on the dual impact of aging and AI, robotics, and automation among older workers. *Organizational Psychology Review*, 11(2), 175–201.

Allan, B. A., Batz-Barbarich, C., Sterling, H. M., & Tay, L. (2019). Outcomes of meaningful work: A meta-analysis. *Journal of Management Studies*, 56(3), 500–528.

Baldacchino, D. (2015). Spiritual care education of health care professionals. *Religions*, 6(2), 594–613.

Bantha, T., & Nayak, U. (2021). The relation of workplace spirituality with employees' innovative work behaviour: The mediating role of psychological empowerment. *Journal of Indian Business Research*, 13(2), 223–235.

Bazeley, P., & Jackson, K. (2013). *Qualitative data analysis with NVivo: SAGE publications limited*. Qualitative data analysis with NVivo: SAGE publications limited.

Bernard, H. R., & Ryan, G. W. (2010). *Analyzing Qualitative Data: Systematic Approaches*. Sage Publications, Inc.

Beverly, D., Williams, J. A., & Kitterlin, M. (2012). Leaders exhibiting high emotional intelligence are more dedicated to their job performance. *Open Journal of Leadership*, 1(4), 37–41.

Brougham, D., & Haar, J. (2018). Smart technology, artificial intelligence, robotics, and algorithms (STARA): Employees' perceptions of our future workplace. *Journal of Management & Organization*, 24(2), 239–257.

Brynjolfsson, E. (2014). *The second machine age: Work, progress, and prosperity in a time of brilliant technologies* (Vol. 236). WW Norton Company.

Bryson, J. J., & Theodorou, A. (2019). How society can maintain human-centric artificial intelligence. In *Human-centered digitalization and services* (pp. 305–323). Springer Nature Singapore.

Creswell, J. W., & Poth, C. N. (2016). *Qualitative inquiry and research design: Choosing among five approaches*. Sage publications.

Daniel, J. L. (2010). The effect of workplace spirituality on team effectiveness. *Journal of management development*, 29(5), 442–456.

Dasa, T. A. (2023). *Spirituality in the age of artificial intelligence*. The Daily Guardian.

Dashenkova, H. M., & Korobkina, T. B. (2024). Humanistic management and psychological support in the field of it: Relevance and development. *Гуманітарний форум*, 2(2), 25–28.

DiCicco-Bloom, B., & Crabtree, B. F. (2006). The qualitative research interview. *Medical Education*, 40(4), 314–321.

Dik, B. J., Byrne, Z. S., & Steger, M. F. (2013). *Purpose and meaning in the workplace*. American Psychological Association.

Dik, B. J., Duffy, R. D., Allan, B. A., O'Donnell, M. B., Shim, Y., & Steger, M. F. (2015). Purpose and meaning in career development applications. *The Counseling Psychologist*, 43(4), 558–585.

Dignum, V. (2018). Ethics in artificial intelligence: Introduction to the special issue. *Ethics and Information Technology*, 20(1), 1–3.

Dimonte, V., Gonella, S., Albanesi, B., Malinverni, E., Campagna, S., & Conti, A. (2023). The contribution of dance movement therapy in promoting nursing students' interpersonal skills during the COVID-19 pandemic: A descriptive phenomenological study. *International Journal of Environmental Research and Public Health*, 20(2), 1376.

Dirkx, J. M. (2013). Leaning in and leaning back at the same time: Toward a spirituality of work-related learning. *Advances in Developing Human Resources*, 15(4), 356–369.

Ellison, C. W. (1983). Spiritual well-being: Conceptualization and measurement. *Journal of Psychology and Theology*, 11(4), 330–338.

Flick, U. (2022). *An introduction to qualitative research*. SAGE Publications Ltd.

Fontana, A., & Frey, J. H. (2005). The interview. *The Sage Handbook of Qualitative Research*, 3(1), 695–727.

Fry, L. W., & Nisiewicz, M. S. (2020). *Maximizing the triple bottom line through spiritual leadership*. Stanford University Press.

George, L. S., & Park, C. L. (2013). Are meaning and purpose distinct? An examination of correlates and predictors. *The Journal of Positive Psychology*, 8(5), 365–375.

Goldschlag, N., & Miranda, J. (2020). Business dynamics statistics of High-Tech industries. *Journal of Economics & Management Strategy*, 29(1), 3–30.

Guillén, M., Ferrero, I., & Hoffman, W. M. (2015). The neglected ethical and spiritual motivations in the workplace. *Journal of Business Ethics*, 128, 803–816.

Hay, D. (2006). *The spirit of the child*. Jessica Kingsley Publishers.

He, X., Wang, W., Liao, L., Ren, Y., Liu, Y., & Xu, J. (2024). The humanistic care ability of nurses in 27 provinces in China: A multi-center cross-sectional study. *Frontiers in Medicine*, 11, 1450783.

Huang, X., & Lai, W. (2006). Clustering graphs for visualization via node similarities. *Journal of Visual Languages & Computing*, 17(3), 225–253.

James, R. (2023). Fit perception and engagement: The mediating role of work meaningfulness. *Vision*, 27(4), 474–484.

Karakas, F. (2010). Spirituality and performance in organizations: A literature review. *Journal of Business Ethics*, 94, 89–106.

Kemeny, T., & Osman, T. (2018). The wider impacts of high-technology employment: Evidence from US cities. *Research Policy*, 47(9), 1729–1740.

Kim, M., & Beehr, T. A. (2018). Organization-based self-esteem and meaningful work mediate effects of empowering leadership on employee behaviors and well-being. *Journal of Leadership & Organizational Studies*, 25(4), 385–398.

Koon, V. Y. (2021). Bibliometric analyses on the emergence and present growth of humanistic management. *International Journal of Ethics and Systems*, 37(4), 581–598.

Kostera, M., & Ludwicki, T. (2021). Learning to coopearate: Implications for humanistic management. *Arts & Cultural Studies Review/Przegląd Kulturoznawczy*, 2021(1), 61–78. https://doi.org/10.4467/20843860PK.21.004.13458

Kostera, M., & Pirson, M. (Eds.). (2017). *Dignity and the organization*. Palgrave Macmillan UK.

Ladkin, D. (2008). Leading beautifully: How mastery, congruence and purpose create the aesthetic of embodied leadership practice. *The Leadership Quarterly*, 19(1), 31–41.

Lee, M. C. C., Idris, M. A., & Delfabbro, P. H. (2017). The linkages between hierarchical culture and empowering leadership and their effects on employees' work engagement: Work meaningfulness as a mediator. *International Journal of Stress Management*, 24(4), 392.

Legere, T. E. (1984). A spirituality for today. *Studies in Formative Spirituality*, 5(3), 375–383.

Liu, H., Zhang, L., Yan, J., Huang, H., Yi, Q., & Peng, L. (2023). The relationship between social support, empathy, self-efficacy, and humanistic practice ability among clinical nurses in china: A structural equation model. *Journal of Nursing Management*, 2023(1), 1378278.

Matheson, A., Dillon, P. J., Guillén, M., & Warner, C. (2021). People mattering at work: A humanistic management perspective. *Humanistic Management Journal*, 6, 405–428.

Mayan, M. J. (2023). *Essentials of Qualitative Inquiry* (2nd ed.). Routledge. https://doi.org/10.4324/b23331

Mazur, B. (2023). Organizational culture in enterprises applying the humanistic and economic paradigm of management.

Melé, D. (2013). Antecedents and current situation of humanistic management. *African Journal of Business Ethics*, 7(2), 52.

Melé, D. (2016). Understanding humanistic management. *Humanistic Management Journal*, 1, 33–55.

Michaelson, C. W., & Tosti-Kharas, J. (2024). *The meaning and purpose of work: An interdisciplinary framework for considering what work is for*. Taylor & Francis.

Mitroff, I. I., & Denton, E. A. (1999). A study of spirituality in the workplace. *MIT Sloan Management Review*. https://sloanreview.mit.edu/article/a-study-of-spirituality-in-the-workplace/

Moberg, D. O. (1984). Subjective measures of spiritual well-being. *Review of religious research*, 25(4), 351–364.

Mustika, R., Pinasthika, A., & Greviana, N. (2024). The importance of learning with patients: post-pandemic takeaways on learning professionalism in Cclinical settings. *The Malaysian Journal of Medical Sciences: MJMS*, 31(1), 140.

Otu, M. S. (2024). Effect of purpose-based career coaching on career decision-making. *Current Psychology*, 43(31), 25568–25594.

Pacey, A., & Segal, H. P. (1999). Meaning in technology. *Nature*, 402(6760), 350–350.

Panch, T., Szolovits, P., & Atun, R. (2018). Artificial intelligence, machine learning and health systems. *Journal of Global Health*, 8(2), 020303.

Pirson, M. (2019). A humanistic perspective for management theory: Protecting dignity and promoting well-being. *Journal of Business Ethics*, 159, 39–57.

Pratt, M. G., & Ashforth, B. E. (2003). Fostering meaningfulness in working and at work. *Positive Organizational Scholarship: Foundations of a New Discipline*, 309, 327.

Rantanen, J., Markkula, S., Konsti, S., Kiuru, N., Mauno, S., & Feldt, T. (2024). Merkity ksellisestä työstä hyvinvointia organisaatioille: MEANWELL-hankkeen loppuraportti.

Rego, A., & e Cunha, M. P. (2008). Workplace spirituality and organizational commitment: An empirical study. *Journal of Organizational Change Management*, 21(1), 53–75.

Rossiter, G. (2010). Perspective on contemporary spirituality: Implications for religious education in Catholic schools. *International Studies in Catholic Education*, 2(2), 129–147.

Stebbins, R. A. (2001). *Exploratory Research in the Social Sciences* (Vol. 48). Sage. https://doi.org/10.4135/9781412984249

Spreitzer, G. M., Cameron, L., & Garrett, L. (2017). Alternative work arrangements: Two images of the new world of work. *Annual Review of Organizational Psychology and Organizational Behavior*, 4(1), 473–499.

Strati, A. (2008). Aesthetics in the study of organizational life. In Barry, D., & Hansen, H. (eds.), *The SAGE Handbook of New Approaches in Management and Organization*, 229–238.

Susskind, D. (2020). *A world without work: Technology, automation and how we should respond*. Penguin UK.

Szostak, M. (2023). Reflexivity in aesthetic situation management. *Discourses on Culture*, 20(1), 161–198.

Szostak, M. (2024). *Humanistic Management, Organisation and Aesthetics: Art of Management and Management of Art*. Routledge. https://doi.org/10.4324/9781003458029

Ul-Haq, S. (2020). Spiritual development and meaningful work: A Habermasian critique. *Human Resource Development International*, 23(2), 125–145.

Vaidyanathan, S. (2020). Spirituality and artificial intelligence: Towards a balanced coexistence. *Journal of Ethics and Information Technology*, 22(4), 259–273.

Van Wingerden, J., & Van der Stoep, J. (2017). The role of meaningful work in employees' work related and general well-being. *International Journal of Human Resource Studies*, 7(4), 23–37.

Vora, D., & Kainzbauer, A. (2020). Humanistic leadership in Thailand: A mix of indigenous and global aspects using a cross-cultural perspective. *Cross Cultural & Strategic Management*, 27(4), 665–687.

Wu, W., Liu, W., Wu, W., & Xia, Y. (2024). Novices' professional identification awakened: Uncovering the impact of positive profession-spotlighting events. *Personnel Psychology*, 77(3), 1195–1234.

Yandong, L., & Wareewanich, T. (2024). Factors influencing employee engagement and innovative work behavior--a case study of hi-tech company in china. *Educational Administration: Theory and Practice*, 30(5), 12408–12422.

Zawadzki, M. (2018). Dignity in the workplace. The perspective of humanistic management. *Central European Management Journal*, 26(1), 171–188.

Zheng, D., Marbut, A. R., Zhang, J., & O'Keefe, L. C. (2022). The contribution of psychological resilience and job meaningfulness to well-being of working cancer survivors. *Workplace Health & Safety*, 70(10), 468–478.

# 5 AI-driven organisational aesthetics

## Cross-paradigmatic perspectives in humanistic management

*Łukasz Sułkowski and Justyna Dziedzic*

### Introduction

The study of organisational aesthetics has emerged as a vibrant field of inquiry, offering valuable insights into how sensory experiences, artistic expressions, and material artefacts shape the dynamics of work life. Scholars increasingly recognise that the aesthetic dimension – encompassing design, symbolism, and embodied practices – fundamentally informs collaboration, meaning-making, and identity construction processes. Despite this growing interest, there remains a need for more profound theoretical clarity about the underlying assumptions that guide the study of aesthetics in organisations. In this regard, the four paradigms of social science (functionalist, interpretive, radical humanist, and radical structuralist) provide a robust conceptual framework for understanding the various ways researchers and practitioners approach and interpret organisational aesthetics.

Proposed initially by Burrell and Morgan (1979) and adapted by many texts (Barley, 1980; Kostera, 1996; Sułkowski, 2009), these paradigms reflect divergent ontological and epistemological stances, each yielding distinct perspectives on social phenomena. Functionalist scholars adopt a realist ontology to measure and optimise aesthetic variables for enhanced productivity or performance. Interpretive researchers, embracing a subjective outlook, focus on how people construct and negotiate aesthetic meanings within organisational settings. By contrast, radical humanists highlight aesthetics as a medium for emancipation, exploring how art and creativity can unmask underlying ideologies and foster liberating forms of expression. Finally, radical structuralists concentrate on the structural constraints that shape and sometimes commodify aesthetic expressions, paying close attention to systemic power imbalances and economic determinants.

In examining organisational aesthetics through these four paradigms, this paper underscores the diverse ways sensory experiences are conceptualised and operationalised in management and organisational studies. By bringing together insights from each paradigm, we seek to illuminate the multifaceted nature of aesthetic phenomena: as a measurable input to organisational processes, a social

DOI: 10.4324/9781003654377-7

construction shaped by culture and communication, a vehicle for emancipation, or a site of structural conflict and domination. Integrating these perspectives enriches our understanding of aesthetics and highlights critical points of tension or convergence among different schools of thought.

This chapter examines how these conceptualisations translate into distinct methodological orientations and empirical focal points, particularly regarding the role of AI in shaping organisational aesthetics. The study investigates how AI-driven aesthetics are framed within each paradigm: as an efficiency-enhancing tool within the functionalist paradigm, as a co-creator of meaning in the interpretive paradigm, as a potential medium for emancipation and ideological critique in the radical humanist paradigm, and as a mechanism of aesthetic standardisation and control in the radical structuralist paradigm. By mapping these theoretical landscapes, the paper comprehensively explains how AI mediates organisational aesthetics' sensory, symbolic, and existential layers, influencing managerial interventions, workplace design, and employees' aesthetic experiences. While AI enables hyper-personalisation and optimised aesthetic management, it raises critical concerns about algorithmic bias, aesthetic commodification, and the reinforcement of dominant power structures. This study, therefore, aims to inspire a more reflexive and multi-paradigmatic engagement with AI-driven aesthetics, encouraging future research that integrates insights from multiple paradigms to address the complex and evolving interplay between technology and aesthetics in contemporary organisational settings.

The *research problem* concerns how AI-driven automation and algorithmic processes impact organisational aesthetic experiences – an area that remains underexplored in management studies. While aesthetics have been widely studied concerning organisational identity, culture, and collaboration, this study focuses on how AI reshapes these experiences through the lens of four paradigms. Specifically, this chapter addresses the following core *research questions*: (RQ1) How does AI shape the conceptualisation of organisational aesthetics within each of the four paradigms? (RQ2) What are AI-mediated aesthetics' managerial and ethical implications in organisational settings? (RQ3) To what extent does AI alter the depth of organisational aesthetics, shaping the layers of sensory, symbolic, and existential meaning within the workplace? By integrating AI into the discourse on organisational aesthetics, this study seeks to bridge a crucial gap in management research. It critically examines whether AI is an enabler of aesthetic diversity and human creativity or a mechanism of aesthetic regulation and structural control.

Regarding *research methods*, this study employs a multi-paradigmatic approach, recognising that AI-driven aesthetics can be interpreted differently depending on the underlying ontological and epistemological stance. The methodological design follows a qualitative, interpretive approach, drawing on discourse analysis and critical theoretical reflections. Functionalist analysis examines how organisations use AI to enhance performance through aesthetic optimisation (e.g., AI-driven workspace design and digital branding algorithms). Quantitative assessments and secondary data sources, such as reports on AI's impact on organisational performance, complement this perspective. Interpretive analysis examines the subjective experiences and social constructions of AI-driven aesthetics through qualitative methods, including semi-structured interviews and ethnographic observations in workplaces that integrate AI. Radical humanist analysis examines the potential of AI for emancipatory aesthetic expression, drawing on critical discourse analysis of AI-generated artistic interventions and participatory aesthetic practices. Radical structuralist analysis: This chapter critically examines AI as a mechanism of aesthetic control and commodification, analysing how AI-generated aesthetics reinforce power structures. It does this through a historical-institutional analysis of aesthetic standardisation in AI-enhanced organisations. To address the third research question on aesthetic depth, this study applies: (1) phenomenological analysis to explore how AI-mediated aesthetics influences embodied sensory experiences and aesthetic perception in workplace environments and (2) semiotic analysis to examine how AI-generated aesthetics reshapes organisational symbolism, affecting more profound layers of meaning and authenticity. By employing a multi-method, paradigmatic approach, this study ensures a nuanced understanding of AI's role in organisational aesthetics, capturing its transformative potential and the risks associated with algorithmic regulation of aesthetic experiences.

## Literature review: conceptual foundation of four paradigms in organisational discourse and aesthetics

The study of organisational aesthetics offers valuable insights into how sensory experiences, artistic expressions, and material artefacts shape management and workplace dynamics. This section critically examines two key strands of literature. The first explores the four paradigms of organisational discourse, analysing how aesthetic considerations are conceptualised within functionalist, interpretive, radical humanist, and radical structuralist perspectives. The second focuses on aesthetic dimensions in organisational management, addressing the role of aesthetics in identity formation, collaboration, and workplace design.

### *Four paradigms in organisational discourse*

Divergent perspectives have long framed the study of organisations and management, each guided by distinctive philosophical assumptions about the nature of reality (ontology), the basis of knowledge (epistemology), and appropriate methods for inquiry (methodology). One of the most enduring frameworks for categorising these perspectives is drawn from the work of Gibson Burrell and Gareth Morgan (1979), who proposed four paradigms in organisation and management sciences: the functionalist, the interpretive, the radical humanist, and the radical structuralist. Although subsequent scholarships have extended and modified this scheme, it remains a touchstone for scholars seeking to comprehend the landscape of organisational theory (Hassard, 1991).

At the most fundamental level, these paradigms are distinguished by whether they adopt an objective or subjective stance, as well as whether their focus is on regulation and stability or radical change (Deetz, 1996). The two "subjective" paradigms (interpretive and radical humanist) assume that social reality is constructed through the meanings and interpretations of individuals and groups. In contrast, the two "objective" paradigms (functionalist and radical structuralist) treat social reality as an external phenomenon that can be observed and measured. Along another dimension, the "regulation" paradigms (functionalist and interpretive) are more inclined towards understanding and explaining organisational order and stability, while the "radical change" paradigms (radical humanist and radical structuralist) emphasise transformation, power inequalities, and the potential or necessity for structural or ideological upheaval.

The functionalist paradigm epitomises an objective perspective oriented towards maintaining order. From a philosophical standpoint, functionalist scholars embrace ontological realism, positing that organisations and social structures exist independently of the observer. The associated epistemological stance is typically positivist or empiricist, meaning researchers aim to uncover universal principles by systematically observing and measuring the external world. Such an approach relies on hypothesis testing, statistical analysis, and quantitative methodologies.

Functionalists conceptualise organisations as tangible entities with identifiable boundaries and internal systems that can be optimised. Within this paradigm, human actors are frequently regarded as rational agents pursuing objectives aligned with the organisation's overarching goals – operational efficiency, profit maximisation, or strategic positioning. As a result, functionalist research often examines how to design processes, structures, and control mechanisms that bolster organisational performance. By identifying cause-and-effect relationships, functionalists seek to generate models and frameworks that can be generalised across contexts, such as contingency theory or systems theory. Their preoccupation with stability, predictability, and the ability to test theories empirically has led to substantial contributions in areas like strategic planning, organisational structure, and human resource management.

In contrast, the interpretive paradigm adopts a subjective view of social reality, contending that organisations are meaningful worlds constructed through language, symbols, and shared interpretations. In this paradigm, the ontological position is relativist, reflecting the belief that multiple, equally valid realities may exist in different social groups or at various times. Epistemologically, knowledge is viewed as emergent from organisational members' lived experiences and interpretive processes. Interpretive researchers, therefore, prioritise understanding how organisational actors make sense of their environment, share meanings and engage in sensemaking.

Empirical studies within the interpretive paradigm often employ qualitative methodologies, including ethnography, case studies, interviews, and discourse analysis. The researcher's goal is less about testing universal laws and more about capturing the richness of organisational culture and practices as they are enacted. Thus, interpretive scholars emphasise reflexivity, acknowledging that researchers themselves are part of the social world under study and are inevitably shaped by, and in turn shape, it. Typical research areas include organisational culture, leadership as a socially constructed process, and the symbolic aspects of organisational change. Scholars within this paradigm argue that understanding the multiplicity of meanings underpinning organisational life gives us deeper insights into why organisations function beyond what purely quantitative or functionalist perspectives can reveal.

The radical humanist paradigm is situated within the subjective dimension yet aligned with the radical change axis. Like interpretive scholars, radical humanists see organisational reality as constructed through human consciousness and intersubjective meanings. However, they adopt a critical stance towards these interpretations, recognising that dominant ideologies and power relations inevitably shape and constrain them. From an ontological standpoint, reality remains fluid and subjective; from an epistemological perspective, radical humanists stress that knowledge involves unveiling how ideological forces shape consciousness to perpetuate certain forms of social or organisational domination.

Consequently, the radical humanist paradigm is primarily concerned with emancipation, challenging the taken-for-granted assumptions and belief systems that hinder personal and collective liberation. Methodologically, researchers in this tradition often employ critical, reflexive, and dialogical approaches, including critical discourse analysis, action research, and participatory research methods. Their investigations aim to reveal power asymmetries, question hegemonic ideologies, and provide alternative narratives that enable individuals to re-envision themselves and their social or organisational structures. Rather than focusing on incremental improvement or maintaining the status quo, radical humanists seek genuine transformation in the consciousness of organisational members, which they view as a precursor to larger-scale societal change.

Lastly, the radical structuralist paradigm shares an objective understanding of social reality with the functionalist tradition – organisations and social systems are accurate, material entities that can be studied and analysed systematically. However, radical structuralists depart from functionalists by emphasising that the structures constituting this reality are imbued with conflict, power struggles, and forms of domination. This paradigm posits that economic and political structures primarily determine societal and organisational dynamics, invariably producing tension and contestation among different groups.

The ontological realism of radical structuralism implies that underlying societal structures – such as class relations, capitalist economic systems, or bureaucratic power – exert a determinative influence on organisational life. Epistemologically, radical structuralists often adopt a critical-objectivist stance, contending that rigorous empirical investigation can reveal how these objective structures systematically advantage some groups while marginalising others. Methodologically, research in this tradition might blend quantitative tools (such as large-scale data on income disparities) with historical and institutional analyses that trace the evolution of structural inequalities.

Like radical humanists, radical structuralists champion radical change but conceptualise it primarily as transforming society's structural underpinnings. Rather than focusing on collective consciousness or interpretive meanings, radical structuralists foreground macro-level factors, such as labour relations, class conflict, and institutional constraints, that shape or even determine individual and organisational behaviours. Examples of radical structuralist inquiries include studies of how global capitalism influences workforce exploitation or examining how regulatory and political frameworks perpetuate systemic discrimination.

Despite their distinctiveness, these four paradigms illustrate how scholars conceive of organisations and pursue knowledge about them. While functionalists seek generalisable principles for managing and improving performance, interpretive scholars reveal the socially constructed realities of organisational members. Radical humanists emphasise how consciousness and meaning-making processes can be shaped by ideologies that restrict human freedom. In contrast, radical structuralists concentrate on structural factors that constrain and enable social action, often leading to conflict and potential upheaval.

Over the years, considerable debate has occurred regarding whether these paradigms are fundamentally incommensurable or if bridges can be built to integrate them (Schultz & Hatch, 1996; Gioia & Pitre, 1990; Hassard, 1991; Deetz, 1996). Scholars advocate a pluralist approach, suggesting that organisational phenomena are too complex and multifaceted to be fully captured by a single set of assumptions (Gioia & Pitre, 1990; Hassard, 1991; Schultz & Hatch, 1996; Deetz, 1996). Others caution that combining paradigms may dilute their philosophical rigour. Nevertheless, awareness of these paradigms enriches management research and practice by making explicit the assumptions underlying various theories and methods (Burrell & Morgan, 1979; Willmott, 1993; Schultz & Hatch, 1996). It prompts critical reflection on how one's choice of theoretical lens shapes the questions asked, the data collected, and the conclusions drawn.

### *Organisational aesthetics: key themes in management and workplace design*

The four-paradigm framework provides a structured approach to classifying different streams of thought while also offering a critical lens for examining the broader purposes and implications of organisational research. This approach enhances scholarly and practical engagement with organisational processes by addressing their philosophical, methodological, and political dimensions, leading to a more comprehensive understanding of their complexity.

Integrating aesthetics into management and organisational practices has garnered increasing attention in recent years, illuminating how sensory perceptions, artistic expressions, and the broader aesthetic experience can profoundly shape organisational life. Organisational aesthetics encompasses both surface aesthetics, based on sensory perception and interactions, and deep aesthetics, grounded in values, paradigms, and organisational identity, shaping meaning-making processes beyond immediate sensory experience (Szostak, 2023). This perspective challenges the dominance of purely rational, logical-analytical frameworks in traditional management theory, underscoring the importance of emotional and tacit knowledge in everyday work-based practices. By highlighting these aesthetic underpinnings, scholars and practitioners gain a more holistic grasp of how individuals coordinate their efforts, collaborate creatively, and construct shared understandings of organisational phenomena (Baldessarelli et al., 2022).

Organisational aesthetics emphasises the sensory reactions evoked by the materials and artefacts surrounding organisational members' daily activities. Far from being mere decorations or superficial add-ons, these aesthetic components—ranging from office layouts and interior design to symbolic elements like logos or artistic installations – carry significant weight in shaping employee engagement, motivation, and sensemaking. By influencing how members feel and perceive their workplace, aesthetic dimensions can enhance creativity, foster a deeper emotional connection, and facilitate more meaningful exchanges among team members. Rather than viewing such artistic and sensory elements as secondary to the rational processes of planning and control, organisational aesthetics recognise them as integral to effective coordination and the co-creation of organisational culture (Mack, 2023). Practically, attending aesthetics can translate into deliberately designing workspaces that stimulate positive emotions, spark curiosity, and support innovative thinking.

Aesthetics in organisation and management has evolved into a rich field of inquiry, encompassing everything from designing workspaces and branding elements to the role of art and sensory experience in shaping employee engagement, communication, and culture. As scholarly interest in organisational aesthetics grows, researchers increasingly draw upon different paradigms with a philosophical and methodological orientation to frame their study and interpretation of aesthetic phenomena.

Moreover, the focus on aesthetic forms of knowing provokes a reconsideration of the epistemological foundations within management scholarship and education. Traditional theories have prioritised measurable outcomes and objective data. Still, aesthetic approaches reveal the inherent value of more subjective forms of knowledge, such as individual tastes, emotional responses, and sensory experiences (Mack, 2023). These practical and embodied forms of knowledge shape how people engage with their work and inform their decision-making processes in subtle yet powerful ways. By acknowledging the legitimacy of aesthetic knowing, scholars and educators open the door to more immersive pedagogies – such as artistic interventions, storytelling, or performance-based methods – that can cultivate management students' creative and reflective capabilities. In this manner, integrating aesthetic experiences within management education fosters richer learning environments that mirror the complexity of organisational life.

From a semiotic perspective, organisational aesthetics can be systematically analysed through typologies that elucidate how signs and symbols generate aesthetic value and meaning. One approach proposes a typology of organisational beauty, outlining various dimensions and variables – such as harmony, simplicity, expressiveness, and coherence – that contribute to an organisation's aesthetic experience (Sastre & Aránega, 2023). Under this framework, researchers can employ a semiotic-based method to identify and validate the elements that render a specific environment aesthetically pleasing, emotionally resonant, or creativity-inducing for its members. This structured examination helps move discussions of aesthetics beyond purely subjective impressions, offering a more robust, empirical basis for understanding how visual, auditory, and spatial cues affect organisational life. By systematically studying how signs and symbols operate, scholars gain insights into how aesthetic values can be enhanced or strategically managed to support organisational goals (Sastre & Aránega, 2023).

A related line of inquiry underscores the historical and theoretical interrelation of aesthetics, management, and spatial organisation. Researchers have revealed how spatial designs – from open-plan offices to flexible, collaborative spaces – incorporate aesthetic considerations that promote or hinder inclusivity, interaction, and well-being (Yusupova, 2022). This work challenges conventional notions of workspace arrangement by demonstrating how aesthetic principles inflect employees' lived experiences, shaping socialisation patterns, communication, and informal learning. In practical application, such findings encourage leaders and organisational designers to move beyond efficiency-centric layout models and consider how a workplace's spatial aesthetics can meaningfully align with corporate values, brand identity, and employee aspirations. Integrating these insights into workplace design can thus have far-reaching implications for employee satisfaction, retention, and overall organisational culture.

Art-driven organisations which create and promote artistic practices present a particularly salient context for applying organisational aesthetics (Araújo & Davel, 2021). In these settings, creative expression and aesthetic engagement lie at the core of the organisational mission, making it especially crucial for leaders to manage and nurture the aesthetic dimension. Managing art-driven organisations entails balancing creative freedom with operational constraints while ensuring the unique aesthetic outputs resonate with internal and external stakeholders. Research suggests that such organisations can provide fertile ground for examining novel management practices, given their openness to experimentation and foundational reliance on creative processes. By studying art-driven organisations, scholars can glean broader lessons about sustaining innovation, harnessing collective creativity, and integrating aesthetic considerations in conventional corporate settings, bridging the gap between art and business.

Although organisational aesthetics has gained scholarly momentum, it also opens new avenues for continued theoretical and empirical research across diverse organisational contexts. For instance, there is a growing need to investigate how aesthetic elements influence remote or hybrid work settings, where physical presence and direct sensory engagement are diminished. Similarly, cross-cultural studies of organisational aesthetics can illuminate how different cultural backgrounds and social norms shape aesthetic preferences and how organisations can navigate these differences sensitively in global or multicultural contexts. Deepening our understanding of such phenomena can enhance global management strategies and enable organisations to design inclusive environments that tap into the creative potential of a diverse workforce (Fryzel & Marcinkowski, 2024).

Critical perspectives in organisational aesthetics also probe potential tensions, contradictions, or ethical issues associated with pursuing aesthetic value within corporate life. On the one hand, aesthetic interventions enrich employees' work experiences, foster organisational pride, and generate social capital. On the other hand, such interventions may inadvertently mask underlying problems or serve as superficial branding efforts without tangible improvements to work conditions. Consequently, researchers must remain alert to the interplay between aesthetics, power dynamics, and organisational politics. This means scrutinising how decisions regarding aesthetic enhancement are made, whose tastes are prioritised, and which stakeholders stand to benefit or feel excluded from such initiatives. Bringing a critical lens to this field ensures that the embrace of aesthetics does not devolve into mere spectacle but instead remains grounded in genuine efforts to support creativity, authenticity, and human well-being (Lütticken, 2023).

In sum, organisational aesthetics represents a dynamic and transformative domain within management studies. This perspective moves beyond conventional managerial rationales that favour efficiency and control by appreciating how material objects, spatial configurations, and sensory experiences contribute to coordination, meaning-making, and creative collaboration. Rather than viewing aesthetics as extraneous or superficial, proponents of this approach emphasise their capacity to enrich employee engagement, spark innovation, and foster workplaces that value human expression. Empirical and theoretical contributions have advanced our understanding of how aesthetics can be intentionally cultivated, from semiotic analyses of beauty and systematic artistic interventions to spatial designs that favour openness, collaboration, and emotional resonance.

Moreover, examining art-driven organisations further highlights how aesthetics can form the cornerstone of an entity's mission, challenging leaders to skilfully blend artistic authenticity with business imperatives (Araújo & Davel, 2021).

The continued exploration of organisational aesthetics is poised to offer deeper insights into how meaning is produced and experienced within ever-evolving organisational landscapes. Rapid technological changes, shifting workforce expectations, and a heightened emphasis on well-being all reinforce the relevance of aesthetics in fostering adaptive, resilient, and human-centric organisations. Researchers may find especially fruitful areas in the study of virtual collaboration, diverse cultural contexts, and critical interrogations of aesthetics as a tool of corporate governance or branding. Ultimately, by integrating aesthetics into our understanding of organisational functioning, we broaden the horizons of management theory and practice. This evolving field invites us to appreciate organisations as systems of rational design and vibrant, engaged communities capable of nurturing creativity, engagement, and transformative experiences (Fryzel & Marcinkowski, 2024; Lütticken, 2023).

## Results: four organisational paradigms, aesthetics, and AI-Driven Design

The analysis identifies how AI influences organisational aesthetics across four distinct paradigmatic perspectives. The findings highlight that each paradigm offers a different ontological and epistemological stance on AI-mediated aesthetics, shaping how organisations conceptualise and engage with aesthetic processes. Expressly, AI is framed as a tool for optimisation in the functionalist paradigm, a co-creator of meaning in the interpretive paradigm, an instrument of emancipation in the radical humanist paradigm, and a mechanism of control and commodification in the radical structuralist paradigm. These insights provide a nuanced understanding of the opportunities and challenges associated with AI-driven aesthetics in organisational settings.

Table 5.1 illustrates how the four paradigms in organisation and management – functionalist, interpretive, radical humanist, and radical structuralist – differ in their ontological and epistemological assumptions, methodological preferences, and approaches to understanding and researching aesthetics in organisations.

Table 5.2 presents a more comprehensive exploration of how the four paradigms (functionalist, interpretive, radical humanist, and radical structuralist) inform distinct approaches to thinking about, investigating, and applying aesthetics in organisational contexts (Szostak & Sułkowski, 2020).

Within the interpretive paradigm, AI is not merely a tool for optimisation but an active participant in shaping organisational aesthetics through symbolic and narrative construction. This perspective emphasises that aesthetic experiences are socially constructed and influenced by human interpretation and interaction with AI-generated designs. AI's role extends to personalising

*Table 5.1* Four organisational paradigms and their approaches to aesthetics

| *Paradigm* | *Ontology & epistemology* | *Focus on aesthetics* | *Methodological orientation* | *Research examples* |
|---|---|---|---|---|
| Functionalist | • Realist ontology<br>• Positivist/empiricist epistemology | • Views aesthetics as an objective factor influencing performance and efficiency<br>• Examines how aesthetic interventions improve productivity, brand image, or customer satisfaction | • Quantitative methods (surveys, statistical analysis, experimental designs)<br>• Emphasis on measurement, causality | • Measuring employee satisfaction or productivity linked to office design<br>• Assessing ROI of aesthetic redesign in corporate settings |
| Interpretive | • Relativist ontology<br>• Constructivist/subjectivist epistemology | • Considers aesthetics as socially constructed meanings<br>• Focuses on symbolic, cultural, and experiential dimensions of aesthetic forms | • Qualitative methods (ethnography, in-depth interviews, participant observation)<br>• Emphasis on subjective experience, narrative, and sensemaking | • Exploring how employees interpret symbolic or artistic elements in their workspace<br>• Investigating the role of art in shaping organisational culture |
| Radical Humanist | • Subjectivist ontology<br>• Critical-subjectivist epistemology | • Sees aesthetics as a means of challenging dominant ideologies and catalysing personal or collective emancipation<br>• Investigates how art and creativity can liberate human potential | • Critical, reflexive, and participatory methods (critical discourse analysis, arts-based inquiry, action research)<br>• Focus on revealing ideology | • Arts-based interventions to expose hidden power structures in creative industries<br>• Using aesthetic tools (e.g., theatre workshops) to promote critical reflection among employees |
| Radical Structuralist | • Realist ontology<br>• Critical-objectivist epistemology | • Analyses aesthetics as embedded in larger power structures and systems of control<br>• Examines how aesthetic strategies support or challenge systemic inequalities or dominance | • Often quantitative or historical-structural analysis<br>• Large-scale data, comparative institutional research, critical theory frameworks | • Assessing how corporate branding aesthetics shape consumer desires and labour discipline<br>• Studying aesthetic labour as a mechanism of social control or worker exploitation |

*Source:* Own elaboration.

*Table 5.2* AI and organisational aesthetics across four paradigms

| *Paradigm* | *AI's role in organisational aesthetics* | *Methodological orientation* | *Research examples* |
|---|---|---|---|
| Functionalist | • AI as a tool to optimise aesthetic efficiency in organisational design<br>• Algorithmic curation of branding and workspace aesthetics for enhanced productivity<br>• AI-driven UX/UI design improving customer engagement | • Quantitative methods (surveys, statistical modelling, experimental studies)<br>• Focus on measurement and causality | • Measuring employee satisfaction with AI-driven workplace design<br>• Assessing the impact of AI-generated branding on consumer perception |
| Interpretive | • AI as a co-creator of aesthetic meaning in organisational settings<br>• Examining AI's influence on symbolic and narrative aspects of aesthetics<br>• AI-mediated personalisation of digital workspaces based on user preferences | • Qualitative methods (ethnography, semi-structured interviews, discourse analysis)<br>• Focus on subjective experience, sensemaking, and symbolic interaction | • Investigating how employees perceive AI-generated aesthetics in digital workspaces<br>• Analysing AI-driven artistic interventions in corporate identity |
| Radical Humanist | • AI as a medium for aesthetic emancipation and creative democratisation<br>• AI-generated art and its role in challenging dominant organisational aesthetics<br>• Critical interrogation of AI's role in reinforcing aesthetic norms | • Critical, reflexive, and participatory methods (arts-based research, action research, critical discourse analysis)<br>• Focus on challenging ideological constraints | • Examining AI-generated art as a tool for social critique in organisations<br>• Using AI in participatory design to foster aesthetic inclusivity |
| Radical Structuralist | • AI as a mechanism of aesthetic control and commodification<br>• Algorithmic bias in aesthetic decision-making reinforcing power structures<br>• AI-driven standardisation of aesthetics as a form of symbolic domination | • Historical-structural and critical analysis (institutional critique, data analysis, comparative studies)<br>• Focus on power asymmetries and systemic inequalities | • Analysing AI's role in reinforcing aesthetic hierarchies in digital marketing<br>• Studying how AI-driven aesthetic automation impacts creative labour and artistic autonomy |

*Source:* Own elaboration.

digital workspaces, adapting visual and auditory elements based on user preferences, and co-producing artistic or branding elements that reflect an organisation's evolving cultural identity. Methodologically, this paradigm relies on qualitative approaches, including ethnography, semi-structured interviews, and discourse analysis, to explore how employees and stakeholders perceive and engage with AI-mediated aesthetics. Studies in this domain investigate how AI-generated aesthetics shape organisational identity, influence the workplace atmosphere, and contribute to sensemaking processes in digital and physical environments.

Table 5.2 illustrates how AI influences organisational aesthetics within the framework of four paradigms. By examining AI's role in shaping aesthetic experiences, decision-making, and power structures, this analysis provides a nuanced understanding of AI's impact on management and organisational discourse. This framework offers a structured way to assess AI's transformative role in shaping organisational aesthetics, providing insights that bridge theoretical perspectives with real-world applications.

The following subsections elaborate on these findings by examining how each paradigm approaches AI-mediated aesthetics, outlining their theoretical assumptions, methodological orientations, and practical implications.

1 Functionalist paradigm

Under the functionalist paradigm, researchers adopt a realist ontology, meaning they regard aesthetics as an external, objective element that can be observed and manipulated. This approach is coupled with a positivist or empiricist epistemology: functionalists believe knowledge is best acquired through systematic observation, measurement, and hypothesis testing. Consequently, their primary concern is how aesthetics can enhance organisational performance, efficiency, or other measurable outcomes.

When studying aesthetics from a functionalist perspective, scholars often explore the practical effects of, for instance, changes in interior design, colour schemes, or ergonomic furniture on employee productivity, job satisfaction, or customer perceptions. Functionalists might conduct large-scale surveys to measure employee attitudes pre- and post-redesign of workspaces, or they may undertake experimental studies that assess the impact of different branding strategies on consumer preferences. The overarching objective is to derive generalisable principles – akin to "universal laws" – that help managers make informed decisions regarding aesthetic interventions.

In functionalist-driven practice, aesthetics is a strategic asset or tool for achieving desired outcomes such as improved customer loyalty or enhanced employee well-being. The focus tends to be on optimising aesthetic variables for organisational gain rather than on the subjective experiences or deeper symbolic meanings that aesthetic elements hold. Although this perspective may overlook the nuanced, interpretive aspects of aesthetic experience, it provides clear, data-driven insights that are often persuasive in managerial decision-making (Szostak & Sułkowski, 2021).

Within the functionalist paradigm, AI is a precision tool for optimising organisational aesthetics, enhancing efficiency, and measuring impact. AI-driven algorithms can analyse vast datasets to identify patterns in consumer preferences, employee satisfaction, or the effectiveness of workspace design. For instance, machine learning models can assess how specific colour schemes or office layouts influence productivity by tracking behavioural data and performance metrics. In branding, AI-powered UX/UI design tools refine aesthetic elements to maximise customer engagement and retention. While this approach offers data-driven insights, it risks reducing aesthetics to a purely instrumental function, overlooking the subjective and symbolic dimensions of aesthetic experience (Szostak & Sułkowski, 2021).

2 Interpretive paradigm

Distinct from the functionalist approach, the interpretive paradigm situates aesthetics within a relativist ontology and a constructivist or subjectivist epistemology. Here, aesthetics is not simply an objective factor influencing organisational performance but a dynamic, socially constructed phenomenon embedded in organisational members' meanings, narratives, and cultural practices. Interpretive scholars thus focus on how employees and stakeholders experience, sense, and talk about aesthetic elements in their organisational environments.

Empirically, interpretive researchers utilise qualitative methodologies such as ethnography, in-depth interviews, participant observation, and narrative analysis. Rather than testing hypotheses about productivity gains, they aim to uncover how specific designs or artistic expressions resonate emotionally with employees or contribute to an organisation's shared sense of identity. For instance, interpretive studies may document how a mural painted in a company lobby becomes a central storytelling device for employees who see it as reflecting the firm's heritage or values. By paying close attention to language and symbolism, interpretive work highlights how aesthetic features become woven into the organisation's cultural fabric, shaping and being shaped by ongoing sensemaking processes.

While this paradigm may not always yield straightforward metrics of interest to functionalists, it offers a deeper appreciation of how aesthetics influences collaboration, motivation, and meaning. Within this framework, even seemingly mundane elements – like the choice of colour for a team's project space – can be significant, reflecting broader organisational values or interpersonal dynamics.

Within the interpretive paradigm, AI is not merely a tool for optimising aesthetics but a co-creator of meaning within organisational settings. Rather than treating aesthetics as a fixed, measurable variable, AI can facilitate sensemaking by mediating personalised aesthetic experiences. For instance, AI-driven workspace personalisation tools enable employees to tailor their digital environments based on individual preferences, thereby reinforcing organisational identity through symbolic and sensory engagement. Similarly, generative AI in corporate branding or artistic interventions can influence how employees and stakeholders interpret an organisation's cultural narrative. While AI offers new avenues for engagement, its algorithmic mediation raises critical questions about authenticity, creativity, and the subjective dimensions of aesthetic experience, as it risks structuring meaning in ways that may standardise or constrain organic sensemaking processes.

3 Radical humanist paradigm

The radical humanist paradigm shares the subjectivist outlook found in the Interpretive tradition but infuses it with a critical-subjectivist epistemology. Radical humanists argue that social and organisational realities, including aesthetics, are shaped by ideologies, power relations, and constraints on human consciousness. In this view, the aesthetic dimension is not merely about beauty or functionality but also about challenging entrenched ways of seeing and freeing individuals from ideological domination.

Under a radical humanist lens, aesthetic interventions – such as theatre workshops, artistic performances, or collaborative art installations – are understood as potential catalysts for transformative change. Researchers employing this paradigm might use arts-based methods or participatory action research to reveal how certain aesthetic norms or "styles" perpetuate inequalities or suppress creative expression among employees. For example, a study of corporate dress codes might investigate how these aesthetic standards reinforce hierarchical structures and limit individual autonomy.

Moreover, radical humanists place a premium on emancipation, explicitly asking the question: how can aesthetics unmask and disrupt taken-for-granted assumptions in organisations, thereby opening new horizons for individual and collective growth? By focusing on the liberatory potential of artistic and aesthetic practices, radical humanists involve participants directly in the creation of knowledge. Rather than simply observing how workers engage with art, they might co-create an art project with employees to provoke critical reflection on organisational values and power structures.

Within the radical humanist paradigm, AI is not merely a facilitator of aesthetic experience but a potential medium for artistic emancipation and ideological critique. AI-generated art, creative algorithms, and digital storytelling tools can challenge dominant aesthetic norms and expose underlying power structures within organisations. For instance, AI-assisted participatory art projects may empower employees to visualise and critique corporate hierarchies, uncovering the aesthetic dimensions of workplace inequality. However, radical humanists remain critical of AI's embedded biases, recognising that algorithmic decision-making can reinforce dominant ideologies and limit authentic creative expression. Thus, while AI offers possibilities for democratising aesthetics, its implementation must be examined through a reflexive and participatory lens to ensure it serves as a tool for liberation rather than aesthetic standardisation.

4 Radical structuralist paradigm

On the opposite side of the objective–subjective divide from radical humanism is the radical structuralist paradigm. While it shares the radical humanists' emphasis on radical change and the critique of power, it adopts a realist ontology and critical-objectivist epistemology. Here, organisations are embedded in structural and systemic forces – economic, political, and social – that shape and constrain behaviour in objective, material ways. In this view, aesthetics is one manifestation of such broader structural forces.

Radical structuralist research on aesthetics may investigate how corporate branding, architecture, and even employee dress codes serve as instruments of power, surveillance, or control. For instance, large-scale studies could examine how specific industries systematically use aesthetic "labour" (e.g., grooming standards for flight attendants or sales associates) to ensure compliance and uphold a brand image that caters to specific market demands. Alternatively, historical or institutional analyses might examine how architectural trends in office buildings reflect broader capitalist imperatives or government policies that drive forms of urban development.

Rather than focusing on individual or small-group sensemaking, radical structuralists aim to reveal how aesthetic phenomena reflect and reproduce systemic inequalities – whether related to class, race, or gender. By foregrounding macro-level constraints, they question whether employees or even managers truly have the agency to define aesthetic standards, or if these standards are primarily dictated by market forces, corporate shareholders, or prevailing ideologies. This paradigm highlights how aesthetics can become entwined with exploitation, commodification, or the legitimisation of hierarchies, paving the way for discussions of potential structural transformations that could redistribute power and resources more equitably.

Within the radical Structuralist paradigm, AI is viewed as a mechanism of aesthetic control and commodification, reinforcing systemic power asymmetries rather than fostering genuine creative autonomy. Algorithmic decision-making in branding, workplace aesthetics, and digital labour platforms standardises aesthetic expectations, often privileging dominant cultural norms while marginalising alternative or subversive expressions. AI-driven surveillance tools, such as facial recognition systems enforcing aesthetic labour standards in service industries, exemplify how technology can entrench corporate discipline and compliance. Moreover, automated content curation in marketing and social media shapes consumer perceptions and reinforces hegemonic aesthetic ideals, consolidating corporate control over cultural production. Radical structuralists, therefore, critically interrogate AI's role in reproducing aesthetic hierarchies, questioning whether technological advancements serve organisational efficiency or merely deepen existing structures of economic and ideological domination.

## Discussion: organisational aesthetics across paradigms: integrating perspectives on AI meaning

The discourse on organisational aesthetics has brought new depth to how scholars and practitioners understand the interplay between sensory experiences, artistic expressions, and organisations' social contexts. Grounded in various philosophical assumptions, four paradigms of social science: functionalist, interpretive, radical humanist, and radical structuralist – offer distinctive ways of conceptualising and researching these aesthetic dimensions, thereby generating diverse insights into how aesthetic forms shape work processes, culture, and human potential.

From a functionalist standpoint, aesthetics is essentially a measurable, objective attribute of organisational life, influencing efficiency and performance. This perspective often seeks quantifiable outcomes by investigating how workspace design or branding strategies directly affect productivity and employee satisfaction. By contrast, the interpretative paradigm adopts a subjectivist lens, focusing on how organisational members construct and negotiate symbolic meanings around aesthetic artefacts and experiences. Qualitative methods, such as interviews and ethnographies, help capture the complexity of these shared interpretations and their role in cultural sensemaking.

The radical humanist perspective highlights how aesthetic practices can catalyse personal and collective emancipation, shedding light on underlying ideologies that shape organisational life. Through artistic interventions or critical discourse analysis, radical humanists explore how aesthetic expressions can subvert entrenched power relations and foster liberating forms of reflection. Ultimately, the radical structuralist approach examines aesthetics within the context of broader control systems, investigating how structures such as capitalism or bureaucratic hierarchies shape and commodify aesthetic expressions. Quantitative and historical-structural analyses often reveal the power dynamics determining which aesthetic forms are promoted and which remain marginalised.

These paradigms illustrate the rich and multifaceted nature of organisational aesthetics. Each offers distinct methodological pathways, from empirical testing and measurement to interpretive inquiry and critical interrogation. By juxtaposing these paradigmatic perspectives, researchers and practitioners can engage more holistically with the aesthetic dimension of organisational life, encouraging integrative approaches that account for efficiency, meaning-making, emancipatory potential, and structural critique. Through this pluralistic lens, organisational aesthetics emerge as a decorative flourish and a powerful medium for understanding and shaping the processes, identities, and values that animate contemporary workplaces.

While each paradigm offers a distinct vantage point, they can fruitfully illuminate complementary facets of organisational aesthetics. A functionalist study on the relationship between workspace aesthetics and productivity may reveal quantitative improvements; interpretive or radical approaches can deepen understanding by examining the qualitative experiences and potential power imbalances that arise from these findings. Similarly, the critical orientations of the radical humanist and radical structuralist paradigms can challenge a purely instrumental use of aesthetics, ensuring that human emancipation, structural inequality, and ethical responsibility remain at the forefront.

Moreover, researchers sometimes blend paradigms to capture the complexity of real-world scenarios. A mixed-methods study might begin with a functionalist-style quantitative survey assessing employee satisfaction with a newly introduced artistic workspace redesign, but then delve into interpretive interviews to grasp the nuanced feelings, stories, and symbolic meanings participants associate with those changes. Adding a critical dimension, the researcher could investigate whether certain voices or roles are marginalised in decisions about aesthetic interventions, revealing how power dynamics influence which aesthetic ideas prevail and which are dismissed (Szostak & Sułkowski, 2024).

Each of the four paradigms sheds light on different dimensions of aesthetics within organisational life. The functionalist paradigm reminds us that aesthetic choices can be systematically analysed to optimise performance, while the interpretive paradigm emphasises the significance of shared cultural meanings and symbolic interactions. The radical humanist perspective reveals the emancipatory potential of aesthetic practices, emphasising the challenge to dominant ideologies and the promotion of human development. In contrast, the radical structuralist lens highlights how broader societal forces and power relations inscribe themselves into aesthetic norms and organisational artefacts. By recognising and thoughtfully integrating these paradigmatic perspectives, scholars and practitioners can develop a more comprehensive and critical understanding of organisational aesthetics, ultimately contributing to more affluent research, nuanced interventions, and ethically grounded management practices.

AI's role in organisational aesthetics spans paradigms, shaping how aesthetics is perceived, implemented, and contested. While functionalist perspectives leverage AI for efficiency in branding and workspace optimisation, interpretive approaches highlight how AI-driven personalisation influences meaning-making and employee identity. Critical paradigms, such as radical humanism and radical structuralism, foreground AI's potential for aesthetic liberation or domination, questioning whether algorithmic curation fosters inclusivity or reinforces systemic biases. By integrating these perspectives, researchers can better assess how AI mediates aesthetic experiences, amplifies or suppresses creative expression, and either democratises or commodifies organisational aesthetics, ensuring a nuanced and ethically informed engagement with technology.

## Conclusion

This chapter addresses three key research questions regarding the impact of AI on organisational aesthetics from four paradigmatic perspectives. Ad RQ1 (*How does AI shape the conceptualisation of organisational aesthetics within each of the four paradigms?*): AI shapes the conceptualisation of organisational aesthetics in distinct ways: within the functionalist paradigm, it serves as a tool for optimisation, enhancing workspace design and branding efficiency; in the interpretive paradigm, it acts as a co-creator of meaning, influencing organisational narratives and visual experiences; from a radical humanist perspective, it offers potential for emancipatory artistic expression while also raising concerns regarding ideological control; and within the radical structuralist paradigm, it functions as a mechanism of aesthetic standardisation and power reinforcement.

Ad RQ2 (*What are AI-mediated aesthetics' managerial and ethical implications in organisational settings?*): The organisational consequences of AI-mediated aesthetics are both promising and problematic. While AI facilitates efficiency in aesthetic management by automating and personalising design processes, it also raises ethical concerns, including the loss of authenticity, the marginalisation of diverse aesthetic expressions, and the mechanisation of artistic creativity. Furthermore, it plays a role in organisational control by standardising visual experience and commodifying aesthetic labour.

Ad RQ3 (*To what extent does AI alter the depth of organisational aesthetics, shaping the layers of sensory, symbolic, and existential meaning within the workplace?*): AI also alters the depth of organisational aesthetics at sensory, symbolic, and existential levels. At the sensory level, it enables hyper-personalisation but risks excessive standardisation. At the symbolic level, it reshapes organisational identity and aesthetic narratives, yet questions of authenticity arise regarding algorithmically curated aesthetics. At the existential level, AI challenges traditional notions of creativity, shifting the role of human intuition and artistic agency. While AI presents new opportunities for managing organisational aesthetics, its broader implications necessitate a critical and reflexive engagement with the evolving relationship between technology and aesthetic experience.

While this study offers a multi-paradigmatic analysis of AI's role in organisational aesthetics, it has *limitations*. The research primarily relies on theoretical frameworks and reflective insights, which, while valuable, may benefit from further empirical validation. Additionally, the rapidly evolving nature of AI means its long-term impact on aesthetics remains uncertain, necessitating continuous reassessment. Another limitation of this study is its focus on conceptual and theoretical perspectives, which may not fully capture organisations' practical challenges when implementing AI-driven aesthetics in real-world settings.

*Future research* should expand empirical investigations into AI-driven aesthetics through longitudinal studies that track its evolving impact on organisational identity, employee experience, and power dynamics. Comparative analyses across industries and cultural contexts would provide deeper insights into how local values and organisational traditions shape AI-mediated aesthetics. Additionally, interdisciplinary approaches integrating insights from design, psychology, and technology studies could further refine our understanding of how AI reshapes aesthetic experience and decision-making in organisational life. Further inquiry could explore the ethical and philosophical dimensions of AI-driven aesthetics, particularly about authenticity, creativity, and agency in organisational contexts. Examining how AI-generated aesthetics influences perceptions of originality and human authorship in design, branding, and workplace environments would provide a critical perspective on the tensions between automation and human creativity. Finally, critical perspectives on AI and aesthetic commodification deserve greater attention. AI's role in shaping market-driven aesthetic preferences, branding strategies, and corporate identities could be explored through a critical lens, focusing on the potential risks of homogenisation and algorithmic bias in aesthetic decision-making. Future research could offer insights into the evolving relationship between technology, aesthetics, and organisational power structures by examining the broader socio-economic implications of AI-driven aesthetics.

## References

Araújo, B. C. de, & Davel, E. P. B. (2021). Gestão de organizações artísticas: Panorama e perspectiva para a produção acadêmica. *Revista de Gestão e Estudos Contemporâneos*, 10(3), 8–39. https://doi.org/10.47456/REGEC.2317-5087.2021.10.3.34532.8-39

Baldessarelli, G., Jones, C., Stigliani, I., Bruni, E., Krabbe, A. D., McBride, M., Jancsary, D. C., Meyer, R. E., & Stephens, J. P. (2022). Not just for show: How aesthetics underpins work within and around organizations. *Academy of Management Proceedings*, 2022(1), Article 13363. https://doi.org/10.5465/AMBPP.2022.13363symposium

Barley, S. R. (1980). Sociological paradigms and organisational analysis. *Sloan Management Review*, 21(4), 92–95.

Burrell, G., & Morgan, G. (1979). Introduction. In G. Burrell, & G. Morgan (Eds.), *Sociological paradigms and organisational analysis: Elements of the sociology of corporate life* (pp. 1–9). Heinemann.

Deetz, S. (1996). Describing differences in approaches to organization science: Rethinking Burrell and Morgan and their legacy. *Organization Science,* 7(2), 191–207. https://doi.org/10.1287/orsc.7.2.191

Fryzel, B., & Marcinkowski, A. (2024). *Organisational aesthetics*. Routledge https://doi.org/10.4324/9781003497103

Gioia, D. A., & Pitre, E. (1990). Multiparadigm perspectives on theory building. *Academy of Management Review,* 15(4), 584–602. https://doi.org/10.5465/amr.1990.4310758

Hassard, J. (1991). Multiple paradigms and organizational analysis: A case study. *Organization Studies,* 12(2), 275–299. https://doi.org/10.1177/017084069101200206

Kostera, M. (1996). *Postmodernizm*. PWE.

Lütticken, S. (2023). Organizational aesthetics: On certain practices and genealogics. *October*, 183(Winter), 17–49. https://doi.org/10.1162/octo_a_00475

Mack, K. (2023). Exploring the aesthetics of organisational life in management education. *Academy of Management Proceedings*, 2023(1), 12668. https://doi.org/10.5465/amproc.2023.12668abstract

Sastre, R., & Aránega, A. Y. (2023). A paradigm change: Aesthetics in the management of organisations. *Journal of Business Research*, 157, 113574. https://doi.org/10.1016/j.jbusres.2022.113574

Schultz, M., & Hatch, M. J. (1996). Living with multiple paradigms: The case of paradigm interplay in organizational culture studies. *Academy of Management Review,* 21(2), 529–557. https://doi.org/10.5465/amr.1996.9605060221

Sułkowski, Ł. (2009). Interpretative approach in management sciences. *Argumenta Oeconomica,* 2(23), 127–149

Szostak, M. (2023). *Sztuka zarządzania – zarządzanie sztuką*. Wydawnictwo Społecznej Akademii Nauk.

Szostak, M., & Sułkowski, Ł. (2020). Manager as an artist: Creative endeavour in crossing the borders of art and organisational discourse. *Creativity Studies*, 13(2), 351–368. https://doi.org/10.3846/cs.2020.11373

Szostak, M., & Sułkowski, Ł. (2021). Identity crisis of artists during the Covid-19 pandemic and shift towards entrepreneurship. *Entrepreneurial Business and Economics Review (EBER),* 9(3), 87–102

Szostak, M., & Sułkowski, Ł. (2024). Creativity management within the aesthetical situation regarding the in-real or digital form of participation in arts: Art receivers' perspective. *Creativity Studies,* 17(1), 41–58

Yusupova, Q. (2022). Aesthetics, management, and the organization of space. In H. H. Antonakis, A. A. Day, & L. T. Epitropaki (Eds.), *Handbook of philosophy of management* (pp. 389–412). Springer. https://doi.org/10.1007/978-3-030-76606-1_20

# Part II

# Leadership and decision-making aesthetics in the AI era

# 6 AI-augmented leadership

## Redefining leaders' style and competencies

*Małgorzata Baran*

### Introduction

Integrating AI into organisational leadership represents a transformative shift in management practices, fundamentally altering how leaders operate and make decisions in contemporary organisations. This technological revolution is reshaping traditional leadership paradigms by enhancing decision-making capabilities, introducing novel approaches to team management, and altering organisational dynamics (Madanchian et al., 2024). AI-augmented leadership enables more precise and expeditious decision-making through sophisticated data analysis and predictive modelling while supporting leaders in addressing organisational challenges and optimising efficiency across various industrial sectors. Research indicates that AI integration significantly enhances several critical elements of leadership practice. Studies by Mitra Madanchian et al. (2024) and Leomar M. Pago (2024) show how AI systems bolster communication processes, streamline collaboration, and transform talent management strategies, even offering personalised leadership development solutions. Moreover, AI technology has demonstrated efficacy in empowering transformational leadership styles by automating routine tasks, thus allowing employees to engage more deeply in complex and creative endeavours. This shift promotes an organisational culture that fosters innovation (Estherita & Shanmugam, 2024).

The evolving relationship between AI and leadership has also prompted substantial changes in organisational structures and employee roles. Traditional leadership models increasingly face challenges as AI-driven analytics and decision-support systems refine strategic planning and mitigate cognitive biases in management processes (Syam & Sharma, 2018). This paradigm shift requires leaders to develop new competencies – such as data literacy, ethical reasoning, and the ability to interpret algorithmic outputs – to leverage AI responsibly and effectively (Raisch & Krakowski, 2021). Additionally, the capacity of AI systems to deliver real-time insights into team dynamics, employee well-being, and productivity metrics allows for leadership that is more attuned to individual and collective needs (Davenport & Kirby, 2016).

DOI: 10.4324/9781003654377-9

Preliminary findings suggest a nuanced impact of AI integration on leadership effectiveness. Although AI holds remarkable promise for enhancing leaders' abilities to build trust, promote professional growth, and strengthen communication channels, it also creates challenges that demand thoughtful management. Implementing AI in leadership practice requires a balanced approach, employing data-driven insights, empathetic engagement, and responsive communication. This equilibrium helps leaders adapt their styles to changing contexts and cultivate greater team resilience. Building on these considerations, the present study examines how AI-driven tools redefine leadership roles and competencies in contemporary organisations, particularly those designed for employee engagement, development, and communication. AI platforms that gauge team sentiment, recommend personalised growth opportunities, and facilitate leader-employee communication via virtual assistants are of special interest. This research investigates how these technologies affect a range of leadership styles – transformational, authentic, servant, transactional, aesthetic, charismatic, visionary, and distributed – while exploring the competencies required of leaders who guide teams in technology-centric settings.

This study's *research problem* revolves around understanding how AI integration transforms traditional leadership paradigms and redefines leadership competencies in modern organisations. A particular focus is placed on how different leadership styles evolve, from transformational to adaptive, in response to AI technologies, while also investigating the balance between technological enhancement and human-centric leadership qualities. The core *research questions* guiding this study are: (RQ1) Which leadership styles are most impacted by AI integration? (RQ2) What new competencies and roles are emerging for leaders in AI-driven contexts?

The *research method* employed in this study is a systematic literature review. According to the methodology outlined by Czakon (2020), the review process was conducted in three stages. In the first stage, publications for analysis were collected from the EBSCO database. Scientific publications (articles, book chapters) containing the phrases ["leadership" or "leader" and "AI-augmented" or "AI-enhanced"] and ["artificial intelligence" or "AI"] were searched. The eligibility criteria stipulated that only studies published within the last ten years in peer-reviewed full-length articles written in English were selected for inclusion. This initial search resulted in over 113 publications. In the second stage, additional selection criteria were applied to focus on publications related to leadership and leadership styles. These criteria narrowed the selection, enabling a more in-depth and substantive analysis in the third stage of the literature review. The final collection of 45 publications was then used for detailed examination. This systematic review explores existing literature on AI-enhanced leadership, focusing on two key areas: (1) how AI augments or reshapes traditional leadership styles and (2) the competencies necessary for effective AI-driven leadership. The review aims to contribute to the emerging concept of hybrid leadership capability, which blends traditional leadership virtues with AI-driven innovation.

## Literature review: conceptual foundations, leadership styles, and competency shifts in the age of AI

The literature review is structured into three thematic sections, providing a comprehensive foundation for understanding AI-enhanced leadership. The first section introduces the conceptual evolution of AI in leadership contexts, tracing how AI has gradually reshaped core practices and roles. The second section examines the transformation of traditional leadership styles under the influence of AI, with a particular focus on the emergence of hybrid and technologically supported leadership models. The third and final section explores the new leadership competencies required in AI-driven environments, including technical skills and human-centric capacities, such as ethical reasoning and emotional intelligence. These sections establish a conceptual and practical framework for analysing how AI redefines leadership in contemporary organisations.

### *The idea of AI-enhanced leadership*

This section delves into the evolution and core concepts of AI-enhanced leadership, exploring how the integration of AI has reshaped leadership practices over time. It examines the key elements that define AI-augmented leadership, with particular attention to its impact on decision-making, employee interaction, and leadership competencies in the digital age.

#### *The evolution and core concepts of AI-enhanced leadership*

Integrating AI into organisational leadership practices represents one of the most significant transformations in modern management history. AI has been highly transformational across sectors for several years, offering unprecedented opportunities to enhance human capacity and redefine legacy practices. The rapid pace at which AI is transforming and reshaping society is remarkable, impacting fields as diverse as healthcare, business, lifestyle, finance, transportation, and education, and revolutionising how we live, work, and interact with the world (Heimans & Timms, 2024; Pago, 2024).

Additionally, recent studies emphasise that AI's influence is not limited to automating tasks or generating predictive insights; it also affects the aesthetic dimension of human-AI interaction, shaping how employees perceive the authenticity and empathy of leaders who use AI-driven communication tools (Hansen et al., 2007; Rosenblat, 2018). For example, personalised messaging systems – often fed by sentiment analysis – have the potential to strengthen empathy by helping leaders quickly detect employee concerns. Nevertheless, they also raise questions about whether the leader's expressions of understanding are truly genuine or algorithmically guided (Milton & Al-Busaidi, 2023).

The concept of AI-enhanced leadership gained prominence as AI technologies evolved rapidly during the late 20th and early 21st centuries. Initially, AI development focused on specific areas, such as basic machine learning and expert systems, primarily utilised in scientific and engineering contexts. Over time, more sophisticated AI tools – including natural language processing, predictive analytics, and robotics – demonstrated potential for direct application in organisational leadership (Elamin, 2024). Accordingly, organisations began integrating AI to improve decision-making processes, boost operational efficiency, and foster innovation. As various industries underwent digital transformation, leaders recognised the need to blend technical expertise with interpersonal skills.

A growing body of literature suggests that AI's role in leadership cannot be fully understood without examining how algorithmic personalisation reshapes interpersonal dynamics. On the one hand, data-driven insights facilitate tailor-made communication strategies, potentially reinforcing empathetic leadership styles (Van Quaquebeke & Gerpott, 2023). On the other hand, the reliance on AI recommendations risks a phenomenon of "AI-mediated empathy", wherein the leader's compassionate response is partly *outsourced* to an algorithm, potentially undermining perceptions of authenticity among team members (Dourish, 2016; Moore & Joyce, 2020).

AI-enabled tools like customer relationship management systems, sentiment analysis platforms, and real-time data dashboards offered new approaches to analysing trends, predicting outcomes, and adapting strategies swiftly. A pivotal catalyst for adopting AI in leadership was the global COVID-19 pandemic, which presented organisations with unprecedented challenges related to remote team management, productivity, and pervasive uncertainty. Many leaders turned to AI solutions during this period, demonstrating the importance of leadership flexibility, resilience, and ethical AI deployment. These factors, in turn, solidified AI-enhanced leadership as an integral aspect of modern business strategies. As Dirani et al. (2020) note, the pandemic created opportunities and obstacles for organisations striving to integrate AI into their leadership frameworks.

Sharma et al. (2020) highlight that AI is rapidly reshaping the landscape of organisational leadership by automating tasks, supporting data-driven decision-making, and personalising employee experiences. This transformation permits leaders to refocus on strategic thinking and innovation; however, it also demands new competencies – such as data analysis and AI ethics – to ensure responsible AI implementation. As Pago (2024) further emphasises, successful AI integration hinges on maintaining a careful balance between technological adoption and a human-centric approach that fosters trust and collaboration in an evolving work environment.

A growing body of literature underscores AI's capacity not to replace but to augment and empower leaders across diverse sectors (Hao et al., 2020). This perspective stresses AI's potential to elevate human capabilities in leadership roles instead of supplanting them. Because AI excels at processing and analysing massive datasets, it can reveal patterns and trends that might escape human detection, providing leaders with deeper insights into market trends, customer behaviours, and organisational performance. According to Milton and Al Busaidi (2023), this proactive stance on strategic planning – guided by AI-driven insights – helps organisations navigate fast-changing business climates with agility and resilience.

*Comparing traditional and AI-enhanced leadership*

Contrasting traditional and AI-enhanced leadership offers insight into how each approach handles decision-making and relationship management. Conventional models rely on intuition, experience, and historical knowledge, which can be effective in stable settings but may fall short in rapidly evolving industries or complex data sets. In contrast, AI-enhanced leadership leverages advanced analytics and predictive models to facilitate quicker, more informed decisions (Gleeson, 2024). While traditional methods prioritise human relationships and emotional intelligence, AI augments these with technology-driven insights into team dynamics and sentiment. However, scholars warn that an over-reliance on AI in relationship management may erode personal engagement and connectedness (Sposato, 2024).

The interplay between AI and relational aspects of leadership has drawn increasing attention. Leaders who use AI to personalise communication may appear responsive – particularly in servant or transformational leadership – yet employees might question whether this responsiveness stems from genuine human insight or algorithmically optimised scripts (Dietvorst et al., 2015). This tension can lead to "algorithm aversion", where employees prefer human-authored feedback and empathic gestures, as automated messages may seem impersonal (Gagliardi, 2006; Dourish, 2016).

The debate on how AI can perform leadership functions typically reserved for humans is captured by Jarrahi et al. (2023), with Parent-Rocheleau and Parker (2021) emphasising the impact of algorithmic management on leadership roles. The rise of human-AI collaboration models also marks significant development, as Van Quaquebeke and Gerpott (2023) introduce "predictive leadership", wherein analytics enable leaders to foresee opportunities and challenges, reshaping strategic planning. Aesthetic leadership scholars highlight that emotional resonance often hinges on subtle cues, such as facial expressions or tone of voice (Hansen et al., 2007). While AI can streamline communication, it risks reducing these spontaneous cues to algorithmic processes that may feel standardised (Strati, 1999). The aesthetic integrity of leadership can be compromised when interpersonal engagement becomes partially delegated to AI systems (Gahlot & Bathla, 2021).

AI-enhanced leadership also demonstrates greater adaptability in technology-driven contexts. Traditional leaders often struggle to respond quickly to technological changes, while AI leaders use tools to recognise problems and opportunities earlier, which is crucial in sectors where rapid innovation offers a competitive edge. However, as AI becomes more integrated into leadership routines, followers may feel a sense of dehumanisation or reduced contact with leaders (Rosenblat, 2018). Some studies show that employees may perceive leaders as overseers of metrics rather than empathetic figures (Moore & Joyce, 2020). This highlights the need to balance AI benefits – such as real-time sentiment analysis – with maintaining humanistic leadership (Van Quaquebeke & Gerpott, 2023).

AI-enhanced leadership extends beyond routine tasks, incorporating ethical and sustainability objectives into decision-making. AI systems provide data that can help conserve energy, minimise waste, and enhance environmental sustainability, aiding organisations in tackling complex challenges while maintaining robust performance in unpredictable markets. Glikson and Woolley (2020) demonstrate how AI supports routine management and strategic decisions, underscoring the need to balance technological potential and human discernment, especially regarding emotional intelligence and interpersonal relationships. As organisations shift towards AI-driven leadership, the literature points to a growing demand for frameworks that integrate AI without sacrificing human qualities. Successful AI-enhanced leadership will depend on balancing technological advances with the essential human aspects of leadership. Ongoing research remains vital for refining best practices, identifying emerging trends, and mitigating risks in AI implementation. By prioritising technical proficiency and human values, organisations can ensure that leadership in the digital era remains innovative, effective, ethical, and sustainable.

### ***Leadership styles through AI***

The second subsection discusses how the development of AI impacts the evolution of traditional leadership styles. Specifically, it examines how AI transforms existing management and team leadership approaches, leading to hybrid models combining human capabilities with advanced technologies. The section then presents changes in various leadership styles, from autocratic to situational, focusing on how AI supports leaders in decision-making, data analysis, and team communication.

#### *The impact of AI development on the evolution of traditional leadership styles*

Leadership styles have evolved significantly in response to technological advancements. Each style reflects unique approaches to organisational management and team guidance, with varying degrees of adaptability to AI integration. Historically, leadership manifested in various styles, reflecting unique approaches to organisational management and team guidance. Over the past few years, AI has been exceptionally transformational and is emerging across diverse sectors. This rapid development offers unprecedented opportunities to enhance human capacity and redefine legacy practices – ultimately reshaping how we live, work, and interact with the world (Heimans & Timms, 2024; Pago, 2024). The integration of AI has transformed established leadership styles, creating hybrid models that combine human capabilities with technological advancements. In particular, leaders can leverage AI-driven data analysis, predictive modelling, sentiment analysis, and automated decision-support mechanisms to complement their strategic thinking. Below is an overview of how each leadership style has evolved under the influence of AI.

Traditionally characterised by centralised decision-making, autocratic leadership has evolved through AI integration to become more evidence-based. While autocratic leaders maintain a clear hierarchy and swift decision-making, AI provides comprehensive data analysis and objective insights. This enhancement helps reduce cognitive bias and lends greater legitimacy to top-down decisions. The collaborative decision-making core of democratic leadership benefits from AI-driven consensus-building tools. These systems aggregate diverse viewpoints, synthesising information from multiple sources and stakeholders. By facilitating more inclusive and data-informed discussions, AI helps maintain the participatory ethos of democratic leadership while improving the quality of collective decisions. Emphasising delegation and autonomy, laissez-faire leadership has been strengthened by AI support systems that offer remote collaboration and data-based recommendations. This approach allows leaders to remain hands-off yet ensure that team members have access to AI-powered guidance and real-time analytics, thus preserving independence without neglecting accountability.

*Advanced leadership styles with AI integration*

In the AI era, leadership styles have evolved with the integration of AI tools. Transformational leadership, combining visionary approaches with data-driven insights, is significantly enhanced by AI. By automating routine tasks and offering real-time feedback, AI fosters a culture of innovation, allowing leaders to inspire teams to pursue ambitious goals backed by predictive analysis of market trends. Studies show that when transformational leaders effectively use AI tools, they are better able to drive change, cultivate innovation, and achieve superior organisational outcomes (Pago, 2024).

Transactional leadership has also adapted to AI, using performance tracking and automated rewards. Objective metrics from AI systems maintain fairness and consistency, reinforcing the structure inherent in this style. In servant leadership, focused on supporting team growth, AI enables personalised development plans through advanced analytics and sentiment analysis, improving job satisfaction and engagement (Madanchian et al., 2024). Aesthetic leadership, which values emotional intelligence and sensory knowledge, benefits from AI tools like sentiment analysis, enhancing leaders' innate capacity for empathy and connection. Charismatic leadership, built on personal influence and emotional connection, is amplified by AI's ability to tailor motivational messages and interventions, although maintaining authentic engagement is still critical. Situational leadership, which emphasises adaptability, gains from AI's real-time data analysis. Leaders can track evolving circumstances and adjust their approach based on performance metrics, market shifts, or team dynamics. Similarly, adaptive leadership thrives with AI integration because it focuses on flexibility and continuous learning. AI's predictive analytics help leaders address challenges early, enabling timely interventions (Estherita & Shanmugam, 2024).

AI-driven decision-making aligns with transformational leadership, using data and predictive tools to guide organisations through change (Estherita & Shanmugam, 2024). In servant leadership, AI provides insights for tailored employee support (Daniels, 2023; Madanchian et al., 2024). Adaptive leaders benefit from AI through feedback loops and performance dashboards, enabling quick responses to disruptions (McKinsey Digital, 2020). By merging AI with these leadership frameworks, leaders can navigate change while staying focused on long-term goals.

### *Leadership impact in AI-enhanced organisations*

The organisational impact of AI-driven leadership styles reaches beyond individual leadership approaches. Personalised assessment, real-time feedback, and predictive talent management algorithms streamline processes like succession planning and high-potential employee identification. Enhanced communication and collaboration tools transcend linguistic and cultural barriers, enabling more effective global team management. Combining AI capabilities with various leadership styles has demonstrated significant potential for enhancing organisational effectiveness and team development. By providing data-driven insights, real-time analysis, and predictive functionalities, AI enables leaders to make more informed decisions while prioritising strategic thinking and innovation (Madanchian et al., 2023). As organisations face increasingly complex challenges, the successful adoption of AI-enhanced leadership hinges on leaders' abilities to preserve fundamental human qualities – empathy, creativity, and ethical decision-making – while harnessing technological advantages. Table 6.1 summarises the most important leadership styles in the context of AI, including their traditional characteristics, methods of AI-enabled enhancement, key benefits, and practical applications.

Adaptive leadership similarly profits from AI's real-time feedback and predictive analytics. As McKinsey reports, leaders who adopt an adaptive mindset alongside AI tools enhance organisational resilience and maintain focus amid volatility. Research by Mitra Madanchian et al. (2024) and Estherita and Shanmugam (2024) underscores that AI-enabled adaptive leaders excel at identifying and responding to early signals of organisational or market challenges, thus ensuring timely intervention. The transformation of leadership through AI is

*Table 6.1* Differences between leadership styles in the context of AI

| *Leadership style* | *Traditional characteristics* | *AI enhancement* | *Key benefits* | *Practical applications* |
|---|---|---|---|---|
| Aesthetic leadership | Sensory knowledge; Emotional intelligence; Tacit understanding; Embodied knowledge | AI-enhanced sensory analytics; Emotional pattern recognition; Advanced feedback systems | Deeper human connections; Enhanced intuitive decision-making; Improved emotional understanding | Experience design tools; Sentiment analysis platforms; Advanced communication systems |
| Autocratic leadership | Centralised decision-making; Clear hierarchy; Swift implementation | Data-driven analysis support; Objective decision-making tools; Predictive modelling | More informed decisions; Reduced bias in decision-making; Enhanced strategic planning | Resource allocation optimisation; Risk assessment automation; Performance monitoring systems |
| Democratic leadership | Collaborative decision-making; Team involvement; Inclusive approach | AI-driven consensus building; Data aggregation tools; Stakeholder feedback analysis | Enhanced group decision quality; Better stakeholder engagement; More efficient collaboration | Digital voting systems; Opinion analysis tools; Collaborative planning platforms |
| Laissez-faire leadership | High team autonomy; Minimal direct supervision; Self-directed teams | AI-powered support systems; Remote collaboration tools; Automated monitoring | Improved team independence; Better resource utilisation; Maintained oversight | Self-service analytics; AI-driven project management; Automated progress tracking |
| Transformational leadership | Vision-driven approach; Innovation focus; Change management | Real-time feedback systems; Innovation support tools; Pattern recognition | Enhanced change implementation; Better innovation management; Improved team development | Predictive analytics; Innovation platforms; Change impact assessment |
| Transactional leadership | Performance-based rewards; Clear expectations; Structured approach | Advanced performance tracking; Automated reward systems; Objective metrics analysis | Fair performance assessment; Transparent rewards; Consistent evaluation | Performance dashboards; Automated compensation systems; KPI tracking tools |

(*Continued*)

*Table 6.1* (Continued)

| *Leadership style* | *Traditional characteristics* | *AI enhancement* | *Key benefits* | *Practical applications* |
|---|---|---|---|---|
| Servant leadership | Focus on team growth; Employee well-being; Support-oriented | Personalised development plans; Well-being monitoring; Individual need analysis | Better team development; Enhanced support systems; Improved employee satisfaction | Learning management systems; Well-being analytics; Career development tools |
| Charismatic leadership | Personal influence; Emotional connection; Inspirational approach | Enhanced communication; Emotion analysis; Impact measurement | Broader reach; More effective inspiration; Better engagement | Communication platforms; Sentiment analysis; Engagement tracking |
| Situational leadership | Adaptive approach; Context-sensitive; Flexible style | Real-time situation analysis; Context-aware recommendations; Adaptive strategy tools | More precise adaptations; Better context understanding; Improved flexibility | Contextual analytics; Decision support systems; Scenario planning tools |

*Sources:* Own elaboration based on Hansen et al., 2007; Katsiroumpa et al., 2024; Abdaljaleel et al., 2024; Sengupta, 2023; Madanchian et al., 2024; Pago, 2024.

reshaping core practices, ranging from daily decision-making and team management to ethical oversight and long-term strategic vision. While AI augments leaders' capabilities by processing complex datasets, identifying emerging trends, and automating routine tasks, it cannot replace the fundamental human elements crucial to effective leadership: empathy, ethical judgment, creativity, and interpersonal connection. Leaders equipped with advanced AI tools and strong relational skills will likely define the future of organisational management, striking a critical balance between technological efficiency and the human-centred values essential for sustainable success. As AI evolves, leaders will increasingly need to combine traditional management principles with modern data analysis methods and change management strategies. This will enable the creation of flexible, innovative, and human-centred organisations where technology supports rather than displaces the essential human aspects of leadership.

The preceding analysis of leadership styles reveals how AI technologies are reshaping traditional approaches to organisational management. As these styles evolve and adapt to technological integration, they necessitate a corresponding evolution in leadership competencies. The following section examines these essential capabilities that leaders must develop to effectively implement AI-enhanced leadership while maintaining human-centric values and ethical oversight. This transition from examining leadership styles to exploring competencies is crucial, as the successful implementation of AI-enhanced leadership requires specific skills and capabilities. While different leadership styles may leverage AI tools uniquely, all leaders in the AI era must develop a common foundation of core competencies to guide their organisations through digital transformation effectively.

### *Ethical and aesthetic challenges in AI-augmented leadership*

One of the most widely discussed issues in the literature is the possibility of amplifying biases through AI systems, particularly in recruitment, employee evaluation, or task allocation (Eubanks, 2018; O'Neil, 2016). Machine learning models can inherit existing patterns of discrimination and stereotypes (O'Neil, 2016), resulting in "algorithmic unfairness" (Jobin et al., 2019) if there is insufficient oversight. From an ethical management perspective, it is essential to monitor whether AI-generated recommendations, such as those related to promotions, align with organisational values, especially the principle of equal treatment (Parent-Rocheleau & Parker, 2021).

Another challenge involves the "black box" problem in advanced AI models (Danks & London, 2017), where even designers cannot fully explain why the system "learned" a particular pattern. This raises accountability issues for leaders: Who is responsible if an applicant is rejected based on an AI-driven assessment, especially if ethical principles are violated (Bryson & Theodorou, 2019)? Regular auditing and validation mechanisms are necessary to ensure accountability and prevent harm (Ananny & Crawford, 2018).

A significant issue is the rise of "algorithmic management", where systems increasingly assess employee performance, suggest rewards or sanctions, and predict turnover (Kellogg et al., 2020). This can shift the balance of power, potentially reducing the leader's direct influence and altering traditional participatory practices. Leaders must critically evaluate how AI models align with ethical standards (Milton & Al-Busaidi, 2023). The widespread collection of employee data (e.g., emails, working hours, IT activity) risks privacy violations and potential misuse (Zuboff, 2019). Surveillance-based systems may foster a "culture of constant monitoring" (Moore & Joyce, 2020), making it crucial for leaders to set precise data collection and usage boundaries, ensuring compliance with legal frameworks like the GDPR.

AI's quantitative nature contrasts with traditional leadership aesthetics, emphasising emotions, intuition, and human empathy (Hansen et al., 2007). When decision-making relies heavily on AI, it may create a disconnect between rationality and the need for emotional engagement, which is central to leadership (Strati, 1999). "Algorithm aversion" describes the preference for human judgment over AI, even when AI is more accurate (Dietvorst et al., 2015), which can be interpreted as a need for relational human contact (Gagliardi, 2006). Leaders may face challenges in maintaining the aesthetic quality of leadership when decisions based on AI are perceived as lacking emotional context (Dourish, 2016). To preserve the aesthetic dimension of leadership, AI-supported decisions should be integrated into a human-centred narrative that aligns with the team's mission and values (Stewart et al., 2020). Emphasising qualitative factors alongside analytical data can make decision-making more authentic and relatable (Barry & Meisiek, 2010). While AI aims for a single optimal solution (Burrell, 2016), leaders who embrace aesthetic leadership might treat data as a starting point, allowing room for intuition, experience, and subjective judgment, thus maintaining creativity and human connection in decision-making (Sutherland & Jelinek, 2015).

### *Leadership competencies in the AI era*

This section explores the evolving leadership competencies required in an era shaped by AI. First, we examine the core competencies that leaders must develop to integrate AI into decision-making and organisational strategy effectively. Then, we discuss the importance of hybrid leadership, where human judgment and AI insights work in tandem to foster innovation and maintain ethical standards.

#### *Core competencies of the leader*

Technological breakthroughs involving AI, the Internet of Things (IoT), and automation drive corporate process shifts, compelling leaders to move from traditional command-and-control paradigms towards more collaborative, flexible, and human-centric approaches (Heimans & Timms, 2024). Unlike past eras, where machinery mostly replaced physical labour, AI now enhances human decision-making by processing vast data sets and uncovering patterns humans might miss (Frick et al., 2021). This evolution has led to AI-augmented leadership: a model in which technology and human judgment coexist, with AI supplying actionable insights while leaders maintain ultimate responsibility for strategic oversight and ethical decision-making. Indeed, as AI systems take on routine or administrative tasks, leadership roles transform accordingly – requiring attention to higher-level responsibilities such as innovation, cultural alignment, and long-term planning (Parent-Rocheleau & Parker, 2021; Wright, 2024). These developments reframe leadership not as a contest between humans and machines but rather as a partnership that leverages the strengths of both (Pago, 2024). AI allows organisations to predict market shifts, appraise competitive threats, and make strategy decisions grounded in empirical evidence (Milton & Al-Busaidi, 2023). However, while AI may free leaders from some operational duties, it raises new challenges regarding data privacy, algorithmic bias, and moral accountability. Leaders must ensure that using AI reflects organisational values and ethical standards, aligning advanced technology with the well-being of employees and stakeholders (Jobin et al., 2019).

Leaders today require AI literacy – a foundational grasp of machine learning, predictive tools, and data analytics – to harness technology's potential effectively (Brynjolfsson & McAfee, 2014). While they need not be technical experts, a basic command of AI's capabilities and limitations enables more informed decisions about its deployment in alignment with strategic objectives (Stewart et al., 2020). Strategic vision ensures that AI adoption goes beyond short-term efficiency gains to reinforce the organisation's broader mission (Devoteam, 2024). Leaders who combine data-driven insights with a clear direction excel in fast-changing markets, anticipating trends and adapting more swiftly than competitors (Walther, 2024). As AI transforms work structures, emotional intelligence and communication skills retain their importance (Northouse, 2019). Technology can enhance communication channels – optimising workflow, automating routine activities, and connecting dispersed teams – but empathy and interpersonal understanding remain central to building trust and fostering a shared sense of purpose (Milton & Al-Busaidi, 2023). This alignment of people and technology is also evident in the emergence of AI tools that personalise leadership development, adjusting content and pace to match an individual's learning style (Stewart et al., 2020).

A critical, evolving challenge for leaders lies in ethical accountability. As AI becomes more sophisticated, so do the implications of data usage, privacy, and fairness. Leaders must proactively mitigate algorithmic biases, ensure data protection, and maintain transparency in AI-driven decisions, especially where automation intersects with sensitive societal issues (Jobin et al., 2019). Safeguarding ethical standards and establishing clear governance protocols engender trust among team members, customers, and the broader community.

Practical applications of these competencies are manifest in real-world cases. Netflix, for example, harnesses AI to analyse vast user data and deliver personalised content suggestions, resulting in higher engagement and satisfaction (Davenport & Kirby, 2016). By combining data-driven insights with a human-focused vision, Netflix continually refines its user experience and content strategy, demonstrating the potential synergy between AI-driven analytics and strategic leadership. In project environments, AI-based tools can serve as automated "assistants", producing progress reports or forecasts and freeing leaders to focus on high-level decisions (Wright, 2024). Such capabilities illustrate how leaders can efficiently manage processes and empower teams, provided they retain a critical perspective on AI outputs and remain vigilant against algorithmic errors or bias.

Change management also becomes an integral leadership function in AI-driven settings. Successful leaders anticipate resistance to new systems, communicate benefits transparently, and provide training that allows teams to adapt. They encourage a culture of continuous learning, foster innovation, and create environments in which teams comfortably integrate AI solutions into daily workflows. By acting as change agents, leaders ensure that AI is welcomed not as a threat but as a tool for growth and improvement (Stewart et al., 2020).

*Towards a hybrid leadership capability*

The emergence of AI-augmented leadership signifies not merely a technological leap but a profound redefinition of how leaders guide teams, cultivate innovation, and shape organisational culture. As discussed throughout this chapter, integrating human qualities – such as empathy, ethical discernment, and creative thinking – with AI-driven insights allows leaders to meet the complex demands of today's business environment (Pago, 2024). However, the key challenge lies in forging a *hybrid leadership capability* that preserves the irreplaceable human dimension while maximising the strategic advantages of AI.

A hybrid leadership model underscores the idea that data analytics, machine learning, and other AI tools should augment human judgment rather than override it. Leaders are responsible for aligning AI outputs with organisational vision, ensuring automated recommendations reflect ethical standards and cultural values (Jobin et al., 2019). By acting as moderators between technology and teams, they reconcile data-driven efficiencies with decision-making's moral and interpersonal aspects. In this capacity, leaders become strategic architects – able to interpret predictive analytics or algorithmic evaluations – and empathetic mentors who inspire engagement and trust.

At the same time, hybrid leadership recognises the broad spectrum of leadership styles – from transformational to servant and beyond – that can benefit from AI support. For instance, *transformational* leaders can leverage advanced analytics to identify untapped opportunities, while *servant* leaders may employ sentiment analysis to tailor individualised support and well-being initiatives (Madanchian et al., 2024). This fluid approach to leadership styles, enhanced by real-time data, empowers organisations to remain agile amid disruptions – capitalising on market signals without relinquishing the human touch that fosters collective motivation and belonging.

Equally crucial is the continuous evolution of leadership competencies, extending to AI literacy, strategic risk management, and heightened change agility. A hybrid leader does not simply adopt technology but learns to interpret, critique, and adapt its outputs within a broader ethical and organisational framework (Devoteam, 2024). This stance includes proactively shaping digital transformation, establishing governance protocols, and nurturing a transparent, learning-oriented culture where team members feel supported by AI tools and reassured that human oversight is firmly in place. Looking ahead, hybrid leadership serves as both the present and future of effective organisational management in an AI-driven age. As algorithms increasingly predict trends or automate routine tasks, leaders focusing on strategic vision, organisational values, and human well-being can propel their organisations forward (Brynjolfsson & McAfee, 2014; Stewart et al., 2020). Their success will not hinge solely on technological savvy but on their ability to harness AI's potential without sacrificing authenticity, empathy, or ethical responsibility.

In sum, a hybrid leadership capability bridges the gap between technology and humanity, ensuring that AI's potential is realised in concert with the qualities that have always distinguished exceptional leadership. By infusing data-driven rigour with a commitment to empathy and organisational ethics, leaders can steer their teams through transformative change, shape resilient cultures, and uphold the central importance of human-centric values in an era increasingly defined by AI.

## Results: impact of AI integration on leadership styles and emerging competencies

In addressing RQ1 (*Which leadership styles are most impacted by AI integration?*), the comprehensive analysis of the literature reveals several key phenomena and insights regarding the transformative impact of AI on leadership practices, competencies, and organisational dynamics. First, integrating AI-driven engagement and communication tools signifies a paradigm shift in organisational operations and leadership roles, moving beyond a simple technological upgrade. While AI demonstrably enhances decision-making through advanced data analysis and predictive modelling (Milton & Al-Busaidi, 2023), its core value lies in its capacity to augment, not supplant, essential human leadership qualities such as strategic thinking, innovation, and the cultivation of authentic human connections (Parent-Rocheleau & Parker, 2021). This augmentation allows leaders to offload routine tasks and leverage data-driven insights, focusing on their roles' more complex and relational aspects (Estherita & Shanmugam, 2024). The shift towards AI-augmented leadership necessitates a re-evaluation of traditional management practices. Second, the evolution of leadership styles in the AI era showcases remarkable adaptability, particularly in employee engagement and development approaches. Traditional styles, including transformational, servant, and adaptive leadership, are not being replaced but are somewhat enhanced through the strategic integration of AI tools (Daniels, 2023). The analysis underscores that successful AI-enhanced leadership achieves a crucial equilibrium between leveraging technological capabilities and upholding human-centric values (Madanchian et al., 2024). Notably: (1) transformational leaders employ AI to fuel innovation and manage change (Madanchian et al., 2024), (2) servant leaders utilise AI for personalised employee growth and well-being (Pago, 2024), (3) adaptive leaders leverage AI for real-time strategic adjustments and enhanced team engagement (Gleeson, 2024). Third, the emergence of hybrid leadership capabilities represents a critical development in organisational management, especially in how leaders utilise AI-driven tools for team engagement and development. This novel paradigm blends traditional leadership competencies with AI literacy (Brynjolfsson & McAfee, 2014), fostering leaders adept at navigating organisational life's technological and human dimensions (Wright, 2024).

The analysis identifies several pivotal developments in response to RQ2 (*What new competencies and roles are emerging for leaders in AI-driven contexts?*). The success of hybrid leadership hinges on several key abilities: interpreting and applying AI-driven insights while maintaining ethical oversight, balancing data-driven decision-making with empathetic engagement, fostering innovation while ensuring responsible AI implementation, and cultivating organisational cultures that embrace technological advancement and core human values. Moreover, beyond conventional management skills, contemporary leaders must cultivate (1) technical literacy in AI and data analytics, (2) ethical reasoning capabilities for AI governance, (3) expertise in change management for digital transformation, and (4) enhanced emotional intelligence to sustain human connections in increasingly automated environments. Successful AI implementation in leadership demands a balanced approach, where data-driven insights are coupled with empathetic engagement and responsive communication. Finally, this analysis reveals several critical implications that will shape the future of leadership development and organisational success. Organisations must prioritise investments in developing leaders capable of effectively synthesising human judgment with the capabilities of AI, acknowledging that neither element is sufficient for optimal leadership in the contemporary era. The future of effective leadership lies in this symbiotic relationship. Leadership development programmes must undergo a necessary evolution, incorporating both technical training in AI applications and a heightened emphasis on uniquely human skills such as emotional intelligence, ethical reasoning, and creative thinking. This dual focus will equip leaders to navigate the complexities of AI-enhanced organisations. The trajectory of organisational leadership's future does not involve a binary choice between human judgment and AI. Instead, it necessitates fostering synergistic relationships between the two. Despite the increasing capabilities of AI, the fundamental importance of human judgment, emotional intelligence, and ethical oversight remains paramount in defining effective leadership. The most successful leaders will be those who can skilfully harness the potential of AI while diligently preserving the essential human elements that underpin effective leadership, such as empathy, trust, and the ability to inspire. Organisations must, therefore, prioritise the development of leaders who can navigate this delicate balance between technological prowess and human-centred values.

## Discussion: evolving leadership styles, emerging competencies, and human-centred challenges in the AI era

In addressing RQ1 (*Which leadership styles are most impacted by AI integration?*), the findings offer significant insights into the evolving landscape of AI-augmented leadership. The study's first key insight highlights that the integration of AI is a transformative paradigm shift rather than a mere technological upgrade. This aligns with the introductory remarks that AI fundamentally alters organisational management practices and decision-making. The enhanced decision-making capabilities through data analysis and predictive modelling are consistently emphasised, but this chapter underscores that AI's primary value lies in its ability to augment, not replace, human leadership qualities. This augmentation allows leaders to concentrate on strategic thinking and human connections, echoing the perspective that AI empowers rather than supplants leaders. Moreover, the research reveals the adaptability of various leadership styles to AI integration. Transformational, servant, and adaptive leadership styles are most significantly impacted. The enhanced capabilities of transformational leadership in driving innovation and change through AI-powered analytics are supported by studies indicating AI's role in fostering innovation (Estherita & Shanmugam, 2024).

Similarly, the benefits of AI for servant leadership through personalised development and well-being monitoring resonate with the human-centric focus of this style (Madanchian et al., 2024). The alignment of adaptive leadership with AI's capacity for real-time strategic adjustments and team engagement underscores the importance of flexibility in technology-driven environments (Gleeson, 2024). This evolution leads to hybrid leadership models that blend technological capabilities with human-centric values, ensuring that essential human elements are maintained. The emergence of hybrid leadership capabilities is a crucial development. This paradigm necessitates leaders who are proficient in traditional leadership competencies and possess AI literacy (Brynjolfsson & McAfee, 2014). The ability to interpret AI-driven insights while maintaining ethical oversight and fostering empathetic engagement is central to this model. This aligns with the increasing demand for frameworks that integrate AI without sacrificing human qualities. The role of leaders as moderators between technology and teams is critical for reconciling data-driven efficiencies with ethical and interpersonal considerations.

Turning to RQ2 (*What new competencies and roles are emerging for leaders in AI-driven contexts?*), the study identifies several pivotal developments. The study underscores the growing importance of new leadership competencies. These include (1) technical literacy in AI and data analytics (Brynjolfsson & McAfee, 2014), (2) ethical reasoning for AI governance (Jobin et al., 2019), (3) change management expertise for digital transformation (Tang, 2019), (4) enhanced emotional intelligence for maintaining human connections in automated environments (Northouse, 2019). These competencies are essential for navigating AI's challenges and opportunities, ensuring responsible AI implementation.

Finally, the analysis points to critical implications for future leadership development. Organisations must invest in developing leaders who synergistically combine human judgment with AI capabilities. Leadership development programmes need to incorporate technical training alongside a focus on uniquely human skills such as emotional intelligence and ethical reasoning. The future of leadership lies in fostering a synergistic relationship between humans and AI, ensuring that technology supports rather than displaces the essential human aspects of leadership. However, the discussion must also acknowledge the ethical and aesthetic challenges highlighted in the literature. The potential for amplifying biases through AI systems necessitates careful oversight and multi-faceted data evaluation (Eubanks, 2018; O'Neil, 2016). The limited transparency of AI models ("black box" problem) (Danks & London, 2017) raises questions about algorithmic accountability (Ananny & Crawford, 2018). The redefinition of power relations through "algorithmic management" (Rosenblat, 2018) and the risks of privacy breaches due to extensive data collection (Zuboff, 2019) require leaders to establish ethical boundaries and governance protocols. Furthermore, the tension between the rationality of AI and the aesthetic dimension of leadership underscores the need for leaders to integrate AI recommendations into human-centred narratives that preserve emotional resonance and authentic human interactions (Hansen et al., 2007). The phenomenon of "algorithm aversion" (Dietvorst et al., 2015) suggests that maintaining personal contact and human-authored feedback remains crucial for team members.

The findings of this literature review reinforce the notion that AI integration is fundamentally reshaping leadership, necessitating an evolution in leadership styles and required competencies. While AI offers unprecedented opportunities for enhancing efficiency and decision-making, the continued importance of human-centric values, ethical considerations, and aesthetic sensitivity cannot be overstated. The successful leaders of the AI era will be those who can effectively harness the power of AI while preserving and nurturing the essential human elements that define effective and sustainable organisational leadership.

## Conclusions

Considering the above discussion, this study addressed two principal research questions: (RQ1) Which leadership styles are most impacted by AI integration? and (RQ2) What new competencies and roles are emerging for leaders in AI-driven contexts? Based on the analysis, transformational, servant, and adaptive leadership styles demonstrate the most significant impact from AI integration, with transformational leadership showing particularly enhanced capabilities in driving innovation and organisational change through AI-powered analytics and automation (RQ1). The emergence of hybrid leadership models enables these styles to leverage AI while maintaining essential human elements of leadership. Regarding new competencies, three critical areas emerge: technical literacy (understanding AI capabilities and limitations), strategic integration (aligning AI with organisational vision), and ethical leadership (ensuring responsible AI deployment) (RQ2). These findings suggest that successful leadership in AI-driven contexts requires a balanced approach combining traditional leadership qualities with new technical and ethical competencies while maintaining the human-centric aspects crucial for organisational success.

Despite the provision of a thorough literature review and theoretical synthesis, it is imperative to acknowledge several inherent *limitations* that may condition the interpretation of the presented findings. These limitations primarily arise from the dynamic and progressive nature of AI and data analytics, alongside the scope and temporal boundaries of the extant scholarly work in this domain. First, it has been recognised that due to the rapid and continuous advancements in AI, data analytics, and associated practices, certain conclusions extrapolated from the literature review (encompassing 2014–2024) may be subject to temporal constraints and potential obsolescence. The field of AI is characterised by perpetual evolution, with the frequent emergence of novel tools, methodologies, and applications. Consequently, the insights derived from the body of literature up to 2024 offer a valuable, yet potentially transient, depiction of the field at that juncture, and future technological developments may necessitate subsequent and updated analyses regarding AI-augmented leadership. Second, the study notes that a significant proportion of the analysed publications exhibit a paucity of longitudinal perspectives. This implies that a substantial segment of the existing research provides insights into AI integration's immediate or short-term effects on leadership paradigms. Conversely, the protracted ramifications for employee well-being, organisational culture, and overall organisational performance within AI-augmented leadership remain comparatively underexplored. A comprehensive understanding of these long-term dynamics necessitates research endeavours that track organisations and their leadership over extended temporal frameworks, which were not extensively represented within the defined scope of this review.

Extending the exigency for longitudinal studies, I posit that *future research* should provide more granular insights into the diachronic evolution of team dynamics, interpersonal trust, and follower engagement under the aegis of AI-enhanced leadership. While the present study identifies the immediate impacts of AI on communication and engagement, a comprehensive understanding of the sustained effects on relational dynamics and team cohesion within AI-driven environments is crucial for a holistic appreciation of AI's role in leadership. Concerns regarding potential dehumanisation and the equilibrium between AI-mediated and authentic empathy underscore the importance of such longitudinal investigations. Another promising avenue for future scholarly inquiry, identified as a limitation of the current body of work, involves investigating emergent hybrid models that synergistically integrate aesthetic and humanistic dimensions with AI-based analytics to formulate best practices for fostering authentic and empathetic relational dynamics. The study alludes to the aesthetic and ethical challenges inherent in AI's role in leadership, and further research is warranted to develop concrete theoretical frameworks and practical strategies for leaders to effectively synthesise data-driven insights with the critical human elements of leadership, such as empathy and emotional intelligence. Finally, this chapter emphasises the critical importance of interdisciplinary collaborations among data science, ethics, and organisational psychology to facilitate the establishment of robust frameworks for algorithmic transparency, fairness, and data privacy, thereby mitigating potential risks of dehumanisation within AI-enhanced workplaces. The ethical dilemmas posed by AI, including algorithmic bias and the inherent opacity of specific AI models (the "black box" problem), necessitate the collective expertise of multiple disciplines to develop efficacious solutions and ensure the responsible and ethical implementation of AI within leadership practices. The current study identifies ethical leadership as a salient and increasingly critical competency, and future interdisciplinary scholarship is essential for providing practical guidance in this complex and evolving landscape. Moreover, future research should examine cross-cultural contexts to explore how AI-augmented leadership unfolds in diverse societal and organisational settings. In addition, longitudinal studies could provide deeper insight into how team dynamics, trust, and follower engagement evolve under AI-enhanced leadership. Another promising direction is investigating new hybrid models that integrate aesthetic and humanistic dimensions with AI-based analytics, offering best practices for nurturing authentic, empathetic relationships. Finally, interdisciplinary collaborations among data science, ethics, and organisational psychology would help establish algorithmic transparency, fairness, and privacy frameworks, thereby mitigating potential dehumanisation risks in AI-enhanced workplaces.

In conclusion, while AI continues to reshape leadership across multiple dimensions – strategic, operational, and relational – maintaining human-centric values remains critical. Leaders who can effectively blend technical prowess, strategic alignment, and empathy stand to create work environments that harness

AI's transformative potential while preserving the vital interpersonal core that defines meaningful and sustainable organisational life.

## References

Abdaljaleel, M., Barakat, M., Alsanafi, M., Salim, N. A., Abazid, H., Malaeb, D., … & Sallam, M. (2024). A multinational study on the factors influencing university students' attitudes and usage of ChatGPT. *Scientific Reports, 14*(1), 1983. https://doi.org/10.1038/s41598-024-52549-8

Ananny, M., & Crawford, K. (2018). Seeing without knowing: Limitations of the transparency ideal and its application to algorithmic accountability. *New Media & Society, 20*(3), 973–989.

Barry, D., & Meisiek, S. (2010). Seeing more and seeing differently: Sensemaking, mindfulness, and the workarts. *Organisation Studies, 31*(12), 1505–1530.

Brynjolfsson, E., & McAfee, A. (2014). *The Second Machine Age: Work, Progress, and Prosperity in a Time of Brilliant Technologies.* W. W. Norton & Company.

Bryson, J., & Theodorou, A. (2019). How society can maintain human-controlled AI. *IEEE Proceedings, 107*(3), 509–517.

Burrell, J. (2016). How the machine 'thinks': Understanding opacity in machine learning algorithms. *Big Data & Society, 3*(1), 1–12.

Czakon, W. (2020). Metoda systematycznego przeglądu literatury. *Przegląd Organizacji, 3*, 57–62.

Daniels, P. (2023). Automated grammar scoring with AI chatbots. *TEFL Praxis Journal, 2*(1), 59–68.

Danks, D., & London, A. J. (2017). Regulating autonomous systems: Beyond standards. *IEEE Intelligent Systems, 32*(1), 88–91.

Davenport, T. H., & Kirby, J. (2016). *Only Humans Need Apply: Winners and Losers in the Age of Smart Machines* (Vol. 1). Harper Business.

Devoteam (2024). Devoteam announces "AMPLIFY", its new bold strategic plan with a vision for 2028 to consolidate its leadership in AI. https://www.devoteam.com/cz/news-and-pr/devoteam-announces-amplify-its-new-bold-strategic-plan-with-a-vision-for-2028-to-consolidate-its-leadership-in-ai/

Dietvorst, B. J., Simmons, J. P., & Massey, C. (2015). Algorithm aversion: People erroneously avoid algorithms after seeing them err. *Journal of Experimental Psychology: General, 144*(1), 114–126.

Dirani, K. M., Abadi, M., Alizadeh, A., Barhate, B., Garza, R. C., Gunasekara, N., Ibrahim, G., & Majzun, Z. (2020). Leadership competencies and the essential role of human resource development in times of crisis: A response to COVID-19 pandemic. *Human Resource Development International, 23*(4), 380–394.

Dourish, P. (2016). Algorithms and their others: Algorithmic culture in context. *Big Data & Society, 3*(2), 1–11.

Elamin, M. O. I. (2024). AI through the ages: Unlocking key opportunities and navigating challenges in the history and future of artificial intelligence. *International Journal of Religion, 5*(12), 1152–1166.

Estherita, A., & Shanmugam, V. (2024, June). Influence of artificial intelligence on transfor mational leadership. In AIP *Conference Proceedings* (Vol. 3112, No. 1), AIP Publishing, Coimbatore.

Eubanks, V. (2018). *Automating Inequality: How High-Tech Tools Profile, Police, and Punish the Poor.* St. Martin's Press.

Frick, N. R. J., Mirbabaie, M., Stieglitz, S., & Salomon, J. (2021). Maneuvering through the stormy seas of digital transformation: The impact of empowering leadership on the AI readiness of enterprises. *Journal of Decision Systems, 30*(2–3), 1–24.

Gagliardi, P. (2006). Exploring the aesthetic side of organisational life. In S. R. Clegg, C. Hardy, & W. R. Nord (Eds.), *The SAGE Handbook of Organization Studies* (pp. 701–724). SAGE Publications.

Gahlot, V., & Bathla, G. (2021). The role of senses in aesthetic leadership. *Advances in Management, 14*(1), 19–24.

Gleeson, B. (2024, April 9). *5 key essentials of adaptive leadership.* Forbes. https://www.forbes.com/sites/brentgleeson/2024/04/09/5-key-essentials-of-adaptive-leadership/ (access 25.01.2025).

Glikson, E., & Woolley, A. W. (2020). Human trust in artificial intelligence: Review of empirical research. *Academy of Management Annals, 14*(2), 627–660.

Hansen, H., Ropo, A., & Sauer, E. (2007). Aesthetic leadership. *The Leadership Quarterly, 18*(6), 544–560.

Hao, M., Lv, W., & Du, B. (2020). The influence mechanism of authentic leadership in artificial intelligence team on employees' performance. *Journal of Physics: Conference Series, 1438*, 012022.

Heimans, J., & Timms, H. (2024). Leading in a world where AI wields power of its own. *Harvard Business Review, 102*(1–2), 71–79.

Jarrahi, M. H., Möhlmann, M., & Lee, M. K. (2023). Algorithmic management: The role of AI in managing workforces. MIT Sloan Management Review.

Jobin, A., Ienca, M., & Vayena, E. (2019). The global landscape of AI ethics guidelines. *Nature Machine Intelligence, 1*(9), 389–399.

Katsiroumpa, A., Moisoglou, I., Konstantakopoulou, O., Kalogeropoulou, M., Gallos, P., & Galanis, P. (2024). Engaging leadership scale (12 items version): Translation and a validation in Greek. *International Journal of Caring Sciences, 17*(3), 1407.

Kellogg, K., Valentine, M., & Christin, A. (2020). Algorithms at work: The new contested terrain of control. *Academy of Management Annals, 14*(1), 366–410.

Madanchian, M., Taherdoost, H., Vincenti, M., & Mohamed, N. (2023). AI-Based Human Resource Management Tools and Techniques; A Systematic Literature Review. *Procedia Computer Science, 229*, 367–377. https://doi.org/10.1016/j.procs.2023.12.039

Madanchian, M., Taherdoost, H., Vincenti, M., & Mohamed, N. (2024). Transforming leadership practices through artificial intelligence. *Procedia Computer Science, 235*, 2101–2111.

McKinsey Digital (2020). Global survey: the state of AI in 2020. McKinsey.com https://www.mckinsey.com/~/media/McKinsey/Business%20Functions/McKinsey%20Analytics/Our%20Insights/Global%20survey%20The%20state%20of%20AI%20in%202020/Global-survey-The-state-of-AI-in-2020.pdf. Accessed 17 Apr 2025

Milton, J., & Al-Busaidi, A. (2023). New role of leadership in AI era: Educational sector. *SHS Web of Conferences*, (Vol. 156, p. 09005). EDP Sciences.

Moore, J., & Joyce, K. (2020). AI-mediated empathy: Ethical considerations in algorithmic leadership. *Journal of Artificial Intelligence Ethics, 5*(2), 145–160.

Northouse, P. G. (2019). *Leadership: Theory and Practice* (8th ed.). Sage Publications.

O'Neil, C. (2016). *Weapons of Math Destruction: How Big Data Increases Inequality and Threatens Democracy.* Crown.

Pago, L. M. (2024). Artificial intelligence empowerment in leadership: A systematic review of positive impacts and applications. *International Journal of Multidisciplinary Research and Analysis*, *7*(8), 4118–4125. https://doi.org/10.47191/ijmra/v7-i08-57

Parent-Rocheleau, X., & Parker, S. (2021). Algorithmic management and leadership: Implications for organisational justice and employee well-being. *Human Resource Management Review, 32*(3), 100850.

Raisch, S., & Krakowski, S. (2021). Artificial intelligence and management: The automation–augmentation paradox. *Academy of Management Review, 46*(1), 192–210. https://doi.org/10.5465/amr.2018.0072

Rosenblat, A. (2018). *Uberland: How Algorithms Are Rewriting the Rules of Work.* University of California Press.

Sengupta, S., Bajaj, B., Singh, A., Sharma, S., Patel, P., & Prikshat, V. (2023). Innovative work behavior driving Indian startups go global–the role of authentic leadership and readiness for change. *Journal of Organisational Change Management, 36*(1), 162–179.

Sharma, G. D., Yadav, A., & Chopra, R. (2020). Artificial intelligence and effective governance: A review, critique and research agenda. *Sustainable Futures, 2*, 100004.

Sposato, M. (2024). Leadership training and development in the age of artificial intelligence. *Development and Learning in Organisations: An International Journal, 38*(4), 4–7.

Stewart, J., Loon, M., & Nachmias, S. (2020). Introduction to volume one: Future of human resource development – disruption through digitalisation. In M. Loon, J. Stewart, S. & Nachmias (Eds.), *The Future of HRD, Volume I* (pp. 1–12). Palgrave Macmillan, Cham. https://doi.org/10.1007/978-3-030-52410-4_1

Strati, A. (1999). *Organisation and Aesthetics.* SAGE.

Sutherland, I., & Jelinek, J. (2015). From bricolage to collage: Reflections on aesthetic leadership. *Organisational Aesthetics, 4*(1), 13–38.

Syam, N., & Sharma, A. (2018). Waiting for a sales renaissance in the fourth industrial revolution: Machine learning and artificial intelligence in sales research and practice. *Industrial Marketing Management, 69*, 135–146. https://doi.org/10.1016/j.indmarman.2017.12.019

Tang, K. N. (2019). *Leadership and Change Management.* Springer.

Van Quaquebeke, N., & Gerpott, F. H. (2023). From managers' use of artificial intelligence to employees' emotions and innovation behavior: A conceptual review. *Human Relations, 76*(3), 629–653.

Walther, C. C. (2024). Where: Humans, technology, and humane technology. In C. C. Walther (Ed.), *Human Leadership for Humane Technology: The New AI: Agency Ignited* (pp. 103–194). Springer Nature Switzerland.

Wright, E. D. (2024). *The Impact of Culturally Competent Leadership on Black Student Graduation Rates*. Sage Graduate School.

Zuboff, S. (2019). *The Age of Surveillance Capitalism: The Fight for a Human Future at the New Frontier of Power.* PublicAffairs.

# 7 Aesthetic dimensions of decision-making process

## AI-powered tools for organisational leaders

*Lucyna Baca-Lönn*

### Introduction

Limited knowledge has been identified regarding aesthetic leadership dimensions significant in organisational leaders' decision processes in the AI era, necessitating further exploration in this area. AI and other smart technologies are discussed as being at the centre of an unprecedented wave of automation, and they are perceived as drivers for transforming decision-making as a cognitive and information-centric process (Kelly, 2012).

Aesthetic leadership dimensions in leaders' decision processes may incorporate the following dimensions: (1) *emotional engagement* of the leaders who foster connections of team members that can strengthen their motivation and commitment to fulfilling their job responsibilities; (2) *creativity and innovation*, allowing leaders to explore novice solutions to problems; (3) *holistic perspective* of organisational challenges, integrating the facts, context, culture, and emotional landscape of the organisation, (4) *identifying organisational purpose* by integrating aesthetic considerations into strategic planning, leaders can align organisational goals with stakeholder values and expectations that strengthen employees' sense of belonging to the organisation. It is presumed that this broader perspective of aesthetic leadership dimensions can lead to more nuanced and effective decisions of aesthetic leaders (Ketelle & Lin, 2019). Moreover, this theoretical descriptive research problem seeks to advance understanding of what benefits and risks the implementation of AI brings to the decision processes of aesthetic leaders and what strategies can be applied to balance human judgment and AI-based insights in aesthetic leaders' organisational decision processes.

Regarding *research methods*, this chapter is based on a qualitative review of literature from 1980 until now in English and Polish, based on phrases: aesthetic leadership, aesthetic leader, and aesthetic dimensions in organisational leaders' decision processes in the AI era. The selection of aesthetic leadership and AI theories in this research stems from their relevance to modern organisational challenges and the evolving nature of leadership in the technological landscape, in which human insights are of significant importance. Aesthetic

DOI: 10.4324/9781003654377-10

leadership involves human subjective evaluations and creative decision-making. In contrast, AI's approach to decision-making is more objective and data-driven, making it an interesting area to explore how humans and AI collaborate or complement each other in leaders' decision processes. Moreover, aesthetic leadership brings emotional and creative aspects, innovation, and challenge into leaders' decision-making to inspire creativity and manage change effectively.

The literature was searched from databases: Google Scholar, EBSCO, JSTOR, and Scopus. An interdisciplinary, multi-paradigm methodological approach integrating the disciplines of management, decision-making, leadership, neuroscience, and computer sciences is applied in this chapter, as complex issues like leaders' decision-making processes require insights from multiple fields. Neuroscience provides insights into the cognitive processes of the leaders, aesthetics offers perspectives on their creative and emotional engagement, leadership theory informs on organisational dynamics, and AI research contributes to leaders' data-driven decision-making and automation (Chen et al., 2020).

This chapter seeks to answer the following research questions: (RQ1) What dimensions of aesthetic leadership are significant in organisational leaders' decision processes supported by AI-powered tools? (RQ2) What benefits and risks does the implementation of AI bring to the decision processes of aesthetic leaders? (RQ3) What strategies can be applied to balance AI-based insights and human judgment in aesthetic leaders' organisational decision processes?

## Literature review: decision-making process, AI, and aesthetic leadership

The literature review has the following structure: first, the generic scientific findings about human decision processes and the two cognitive systems of information processing, intuition and reasoning, applied by human beings, are presented. Then, the concept of human reasoning propensity (pr) is introduced in the continuum between extreme attitudes – intuitive propensity and analytical propensity in the decision-making processes. Finally, aesthetic dimensions that can assist organisational leaders' decision-making processes, supported by AI tools in aesthetic leadership, are described.

### *Leaders' decision-making*

There is consistent research on the nature of decision-making, especially the role of cognition, intuition, and emotion in human decision processes (Soosalu, 2019). The human decision-making processes are connected with cognition and intuition, and different types of information processing, which are defined as analytical and intuitive (Kahneman, 2003). The generic distinction between these two information processing types is that the analytical type involves conscious, cognitive, logical, and reason-oriented thinking. In contrast, the intuitive type is associative, heuristic[1], tacit, and implicit (Kahneman, 2011). Two cognitive systems in human decision-making have been identified: intuition-system 1 and reasoning-system 2, with different processes and content inherent in them (Kahneman, 2003).

As shown in Figure 7.1, according to Kahneman (2003), intuitive decision-making refers to concepts and percepts that language can evoke. The perceptual system and the intuitive operations of System 1 generate impressions of the attributes of objects of perception and thought in the decision processes. In contrast, judgments are intentional and explicit even when not overtly expressed. System 2 is involved in all decision-making processes, whether they originate in impressions or deliberate reasoning. The term intuitive is applied to judgments directly reflecting impressions, which are not modified by System 2.

According to the past view of scholars and practitioners, effective decision-making must occur under the most rational conditions (Sayegh et al., 2004). However, recent conceptions of the decision-making processes include constructs of emotions and intuition (Hodgkinson et al., 2008), which constitute an integral part of aesthetic leadership. A presumption can be made that every individual displays a reasoning propensity pr € (0,1), embedding his/her habitual attitude, including character, beliefs, values, and experiences, in processing the information referring to the specific task. The reasoning propensity can take values in a continuum between two extreme attitudes, called "intuitive propensity" (pr = 0) and "analytical propensity" (pr = 1), assuming that both are involved in

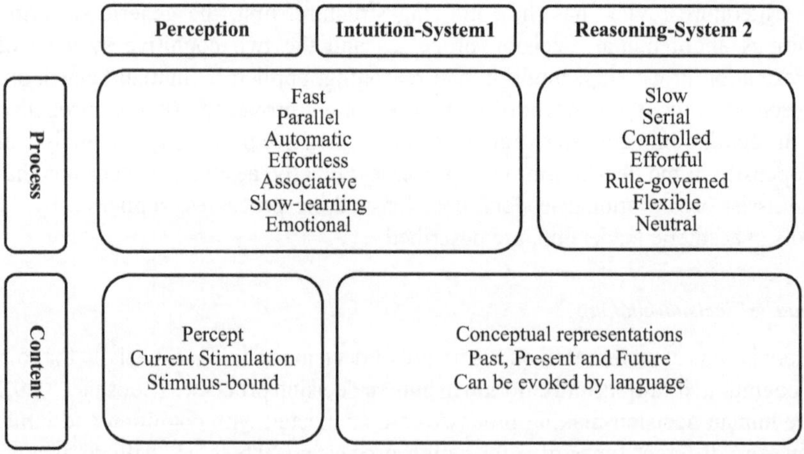


*Figure 7.1* Two cognitive systems of information processing: intuition-system 1 and reasoning-system 2.

*Source:* Kahneman (2003)

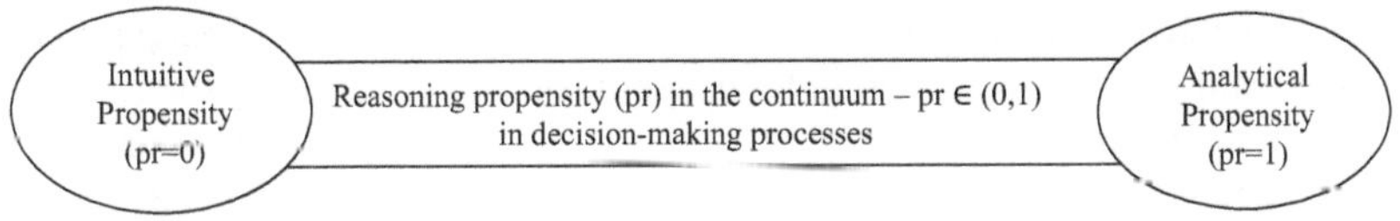


*Figure 7.2* Reasoning propensity (pr) in the continuum between extreme attitudes – intuitive propensity and analytical propensity in the decision-making.

*Source:* Own elaboration based on Bizzarri & Mocenni (2022)

any decision-making, with different magnitude (Bizzarri & Mocenni, 2022) (see Figure 7.2).

In Figure 7.2, the individual's reasoning propensity (pr) in the continuum $pr \in (0,1)$ is presented as embedding a person's habitual attitude, character, beliefs, values, and experiences in decision-making. Reasoning propensity (pr) takes values in a continuum between two extreme attitudes, defined as "intuitive" ($pr = 0$) and "analytical" ($pr = 1$), assuming in this way that both are always involved in any human decision process with different immensity (Bizzarri & Mocenni, 2022). Much of cognition and human decision-making does not directly result from deliberate information gathering and processing but arises from the subconscious in the realm of intuition[2] (Dane et al., 2012).

Effective leaders excel in decision-making[3], team management, and conflict resolution (Klus & Müller, 2021). Leaders tend to make rational, justifiable, and information-based decisions. As rational thinking is agreed to be the managerial standard for decision-making, leaders aspire to get as precise and complete information as possible in their decision-making processes[4] (Butcher, 1998). However, the rational decision-making model has been the subject of criticism because of: (1) humans' inability to act in the entirely rational manner that underpins the model (Buchanan & O'Connell, 2006); (2) the lack of non-rational human factors that play a role in organisational decision making in that model (Andrade & Ariely, 2009); (3) the limited applicability of the model in decision-making contexts characterised by complexity and uncertainty (Thomas & Mengel, 2008). Moreover, complete information hardly exists or is too extensive to be processed by leaders (Simon, 1990), with no guarantee that a rational decision is the best option in a specific context (Kerschbaum, 2025). The data can be inaccurate, incomplete, or confusing (Figueiredo, 2021). The interconnectedness and dynamism of the organisations favour leadership approaches beyond the cognitive and rational dimensions, incorporating the aesthetic, emotional, and sensory aspects of human experience (Strati, 1999; Szostak, 2024).

Purely rational decision-making relies on logic and analysis, whereas aesthetic judgment, inherently subjective and shaped by individual preferences, cultural norms, and contextual factors, requires leaders to consider their choices' emotional and experiential impact on the environment (Gagliardi, 2006). Phenomenological values referring to lived experience, subjective interpretation, and embodied understanding constitute a central part of the decision-making process. Phenomenological values highlight the significance of considering the full spectrum of human experience, including emotions, perceptions, and intuitions, when making decisions in an organisational context (Szostak, 2024). The phenomenological approach implies recognising that decision-making is more than a cognitive activity as it is connected with the leader's embodied presence, emotions, intuition, and the social and cultural context in which the decisions are taken (Küpers, 2005). A phenomenological perspective on decision-making stresses the role of intuition and tacit knowledge, defined as the unarticulated, experiential knowledge individuals accumulate through their experiences (Polanyi, 1966). Tacit knowledge informs intuitive decision-making, in which leaders rely on their instincts rather than cognitive analysis (Szostak, 2024). From a phenomenological approach, intuition is regarded as a legitimate form of knowing that stems from the leader's profound engagement with their environment rather than as irrational knowing (Sadler-Smith, 2008). The phenomenological perspective integrates emotions perceived not as reactions to external factors but as integral components of how individuals make sense of the environment (Damasio, 1994). Emotional awareness allows leaders to understand the influence of their decisions on the well-being and motivation of their staff, fostering an empathetic and responsive leadership style (Goleman et al., 2002). Emotions provide critical insights into the values and principles that should guide action, supporting decision processes with ethical and moral considerations (Ladkin, 2008). Phenomenological values encourage a more holistic approach to decision-making, focusing on decision-making, which includes interpersonal dynamics, power relations, and communicative practices in organisational decision-making (Van Manen, 2016). Consequently, tacit and explicit knowledge create new knowledge in the organisation (Nonaka & Takeuchi, 1995). There are opinions that these two types of knowledge are not separate, and they constitute mutually complementary entities that interact with each other and even transform one into the other under specific conditions (Nonaka et al., 2021).

Aesthetic dimensions can assist organisational leaders' decision-making processes (Keenan, 2016, p. 19). Aesthetics dimensions in leaders' decision-making may include: (1) *emotional engagement*: leaders who incorporate aesthetics into their decision-making processes can foster deeper emotional connections with the environment that can lead to increased motivation and commitment among team members; (2) *creativity and innovation*: aesthetic considerations encourage creativity, allowing leaders to explore unconventional solutions to problems. Aesthetic leaders question the status quo and drive creativity, which helps their organisation stay relevant and identify efficiencies; (3) *holistic perspective:* aesthetic leadership promotes a holistic view of organisational challenges, considering the facts, context, culture, and emotional landscape of the organisation. This broader perspective can lead to more nuanced and effective decisions (Ketelle & Lin, 2019); (4) *identifying organisational purpose:* by integrating aesthetic considerations into strategic planning, leaders can align organisational goals with stakeholder values and expectations that strengthen a sense of belonging among employees. Organisational purpose is the term describing the reason why an organisation exists from *a goal-based view* that relates to purpose as an organisational objective defined by the firm itself or from *a duty-based view* referring to ethical and moral positions, including values, social and environmental duties as core to the firm's existence (George et al., 2021). The aesthetic recognition of organisational purpose complements implementing purposeful organising into the three dimensions of activities – framing purpose, formalising purpose, and realising purpose as a basis of purpose-driven organisational strategy (George et al., 2021).

Aesthetic perceptions can serve as a guiding framework for decision-making, allowing leaders to make choices that resonate with their vision and the collective identity of the organisation (Kerschbaum & Peschl, 2023). Leaders' emotional engagement as an aesthetic dimension in leaders' decision-making refers to their emotional intelligence, including four areas: (1) *self-awareness* – the ability to understand personal feelings and how they influence individual performance; (2) *self-management* – controlling the emotions and feelings to set target-oriented incentives and initiatives to increase performance; (3) *relationship management* – the management of interactions to develop productive cooperation with the environment; (4) *social awareness* – the ability to analyse and understand other humans and situations to use the gained information (Crummenerl et al., 2019, p. 4). The above-mentioned areas of leaders' emotional intelligence play a crucial role in strengthening their connection with team members and enhancing their engagement and commitment to their job responsibilities. Recognising feelings and emotions as a legitimate source of knowledge (Taylor, 2002) is an important aspect of studying aesthetics in organisational life.

However, leaders' decision-making processes are interconnected with AI resources in Economy 4.0 and Economy 5.0. It has been found that AI has the potential to change leaders' decision-making by offering data-driven insights and real-time analysis, freeing them from routine responsibilities and creating space for strategic thinking and innovation (Madanchian et al., 2024; Agrawal et al., 2019).

### *Leaders and AI*

The application of AI in the decision-making processes of aesthetic leaders brings substantial value through enhanced personalisation, improved data analysis, and efficiency in organisational operations. Implementing AI in leadership accelerates leaders' decision-making processes and enables them to make more efficient and strategic decisions (Shamim, 2022). AI-supported decision-making systems allow leaders to manage the workforce more effectively and achieve organisational targets more efficiently (Daft, 2016).

Regarding personalisation, AI technologies enable aesthetic leaders to tailor experiences based on individual user preferences and behaviours. By analysing data, AI can create customised recommendations that resonate with consumers, leading to higher organisational engagement and conversion rates. Moreover, AI is positively changing the conventional decision-making models by organisational leaders (Kaggwa & Farayola, 2023) by supporting their limited working memory, short attention span, and decision fatigue, especially when making decisions under pressure (Purdy & Williams, 2023).

AI can support aesthetic leaders with enhanced data analysis, processing a real-time data overload, and transforming the landscape of leadership and leaders' decision-making processes. As organisations face increasing complexity and an overload of data, leaders are applying AI to enhance their decision-making capabilities. AI has become a decision-making tool that assists leaders by instantly processing vast amounts of data, identifying patterns, and generating insights that support leaders' decision-making processes (Peng, 2022). This capability is particularly beneficial in areas such as: (1) *predictive analytics:* AI analyses historical data to forecast future trends, enabling leaders to anticipate market changes and customer behaviours with substantial accuracy; (2) *risk assessment*: by evaluating potential risks associated with various decisions, AI supports leaders to choose informed options that consider long-term impacts; (3) *resource allocation:* AI optimises the distribution of resources by analysing data to determine the most effective use of assets. With the advancement of AI technology analysing large amounts of user data, such as purchasing behaviours, social media interactions, and personal preferences, AI can depict broader public aesthetic trends (Panda, 2023). Decision-making models have been formulated that showcase the integration of AI in organisational decision processes. This involved examining how the principles of participative leadership could be incorporated into AI-driven decision frameworks for transparent governance (Sarioguz & Miser, 2024).

However, data analytics are incapable of aesthetic judgment, but it is said that they rather provide an objective standard of aesthetic judgment. The data collected in the market reflects the reality of consumer preferences, significantly influenced by marketing strategies and sociocultural environments. Consequently, AI reproduces and reinforces existing aesthetic preferences rather than creating new aesthetic standards (Chen, 2024).

Enhanced efficiency constitutes a value that brings the application of AI to the decision-making processes of aesthetic leaders. AI supports the automation of routine tasks and allows aesthetic leaders to focus on complex and creative aspects of their work, accelerating the design process and improving the quality of outputs by minimising human error. Implementing AI in the leaders' decision-making enables them to pursue their strategic planning in an informed manner and adapt the organisation to necessary changes agilely (Kitsios & Kamariotou, 2021; Ifitri et al., 2024).

AI's ability to analyse large datasets in seconds has given rise to data-driven decision-making, which is optimal and more accurate (Al-Bayed et al., 2024). Leaders can also use AI to simulate different scenarios and their potential outcomes, enabling them to make proactive rather than reactive decisions. Consequently, this evolution has led to a more agile and adaptive leadership, where new data and evolving market conditions inform decisions. AI-supported decisions can be made instantly, allowing brands to take advantage of cultural moments, trends, and short-lived opportunities that traditional decision-making modes might lack.

Moreover, it has been recognised that AI is helping to eliminate biases in decision-making. By relying on data and algorithms rather than subjective opinions, AI reduces the likelihood of decisions being influenced by unconscious bias, leading to more objective and fair outcomes. As a result, leadership in the AI era is becoming more inclusive and equitable, with decisions based on merit and performance rather than personal preferences or biases.

A collaborative, symbiotic relationship between leaders and AI in organisational decision-making processes can be observed (Wang, 2021). The ability of AI to efficiently collect, process, and analyse data and provide real-time results can enhance efficiency and support leaders in making data-driven and evidence-based decisions (Garrigan et al., 2018; Wang, 2021). As presented above, there are significant benefits of implementing AI in the aesthetic leaders' decision processes, but there are also risks related to it, including: (1) ethical concerns, (2) overreliance on technology, and (3) lack of transparency. The unintended negative consequences emerge from over-reliance on AI systems in sensitive decision-making contexts without a clear understanding of the limitations and safe use of the AI models (Nassar & Kamal, 2021).

AI systems can inadvertently perpetuate biases in their training data, leading to ethical dilemmas combined with representation and inclusivity. Aesthetic standards influenced by biased algorithms may reinforce societal norms rather than challenge them. Leaders must ensure that AI systems are transparent and aligned with ethical principles to avoid unintended consequences and maintain trust within their organisations. Ethical concerns arise with data privacy and the security of the processed data. Leaders must prioritise protecting sensitive information and implement robust security measures to prevent data breaches and misuse.

Overreliance on technology constitutes another risk, referring to the application of AI tools in the aesthetic leaders' decision-making. Overreliance occurs when individuals trust and agree with AI conclusions even when incorrect (Vasconcelos et al., 2023). There is a danger that leaders may become overly dependent on AI insights, neglecting their own judgment and emotional intelligence. Critical thinking remains essential for effective leadership and balancing human intuition and machine-generated data. This overreliance on AI raises questions about the extent to which it may shape human thinking patterns, influence higher-order thinking skills, and impact the overall cognitive abilities of individuals (Dong et al., 2020). The concept of "AI-Minds" was introduced to describe the excessive reliance on AI technologies in gathering information, knowledge, and decision-making, which can have negative implications for human cognitive processes (Siemens et al., 2022). Moreover, overreliance on AI raises reflections about the magnitude to which it may shape human thinking patterns and influence higher-order thinking skills and the cognitive abilities of individuals (Dong et al., 2020).

Lack of transparency in reaching conclusions by AI-supported tools may be the subsequent risk, combined with the application of generative AI in leaders' decision processes. Many AI algorithms operate as "black boxes", making it difficult for leaders to understand how conclusions are reached. This lack of transparency can erode stakeholders' trust and complicate organisational accountability.

However, AI-assisted data-driven decision-making may conflict with value-based aesthetic decision-making, and a correct balance between AI-driven insights and human judgment is important. AI can be seen as a valuable tool providing insights and efficiency, but it cannot be considered a replacement for human judgment. Human intuition, critical thinking, creativity, and ethical considerations are irreplaceable and essential in complex or nuanced situations.

A question arises about what strategies organisations can use to balance AI-based insights and human judgment in aesthetic leaders' decision processes. It is suggested that to balance human judgment and AI-based insights in organisational leaders' decision-making, businesses can implement strategies that capitalise on the advantages of both while minimising their potential drawbacks. These strategies include: (1) defining clear roles and objectives of the leaders and AI tools, (2) implementing collaborative workflows, using AI as a support tool, maintaining human oversight, and (3) developing human skills.

Clear roles and objectives are key: it has been noticed that AI is effective at analysing large datasets, identifying patterns, and generating predictions, whereas human judgment is optimal at interpreting insights, applying context, and making final decisions in ethically charged or complex situations. When it comes to implementing collaborative workflows, training and understanding should be mentioned as a strategy to support teams in comprehending the strengths and weaknesses of the AI tool in an organisational context. Moreover, establishing explicit goals for AI implementation in an organisation plays a pivotal role in balancing human and AI insights in the leaders' decision processes.

An explicit role of AI as a support tool in the organisational context constitutes another strategy for merging human judgment with AI in leaders' decision-making. Implementing AI for routine tasks and data analysis allows leaders to focus on strategic objectives and creative problem-solving. Human oversight regarding ethical guidelines, review and audits of AI systems, and prioritising transparency in AI decision-making processes is specified as a strategy for integrating human insight and AI analysis in the leaders' decision processes.

With the growing importance of AI in human decision-making within an organisational context, the development of human skills, including critical thinking, complex problem-solving, emotional intelligence, interpersonal communication, adaptability, lifelong learning, ethical reasoning, and decision-making, is becoming of major importance. It is advised that business leaders should be the experts in their industries to prevent over-reliance on AI and maintain critical decision-making skills. This includes direct engagement with customers, employees, competitors, and regulators.

Leaders' strategic decisions are predominantly characterised by uncertainty, complexity and equivocality, which must be handled to make appropriate decisions (Jarrahi, 2018). Both humans and AI can minimise the challenging factors and make controllable decisions. The different approaches to uncertainty, complexity, and equivocality show the complementarity of humans and AI (Jarrahi, 2018), which can create a balanced partnership between them in the leaders' decision-making in the organisational context. Including intelligent systems generates a shift in the competencies and demands on humans in the process (Logg et al., 2019).

### *Aesthetic leadership*

Leadership is a matter of the aesthetic functioning of human beings (Ladkin, 2008) and is observed as a phenomenon on an individual and intrapersonal level as well as an interpersonal level, with the leaders interacting with their teams (Koeleman, 2014). Aesthetic leadership is a style of leadership underscored by sensory, somatic, and emotional awareness and a strong moral purpose focused on being fair, just, and truthful (Katz-Buonincontro, 2011). Aesthetic leadership synthesises transformational, charismatic and authentic leadership and uses aesthetics as a means (Polat & Öztoprak-Kavak, 2011).

Aesthetic leadership is an underexplored aspect of organisational life that can significantly impact how leaders interact with their teams and make decisions (Hansen et al., 2007; Mannix & Daly, 2015). Traditional leadership theories prioritise rationality and metrics, but recent research suggests that integrating aesthetic dimensions can enhance leaders' decision-making and organisational performance. It has been noticed that the decision-making processes cannot be reduced solely to rational aspects (Hansen et al., 2007) and that decision models have been incapable of delineating the emotions, feelings, and personal experiences of people in an organisation. Aesthetic factors, such as emotions, intuition, symbols, and sense perception, seem to have an equally important role in organisational behaviour as cognitive activities (Guillet de Monthoux, 2004).

Aesthetic leadership values the significance of leadership's sensory and emotional dimensions, which can influence leaders' actions, decisions, and overall organisational climate (Hansen et al., 2007; Szostak, 2024). This perspective challenges the traditional, rationalist views of leadership based on logical reasoning and objective decision-making by highlighting the significance of affective and embodied knowledge in effective leadership practices (Ladkin & Taylor, 2010; Szostak, 2024). Leaders attuned to the aesthetic dimensions of their environment and interactions are more appropriately equipped to create conditions that foster creativity, innovation, and engagement within their organisations (Taylor & Ladkin, 2009). Aesthetic experiences in leadership can be perceived through the sensory perception and appreciation of qualities such as harmony, beauty, and rhythm (Ladkin, 2008).

Integrating aesthetics into leadership phenomenon refers to the role of embodied knowledge, understood as the tacit, non-verbal knowledge embedded in bodily practices and sensory experiences (Merleau-Ponty, 2005). It has been noticed that efficient leadership integrates cognitive activity and responds to the aesthetic cues in the organisational environment (Ropo et al., 2007). A leader's ability to sense a team's mood, anticipate their followers' unspoken concerns or apply space and movement efficiently draws on embodied knowledge (Hansen et al., 2007). Such skills can be developed through practice and reflection, and they highlight the significance of aesthetic sensibility in leadership.

Aesthetic leadership is focused on the development of leadership qualities that contribute to a leader's general self-awareness as well as emotional and sensory awareness (Ketelle & Lin, 2019). This approach recognises that decisions are not solely based on data and logic but are influenced by the leader's intuition, creativity, and interpersonal dynamics. The concept of the aesthetic intelligence of a leader has been developed in which the following elements are included: (1) *to be present* – aesthetic leaders are conscious of themselves and of others and are aware of the environment they operate in; (2) *to be authentic* – it corresponds to configuring self with topic, time, audience, and intention. It is about assimilating the clarity of intention and delivering on that intention; (3) *to synthesise* – combining divergent encounters from the visual, cognitive, kinesthetic, auditory, and spatial to apprise thought and action (Goodwin & Mucha, 2008). Synthesising aesthetic leaders respect tacit knowledge that refers to sensory/aesthetic knowing and is gained from deep, indefinable know-how that defies logical explanation (Hansen et al., 2007). A significant feature of aesthetic leadership is how followers view the leadership qualities. Aesthetic leaders are not self-appointed but emerge from colleagues' perceptions (Guillet de Monthoux et al., 2007). Aesthetic leadership is a value-oriented ideological leadership model focusing primarily on moral behaviours (Mumford & Fried, 2014).

Organisational leaders face significant aesthetic decision-making challenges as we integrate AI across various industry sectors. Implementing AI into organisational frameworks imposes a re-evaluation of leadership strategies to ensure aesthetic dimensions are at the forefront of leaders' decision processes. The importance of real-world human experience, intuition, and human skills in decision-making in complex and non-standardised tasks is acknowledged in Industry 5.0

(Nahavandi, 2019), as human judgment is essential to evaluate them properly (Agrawal et al., 2019).

At the same time, AI has transformed leaders' decision-making processes by providing real-time data analytics and predictive models that allow leaders to anticipate future trends and outcomes. AI's ability to analyse large datasets in seconds has given rise to data-driven decision-making (Reez, 2020), which is faster and more accurate. Leaders can apply AI to simulate different scenarios and their potential outcomes, enabling them to make proactive rather than reactive decisions. However, the maintenance of fundamental human traits in leadership remains crucial. Empathy, inventiveness, and decision-making require the correct balance between AI-driven insights and human judgment (Madanchian et al., 2024).

## Results: aesthetic dimensions in organisational leaders' decision processes

The intersection of aesthetics and leadership in the context of AI is gaining attention in scientific literature as organisations navigate the complexities of decision-making processes. Integrating aesthetics and AI is crucial because aesthetics is considered a quintessentially human domain (Manovich & Arielli, 2021). Leaders and decision-makers accept AI as an augmentation tool in decision-making that human beings should control (Duan, 2019).

Based on the literature review, the current knowledge referring to the research area can be structured as follows: (1) human decision processes and two cognitive systems of information processing – intuition and reasoning- applied by human beings, (2) the concept of human reasoning propensity (pr) in the continuum between extreme attitudes – intuitive propensity and analytical propensity in the decision-making processes, (3) aesthetic dimensions that can assist organisational leaders' decision-making processes supported by AI tools in aesthetic leadership. This theoretical research fills the gap in the scientific literature regarding integrating aesthetic leadership dimensions with leaders' rational decision models supported by AI tools.

Based on the critical analysis of the literature on the subject, the following aesthetic dimensions in organisational leaders' decision processes supported by AI-powered tools have been identified: (1) *emotional engagement*, (2) *creativity and innovation*, (3) *holistic perspective* (Ketelle & Lin, 2019), and (4) *identifying organisational purpose.* Integrating those aesthetic dimensions with the leaders' rational decision model supported by AI resulted in *a balanced leaders' human-centred decision model* as an added value of this chapter (Figure 7.3).

Effective decision-making (Figure 7.3) requires the emotional engagement of the leaders with their team members and the cultivation of their creative, problem-solving mindset (Ketelle & Lin, 2019). A holistic perspective is expected from leaders when making decisions, which entails applying the

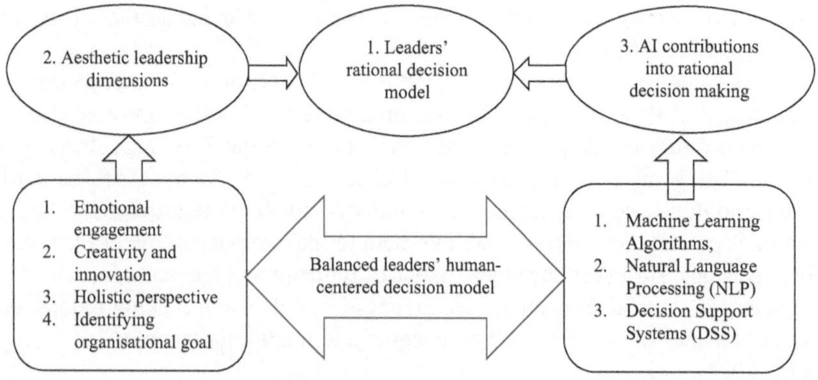


*Figure 7.3* A balanced leader's human-centred decision model - integrating aesthetic leadership dimensions with leaders' rational decision model supported by AI.

*Source:* Own elaboration based on Keenan (2016) and Peifer et al. (2022)

explicit and tacit knowledge they have gathered through "learning, training, practice and feedback" (Wilford, 2011, p. 19).

Incorporating aesthetic dimensions into leadership decision-making enriches the process by acknowledging the interplay between emotional engagement, creativity and innovation, and a holistic perspective in identifying organisational goals. Integrating aesthetic experiences into decision-making can enhance creativity and innovation by allowing leaders to explore diverse perspectives and ideas. Leaders who understand and leverage these aspects can create more dynamic, engaging, and effective organisational environments. By moving beyond traditional rational frameworks, aesthetic leadership offers a holistic approach that recognises the complexity of human interactions in decision-making contexts. Apart from the above, human agency constitutes a key aspect of aesthetic leadership in which aesthetic dimensions shift the focus from individual leaders to collective team interactions. This perspective encourages collaboration and shared responsibility in decision-making, emphasising the role of all members in shaping outcomes (Samier, 2008).

Several key aspects distinguish a leader's rational decision model, supported by AI and integrate aesthetic dimensions from models without aesthetic dimensions. The leaders' rational decision model with integrated aesthetic leadership dimensions is characterised by: (1) *aesthetic influence*, which incorporates visual appeal and emotional engagement, enhancing user experience and fostering trust in decision-making processes; aesthetic dimensions can trigger intuition and motivate creative problem-solving by engagingly presenting data; (2) *humanistic approach* – referring to humanistic values by incorporating elements that resonate with human emotions and creativity, leading to empathetic and inclusive decision-making environments; (3) *AI integration*, which can improve aesthetic design by analysing patterns and suggesting augmentations based on empirical evidence, ensuring that aesthetic decisions are data-driven and complement cognitive knowledge (Manger, 2017). Aesthetic dimensions can influence decision-making by enhancing intuition and creativity, improving emotional intelligence and collaboration within decision-making teams. Leaders who incorporate aesthetics into their decision-making models may prioritise user experience and emotional intelligence, leading to collaborative and inclusive decision-making environments.

The following aspects characterise a leader's rational decision model without aesthetic leadership dimensions: (1) *functionality focus:* this model prioritises efficiency and accuracy over the visual appeal, focusing on delivering objective insights and data-driven decisions; (2) *data-driven approach* – it relies on AI's analytical capabilities to provide objective data analysis, limiting subjective biases and ensuring decisions based on empirical evidence; (3) *rational decision-making process* – it involves a systematic approach to decision-making and include following steps – identifying the problem, gathering information, evaluating alternatives, and selecting the best option based on logical reasoning and analysis (Uzonwanne, 2016). Non-aesthetic models focus on objective data analysis, which can lead to more efficient and accurate decision-making processes. However, they may lack the creative and intuitive elements that aesthetics can provide. Leaders who prefer functionality over aesthetics may prioritise speed and accuracy, leading to prompt decision-making cycles but with less emphasis on user experience or emotional intelligence.

Aesthetic leadership contributes to humanising organisational strategies to become more human-centric and future-focused through six practices, including coping with complexity, adapting dynamically to reality, embracing "dynamic duality", empathising with others, narrating stories, and living with nature (Nonaka & Takeuchi, 2021). AI's integration into leadership decision processes necessitates a balanced approach to harness its benefits while preserving vital human qualities, shaping a more adaptable and sustainable future for leadership. AI-powered technologies can improve decision-making in real-time tracking, enhanced prediction of business developments, and emerging generative AI tools that can advise leaders' decision-making (Purdy & Williams, 2023). Integrating AI into leaders' decision-making processes is not about replacing human judgment but augmenting it. Leaders are equipped with real-time insights to make more accurate and optimal decisions. The integration of AI into the decision-making processes of aesthetic leaders offers significant advantages in personalisation, data analysis, and operational efficiency. However, it brings challenges related to bias, overreliance, and transparency of the application of AI that must be carefully managed. We must bear the risks of overreliance on AI-generated ideas, maintaining harmony between AI and human judgment, balancing AI with human intuition, enhancing, not replacing, human knowledge, and the challenge of data privacy and security. AI has become an integral part of the leaders' decision-making processes, whereas the reliability of information technologies on which those decisions are based can be questionable, and data falsification is possible (Gyöngyössy et al., 2024).

## Discussion: balanced leader's human-centred decision model – challenges and benefits

After providing a comprehensive literature review on the intersection of leaders' decision-making, leaders and AI, and aesthetic leadership, the discussion will evolve around the necessity of a *balanced leader's human-centred decision model*, integrating aesthetic leadership dimensions with leaders' rational decision model supported by AI (Figure 7.3). Based on a critical literature review, the following aesthetic dimensions in organisational leaders' decision processes supported by AI-powered tools have been identified: (1) *emotional engagement,* (2) *creativity and innovation,* (3) *holistic perspective* (Ketelle & Lin, 2019), and (4) *identifying organisational purpose* and they incorporation into leaders decision making is fundamental for balanced leaders' human-centred decision processes. In contrast to the knowledge's cognitive penetrability and linear rationality, aesthetic knowledge originates from empirical knowledge and understanding (Hansen et al., 2007). Aesthetic leaders' emotional insights, aesthetic considerations that encourage creativity and innovation in organisations, and their holistic perspectives supplement the rational decision processes. Integrating aesthetic dimensions with leaders' rational decision models complemented by real-time data analytics and predictive models from AI Machine Learning Algorithms, natural language processing, and decision support systems can enhance organisational leaders' decision-making. Moreover, aesthetic leadership is positioned as one of the ideological models of leadership that are value-oriented and focused primarily on moral behaviours (Mumford & Fried, 2014). There are claims that AI is positively changing the conventional decision-making models of organisational leaders (Kaggwa & Farayola, 2023) by supporting their restricted working memory, limited ability to concentrate, and decision fatigue in stressful situations (Purdy & Williams, 2023).

At the same time, the leaders face *challenges* of maintaining aesthetic standards based on machine-driven knowledge. Leaders should combine data-driven AI recommendations with their intuition and emotional intelligence to make informed and sound decisions. This balance is crucial as AI systems can perpetuate biases or generate ethically questionable recommendations, necessitating a vigilant moral compass among leaders. That is why the implementation of AI must be human-centred (Peifer et al., 2022) and support the leaders' decision-making.

There are significant *benefits* of integrating AI in the aesthetic leaders' decision processes, but there are risks related to it, which include: (1) ethical concerns, (2) overreliance on technology, and (3) lack of transparency, which needs to be carefully considered by the leaders. Research presented the unintended negative consequences of over-reliance on AI systems in sensitive decision-making contexts without understanding the limitations and safe application of the AI models (Nassar & Kamal, 2021). The question of how we can get reliable, legally congruent information with AI support to make informed and sound decisions in line with the organisation's goals and values is fundamental (Gyöngyössy et al., 2024).

The future of leadership will hinge on the balance of human and AI insights, ensuring that technology enhances rather than diminishes the human experience within organisations. Future leaders must cultivate adaptability, AI literacy, and empathetic leadership to harness the synergies between human insight and machine precision. This holistic approach will position leaders to navigate complexities effectively while fostering a culture that values human connection and technological advancement. Successful leaders must integrate their intuitive understanding of aesthetics with the analytical capabilities of AI, ensuring that decisions reflect human sensibilities complemented by data-driven insights. Leaders must be vigilant about the potential risks of over-relying on AI, which lacks the emotional intelligence necessary for nuanced decision-making. The complementarity of humans and AI in organisational decision-making can be observed. However, sound and strict strategies need to be applied in organisations to balance human and AI-based insights in aesthetic leaders' decision processes to maintain a balanced leader's human-centred decision model – integrating aesthetic leadership dimensions with leaders' rational decision model supported by AI.

## Conclusion

Answering on the first research question (*What dimensions of aesthetic leadership are significant in organisational leaders' decision processes supported by AI-powered tools?*), it can be stated that aesthetic leadership dimensions significant in organisational leaders' decision processes supported by AI-powered tools include: (1) *emotional engagement*, which assists leaders in deeper emotional connections with the environment leading their team members to increased motivation and commitment to the work responsibilities; (2) *creativity and innovation* allowing leaders to explore unconventional solutions to challenges, question the *status quo* driving creativity, and efficiency; (3) *holistic perspective* enabling aesthetic leaders to promote a holistic view on organisational challenges and leading to nuanced and effective decisions; (4) *identifying organisational purpose*, where aesthetic considerations integrated into strategic planning, can align organisational goals with stakeholders' values and expectations and strengthen a sense of belonging of the employees.

Regarding the second research question (*What benefits and risks does the implementation of AI bring to the decision processes of aesthetic leaders?*), it can be concluded that the application of AI in the decision-making processes of aesthetic leaders brings substantial value through enhanced personalisation, improved data analysis, and efficiency in organisational operations. AI's ability to analyse large datasets in seconds has optimised leaders' data-driven decision-making. Moreover, it has been recognised that AI is helping to eliminate biases in leaders' decision-making. It is said that by relying on data and algorithms rather than subjective opinions, AI reduces the likelihood of decisions being influenced by unconscious bias, leading to more objective outcomes. Apart from the benefits of implementing AI in the aesthetic leaders' decision processes, there are risks related to it, which include (1) ethical concerns, (2) overreliance on technology, and (3) lack of transparency. Aesthetic standards influenced by biased algorithms may reinforce societal norms rather than challenge them. AI systems need to be transparent and aligned with the organisation's ethical principles to maintain trust within the firm. Ethical concerns arise when it comes to the protection of sensitive information and implementing robust security measures to prevent data breaches and misuse. Overreliance on technology is regarded as another risk, referring to the application of AI tools in aesthetic leaders' decision-making. There is a danger that leaders may become overly dependent on AI insights, neglecting their judgment and emotional intelligence, making critical thinking essential for effective leadership and balancing human intuition and machine-generated data. The concept of "AI-Minds" was formulated to describe the excessive reliance on AI technologies in gathering information, knowledge, and decision-making, which can negatively affect human cognitive processes. Apart from that, limited transparency in reaching conclusions by AI tools constitutes the next risk, combined with the application of generative AI in leaders' decision processes. AI algorithms make it difficult for leaders to understand how conclusions are reached, which can reduce trust among stakeholders within organisations.

Responding to the third research question (*What strategies can be applied to balance AI-based insights and human judgment in aesthetic leaders' decision processes?*), a statement can be made that to balance human and AI-based insights in organisational leaders' decision-making, businesses can implement strategies that include: (1) defining clear roles and objectives of the leaders and AI tools, (2) implementing collaborative workflows, using AI as a support tool, maintaining human oversight, and (3) developing human skills. Clear roles and objectives are substantial as AI tends to be effective at processing large datasets, identifying patterns, and generating predictions, whereas human insight is optimal at interpreting complex perceptions, applying context, and making ethical decisions. Implementing collaborative workflows, using AI as a support tool, and maintaining human oversight seem effective strategies for balancing AI-based insights and human judgment in aesthetic leaders' decision processes. Developing human skills, including critical thinking, complex problem-solving, emotional intelligence, interpersonal communication, adaptability, lifelong learning, ethical reasoning, and decision-making, is significant in balancing human and AI insights in leaders' decision-making processes.

To summarise the above-mentioned considerations, a conclusion can be made that leaders' AI-assisted data-driven decision-making can simulate different scenarios and their potential outcomes, enabling leaders to make proactive and informed decisions. AI practices positively correlate with the leaders' decision-making accuracy regardless of the organisation structure (El Emary et al., 2020). The role of aesthetics in leadership decision-making processes emphasises the importance of sensory experiences, creativity, and emotional intelligence in effective leadership. The human-AI symbiosis in leaders' decision processes requires proactively identifying areas in which AI can augment rather than replace humans in decision-making or manage them algorithmically. AI can extend leaders' cognition when dealing with complexity, whereas humans can contribute with a holistic, intuitive approach in dealing with uncertainty and equivocality in organisational decision-making processes (Jarrahi, 2018).

The *limitations* of this research can be listed as follows: (1) the reliance on a critical literature review resulting in the findings not being supported by original empirical research; (2) integrating aesthetic leadership dimensions including emotional engagement, creativity and innovation, holistic perspective, identifying organisational purpose with leaders' rational decision model supported by AI can be inherently subjective, resulting in varying interpretations across different organisational contexts; (3) development stage of strategies that organisations can apply to balance human and AI-based insights in aesthetic leaders' decision processes.

*Future research directions* relating to the above considerations may include: (1) the empirical research regarding aesthetic dimensions of leaders' decision-making process supported by AI tools, (2) the concept of "AI-Minds" with the excessive reliance on AI technologies in gathering information, knowledge, and decision-making, which can result in negative implications for human cognitive processes, (3) decision-making models and principles integrating leaders' aesthetic insights and AI support for transparent governance in organisational leaders' decision-making processes.

## Notes

1 Heuristic – *heuriskein* (ancient Greek) and *heurisricus* (Latin) – to find out, discover. The notion of a heuristic has played a crucial role in the A1 researchers' descriptions of their work. Heuristics constitute simple strategies that humans and even machines use to quickly form judgments, make decisions, and find solutions to complex problems. A heuristic is a strategy that ignores part of the information, with the goal of making decisions more quickly, frugally, and accurately than more complex methods (Gigerenzer & Gaissmaier, 2011, p. 454).

2 Intuition in a decision-making context is defined as a capacity for generating direct knowledge or understanding and making a decision without relying on rational concepts or logical inference (Sadler-Smith & Shefy, 2004).

3 Decision is defined here as a commitment to a course of action intended to yield results that are satisfying for specified individuals (Yates & Tschirhart, 2006).

4 Decision-making process – the method applied by decision-makers to establish and select among options relating to the matter under consideration, enabling a commitment to a course of action to be made (Choo, 1998).

## References

Agrawal, A., Gans, J. S., Goldfarb, A. (2019). Exploring the impact of artificial intelligence: Prediction versus judgment, *Information Economics and Policy*, 47, 1–6.

Al-Bayed, M. H. et al., (2024). AI in leadership: Transforming decision-making and strategic vision, *International Journal of Academic Pedagogical Research (IJAPR)*, 9(8), 1–7.

Andrade, E., & Ariely, D. (2009). The enduring impact of transient emotions on decision making, *Organizational Behavior and Human Decision Processes*, 109, 1–8.

Bizzarri, F., & Mocenni, C. (2022). *Awareness,* Academia Letters, Article 4688, 1–9.

Buchanan, L., & O'Connell, A. (2006). A brief history of decision-making, *Harvard Business Review*, 84(1), 32–41.

Chen, H. (2024). A Study of artificial intelligence's impact on aesthetic standards and its potential social dilemmas, *Journal of Sociology and Ethnology*, 6(5), 35–42.

Chen, X., Chen, J., Cheng, G., Gong, T. (2020). Topics and trends in artificial intelligence assisted human brain research, *PLoS ONE,* 15(4), 1–27.

Choo, C. W. (1998). *The knowing organization: How organizations use information to construct meaning, create knowledge and make decisions.* New York: Oxford University Press.

Crummenerl, C., Buvat, J., Sengupta, A., Shah, H., Khadikar, A., & Pendlebury-Green, A. (2019). Emotional intelligence: The essential skillset for the age of AI, *Capgemini Research Institute*, 2019, 35.

Daft, R. L. (2016). Management. Mason, OH: Thomson Learning/South-Western.

Damasio, A. R. (1994). *Descartes 'error: Emotion reason, and the human brain.* New York: Avon Books.

Dane, E., Rockmann, K. W., & Pratt, M. G. (2012). When should I trust my gut? Linking domain expertise to intuitive decision-making effectiveness, *Organizational Behavior and Human Decision Processes*, 119(2), 187–194.

Dong, Y., Hou, J., Zhang, N., Zhang, M. (2020). *Research on how human intelligence, consciousness, and cognitive computing affect the development of artificial intelligence.* Complex.

Duan, Y., Edwards, J. S., & Dwivedi, Y. K. (2019). Artificial intelligence for decision making in the era of big data – evolution, challenges and research agenda, *International Journal of Information Management*, 48, 63–71.

El-Emary, I., Al Otaibi, S., & Al Amri, W. (2020). The effect of using artificial intelligence on the quality of decision-making in various organizations: A critical survey study, *Bioscience Biotechnology Research Communications*, 13(4), 2042–2049.

Figueiredo, J. (2021). Tacit knowledge, action, learning, and spirits of science. Academia Letters, Article 1701. https://doi.org/10.20935/AL1701

Gagliardi, P. (2006). Exploring the aesthetic side of organisational life. In S. R. H. C. Clegg, C. Hardy & W. R. Nord (Eds.), *Handbook of organization studies* (Second ed., pp. 701–724). London: Sage.

Garrigan, B., Adlam, A. L. R., & Langdon, P. E. (2018). Moral decision-making and moral development: Toward an integrative framework, *Developmental Review*, 49, 80–100.

George, G., Haas, M. R., McGahan, A. M., Schillebeeckx, S. J. & Tracey, P. (2021). Purpose in the for-profit firm: A review and framework for management research, *Journal of Management*, 49(6), 1841–1869. https://doi.org/10.1177/01492063211006450.

Goleman, D., Boyatzis, R., & McKee, A. (2002) *Primal leadership: Realizing the power of emotional intelligence*. Boston, MA: Harvard Business School Press.

Goodwin, C. A., & Mucha, R. T. (n.d.). *Aesthetic Intelligence: What Business Can Learn from the Art,* 2008.

Guillet de Monthoux, P. (2004). *The art firm: Aesthetic management and metaphysical marketing.* Stanford, CA: Stanford University Press.

Guillet de Monthoux, P., Gustafsson, C., & Sjostrand, S. (Eds.) (2007). *Aesthetic leadership: Managing fields of flow in art and business.* New York: Palgrave Macmillan.

Gyöngyösi, S., Szabó, G., Barkóczy, P., & Cseh, J. (2024). A vértesszőlősi bronzkincs és szórvány csüngő archaeometallurgiai vizsgálata / Archaeometallurgical examination of the bronze hoard and stray-find pendant of Vértesszőlős (in Hungarian with English abstract), *Archeometriai Műhely* XXI/4 423–444. doi: 10.55023/issn. 1786-271X.2024-032

Hansen, H., Ropo, A., & Sauer, E. (2007). Aesthetic leadership, *The Leadership Quarterly*, 18, 544–560.

Hodgkinson, G. P., Langan-Fox, J., & Sadler-Smith, E. (2008). Intuition: A fundamental bridging construct in the behavioral sciences, *British Journal of Psychology*, 99(1), 1–27.

Ifitri, M., Aryani, N. F., Fajar, W., & Herman, H. (2024). Digital transformation in human resource management: The impact of AI and automation on employee competency development, *Indo-Fintech Intellectuals, Journal of Economics and Business*, 4(5), 2317–2328.

Jarrahi, M. H. (2018). Artificial intelligence and the future of work: Human-AI symbiosis in organizational decision making, *Business Horizons,* 61(4), 577–586.

Kaggwa, S., Farayola, O. (2023). AI in decision making: Transforming business strategies, *International Journal of Research and Scientific Innovation*, 10(12), 423–444.

Kahneman, D. (2003). A perspective on judgment and choice: Mapping bounded rationality. *American Psychologist,* 58(9), 697–720. https://doi.org/10.1037/0003-066X. 58.9.697

Kahneman, D. (2011). *Thinking, fast and slow*. London: Penguin Books.

Katz-Buonincontro, J. (2011). *How might aesthetic knowing relate to leadership? A review of literature.* International Journal of Education & the Arts, 12(SI 1.3), 1–18.

Keenan, T. M. (2016). *The use of aesthetic knowledge in decision-making processes in mega projects,* PhD dissertation, QUT Business School, Australia.

Kelly, K. (2012). *Better than human: Why robots will—and must—take our jobs*, Wired.

Kerschbaum, C., & Peschl, M. F. (2023). The power of aesthetic alignment in future-oriented organisations: The case of patagonia. *ENTRENOVA - ENTerprise REsearch InNOVAtion*, *9*(1), 387–399. https://doi.org/10.54820/entrenova-2023-0035

Kerschbaum, C. (2025). A beautiful strategy – bridging the gap between the (aesthetic) perception and (strategic) realization of the organisations' purpose, *VINE Journal of Information and Knowledge Management System*, 55(1), 1–14. https://doi.org/10.1108/VJIKMS-09-2021-0210.

Ketelle, D., & Lin, B. (2019). Aesthetic leadership and school leadership preparation: Cultivating aesthetic awareness through an arts-based leadership development curriculum, *AASA Journal of Scholarship and Practice*, 16(2), 6–17.

Kitsios, F., & Kamariotou, M. (2021). Artificial intelligence and business strategy towards digital transformation: A research agenda, *Sustainability*, 13(4), 2025.

Klus, M. F., & Müller, J. (2021). The digital leader: What one needs to master today's organisational challenges. *Journal of Business Economics*, 91(8), 1189–1223.

Koeleman, M. (2014). *Aesthetics at the heart of leadership. An exploration of business meaning and practices*. Master-thesis Business Administration, Rotterdam School of Management.

Küpers, W. (2005). Phenomenology of embodied implicit and narrative knowing. *Journal of Knowledge Management,* 9(6), 114–133. https://doi.org/10.1108/13673270510630006

Ladkin, D. (2008). Leading beautifully: How mastery, congruence and purpose create the aesthetic of embodied leadership practice, *The Leadership Quarterly*, 19, 31–41.

Logg, J. M., Minson, J. A., & Moore, D. A. (2019). Algorithm appreciation: People prefer algorithmic to human judgment, *Organizational Behavior and Human Decision Processes*, 151, 90–103.

Madanchian, M., Taherdoost, H., Vincenti, M., Mohamed, N. (2024). Transforming leadership practices through artificial intelligence, *Procedia Computer Science*, 235, 2101–2111. https://doi.org/10.1016/j.procs.2024.04.199

Manger, D. (2017). The aesthetic dimension of decision making, *International Journal of Humanities, Arts and Social Sciences*, 3(5), 223–230.

Mannix, J., & Daly, J. (2015). Aesthetic leadership: Its place in the clinical nursing world, *Journal of Mental Health Nursing*, 36, 357–361.

Manovich, L., & Arielli, E. (2021). Artificial aesthetics: Generative AI, art and visual media, *Attribution-NonCommercial-NoDerivatives,* 4(0). https://manovich.net/index.php/projects/artificial-aesthetics

Merleau-Ponty, M. (2005). *Phenomenology of perception.* New York and London: Routledge Classics.

Mumford, M., & Fried, Y. (2014). Give them what they want or give them what they need? Ideology in the study of leadership, *Journal of Organizational Behavior*, 35(5), 622–634.

Nahavandi, S. (2019). Industry 5.0—A human-centric solution, *Sustainability,* 11(16), 4371. MDPI AG.

Nassar, A., & Kamal, M. (2021). Ethical dilemmas in AI-powered decision-making: A deep dive into big data-driven ethical considerations, *International Journal of Responsible Artificial Intelligence*, 11(8):1–11.

Nonaka, S., Majima, K., Aoki, S. C., Kamitani, Y. (2021). Brain hierarchy score: Which deep neural networks are hierarchically brain-like?, *iScience*, 24(9), 103013. https://doi.org/10.1016/j.isci.2021.103013.

Nonaka, I., & Takeuchi, H. (1995). *The knowledge-creating company: How Japanese companies create the dynamics of innovation*. New York: Oxford University Press.

Nonaka, I., & Takeuchi, H. (2021). Humanizing strategy, *Long Range Planning*, 54(4), 102070. https://doi.org/10.1016/j.lrp.2021.102070

Panda, V., et al., (2023). Turning Data into Insights: Leveraging Artificial Intelligence for Better Understanding of Social Media Consumer Behaviour, *International Conference on Sustainable Emerging Innovations in Engineering and Technology (ICSEIET)*, IEEE.

Peifer, Y., Jeske, T., & Hille, S. (2022). Artificial intelligence and its impact on leaders and leadership, *Procedia Computer Science*, 200, 1024–1030.

Peng, B. (2022). Digital leadership: State governance in the era of digital technology, *Cultures of Science*, 5(4), 210–225.

Polanyi, M. (1966). *The tacit dimension*. London: Routledge & Kegan Paul.

Polat, S., & Öztoprak-Kavak, Z. (2011). Aesthetic leadership (AL): Development and implementation of aesthetic leadership scale (ALS) of the school directors, *Educational Research and Reviews*, 6(1), 50–61.

Purdy, M., & Williams, M. (2023). How AI Can Help Leaders Make Better Decisions Under Pressure, *Harvard Business Review*, 2023.

Reez, N. (2020). Foresight-based leadership. Decision-making in a growing AI environment. In Jacobs, G., Suojanen, I., Horton, K., & Bayerl, P. (eds.), *International security management: New solutions to complexity* (pp. 323–341). Cham: Springer International Publishing. https://doi.org/10.1007/978-3-030-42523-4_22

Sadler-Smith, E., & Shefy, E. (2004). The intuitive executive: Understanding and applying 'gut feel'in decision-making, *The Academy of Management Executive*, 18(4), 76–91.

Samier, E. (2008). On the Kitschification of educational administration: An aesthetic critique of theory and practice in the field. *International Studies in Educational Achievement*, 36(3), 3–18. https://doi.org/10.1016/b978-0-08-037268-6.50001-7

Sarioguz, O., & Miser, E. (2024). Artificial Intelligence and participatory leadership: The role of technological transformation, in business management and its impact on employee participation, *International Research Journal of Modernization in Engineering Technology and Science*, 6, 1618–1633.

Sayegh, L., William, P. A., & Perrewé, P. L. (2004). Managerial decision-making under crisis: The role of emotion in an intuitive decision process, *Human Resource Management Review*, 14(2), 179–199.

Shamim, M. (2022). The digital leadership on project management in the emerging digital era, *Global Mainstream Journal of Business, Economics, Development & Project Management*, 1(1), 1–14.

Siemens, G., Marmolejo-Ramos, F., Gabriel, F., Medeiros, K., Marrone, R., Joksimovic, S., & De Laat, M. (2022). *Human and artificial cognition, Computers and Education: Artificial Intelligence*, 3, 10010.

Simon, H. A. (1990). Invariants of human behavior. *Annual Review of Psychology*, 41, 1–19. https://doi.org/10.1146/annurev.ps.41.020190.000245

Soosalu, G., Henwood, S., & Deo, A. (2019). Head, heart, and gut in decision making: Development of a multiple brain preference questionnaire, *SAGE Open*, 9(1), 1–17.

Szostak, M. (2024). Phenomenological perspectives in dialectical leadership: Influence of aesthetic experiences on managing organisational complexity and paradoxes, *Discourses on Culture*, 22(1), 41–76. https://doi.org/10.2478/doc-2024-0009

Taylor, S. (2002). Overcoming aesthetic muteness: Researching organizational members' aesthetic experience, *Human Relations*, 55(7), 821–840.

Thomas, J., & Mengel, T. (2008). Preparing project managers to deal with complexity-Advance project management education, *International Journal of Project Management*, 26, 304–315.

Uzonwanne, F. (2016). Rational model of decision making. In A. Farazmand (Ed.), *Global encyclopedia of public administration, public policy, and governance*. Cham: Springer. https://doi.org/10.1007/978-3-319-31816-5_2474-1

Vasconcelos, H., Jörke, M., Grunde-McLaughlin, M., Gerstenberg, T., Bernstein, M. S., & Krishna, R. (2023). *Explanations Can Reduce Overreliance on AI Systems During Decision-Making.* Proc. ACM Hum.-Comput. Interact. 7(CSCW1), Article 129.

Wang, Y. (2021). Artificial intelligence in educational leadership: A symbiotic role of human-artificial intelligence decision-making, *Journal of Educational Administration*, 59(3), 256–270.

Wilford, A. (2011). Why the era of complex project management has emerged. In ICCPM (Ed.), *Complex project management: Global perspectives and strategic agenda to 2025 compendium of working papers* (pp. 17–20). Canberra: International Centre for Complex Project Management.

Yates, J. F., & Tschirhart, M. D. (2006). Decision-making expertise. In E. K. A., N. Charness, P. J. Feltovicj & R. R. Hoffman (Eds.), *The Cambridge handbook of expertise and expert performance* (pp. 421–438). New York: Cambridge University Press.

# 8 Textual charisma in leadership

## Aesthetic depth in navigating AI challenges through critical thinking

*Justyna Dziedzic and Iga Maria Lehman*

### Introduction

The role of critical thinking and "textual charisma" in contemporary management emphasises their importance for fostering ethical, inclusive, and innovative leadership. "Textual charisma", defined as a combination of linguistic sensitivity and stylistic uniqueness (Lehman, 2024), enables leaders to craft authentic and engaging communication that profoundly resonates with their audiences. Central to this analysis is relational reflexivity – a dynamic approach that allows leaders to tailor their messages to audience expectations and socio-cultural contexts. We contend that critical thinking, framed through "textual charisma", enhances managerial effectiveness by strengthening ethical decision-making, creativity, and inclusiveness within organisational environments. Particular emphasis is placed on how critical thinking serves as a tool for leaders to navigate the rapidly evolving landscape of technologies, such as AI.

We situate these issues within the broader context of aesthetics, which gains renewed significance in the era of AI. In management and communication, aesthetics encompasses visual elements, as well as linguistic and cultural dimensions, becoming a means of expressing values and creating emotional connections. In this context, "textual charisma" is an aesthetic medium through which leaders harmonise analytical precision with creative expression, imbuing their communication with a distinctive character.

The *research problem* of this study lies in understanding how critical thinking, reframed through the lens of textual charisma, can empower leaders to navigate the ethical, relational, and communicative complexities introduced by AI-driven environments. By examining the integration of aesthetic communication, relational reflexivity, and contextual judgment, this study aims to identify how leaders can maintain authenticity and inclusivity while leveraging automation for strategic decision-making. This approach highlights the need for a renewed managerial paradigm that balances humanistic insight with technological precision. This chapter addresses the following *research questions*: (RQ1) How does critical thinking, framed through "textual charisma", support managerial

DOI: 10.4324/9781003654377-11

effectiveness by fostering linguistic sensitivity, stylistic uniqueness, and aesthetic communication? (RQ2) What challenges do managers face in integrating critical thinking, relational reflexivity, and aesthetics into their leadership practices? (RQ3) To what extent does critical thinking, supported by "textual charisma" and an aesthetic approach, promote ethical and inclusive organisational outcomes in the context of AI-related challenges and opportunities? (RQ4) How does the interplay between AI-driven tools and textual charisma influence leaders' ability to maintain authenticity while leveraging automation for efficiency? (RQ5) In what ways does the integration of AI into leadership communication reshape the role of critical thinking in decision-making, particularly in balancing data-driven insights with human intuition?

From the *methodology* point of view, in this chapter, we conduct a systematic literature review to explore how critical thinking enhances managerial practices, addresses challenges, and fosters authenticity and reflective decision-making in the context of increasing reliance on AI technologies. To complement these theoretical insights, we examine decision-making processes and the broader implications of AI in managerial contexts. Employing a critical content analysis methodology, we identify patterns, contradictions, and gaps in existing literature. Through triangulating insights from academic frameworks, we comprehensively examine the pivotal role critical thinking plays in navigating AI-related challenges. Our analysis is based on a narrative literature review and a critical content analysis of key publications on critical thinking, textual charisma, and the integration of AI in leadership communication. Selection criteria for materials include their recency (publications from 2010 to 2024), relevance to academic debates, and contributions to the ethical and aesthetic dimensions of management in the AI context. Special attention is given to work addressing relational reflexivity, leadership communication aesthetics, and AI-driven models of management decision-making.

We emphasise that aesthetics in the context of AI require sensitivity to form and style, alongside a critical awareness of how technologies influence creative and communicative processes. The adopted *research method* of critical content analysis, supported by a narrative literature review, enables the exploration of gaps in existing research, allowing for the proposal of new perspectives on management in the technological era, where aesthetics, ethics, and innovation are deeply interconnected. This study draws on over 50 sources, including peer-reviewed journal articles, reports from international organisations, such as the OECD, Deloitte, PwC, Lewiatan Confederation, McKinsey & Company, and the World Economic Forum, as well as scholarly monographs and case studies. This diverse corpus provides a comprehensive foundation for examining the intersection of critical thinking and textual charisma with AI-driven leadership communication.

This exploratory study aims to identify research gaps and introduce new perspectives on management and critical thinking in AI-driven environments.

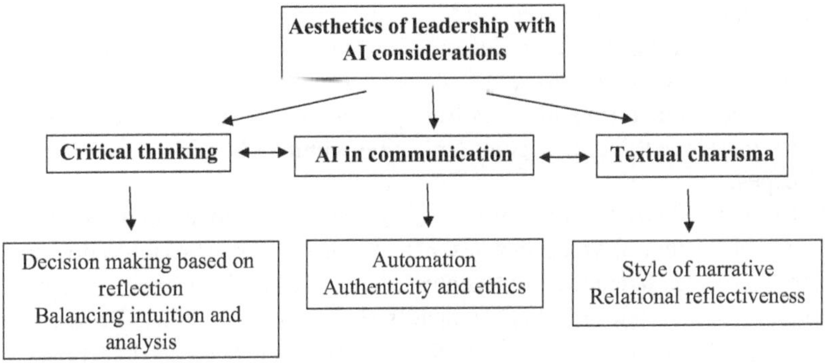


*Figure 8.1* Analytical model for critical analysis of reports.

*Source:* Own elaboration

To systematically analyse the research material, we developed a conceptual model (Figure 8.1) that integrates critical thinking, AI-driven communication, and textual charisma as key dimensions of leadership aesthetics. This framework provides a structured approach to examining how decision-making, automation ethics, and narrative coherence influence the balance between AI-driven precision and human authenticity in leadership practices. The conceptual model (Figure 8.1) visually represents the interplay between critical thinking, AI-driven communication, and textual charisma in leadership aesthetics. It illustrates how reflective decision-making, ethical considerations in automation, and narrative coherence balance AI's analytical capabilities and the human-centric authenticity essential in effective leadership. The framework will guide the interpretation of empirical examples in the subsequent chapters, highlighting how aesthetic and ethical dimensions interplay with technological mediation in leadership narratives.

## Literature review: critical thinking and textual charisma in leadership

This section examines how critical thinking and textual charisma shape leadership communication in the AI era. It explores how leaders balance technological precision with human creativity, ensuring AI enhances rather than undermines authenticity and ethical integrity.

### *Textual charisma and AI: the symbiotic potential*

Textual charisma in leadership communication derives from linguistic sensitivity and stylistic uniqueness (Lehman, 2024; Lehman & Tienari, 2024). Linguistic sensitivity, epitomised by relational reflexivity, enables leaders to frame their messages in alignment with their audiences' needs and socio-cultural contexts.

Relational reflexivity involves continuously repositioning oneself to address audience expectations, cultural contexts, and diverse identities (Cunliffe, 2022; Hibbert et al., 2014). By fostering shared understanding and emotional resonance, leaders transform audiences from passive recipients to active co-creators of meaning, embedding their communication within cultural and organisational landscapes.

Relational reflexivity arises from the writer's intent to establish credibility and craft an authorial voice that resonates with readers. Through ethos-driven and pathos-driven language, leaders create authentic and inclusive messages that meaningfully connect with their audiences (Lehman et al., 2024; Brown et al., 2012). Stylistic uniqueness, in turn, elevates communication by fostering creativity and emotional resonance (Lehman, 2024; Van Maanen, 1995a,b). Leaders craft distinctive yet inclusive narratives that align with their audience's values and aspirations by employing rhetorical devices, such as metaphors, personal anecdotes, and dialogical structures. Textual charisma thus becomes a cornerstone of leadership communication, bridging personal authenticity with collective purpose.

As AI tools become integral to leadership practices, they offer opportunities to enhance these qualities while introducing challenges. AI tools such as natural language generation systems and sentiment analysis software provide new ways to refine linguistic sensitivity and explore stylistic uniqueness. For instance, sentiment analysis enables leaders to gauge real-time audience reactions, fostering inclusivity and engagement. Similarly, generative AI suggests diverse stylistic approaches, helping leaders maintain an authentic voice while enhancing clarity and impact.

However, the integration of AI demands vigilance. While AI excels in analytical precision, it relies on predefined algorithms that may lack the nuance and ethical sensibilities inherent to human judgment. Leaders must critically assess AI outputs to ensure their communication remains authentic and culturally appropriate. Leaders can craft messages that balance technological innovation with human-centred values by harmonising AI's capabilities with textual charisma's relational and creative depth. We assert that AI tools can fortify the core pillars of textual charisma by amplifying relational reflexivity, enriching stylistic uniqueness, and enabling dialogical writing. These capabilities provide leaders with dynamic opportunities to refine their communication strategies and foster more profound engagement with their audiences through the following mechanisms:

1 *Enhancing relational reflexivity*: AI-driven tools can analyse audience sentiment, cultural preferences, and language patterns, providing leaders with actionable insights to tailor their messages. For example, sentiment analysis tools enable leaders to gauge audience reactions in real time, allowing for dynamic adjustments to communication strategies. By leveraging these insights, leaders can frame their messages to resonate more deeply with their audiences, fostering inclusivity and engagement.

2 *Augmenting stylistic uniqueness*: Generative AI tools, such as GPT models, can assist in crafting stylistically diverse and contextually relevant content. By suggesting metaphors, rhetorical structures, or alternative phrasing, these tools empower leaders to explore innovative ways of expressing ideas. While AI cannot replicate the depth of human creativity, it can act as a collaborative partner, sparking ideas that enhance stylistic distinctiveness.
3 *Facilitating dialogical writing*: AI systems that support iterative writing processes, such as collaborative editing platforms, enable leaders to engage with feedback from multiple stakeholders. This iterative approach mirrors dialogical writing's ethos, transforming communication into a shared endeavour where AI tools mediate between leader input and audience interpretation.

### *Challenges and aesthetic considerations in AI-driven leadership communication*

The idea of aesthetics in leadership goes beyond visual or artistic elements; it involves a broader perspective on how sensory experiences, emotional responses, and the physical presence of leaders shape both their actions and how others perceive them (Szostak, 2024). While AI offers substantial benefits, it also introduces challenges requiring critical thinking (Russell & Norvig, 2022; Brynjolfsson & McAfee, 2018) to establish a charismatic authorial presence effectively. We contend that these challenges are particularly significant in the following areas:

1 *Mitigating bias*: AI-generated insights and content may reflect biases embedded in the datasets on which these systems are trained. These biases often stem from historical inequalities or systemic prejudices, which can inadvertently perpetuate discriminatory narratives when left unchecked. For instance, sentiment analysis tools may produce skewed results if the underlying training data lacks diversity or misrepresents certain groups. Leaders must critically assess AI outputs to ensure inclusivity and fairness, utilising textual charisma – particularly relational reflexivity – to identify and challenge implicit biases. By framing their messages to counteract discriminatory assumptions, leaders can promote equity and social responsibility in their communication.
2 *Balancing automation and authenticity*: The increasing reliance on AI for content creation and analysis risks eroding the authenticity and emotional resonance central to textual charisma. While AI can enhance efficiency and generate stylistically varied content, it lacks the depth of human creativity and the ability to convey personal experiences or emotions. Overusing AI tools may lead to communication that feels impersonal or mechanistic, undermining the trust and connection between leaders and their audiences. To address this, leaders must maintain a human touch, ensuring AI-generated content is a supplement rather than a substitute for their unique stylistic

voice. This balance requires reflective perception, allowing leaders to discern where AI can add value, and their input is indispensable for fostering genuine engagement.

3 *Maintaining contextual ethics*: Although AI excels in processing vast data and providing analytical insights, it lacks the contextual judgment necessary to navigate complex ethical dilemmas. For example, AI may suggest optimal solutions or strategies based on statistical data but conflict with organisational values, cultural norms, or broader societal expectations. Leaders must critically evaluate AI-driven recommendations using moral intuition and ethical reasoning, ensuring alignment with principles of transparency, fairness, and the greater social good. Textual charisma reinforces this capacity by enabling leaders to articulate these nuanced ethical considerations clearly and persuasively, fostering trust and integrity in their communication.

These ethical challenges underscore the importance of critical thinking as a vital leadership skill. By integrating critical thinking with textual charisma, leaders can navigate the complexities introduced by AI while upholding their commitment to transparency, inclusion, and organisational integrity. This interplay between technological innovation and human-centred values ensures that AI-driven tools enhance communication and align with ethical and cultural standards, fostering trust and authenticity in leadership practices.

### *Critical thinking, AI, and the evolution of leadership communication*

Critical thinking has been widely explored in management, focusing on improving decision-making processes, fostering ethical leadership, and enhancing organisational outcomes. This section synthesises key themes and insights from the existing literature, underscoring how critical thinking aligns with a human-centred approach to management. Effective decision-making is a cornerstone of managerial success, and critical thinking provides a robust framework for addressing complex challenges. Ennis (2011) outlines the dispositions and abilities essential for critical thinking, highlighting their application in ethical and transparent decision-making. Similarly, Kahneman (2011) contrasts intuitive and analytical thinking, offering insights into how managers can navigate cognitive biases to make sound decisions. Critical thinking is integral to ethical leadership, as it equips managers with the tools to evaluate the moral implications of their choices. Paul and Elder (2019) emphasise that ethical reasoning is a fundamental component of critical thinking that fosters a culture of accountability and trust within organisations. Case studies, such as those of Unilever and Patagonia, illustrate how critical thinking guides leaders in balancing profitability with ethical responsibilities (Unilever, 2023; Fast Company, Inc., n.d.).

The impact of critical thinking on organisational performance has been extensively documented. Fisher (2011) and McKee (2017) argue that managers who employ critical thinking are better positioned to drive innovation and adaptability, which are essential for sustainable growth. The case of IBM's digital transformation demonstrates how strategic critical thinking can realign business operations with evolving market demands, ensuring long-term success (Forbes, n.d.). The theoretical underpinnings of critical thinking in management are deeply rooted in education and philosophy. Brown and Keeley (2016) advocate for questioning as a critical skill, while Lipman (2003) explores its role in fostering reflective thinking.

Halpern (2013) extends this discussion to applied contexts, demonstrating how critical thinking translates into practical problem-solving in organisational settings. Despite its recognised importance, integrating critical thinking into managerial practices faces several challenges. These include resistance to change, limited training opportunities, and the persistence of traditional hierarchical models. Addressing these barriers requires a concerted effort to embed critical thinking into organisational culture, supported by case studies and empirical research (Mumford & Frese, 2015; Walshe & Tait, 2019). By connecting these perspectives, the literature underscores the transformative potential of critical thinking in management. It enhances decision-making and ethical leadership and supports the development of inclusive and innovative organisational cultures.

The Future of Jobs Report (World Economic Forum, 2023) identifies critical thinking as a top skill required in the evolving workforce, particularly as automation and AI disrupt traditional roles. Similarly, McKinsey Global Institute (2017) highlights how critical thinking supports workforce transitions in an era of automation, focusing on skills that balance technological efficiency with human adaptability. A key concern Deloitte Insights (2019) addresses is the emphasis on human-centred leadership in an AI-driven world. Deloitte underscores the importance of managers fostering trust and accountability while navigating technological transformations. This aligns with findings from PwC (2021), highlighting that ethical decision-making remains a core managerial challenge when adopting AI systems. Managers are tasked with balancing algorithmic precision with contextual ethics to ensure transparent and responsible outcomes.

The OECD's Skills for 2030 report (2022) further supports the need for adaptive skills, such as critical and logical thinking, to address the complexities of a digitised world. OECD identifies that while AI excels in data processing and pattern recognition, it lacks human capabilities such as empathy-driven reasoning, moral intuition, and creative problem framing – skills essential for navigating ambiguity and ethical dilemmas. Key sources include Paul and Elder's (2019) critical thinking model, which identifies fundamental components such as clarity, accuracy, and logical reasoning. Additionally, Ennis's (2011) dispositions for critical thinking provide a foundation for understanding reflective inquiry, scepticism, and analytical judgment. Integrating these theoretical frameworks enables a structured analysis of critical thinking as an essential managerial competency.

The growing use of algorithms in decision-making raises demands for accountability, requiring decision-makers to justify automated outcomes based on clear guiding principles (Binns, 2018). The essence of Communities of Practice lies in the process of "thinking together", where members collaboratively shape their understanding of shared problems, facilitating the exchange of tacit knowledge and professional learning (Pyrko et al., 2017). Machine behaviour is an emerging interdisciplinary field, emphasising that AI systems should be studied as engineering artefacts and autonomous agents with distinct behavioural patterns that interact with and shape social, economic, and political systems. It highlights the need for a broad research agenda to understand the implications of AI-driven decision-making, address ethical concerns, and establish frameworks for the responsible integration of AI into society (Rahwan et al., 2019). A study (Lee et al., 2025) conducted on 319 knowledge workers who regularly use generative AI tools, such as ChatGPT and Copilot, found that individuals with higher trust in AI technology exhibited lower engagement in critical thinking compared to those who placed greater confidence in their abilities. The latter group was likelier to verify, refine, and critically integrate AI-generated responses.

### *Textual charisma in leadership: rhetoric, dialogue, and authority*

Textual charisma operates as a dynamic force in leadership, shaped by rhetorical, dialogical, and authoritative dimensions. By engaging readers through carefully constructed arguments, fostering collaborative dialogues, and anchoring collective action in textually mediated practices, writing emerges as a transformative tool for leadership within management and organisational research. This review examines foundational studies that elucidate how writing influences leadership by leveraging these textual elements.

Locke and Golden-Biddle's (1997) exploration of rhetorical elements in scientific work reveals how persuasive features enable scholarly texts to resonate with audiences. They argue that scientific outputs are not merely factual compilations but carefully constructed arguments that engage readers through rhetorical strategies. Analysing 82 articles from the *Academy of Management Journal* and *Administrative Science Quarterly*, they identify two pivotal insights: (1) texts reflect their relationship to the social realities of their creation, and (2) the objectivity claimed in scientific reporting is often a "pretence" (pp. 1059–1060). These findings underscore the importance of rhetorical sophistication, suggesting that *textual charisma* in leadership relies on crafting arguments that resonate with and persuade audiences effectively.

Helin's (2019) conceptualisation of "dialogical writing" emphasises written communication's emergent, unfinished, and relational nature, particularly in collaborative contexts. Helin presents dialogical writing as responsive to prior discourse and future possibilities by drawing on literature about performative utterances and integrating fieldwork into the writing process. Her work identifies three key dimensions that contribute to textual charisma: (1) the generative potential of integrating writing with fieldwork, (2) the inseparability of spoken and written language, and (3) a reimagined notion of authorship as a collaborative dialogue (pp. 12–13). Extending her perspective, writing can be viewed as a dialogue between writer and reader, where leadership emerges through the author engaging with their audience to co-construct meaning (see Lehman & Sułkowski, 2023).

Kuhn's (2008) concept of "authoritative text" enriches the leadership discussion by examining how written communication mediates organisational practices. Adopting a discursive lens, Kuhn explores the interplay between "concrete" and "figurative" texts and their role in shaping co-oriented, distributed actions. This demonstrates how individuals and collectives participate in textually mediated practices that redefine organisational operations. In this context, leadership emerges through the ability to create and mobilise texts that align collective actions with organisational goals.

While the textual strategies outlined above – rhetorical sophistication, dialogical writing, and authoritative text – underscore the transformative potential of writing in leadership, they gain greater significance when integrated with critical thinking. As AI increasingly shapes decision-making processes, the intersection of textual charisma and critical thinking becomes pivotal. AI excels in enhancing analytical reasoning but often lacks the ethical sensibilities, creativity, and relational understanding central to effective leadership. Leaders can navigate these complexities by leveraging critical thinking, ensuring that authoritative texts and AI-driven insights align with ethical principles and organisational goals. This synthesis highlights the importance of human oversight in maintaining accountability, fostering innovation, and achieving human-centred organisational outcomes, as the World Economic Forum (2023) emphasises. In this light, textual charisma and critical thinking operate as complementary forces, enabling managers to adapt to an evolving digital landscape while anchoring their practices in ethical and reflective decision-making.

## Results: the aesthetics of leadership – bridging critical thinking, textual charisma, and AI

The results presented in this section are deeply rooted in aesthetics as they explore how leaders craft meaningful, engaging, and ethical communication in AI-driven management. In this framework, aesthetics extends beyond superficial virtuosity (such as external or performative aspects), encompassing linguistic sensitivity, stylistic uniqueness, and the emotional resonance of messages. This study's results in this context highlight key areas: (1) textual charisma and leadership and the role of relational reflexivity and (2) balancing innovation and authenticity in AI-driven leadership communication, particularly in harmonising human intuition with automation while maintaining ethical and relational depth.

### *Balancing innovation and authenticity in AI-driven leadership communication*

The findings highlight how leaders, by leveraging critical thinking and textual charisma, create aesthetically coherent communication strategies that align with organisational values and cultural contexts. Table 8.1 presents key findings from reports on the impact of AI on leadership, highlighting the importance of critical thinking, ethical challenges in decision-making, and the role of AI in shaping leadership communication. The analysis highlights the potential benefits of AI and the risks associated with automating decision-making processes and compromising authenticity in leadership interactions. While AI-driven tools enhance efficiency and adaptability in leadership communication, maintaining authenticity requires a strategic and intentional approach. Rather than replacing a leader's unique style, AI can serve as a complementary aid that refines messaging while preserving personal voice and values. Customisation features in AI-driven writing assistants enable leaders to infuse their distinct tone, preferred rhetorical strategies, and relational nuances into AI-generated content, ensuring that the output aligns with their communication style. Additionally, AI-supported real-time feedback mechanisms, such as sentiment analysis and engagement analytics, can help leaders fine-tune their messaging to resonate with audiences without compromising authenticity. The key lies in critical oversight and selective integration, where leaders actively curate, edit, and personalise AI-generated content, ensuring that it enhances rather than dilutes their human-centred leadership approach.

Analysis of reports has shown that AI enhances the efficiency of decision-making. However, it requires conscious management by leaders, both in terms of their competencies and understanding of the role of AI in the decision-making process. AI is a valuable tool for managers, but it should be utilised to support thought processes. Critical thinking competencies are crucial in evaluating the data and solutions that AI provides through algorithmic thinking. Textual charisma, therefore, requires authenticity, which entails a particular obligation to balance technology and human involvement. Human intuition and reflexivity distinguish leaders' communication in this process, and AI should be treated as a tool that supports and provides the necessary data and information. Therefore, future leaders must combine AI with critical thinking skills and cultivate textual charisma to build engagement and authority in the digital world. Reports indicate that AI supports critical thinking but cannot replace reflective analysis of leaders; authenticity and textual charisma are crucial for effective leadership in the digital age. Leaders who use AI to analyse data but maintain a human approach to communication are more effective and trustworthy.

*Table 8.1* Summary of findings from selected reports on AI and leadership competencies

| *McKinsey and Company (2024) – AI in leadership* | *Lewiatan Confederation (2023) – Competences of the future of leaders* | *World Economic Forum (2024) – AI-driven leadership* |
|---|---|---|
| The state of AI in early 2024 report indicates that 78% of business leaders see critical thinking as a key competency in the AI era. AI provides leaders with vast data, but interpreting results and making decisions requires reflective thinking. McKinsey emphasises that the effectiveness of AI in management depends on the ability of leaders to combine technology with ethical decision-making. | The forecast of the demand for competencies and qualifications in selected industries in connection with economic changes analyses which skills will be crucial for leaders in the coming years. It points to the growing importance of digital competence, critical thinking and adaptability in the AI era. | A report by *the World Economic Forum (2024)* indicates that AI increases leaders' effectiveness, enabling them to process information faster and better personalise communication. However, the misuse of AI can undermine relational reflexivity, leading to shallow human relationships and automated decisions without deeper contextual analysis. |
| **Critical thinking**<br>Leaders use AI as a supporting tool but must also make key decisions based on their analysis and intuition.<br>The report highlights the risk of over-reliance on AI, which can lead to mechanical decision-making without reflection on context and ethical implications.<br>A leader's effectiveness is based on the ability to filter AI-generated data and identify algorithmic biases. | **AI in decision-making**<br>Leaders are using AI to analyse big data, but the report highlights that the ability to interpret results remains crucial.<br>The risk of "blind trust" in AI, i.e., making decisions based on algorithmic recommendations without questioning them, was indicated.<br>The report suggests that critical thinking training should include an analysis of AI's risks and ethical aspects. | **AI in decision-making**<br>Leaders use AI for data processing and analysis, but the WEF report warns against unwittingly transferring algorithmic biases into management decisions.<br>Automating decision-making processes can lead to AI making decisions based on patterns and historical patterns rather than considering dynamically changing conditions.<br>A lack of critical analysis of AI-generated data can lead to wrong conclusions, especially in the organisation's recruitment, talent management, or internal communication. |

(*Continued*)

*Table 8.1* (Continued)

| *McKinsey and Company (2024) – AI in leadership* | *Lewiatan Confederation (2023) – Competences of the future of leaders* | *World Economic Forum (2024) – AI-driven leadership* |
|---|---|---|
| **Textual charisma and relational reflexivity of leaders** | **Textual charisma and relational reflexivity of leaders** | **Textual charisma of leaders and AI** |
| Leaders should use AI to personalise communication but maintain their unique narrative style and contact with their audience. Leaders who retain elements of textual charisma (e.g., storytelling, metaphors, emotional appeals) are better perceived by their audiences. | Leaders need to develop persuasive storytelling skills in the age of remote communication and digital tools. | AI can support leaders in creating dynamic narratives, but too much use of AI in communication can decrease the message's authenticity. |
| While AI can make content creation easier, leaders fear losing authenticity if they rely solely on automation. | The growing role of storytelling in building the leader's authority, crucial in managing dispersed teams of organisations, was indicated. | Leaders must balance automation and authenticity, not just to become curators of AI-generated content. |
| We indicate examples of companies that use AI to generate personalised emails and tailor content to recipients, which increases their engagement. | AI can help analyse sentiment, e.g., determine the emotions of recipients on social media, which allows leaders to adapt messages to current needs. | Introducing AI into organisational communication can help analyse sentiment and personalise content, but it will not replace the intuitive adjustment of tone and emotion in an interpersonal relationship. |

*Source:* Own elaboration based on McKinsey and Company (2024); Lewiatan Confederation (2023); and World Economic Forum (2024).

***Textual charisma and leadership: the role of relational reflexivity***

Aesthetics emerge as a vital dimension of leadership. It enables the fusion of creativity, empathy, and ethical reflection, transforming leadership practices into a harmonious interplay of human-centred values and technological innovation. This perspective underscores the transformative potential of aesthetics in redefining leadership as a practice that integrates beauty, meaning, and purpose into organisational communication. Aesthetics emerge as a vital dimension of leadership. It enables the fusion of creativity, empathy, and ethical reflection, transforming leadership practices into a harmonious interplay of human-centred values and technological innovation. This perspective underscores the transformative potential of aesthetics in redefining leadership as a practice that integrates beauty, meaning, and purpose into organisational communication.

The findings are reflected in the proposed models of critical thinking dimensions for leaders and AI and in the tables outlining key competencies, which provide a structured framework for ethical, adaptive, and creative leadership in the digital age. This study identifies three primary outcomes, demonstrating how critical thinking and textual charisma shape leadership communication, how AI integration presents both opportunities and challenges, and how strategic approaches can help leaders maintain authenticity and ethical integrity in an AI-driven landscape:

1 *Enhancing managerial practices through critical thinking and textual charisma.* This study identifies critical thinking, framed through textual charisma, as a key enabler of fostering deeper engagement, creativity, and trust in organisational communication. Results demonstrate that managers who integrate linguistic sensitivity and stylistic uniqueness into their practices create stronger emotional connections with their teams, enhance collaboration, and promote a shared sense of purpose. Textual charisma amplifies the expressive power of managerial messages, allowing leaders to inspire reflection, authenticity, and inclusivity in organisational culture. Furthermore, the findings suggest that, as expressed through textual charisma, critical thinking enables managers to engage critically with AI-driven tools and insights. This capacity supports the development of meaningful, aesthetically coherent communication strategies, ensuring that technological advancements are aligned with human-centred and creative leadership practices.
2 *Overcoming challenges and promoting authenticity and reflective perception outcomes in AI.* The second part of the findings examines the challenges managers encounter in integrating critical thinking into their leadership practices, particularly in the context of AI implementation. These challenges include navigating the dynamic interplay between human judgement and machine intelligence, ensuring transparency, and addressing potential biases in AI-generated data. Despite these challenges, the results underscore that

> critical thinking and relational reflexivity empower managers to build ethical, sustainable, and inclusive organisational cultures. The findings highlight the role of critical thinking in fostering a balance between technological advancements and human-centred values, with managers leveraging their unique voices to cultivate creativity and ethical decision-making.

Through a critical lens, this chapter proposes pathways for integrating critical thinking into management practices, suggesting strategies for managers aiming to foster human-centred organisational cultures. The model (Figure 8.2) presents the core dimensions of critical thinking essential for both leaders and AI systems in decision-making processes. The model illustrates the interdependencies between leaders' critical thinking skills and AI competencies, highlighting their role in achieving effective, ethical, and value-driven decisions. It demonstrates how combining these elements influences organisational outcomes, balancing human intuition and creativity with AI's analytical precision.

Table 8.2 presents the critical and logical thinking competencies unique to leaders, emphasising their ability to navigate complex and ambiguous decision-making contexts where artificial intelligence alone is insufficient. It

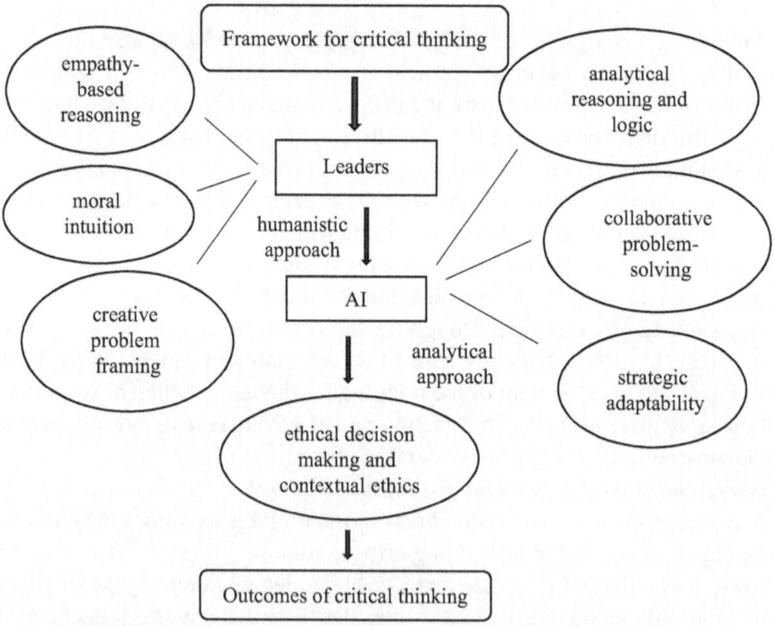


*Figure 8.2* Model of core dimensions of critical thinking for leaders using AI.

*Source:* Own elaboration

highlights how leaders' empathy-driven reasoning, moral intuition, and contextual ethics complement AI's analytical capabilities. These dimensions ensure that decision-making processes consider human well-being, ethical principles, and creative problem-solving, reinforcing human judgment's indispensable role in leadership.

*Table 8.2* Leader critical and logical thinking competencies

| *Core dimensions* | *Definition* | *Relevance* | *Key skill* |
|---|---|---|---|
| Empathy-driven reasoning | Understanding and considering decisions' emotional and social context ensures they account for human well-being. | AI can process data but cannot grasp nuanced human emotions, interpersonal dynamics, or cultural subtleties. Managers with empathy-driven reasoning can anticipate how decisions will affect employees, clients, and stakeholders on a personal level. | Translating abstract data into actionable insights prioritising emotional intelligence and fostering trust and engagement within teams. |
| Moral intuition | The ability to draw on moral principles to navigate decisions without clear guidelines. | While AI can follow predefined rules, it cannot rely on innate moral sensibilities to guide decisions in ambiguous scenarios. | Applying personal moral judgment to complex, ambiguous situations. |
| Contextual ethics | The ability to apply situational judgement to ethical dilemmas, factoring in cultural norms and historical context. | AI cannot weigh ethical trade-offs dynamically. Managers ensure ethical decisions remain culturally and contextually appropriate. | Identifying unintended consequences and adapting ethical principles to fit real-world complexities. |
| Creative problem framing | The ability to reframe problems in novel ways to uncover unique solutions beyond AI's predictive capabilities. | AI excels at optimising within predefined parameters but needs more ingenuity to question those parameters or redefine problems creatively. Managers can leverage their imagination to explore unconventional paths and inspire innovation. | Challenging the status quo, envisioning alternatives, and fostering a culture of innovation within teams. |

*Source:* Own elaboration.

Table 8.3 outlines AI's critical and logical thinking competencies, emphasising its role in enhancing decision-making processes through analytical precision, ethical evaluation, and strategic adaptability. It highlights how AI's capabilities – from analytical reasoning to collaborative problem-solving – support managerial decision-making. While AI excels at processing vast amounts of data, identifying patterns, and providing evidence-based recommendations, its reliance on predefined logic underscores the need for human oversight to address ethical, contextual, and creative challenges.

The integration of AI tools into leadership practices offers practical opportunities to amplify textual charisma while addressing its challenges:

1 *Interactive narrative framing:* Leaders can use AI to craft narratives that engage audiences as active participants. For instance, adaptive storytelling

*Table 8.3* AI critical and logical thinking competencies

| *Core dimensions* | *Definition* | *Relevance* | *Key skill* |
|---|---|---|---|
| Analytical reasoning and logic | The ability to evaluate data, identify patterns, and distinguish between correlation and causation. | Managers must assess AI outputs critically, understanding their foundations and limitations (e.g., algorithm biases). | Breaking down complex problems into manageable parts and questioning underlying assumptions. |
| Ethical decision-making | Applying moral principles to evaluate the impact of decisions on stakeholders. | As AI becomes central to decision-making, managers must balance efficiency with ethical considerations. | Identifying ethical dilemmas, assessing risks, and making decisions that align with human values. |
| Strategic adaptability | The capacity to integrate AI-driven insights with human judgment for long-term planning. | Managers must adapt to rapid technological changes while maintaining organisational stability. | Combining AI forecasts with a strategic vision to craft sustainable and innovative solutions. |
| Collaborative problem-solving | Engaging diverse teams to address challenges through inclusive decision-making. | AI thrives on data diversity, and managers must leverage human collaboration to ensure comprehensive data interpretation. | Facilitating dialogue, integrating diverse perspectives, and fostering trust among team members. |

*Source:* Own elaboration.

platforms allow dynamic adjustments to content based on audience feedback, fostering a dialogical and inclusive communication style.

2 *Ethical decision-making frameworks:* AI tools can assist leaders in modelling ethical scenarios, providing data-driven insights into potential outcomes. Leaders can then draw on textual charisma to present these insights in ways that emphasise empathy, moral reasoning, and contextual sensitivity.
3 *Cross-cultural communication:* NLP tools that support multilingual and multicultural communication enable leaders to craft messages that resonate across diverse audiences. By integrating relational reflexivity with AI-driven linguistic analysis, leaders can ensure their messages bridge cultural divides and foster global inclusivity.

## Discussion: the human edge in AI-driven leadership

The findings underscore the vital role of critical thinking in mitigating the limitations of AI in contemporary managerial decision-making processes. While AI excels at analytical reasoning, identifying patterns, and providing data-driven recommendations, its reliance on predefined algorithms creates gaps that require human oversight (World Economic Forum, 2023). This gap highlights managers' need to employ critical thinking skills – such as empathy-driven reasoning, moral intuition, and contextual ethics – to ensure decisions are ethical, inclusive, and aligned with organisational values (Paul & Elder, 2019; OECD, 2022).

One key aspect emerging from the analysis is the importance of empathy-driven reasoning, which remains beyond AI's capabilities. As noted by Deloitte Insights (2019), AI cannot grasp decision-making's emotional and social dimensions, which are crucial for fostering trust and employee engagement. Managers with empathy-driven reasoning can anticipate the personal implications of decisions for stakeholders and adjust their strategies accordingly. This competency is particularly relevant in organisations striving to balance technological efficiency with human well-being.

Furthermore, the analysis reveals that moral intuition is pivotal in navigating ambiguous scenarios where ethical guidelines are absent or unclear. While AI can apply predefined ethical principles, it lacks the innate moral sensibility needed to evaluate complex, context-dependent dilemmas (PwC, 2021). Human leaders bridge this gap by applying personal judgment and reflecting on their decisions' broader social and cultural implications. This reinforces the findings by Ennis (2011), who emphasised the importance of reflective inquiry in ethical decision-making.

Another key insight is the concept of creative problem framing, where critical thinking enables managers to challenge assumptions and reframe problems in novel ways. AI operates within predefined boundaries, optimising solutions based on existing parameters (Kahneman, 2011). However, as the literature demonstrates, innovation often requires stepping outside these boundaries and exploring unconventional pathways. Managers leverage their creativity to envision alternatives, fostering a culture of adaptability and innovation (Fisher, 2011; McKee, 2017).

Textual charisma also emerges as a crucial framework for bridging the gap between AI-driven insights and human-centred leadership. Through its core components – linguistic sensitivity, stylistic uniqueness, and relational reflexivity – textual charisma enables managers to craft compelling messages that resonate deeply with their audiences. AI tools can provide valuable analytical support, such as sentiment analysis or content generation, but lack the nuanced understanding required to adapt messages to diverse cultural contexts or emotional landscapes. Managers with textual charisma can integrate these insights with their creative and empathetic communication styles, fostering trust, inclusivity, and alignment with organisational values. This dynamic interplay ensures that managerial communication remains impactful and authentic in an AI-driven era.

The results also highlight collaborative problem-solving as an area where human judgment and AI intersect. AI thrives on data diversity, offering insights that inform decision-making processes. However, as noted in the OECD's Skills for 2030 report (2022), integrating diverse human perspectives remains essential for interpreting data holistically and addressing complex organisational challenges. Managers are key in facilitating inclusive dialogue, fostering trust, and synthesising insights to create actionable strategies.

While critical thinking is fundamental to managerial effectiveness, several challenges to its integration persist. Resistance to change, limited training opportunities, and overreliance on AI-driven processes can impede the development of critical thinking skills in organisational settings (Walshe & Tait, 2019). Addressing these barriers requires a systemic effort to embed critical thinking into leadership development programs and organisational culture.

The interplay between AI's analytical precision and human critical thinking creates a synergistic approach to decision-making. By combining AI-driven insights with human judgment, managers can navigate the complexities of the modern business environment while ensuring ethical, innovative, and human-centred outcomes. This aligns with the growing recognition that human capabilities – such as empathy, moral reasoning, and creativity – remain irreplaceable in the era of AI (World Economic Forum, 2023; Paul & Elder, 2019).

## Conclusion

This chapter highlights the emerging significance of critical thinking and textual charisma as leadership tools in an era increasingly influenced by artificial intelligence. While these concepts offer transformative potential for fostering inclusivity, creativity, and ethical decision-making, their integration into leadership practices is far from straightforward. Beyond theoretical considerations, the real-world application of these ideas reveals opportunities and constraints that merit further exploration.

Addressing the first research question (*How does textual charisma shape leadership communication in AI-driven environments?*), it can be said that textual charisma ensures authenticity, engagement, and adaptability in AI-driven leadership communication. By integrating linguistic sensitivity, rhetorical strategies, and relational reflexivity, leaders maintain a human-centred voice, preventing AI-driven messages from becoming impersonal or mechanical. Regarding the second research question (*In what ways can AI tools support or challenge ethical and creative managerial dialogue?*), AI enhances communication through sentiment analysis, stylistic refinement, and audience adaptation. However, it also poses risks such as bias, loss of authenticity, and over-reliance on automation. Leaders must critically evaluate AI outputs, ensuring they align with ethical and creative values. Regarding the third research question (*How can leaders integrate AI-driven communication while maintaining authenticity and relational depth?*), leaders should use AI as a support tool, not a substitute, refining AI-generated content to preserve their unique style and ethical stance. They can balance technological efficiency and genuine engagement by leveraging real-time audience feedback and relational reflexivity. Referring to the fourth research question (*How does the interplay between AI-driven tools and textual charisma influence leaders' ability to maintain authenticity while leveraging automation for efficiency?),* AI enhances linguistic precision; however, leaders must actively shape AI-generated content to ensure authenticity is maintained. Through relational reflexivity and stylistic uniqueness, textual charisma ensures AI-assisted communication remains personal and aligned with organisational values. AI tools support refinement, but critical oversight is essential to prevent impersonal or biased messaging. Regarding the fifth research question (*In what ways does the integration of AI into leadership communication reshape the role of critical thinking in decision-making?),* AI improves efficiency and data analysis; however, leaders must apply critical thinking – encompassing moral intuition, contextual ethics, and creative framing – to ensure ethical, human-centred decisions. While AI-driven insights aid decision-making, reflective judgement is crucial to mitigating bias and maintaining organisational integrity.

A central *limitation* of this study lies in the challenge of operationalising abstract concepts, such as textual charisma and relational reflexivity, into measurable, practical frameworks for leadership development. These constructs' dynamic and context-dependent nature makes it difficult to establish universal guidelines, leaving their application highly reliant on individual interpretation and situational awareness. Moreover, while the discussion incorporates AI's potential as a creative partner, it acknowledges that the technology is limited by its dependence on preexisting data and algorithms. This constraint presents significant challenges for leaders who use AI tools to foster innovative and culturally sensitive communication. Another limitation stems from the evolving nature of AI. As technology continues to develop, new ethical and aesthetic dilemmas are likely to emerge, potentially outpacing the frameworks proposed in this chapter. Future research could address how these rapid advancements reshape the balance between human creativity and machine-generated insights, particularly in cross-cultural and interdisciplinary contexts. The findings underscore the necessity of integrating critical thinking into leadership training, yet they also reveal structural barriers within organisations, such as hierarchical resistance and insufficient emphasis on reflective practice. While this chapter explores theoretical pathways for overcoming these challenges, practical strategies for embedding critical thinking and textual charisma into organisational cultures remain underdeveloped and require further empirical validation.

Despite these limitations, this chapter offers a foundation for *future research directions* regarding reimagining leadership communication at the intersection of ethics, aesthetics, and technology. It calls for leaders to embrace their roles as cultural intermediaries who can harmonise human values with technological innovation. By continuing to refine our understanding of critical thinking and textual charisma, we open new avenues for creating leadership practices that are not only effective but also deeply humane. Future research should explore how AI-driven communication influences long-term leadership effectiveness, particularly in maintaining authenticity and relational depth. Comparative analyses of AI-integrated leadership across industries could provide insights into sector-specific challenges and best practices. Further research should also examine the evolution of textual charisma in AI-mediated environments, exploring how generative AI tools influence linguistic creativity and rhetorical strategies. Finally, interdisciplinary studies incorporating management, linguistics, and AI ethics could refine frameworks for integrating AI into leadership communication while preserving human-centred values.

## References

Binns, R. (2018). Algorithmic accountability and public reason. *Philosophy & Technology*, 31(4), 1–14. https://doi.org/10.1007/s13347-017-0263-5

Brown, A. D., Ainsworth, S., Grant, D. (2012). The rhetoric of institutional change. *Organization Studies*, 33(3), 297–321.

Brynjolfsson, E., & McAfee, A. (2018). Machine, Platform, Crowd: Harnessing Our Digital Future. W.W. Norton & Company.

Brown, P., & Keeley, S. M. (2016). *Asking the right questions: A guide to critical thinking* (12th ed.). Pearson. Retrieved from https://www.pearson.com/us/higher-education.html

Cunliffe, A. L. (2022). Must I grow a pair of balls to theorize about theory in organization and management studies? *Organization Theory*, 3(3), 1–28.

Cunliffe, A. L., & Karunanayake, G. (2013). Working within hyphen-spaces in ethnographic research: Implications for research identities and practice. *Organizational Research Methods*, 16, 364–392.

Deloitte. (2019). *Leading the social enterprise: Reinvent with a human focus. Deloitte Insights*, Retrieved from https://www2.deloitte.com

Ennis, R. H. (2011). *The nature of critical thinking: An outline of critical thinking dispositions and abilities*. Retrieved from https://education.illinois.edu/docs/default-source/faculty-documents/robert-ennis/thenatureofcriticalthinking_51711_000.pdf

Fisher, A. (2011). *Critical thinking: An introduction* (2nd ed.). Cambridge University Press. Retrieved from https://www.cambridge.org

Halpern, D. F. (2013). *Thought and knowledge: An introduction to critical thinking* (5th ed.). Routledge. Retrieved from https://www.routledge.com

Helin, J. (2019). Dialogical writing: Co-inquiring between the written and the spoken word. *Culture and Organization*, 25, 1–15.

Hibbert, P., Sillince, J., Diefenbach, T., & Cunliffe, A. (2014). Relationally reflexive practice: A generative approach to theory development in qualitative research, *Organizational Research Methods,* 17(3), 278–298.

Kahneman, D. (2011). *Thinking fast and slow*. Farrar, Straus and Giroux. Retrieved from https://us.macmillan.com

Kuhn, T. (2008). A communicative theory of the firm: Developing an alternative perspective on intra-organizational power and stakeholder relationships. *Organization Studies*, 29(8–9), 1227–1254.

Lee, H. -P., Sarkar, A., Tankelevitch, L., Drosos, I., Rintel, S., Banks, R., & Wilson, N. (2025). *The impact of generative AI on critical thinking: Self-reported reductions in cognitive effort and confidence effects from a survey of knowledge workers*. Microsoft Research.

Lehman, I. M. (2024). *Charismatic leadership in organizations: A critique of texts* (1st ed.). Routledge.

Lehman, I. M., & Sułkowski, Ł. (2023). Reader perceptions of authorial voice in top-tier management journals: The case of doctoral students of management from Eastern Europe. *Journal of Management Education*, 47(4), 349–387. https://doi.org/10.1177/10525629231170619

Lehman, I. M., Tienari, J., Hyland, K., & Alejandro, A. (2024). Forum: The case for reflexive writing practices in management communication and organization studies. *Management Communication Quarterly*, 38(3), 698–729.

Lehman, I. M., & Tienari, J. (2024). What do you mean? Linguistic sensitivity and relational reflexivity in scholarly writing. *Organization*, 32(3), 464–475. https://doi.org/10.1177/13505084241233956

Lewiatan Confederation. (2023). Forecast of demand for competencies and qualifications in selected industries in connection with economic changes. *Lewiatan Confederation*. https://lewiatan.org/wp-content/uploads/2023/07/prognoza_zapotrzebowania_na_kompetencje.pdf

Lipman, M. (2003). *Thinking in education* (2nd ed.). Cambridge University Press. Retrieved from https://www.cambridge.org

Locke, K., & Golden-Biddle, K. (1997). Opportunities for contribution: Structuring Intertextual coherence and "problematizing" in organizational studies, *Academy of Management Journal,* 40, 1023–1062.

McKee, A. (2017). *Management: A focus on leadership and critical thinking*. Routledge. Retrieved from https://www.routledge.com

McKinsey Global Institute. (2017). *Jobs lost, jobs gained: Workforce transitions in a time of automation*. McKinsey & Company. Retrieved from https://www.mckinsey.com

McKinsey & Company. (2024). *The state of AI in early 2024*. McKinsey & Company. https://www.mckinsey.com/capabilities/quantumblack/our-insights/the-state-of-ai

Mumford, M. D., & Frese, M. (2015). *The psychology of planning in organisations: Research and applications*. Routledge. Retrieved from https://www.routledge.com

OECD (2022). *Skills for 2030: Preparing for a changing world of work*. OECD Publishing. Retrieved from https://www.oecd.org

Paul, R., & Elder, L. (2019). *Critical thinking: Concepts and tools* (8th ed.). Foundation for Critical Thinking. Retrieved from https://www.criticalthinking.org

Pw, C. (2021). *AI and the future of work: A matter of choices*. PwC. Retrieved from https://www.pwc.com

Pyrko, I., Dörfler, V., & Eden, C. (2017). Thinking together: What makes communities of practice work? *Human Relations,* 70(4), 389–409. https://doi.org/10.1177/0018726716661040

Rahwan, I., Cebrian, M., Obradovich, N., Bongard, J., Bonnefon, J. -F., Breazeal, C., Crandall, J. W., Christakis, N. A., Couzin, I. D., Jackson, M. O., Jennings, N. R., Kamar, E., Kloumann, I. M., Larochelle, H., Lazer, D., McElreath, R., Mislove, A., Parkes, D. C., Pentland, A. S., Wellman, M. (2019). Machine behaviour. *Nature,* 568(7753), 477–486. https://doi.org/10.1038/s41586-019-1138-y

Russell, S., & Norvig, P. (2022). *Artificial intelligence: A modern approach* (4th ed.). Pearson.

Szostak, M. (2024). Phenomenological perspectives in dialectical leadership: Influence of aesthetic experiences on managing organisational complexity and paradoxes. *Discourses on Culture*, 22(1), 41–76. https://doi.org/10.2478/doc-2024-0009

Unilever. (2023). *Sustainable living plan*. Unilever. Retrieved from https://www.unilever.com/sustainable-living?

Van den Brink-Budgen, R. (2010). *Critical thinking for students: Learn the skills of critical assessment and effective argument* (4th ed.). How to Books. Retrieved from https://www.amazon.com\

Van Maanen, J. (1995a). Style as theory. *Organization Science,* 6(1), 133–143.

Van Maanen, J. (1995b). Fear and loathing in organization studies. *Organization Science,* 6(6), 687–692.

Walshe, N., & Tait, E. (2019). *Critical thinking and reasoning: Current research, theory, and practice*. Routledge. Retrieved from https://www.routledge.com

World Economic Forum. (2023). *The future of jobs report*. World Economic Forum. Retrieved from https://www.weforum.org

World Economic Forum. (2024). *AI-Driven Leadership: The impact of artificial intelligence on leadership strategies*. World Economic Forum. https://www.weforum.org/reports/ai-driven-leadership

# Part III

# Human resources, user experience, and organisational communication

# 9 Perception of implementing AI in HRM by organisational actors

## Humanisation or dehumanisation?

*Joanna Cewińska*

## Introduction

AI transforms work processes and how they are organised and executed. The literature on the subject emphasises that adopting advanced technologies usually leads to higher work efficiency, but also indicates the risks associated with their use. Research to date studies dedicated to using AI in human resource management (HRM) highlights that advances in the use of technology in HRM are observed across the various functions of HRM – recruitment, performance review, onboarding, employee engagement, and self-service. At the same time, attention is drawn to the fact that AI research in HRM is still in its infancy, and the area of research is scattered and fragmented (Pan & Froese, 2023). Many problems in HRM are worth addressing. Research on AI in HRM continues to grow, creating opportunities for further discoveries (Prikshat et al., 2023).

This chapter analyses the manifestations of humanisation and dehumanisation resulting from using AI-supported solutions in HRM practices. AI is forecast to be used increasingly in various areas as it offers convenient solutions. AI in HRM has many applications but poses problems that must be addressed to ensure responsible use. Its application must be controlled and used for a fair and appropriate purpose, protecting people and values important to society (Tomasz, 2022). While companies are enthusiastically implementing AI and digital technologies in many areas of HRM, their understanding of the impact of such innovations on employees is often not seen as a priority or lags behind (Rogovsky & Cooke, 2021). The use of AI depends, to a large extent, on employees' attitudes towards the technology. They may delay the introduction of change or drive it and willingly engage in it. Knowing employee attitudes is important for the management process.

The *research problem* is, therefore, the perception of the application of AI-based solutions by organisational actors to identify the benefits and risks of using AI in HRM. The factors diagnosed were classified as manifestations of humanisation and dehumanisation. This chapter answers the following partial *research questions*: (RQ1) How can AI be used to ensure the effectiveness

DOI: 10.4324/9781003654377-13

of HRM and counteract its negative effects? (RQ2) Which AI-based solutions implemented within HRM may lead to the humanisation of the organisational environment? (RQ3) Which AI-based solutions implemented within HRM may lead to the dehumanisation of the organisational environment?

Regarding *research methods*, the theoretical part is based on a narrative review of scientific literature from 2020 to 2025 in English. The literature was collected from the ScienceDirect database and ResearchGate with keywords such as humanisation of HRM, dehumanisation of HRM, and AI in HRM. A narrative review aims to synthesise the existing literature on a topic in a descriptive manner, is not subject to a strict methodological framework, and is unstructured, so it allows for a flexible approach to interpreting its findings (Ferrari, 2015; Orlowska, Mazur & Laguna, 2017; Juntunen & Lehenkari 2019). It can provide a basis for further research. A limitation is the lack of specific criteria for selecting literature and analysis methods, which may lead to bias. It is more difficult to reproduce and verify the results obtained in this case. Narrative reviews are typical in the humanities and social sciences, including management research (Juntunen & Lehenkari, 2019).

The empirical study used the description technique (written statement) according to the disposition (Lutyński, 1994). This technique made it possible to penetrate the way of reasoning of the subjects, present situations from their lives and express a subjective attitude towards them (Lutyński, 1994). The choice of research technique was influenced by the fact that a written statement (as opposed to a face-to-face interview) provided a sense of anonymity and the associated freedom of presenting opinions, which increased the likelihood of collecting candid information. The investigation involved 115 second-cycle (master's) students of the Business Logistics II course (53 full-time students, 24 females and 29 males; 62 part-time students, 29 females and 33 males) of the Faculty of Management at the University of Łodz. Respondents were selected because they had taken classes on HRM (including the use of AI in HRM) and had work experience. The selection of respondents was purposive. Respondents were informed about the purpose of the research and the relevance of their opinions to the research objectives. The respondents answered the question at home. They had several days to reflect and respond. This increased the likelihood of obtaining reliable, comprehensive opinions. The survey was conducted at the turn of January and February 2024. Responses were coded and analysed. Respondents' opinions were read at least twice to avoid omitting important issues for the research. Examples of humanisation and dehumanisation were highlighted. In brackets next to the quotes is the code (number) of the written statement (of the respondent), the gender of the respondent (f – female, m – male), age, length of service, and position held (employee).

## Literature review: AI in HRM – humanisation or dehumanisation

This section introduces the concept of HRM, the benefits and barriers of using AI in HRM, and the manifestations of humanisation and dehumanisation of working relationships resulting from using AI in HRM.

HRM is an approach to employment management that seeks to gain a competitive advantage by strategically deploying a competent workforce, utilising a diverse range of cultural, structural, and human approaches (Storey, 1995). It offers a strategic, coherent, and comprehensive perspective on the challenges involved in managing and developing human resources within a business structure, with each aspect of the process playing an integral role in overseeing the organisation as a whole (Armstrong, 1996). HRM encompasses recruitment, training, performance management, employee relations, benefits, compensation, and labour compliance, as well as knowledge management, organisational development, sourcing (human resource planning, recruitment and selection, and talent management), learning and development, reward management, employee relations, employee welfare, health and safety, and employee service delivery (Armstrong & Taylor, 2020). HRM involves the processes of hiring, training, evaluating, and remunerating employees while ensuring compliance with labour relations, health and safety regulations, and ethical standards (Dessler, 2018).

***Benefits and barriers to the use of AI in HRM***

In the era of intensive technological development, there are hopes that modern technologies will ensure a high-quality life full of comfort, make workplaces more inclusive and safer for employees, as well as increase their job satisfaction and well-being, and improve HRM processes (Cockburn, 2021; Malik at al., 2022; Olajide & Sposato, 2022; Weber, 2023). On the other hand, attention is paid to factors that can destabilise work and be a source of fear and prejudice related to using these technologies (Heinold et al., 2023; Malik et al., 2022; Malin et al., 2023). One of these technologies is AI.

AI refers to the technology used to perform tasks requiring a certain level of intelligence. Core AI technologies provide greater accuracy and stability to everyday processes, using an algorithm that combines high-quality data with fast computing services (*A definition of* AI, 2019). AI technologies offer significant opportunities to streamline HR functions such as self-service transactions, recruitment and talent acquisition, payroll, reporting, and access policies and procedures. We live in an era where AI capabilities are reaching new heights and significantly impact how we do business. HR directors believe combining AI with HR administration functions will benefit and improve the overall employee experience (Olajide & Sposato, 2022; Zhang & Chen, 2023).

AI transforms HRM practices, improving efficiency and accuracy and aiding decision-making. AI can be key in recruitment, talent acquisition, employee engagement, and retention. AI can also improve employee learning and development programmes by implementing training or improving workplace culture. By analysing employee data, AI algorithms can identify knowledge gaps and recommend training programmes to fill them. AI-based learning platforms can personalise learning experiences to match individual employee needs. AI can also significantly impact performance management (*Artificial intelligence for worker management*, 2022; Fritts & Cabrera, 2021; *The new age*, 2018).

AI technologies offer significant opportunities to improve HR functions, such as self-service transactions, employee recruitment (including talent acquisition), training and career planning, incentive systems management, and reporting. The use of AI reduces the time HR professionals spend on administrative tasks, reviewing and updating employee information data processing, reduces the burden on shared service centres and helpdesks by performing HR transactions and responding to routine queries, and can reduce the bias of HR decisions. AI allows HR to automate repetitive tasks and help HR teams do more creative and strategic work for the company's success (Altenried, 2019).

AI-powered HR applications have much potential to increase employee productivity and help HR professionals become competent consultants who increase employee productivity. AI can support managers. It allows for optimisation in work organisation by both employers and employees. Algorithms can predict future customer demand so that the shift work plan considers meeting staffing needs and avoiding the negative effects of staff shortages. Algorithmic management can also assign tasks to workers based on their abilities and skills (*Artificial*, 2022). Despite the perception of the dangers of using AI, the fascination with this technology is not conducive to a critical look at its use. AI-driven solutions can deprive people of their subjectivity and contribute to the dehumanisation of HRM processes.

There are many psychosocial risks associated with the use of AI in HRM. They often focus on employees feeling less independent because their decision-making power has been limited. They feel that they no longer have control over their work. They also feel pressured to work faster, resulting in work-related stress, health problems, and accidents (*Artificial*, 2022). Trying to impose artificial values using algorithms may seem alienating to some people, negatively affecting the employee-employer relationship.

### *Humanisation and dehumanisation of work*

As the considerations show, AI in HRM can contribute to the humanisation and dehumanisation of work. Humanisation means adapting the sphere of life to the needs and capabilities of a human being, following the principles of humanism, and taking care of the individual's subjectivity. Therefore, if AI supports HRM processes, facilitates the performance of tasks by employees and helps shape a safe work environment, we can talk about the humanisation of work. Unfortunately, the consequence of using AI in HRM may also be the dehumanisation of HR processes – employees may feel reduced to data and performance indicators, which lowers their sense of value in the organisation. AI-based solutions may deprive people of subjectivity and cause their objectification, "bypassing the human" (Haslam & Stratemeyer, 2016; Kronfeldner, 2021).

In the most general sense, the dehumanisation of people, organisations and societies refer to their tendency to become less human. Dehumanisation can refer to the replacement of human activity by automated production and organisational processes that operate differently from human sense-making and reflexivity (Al-Amoudi, 2022). In connection with technology development, we can talk about algorithmic dehumanisation. Algorithmic dehumanisation is the act of using algorithms and data in a way that results in the intentional or unintentional treatment of individuals and/or groups as less than fully human, thereby violating human rights, including liberty, equality, and dignity. Algorithmic dehumanisation is particularly problematic for human resource management and the future of work, managerial decision-making, ethics, law regulation, and fundamental values (Schultz et al., 2025). AI may be increasingly dominant, reducing workers' self-determination, control, and professional future. This can lead to feelings of powerlessness or dehumanisation for human workers, especially when algorithmic decisions remain opaque, and workers cannot challenge the algorithm (Schultz et al., 2025). Using AI in HRM can increase efficiency and optimise costs, but it can also lead to excessive control, standardisation, and reduced employee autonomy. Philip Brown, a sociologist, described this trend as digital Taylorism – "work on the tape of the 21st century" (OSHA, 2025).

Digital Taylorism primarily concerns the negative consequences of computer-assisted, Taylorist work organisation and assumes a systematic reduction in autonomy. The idea of "digital Taylorism" also implies increased monitoring by management in highly digitised workplaces (Altenried, 2019; Kirchner et al., 2023). Through digital Taylorism, companies use their control over technology to reconfigure workplaces and positions and then monitor and manage employees in new ways, often through measures that weaken or suppress workers' association power (Brishen, 2023, p. 80). Monitoring of tasks performed by employees, measuring the time of their activities, is reflected in the following relationship:

> The company treats us like robots. It automates our movements, organizes work in the most routine and monotonous way possible, controls and calculates all our activities, sets the pace of work in advance, does not take into account the fact that employees are in different health conditions, of different ages, have different genders, different needs and their psycho-physical condition changes...
>
> (Koc, 2020)

The audit applies not only to stationary but also to remote work. The practice of excessive control of a remote worker includes tracking browser or application history, observing emails and social media posts, recording the performance indicator, i.e. examining the frequency and even speed of keyboard and mouse use, and recording every keystroke by the employee (Koc, 2020).

The risk of dehumanisation of work and digital Taylorism may cause employees' fear and resistance to AI implementation. Human resource managers should recognise that resistance to AI stems from diverse and interrelated fears of losing their jobs and outdated skills, threatening their identity or professional values. People may feel uncomfortable because AI can raise concerns about job safety or ethical issues (Golgeci et al., 2025). Therefore, it can be concluded that the perception of AI by employees may affect the possibility of accelerating or slowing down changes related to the use of new technologies (Czakon & Meyer, 2024).

Open and transparent communication about AI and its role in the organisation is important. Human resource professionals and other leaders can promote collaboration between employees and AI systems, showing how AI can enhance human capabilities, improve decision-making, and reduce routine tasks. This synergistic – rather than complementary – approach strengthens employees' sense of security and helps to counteract their resistance. By promoting AI as a tool to assist employees, human resource managers can highlight their role in enhancing creativity and other human-centric skills in decision-making and in replacing monotonous, dull, or repetitive work. HR initiatives such as training and experiential learning can help debunk AI myths, misconceptions, and prejudices. Once employees see the benefits of their collaboration with AI, their trust and acceptance of the technology increase. Investing in reskilling and upskilling is important to equip employees with the skills they need to work with AI. This means offering training programs to help them develop the skills they need to work effectively with AI. Managers should be open about their organisation's plans for AI and what they mean for employee roles and the future. In order to help a sustainable transition to human-AI collaboration, new employee roles and career paths need to be defined and supported with guidelines and standards for using AI in organisations (Golgeci et al., 2025).

## Results: AI in HRM – nothing more, nothing less

This section presents the results of an empirical study using the description technique (written statement). The findings are framed in a model of the humanising and dehumanising consequences of using AI-supported solutions in HRM.

### *Empirical study: employee opinions on the use of AI in HRM*

A total of 115 people participated in the study, nearly 90% of whom were under 30 years old, held non-managerial positions, and had between one and six years of professional experience. The respondents predominantly belonged to Generation Z, making the group relatively homogeneous. No significant differences were observed between the responses of men and women. All participants provided examples of AI applications in HRM and the associated benefits and risks. They highlighted that AI has the potential to both humanise and dehumanise work. Participants most frequently cited the use of AI in employee recruitment, career planning, training, HR administration, and talent management, with some also mentioning its role in onboarding. The benefits of AI in HRM include greater efficiency in HR processes and faster recruitment. The findings confirm that the possibility of using AI to humanise human resource management (reducing bias in assessing job applicants and employees, personalising training, analysing the emotional state of employees, and managing their well-being) is generalised. Among the risks, they mentioned the possibility of job loss, excessive control, bias, lack of empathy, standardisation of processes, and the decline of interpersonal relationships. The risks of dehumanising personnel management when introducing AI are highlighted, which may be due to the risks identified (over-control, risk of violating employee privacy, loss of the human element in relationships, automated decisions, and overlooking employees' life contexts).

In humanisation, AI can be seen as a tool for supporting employee development and improving work-life balance. It can provide personalised career paths, assist in skill development, and tailor working conditions to individual preferences, enhancing the overall employee experience. However, concerns about dehumanisation also arise with the use of AI. AI may diminish the focus on individual employee needs, as standardised procedures might fail to account for personal characteristics and requirements. Additionally, AI cannot understand human emotions and behaviour, which could result in inaccurate assessments of employees. In humanisation, AI can be seen as a tool for supporting employee development and improving work-life balance. It can provide personalised career paths, assist in skill development, and adapt working conditions to individual preferences, enhancing the overall employee experience. However, concerns about dehumanisation also arise in the use of AI. It may lead to a neglect of individual approaches to employees, as standardised procedures might fail to consider personal characteristics and needs. Furthermore, AI cannot understand human emotions and behaviour, which could result in inaccurate assessments of employees (12, f, age: up to 30 years, seniority 1–5 years, employee):

> AI algorithms can reflect existing biases and social inequalities, leading to unfair decisions dictated by a lack of empathy and interpersonal communication. AI tools use a large amount of data on employees, among others, for their functioning, which may pose the risk of violating their privacy, especially when it is inadequately protected and used in violation of legal regulations. Too much automation without proper oversight can lead to the loss of the human element in human resource management, which can affect employee engagement. Algorithms may lack empathy, contextual understanding or the ability to respond appropriately in emotionally sensitive situations.
>
> (18, f, age: up to 30 years, seniority 1–5 years, employee)

> The introduction of AI into HRM can be both an opportunity and a risk. Given the rapid advancement of technology and AI's potential to assist and streamline our work, it is easy to become overly reliant on it. AI is an excellent

> support tool—thanks to machine learning algorithms, it can analyse vast amounts of data, improving the forecasting of HR trends. It can also personalise employee experiences, tailor training programmes, and support career development. AI is a revolutionary invention; however, its excessive use, particularly in human resource management, poses a risk and leads to dehumanisation. Ultimately, humans should have the final say, while AI should remain a tool that supports decision-making rather than replacing human judgment.
> (58, m, age: up to 30 years, seniority 6–10 years, employee)

> One of the key benefits of using AI in HR is the improvement of recruitment and candidate selection processes. Machine learning algorithms can analyse vast datasets, enabling the identification of suitable candidate profiles with greater accuracy and speed than traditional human-led methods. AI can also aid in talent identification by analysing data and patterns that might be overlooked or unnoticed by the human eye. Additionally, it can support the personalisation of the employee experience by providing tailored development plans or career path recommendations, ultimately increasing employee engagement. However, algorithms based on historical data can internalise existing injustices or biases, leading to personnel decisions based on opaque and biased criteria and may result in unequal treatment of candidates or employees. Furthermore, uncontrolled use of AI in HR can lead to the dehumanisation of workplace relationships. While automation of processes may bring efficiency, eliminating the human element in interpersonal interactions could weaken team bonds and lower employee trust and job satisfaction.
> (60, f, age: 31–40 years, seniority 16–20 years, employee)

> More and more tasks can be done using AI tools. This streamlining of the work of people in HR departments speeds up the execution of various activities and, at the same time, frees up time that can be spent on creative work or getting more involved in scope projects. Therefore, it can be said that the 'dehumanisation' of certain tasks performed with the help of AI flows into an increase in the humanisation of HR departments.
> (68, m, age: up to 30 years, seniority 1–5 years, employee)

Interestingly, the issue of resistance to AI was rarely mentioned in the responses. This may be because the respondents predominantly represented Generation Z, who were born and raised during an era of rapid technological development and view technology as an integral part of reality. From a young age, they have been using technology, influenced by the rise of the internet, which provided access to vast amounts of information and created opportunities for online communication. Generation Z considers technology to be an inseparable part of their reality.

Respondents emphasised the importance of preparing employees to implement this technology to prevent the negative consequences of using AI. They also highlighted the need to develop interpersonal skills that foster human relationships. This is reflected in the following statements:

> In the context of these challenges, it is essential to establish appropriate regulatory and ethical frameworks. Such regulations should oversee and monitor the use of AI in HRM. Implementing responsible practices, such as auditing algorithms for bias and strictly adhering to ethical principles, may be crucial in minimising the risks of dehumanisation and discrimination in personnel management processes. It is also worth emphasising the importance of strengthening the focus on developing soft and interpersonal skills among HR professionals. These skills, alongside careful judgement, can counterbalance the potentially dehumanising effects of AI's growing role in this field.
>
> (60, f, age: 31–40 years, seniority 16–20 years, employee)

> The identified risks highlight the need for caution and appropriate monitoring when integrating AI into HRM to avoid potentially harmful consequences for employees and organisations. Ensuring that AI development in HRM aligns with ethical principles and human rights is essential. Establishing clear regulatory standards, transparent procedures, and oversight mechanisms for AI applications can help mitigate the risk of dehumanisation and ensure that employee-related decisions are made fairly and in accordance with their rights. Additionally, continuous education and awareness-raising among employees about AI are crucial to enabling them to fully understand the impact of this technology on both their professional and personal lives.
>
> (92, m, age: up to 30 years, seniority 1–5 years, employee)

> Therefore, with proper adaptation and oversight, the use of AI in human resource management emerges as a significant opportunity for improving efficiency.
>
> (69, m, age: up to 30 years, seniority 1–5 years, employee)

Whether certain practices contribute to the humanisation of work or, conversely, lead to its dehumanisation ultimately depends on people:

> Regarding interpersonal relationships, humans should always play a decisive role. No one understands another person as well as a fellow human being. Take, for example, the recruitment process. AI selects candidates based purely on data—information from a CV or results from an assessment conducted for the position. However, this does not always guarantee the best choice, as knowledge and qualifications do not necessarily translate into future job performance. There is a possibility that a candidate who appears weaker "on paper" may perform better than the one AI deems ideal for the role. This is why the human factor is crucial in such situations. A person will

> not only consider a candidate's education but also their character, personality, and interests. Another key difference is that humans rely on instinct and intuition when making decisions. In my view, this set of human attributes plays a determining role in making the right choice.
>
> Another example is a decline in an employee's productivity. AI may conclude that the employee is no longer suitable for their position and issue a decision based solely on performance metrics. On the other hand, a human would approach the situation differently, investigating the underlying causes of the decline. It could turn out that the employee is facing serious family issues, preventing them from fully concentrating on work. Naturally, not all employers will respond in the same way, but in my opinion, the right approach is to talk to the employee and attempt to find a solution rather than immediately writing them off. Ultimately, humans should have the final say, while AI should support human decision-making.
>
> (58, m, age: up to 30 years, seniority 6–10 years, employee)

One of the respondents shared a particularly thought-provoking perspective. She pointed out that technology itself is not the real threat to people—instead, it is humans who contribute to the dehumanisation of their environment:

> I fully support the development of artificial intelligence and its application in HR. I also believe that the threat of dehumanisation is real, but it does not stem from AI itself—it comes from people and their thirst for power and control. This can be observed today in armed conflicts, where AI plays no role, but humans do. Perhaps, if humans lose empathy for one another, will AI show it to us first?.
>
> (71, f, age: up to 30 years, seniority 1–5 years, employee)

***Consequences of the perception of AI in HRM***

Respondents have a relatively optimistic attitude towards new technologies in HR ("fascinating", "great opportunities"), listed both the benefits and risks of using new technologies in HR, and believed that it is necessary to ensure a balance between the social and technical systems, but did not present specific proposals for action.

The ultimate result of the study is a model of humanising and dehumanising consequences of using AI-supported solutions within HRM (Figure 9.1). Using AI in HRM can lead to the dehumanisation or humanisation of workplace relationships. If the use of AI results in dehumanisation, the consequence can be digital Taylorism and resistance to change (AI implementation). If we can demonstrate the positive aspects of using AI in HRM, we can talk about the humanisation of work. Then, the pace of implementation of new technologies

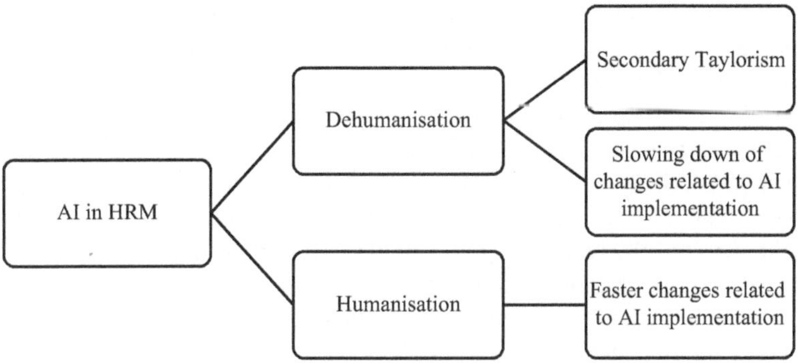


*Figure 9.1* Model of consequences of the perception of AI in HRM.

*Source:* Own elaboration

can be faster. Employees understand why AI technologies are implemented and are prepared for it.

## Discussion: AI in HRM – today and tomorrow

The research presented in this chapter is part of the discussion on using AI in organisations. They confirm the potential benefits and negative effects of implementing AI in the work environment and for HRM, as described in previous studies. Research shows that employees have different opinions about AI in HRM and attitudes towards new technologies. Czakon and Meyer (2024) highlight that one of the behavioural factors that hinders the desire to embrace digital transformation and transform the way organisations operate is the (mis)perception of technology (Czakon & Meyer, 2024). Therefore, it can be concluded that the perception of AI by employees may affect the possibility of accelerating or slowing down changes related to the use of new technologies. AI in HRM can be effective if it can counteract the negative consequences of implementing this technology reported by its users (employees). The negative effects of using AI can be identified with the negative consequences of classical management – a trend in the organisation of scientific work referred to as digital Taylorism. To counteract these negative effects, it is crucial to balance Taylorism's efficiency and standardisation principles in the digital age and employee well-being and job satisfaction (Czakon & Meyer, 2024).

It is important to respond to the diverse needs of employees to prevent the inhumane impact of digital Taylorism at work. An open, continuous dialogue with employees can help with this. On this basis, ways to prevent adverse situations and solve problems can be individualised (Heinold et al., 2023). It is necessary to make employees aware of the role of AI in business practice and how it can be used. If employees understand the role of technology, their sense of security will increase. As such, workers should upskill using AI (Breque et al., 2021). Employees should also be able to retrain to prevent deskilling (Heinold et al., 2023, p. 2) and job losses.

Training can help debunk myths, misconceptions, and biases about technology. Once employees see the benefits of working with AI, their trust and acceptance of AI are likely to increase. Without a clear understanding of the results and benefits of AI in HR management, it is not easy to convince an organisation's stakeholders to fully reap the significant benefits of investing in AI in HR (Prikshat et al., 2023). Employee training is important because using AI systems does not automatically lead to systematic upskilling of employees. While AI systems can bring many benefits in the workplace, their use must be accompanied by upskilling and reskilling efforts (Morandini et al., 2023, p. 127)

In the new symbiotic human-robot relationship, the roles of "partners" must be defined (Huang et al., 2022). An attempt to impose artificial values using algorithms may seem alienating to some, negatively affecting the employee-employer relationship. It is necessary to take a critical look at the development of technology and provide upskilling and reskilling opportunities to develop competencies that give humans an edge over robots (Cockburn, 2021; Breque et al., 2021; Heinold et al., 2023). Broad, nationwide approaches to upskilling and educating all citizens at different levels of AI literacy correlate with higher AI readiness (Rigley et al., 2023).

Working with employees to build trust is important to ensure the positive impact of AI-powered workforce management systems. It starts with consulting employees and allowing them to participate in developing and implementing algorithmic management systems (*Artificial intelligence for worker management*, 2022). It is necessary to systematically identify psychosocial risks, such as emotional demands, lack of autonomy, ethical conflicts, poor social relations, and job insecurity. Identifying psychosocial risk factors and determining workers' exposure to these factors allows workplaces and organisational interventions to be designed in the best way to address risks (Breque et al., 2021; Cockburn, 2021; Eurofound, 2021; Heinold et al., 2023). To facilitate the process of integrating employees with AI, it is worth involving them in the design, development, and decision-making about the use of technology. Employee participation can counteract resistance from employees and help build trust in AI (Li & Xiang, 2024).

## Conclusion

The results of the investigations undertaken allow for the answering of the research questions posed. AI technologies can be used if they offer significant opportunities to improve the HRM function, reduce the time to complete administrative and analytical tasks, reduce the workload, and prevent bias in HRM assessments and decisions. AI should provide the ability to automate repetitive tasks, allowing employees to engage in more creative and strategic work that contributes to the company's success (RQ1). The humanisation of the work environment can be fostered by AI-based solutions implemented as part of HRM, such as upskilling and reskilling, communication with employees to explain the role of AI at work and how it is used, nurturing trust, and building a pro-technology culture (RQ2). If, as a result of using AI, people feel objectified, treated as part of the mechanism, deprived of agency and freedom, and their role is limited to following orders, work will be dehumanised. The reason for the dehumanisation of the organisational environment may be solutions based on artificial intelligence, such as unjustified replacement of human work by AI, lack of understanding of the specific situations of the employee, resulting in lower commitment and efficiency conditioned by objective circumstances, limitation of interpersonal relationships and a sense of security, excessive control by AI and standardisation, lack of development opportunities, improper communication between employees and managers (RQ3).

The research carried out has some *limitations*. Respondents were overwhelmingly Gen Z, making the group relatively homogeneous (nearly 90% were under 30, held non-managerial positions, and had between one and six years of work experience). The research was focused on obtaining qualitative data, so their results cannot be generalised to the entire population. The descriptions were varied in terms of the account details. The respondents paid attention to selected problems that were important to them. As such, they did not consider all aspects of implementing AI into HRM.

Regarding *future research directions*, counteracting dehumanisation and digital Taylorism is key to taking full advantage of new technologies. For this to happen, it is necessary to examine the attitudes and opinions of employees and diagnose the causes of their fears and resistance. The specific issues related to the use of AI in HRM indicated by the respondents can be used to develop and implement appropriate management solutions aimed at counteracting dehumanisation and accelerating the processes of AI integration, not only in HRM. Further research on the use of new technologies, the challenges of robotisation and the humanisation of work in the robotic environment may be interesting. Future research may cover diverse groups of respondents and other areas of the organisation's functioning. It would be valuable to examine how employees are trained in using new technologies, how their effectiveness is assessed, and how employee attitudes evolve in implementing the humanisation of work in a robotic environment. Studying the relationship between robots and humans in mixed teams will undoubtedly be important. The research he presented has limitations that are characteristic of qualitative research. The sample consisted of a minor, homogeneous group; the results cannot be generalised to the broader population. Respondents' statements varied, with some more detailed accounts and others more concise. This may have been due to a reluctance to share their experiences, especially if they triggered negative emotions.

## References

*A definition of AI: Main capabilities and scientific disciplines* (2019). High-Level Expert Group on Artificial Intelligence, European Commission B-1049 Brussels, Document made public on 8 April.

Al-Amoudi, I. (2022). Are post-human technologies dehumanizing? Humanenhancement and artificial intelligence in contemporary societies. *Journal of Critical Realism*, 21:5, 516–538, https://doi.org/10.1080/14767430.2022.2134618

Altenried, M. (2019). On the last mile: Logistical urbanism and the transformation of labour, Work Organisation, Labour & Globalisation, 13(1) (Spring 2019), 114–129. https://www.jstor.org/stable/10.13169/workorgalaboglob.13.1.0114

Armstrong, M. (1996). *A Handbook on Personnel Management Practice* (5th ed.). London: Kogan Page.

Armstrong, M., & Taylor, S. (2020). *Armstrong's Handbook on Human Resource Management Practice*. (15th ed.). London: Kogan Page.

*Artificial intelligence for worker management: implications for occupational safety and health. Report* (2022). European Agency for Safety and Health at Work DOI: 10.2802/76354

Breque, M., De Nul, L., & Petridis, A. (2021). *Industry 5.0: towards a sustainable, human-centric and resilient European industry*. In *Komisja europejska, dyrekcja generalna ds. badań naukowych i innowacji,* Urząd Publikacji Unii Europejskiej. European Commission. https://data.europa.eu/doi/10.2777/308407

Brishen, R. (eds). (2023). *Inductive knowledge and digital taylorism in: Data and democracy at work: advanced information technologies, labor law, and the new working class.* MIT Press, p. 57–80. DOI: https://doi.org/10.7551/mitpress/11253.001.0001

Cockburn, W. (2021). OSH in the future: Where next? *European Journal of Workplace Innovation,* 6(1), 84–97. https://doi.org/10.46364/ejwi.v6i1.813

Czakon, W., & Meyer, N. (2024). Why is digital transformation so slow? The shadow of dehumanization 2.0. *Central European Management Journal*, 32(3), 339–349. https://doi.org/10.1108/CEMJ-03-2024-0073

Desseler, G. (2018). Human Resource Management.(16th ed.), Pearsonandbook on Human Resource, New York.

Ferrari, R. (2015). Writing narrative style literature reviews. *Medical Writing*, 24(4), 230–235. https://doi.org/10.1179/2047480615Z.000000000329.

Fritts, M., & Cabrera, F. (2021). AI recruitment algorithms and the dehumanization problem. *Ethics and Information Technology,* 23(4), 791–801. doi: 10.1007/s10676-021-09615-w.

Golgeci, I., Ritala, P., Arslan, A., McKenna, B., & Ali, I. (2025). Confronting and alleviating AI resistance in the workplace: An integrative review and a process framework. *Human Resource Management Review*, 35(2), Article 101075. Advance online publication. https://doi.org/10.1016/j.hrmr.2024.101075

Haslam, N., Stratemeyer, M. (2016). Recent research on dehumanization. *Curr Opin Psychol,* 11, 25–29. https://doi.org/10.1016/j.copsyc.2016.03.009

Heinold, E., Rosen, P.H., & Wischniewski, S. (2023). Advanced robotics and AI-based systems in the workplace: OSH challenges and opportunities originating from actual implementations. European Agency for Safety and Health at Work, EU-OSHA. Available from: https://osha.europa.eu/en/publications/advanced-robotics-and-ai-based-systems-workplace-osh-challenges-and-opportunities-originating-actual-implementations

Huang, S., Wang, B., Li, X., Zheng, P., Mourtzis, D., & Wang, L. (2022). Industry 5.0 and Society 5.0—Comparison, complementation and co-evolution. *Journal of Manufacturing Systems*, 64, 424–428. https://doi.org/10.1016/j.jmsy.2022.07.010

Juntunen, M., & Lehenkari, M. (2019). A narrative literature review process for an academic business research thesis. *Studies in Higher Education*, 46(2), 330–342. https://doi.org/10.1080/03075079.2019.1630813

Kirchner, S., Meyer, S.A., Tisch, A. (2023). Digital Taylorism for some, "digital self-determination" for others? Inequality in job autonomy across different task domains. *Zeitschrift für Sozialreform - Journal of Social Policy Research*, 69(1), 57–84, https://doi.org/10.1515/zsr-2022–0101

Koc, J. (2020). Digital Taylorism in companies. Maximum supervision, high efficiency. https://www.pulshr.pl/prawo-pracy/cyfrowy-tayloryzm-w-firmach-maksymalnynadzor-wysoka-efektywnosc,77412.html Access: 18.02.2025.

Kronfeldner, M. (2021). Introduction: Mapping dehumanization studies. In M. Kronfeldner (Ed.), *The Routledge handbook of dehumanization* (pp. 1–36). Routledge/Taylor & Francis Group. https://doi.org/10.4324/9780429492464-chapter1

Li, Y., Xiang, B. (2024). Reducing organizational inequalities associated with algorithmic controls. *Discov Artif Intell*, 4, 36. https://doi.org/10.1007/s44163-024-00137-0

Lutyński, J. (1994). *Metody badań społecznych. Wybrane zagadnienia*, Łódzkie Towarzystwo Naukowe, Łódź

Malik, N., Tripathi, S., Kar, A., & Gupta, S. (2022). Impact of artificial intelligence on employees working in industry 4.0 led organizations. *International Journal of Manpower*, 43(2), 334–354. https://doi.org/10.1108/IJM-03-2021-0173

Malin, C., Kupfer, C., Fleiss, J., Kubicek, B., & Thalmann, S. (2023). In the AI of the beholder-a qualitative study of HR professionals' beliefs about AI-Based chatbots and decision support in candidate pre-selection. *Administrative Sciences*, 13(11). https://doi.org/10.3390/admsci13110231

Melé, D. (2016). Understanding humanistic management. *Humanistic Management Journal*, 1(1), 33–55. https://doi.org/10.1007/s41463-016-0011-5

Morandini, S., Fraboni, F., De Angelis, M., Puzzo, G., Giusino, D., Pietrantoni, L. (2023). The impact of artificial intelligence on workers' skills: Upskilling and reskilling in organisations. *Informing Science: The International Journal of an Emerging Transdiscipline*, 26, 039–068. https://doi.org/10.28945/5078

Olajide, O., & Sposato, M. (2022). Opportunities and risks of artificial intelligence in recruitment and selection. *International Journal of Organizational Analysis*, 30(6), 1771–1782. https://doi.org/10.1108/IJOA-07-2020-2291

Orłowska, A., Mazur, Z., & Łaguna, M. (2017). Systematyczny przegląd literatury: Na czym polega i czym różni się od innych przeglądów? *Ogrody Nauk i Sztuk*, 7(7) (lip. 2017), 350–363. https://doi.org/10.15503/onis2017.350.363

OSHA (2025) *Cyfrowy tayloryzm*. EU-OSHA thesaurus. https://osha.europa.eu/pl/tools-and-resources/eu-osha-thesaurus/term/70047i

Pan, Y., & Froese, F. J. (2023). An interdisciplinary review of AI and HRM: Challenges and future directions. *Human Resource Management Review*, 33(1), 100924. https://doi.org/10.1016/j.hrmr.2022.100924

Prikshat, V., Islam, M., Patel, P Malik, Ashish Budhwar, P., & Gupta, S. (2023). AI-Augmented HRM: Literature review and a proposed multilevel framework for future research. *Technological Forecasting and Social Change*, 193(C). https://doi.org/10.1016/j.techfore.2023.122645

Rigley, E., Bentley, C., Krook, J., & Ramchurn, S. (2023). Evaluating international AI skills policy: A systematic review of AI skills policy in seven countries. *Global Policy*, 15(1). https://doi.org/10.1111/1758-5899.13299

Rogovsky, N., & Fang L.C., eds. (2021). *Towards a Human-Centred Agenda: Human Resource Management in the BRICS Countries in the Face of Global Challenges*. Geneva

Schultz, M.D., Clegg, M., Hofstetter, R., & Seele, P. (2025). Algorithms and dehumanization: A definition and avoidance model. *AI & Society*, 40, 2191–2211. Received: 2 August 2024 / Accepted: 28 October 2024 https://doi.org/10.1007/s00146-024-02123-7

Słapczyński T. (2022). Artificial Intelligence in science and everyday life, its application and development prospects. *ASEJ - Scientific Journal of Bielsko-Biala School of Finance and Law*, 26(4), 78–85. https://doi.org/10.19192/wsfip.sj4.2022.12

Storey, J (ed). (1995). *Human Resource Management: A critical text.* Routledge, London.

*The new age: Artificial intelligence for human resource opportunities and functions* (2018). Ernst & Young LLP.

Tomasz, S. (2022). Artificial Intelligence in science and everyday life, its application and development prospects. *ASEJ* 26(4). https://doi.org/10.19192/wsfip.sj4.2022.12

Weber, P. (2023). Unrealistic optimism regarding artificial intelligence opportunities in human resource management. *International Journal of Knowledge Management, 19*(1), 1–19. https://www.igi-global.com/gateway/article/317217

Zhang, J., & Chen, Z. (2023). Exploring human resource management digital transformation in the digital age. *Journal of the Knowledge Economy*, 15(1), 1482–1498. https://doi.org/10.1007/s13132-023-01214-y

# 10 Impact of AI-supported solutions on humanistic management practices

## Sensory and emotional well-being of elderly employees

*Marlena Kondrat*

### Introduction

Today's reality is characterised by changes of a powerful intensity, which poses an enormous intellectual and developmental challenge to modern man. This is reflected in the various activities undertaken by the individual, which depend on various external conditions. The development of modern civilisation is a source of transformation for society, including older people. The ageing process of the population affects the whole world – but especially developed countries, and in the coming years, it will condition decisions taken by many countries at the social and economic levels. This forces them to become more active in various areas, including work. At the same time, a large group of senior citizens withdraw from active life because they require support and various kinds of assistance.

This chapter's *research problem* addresses the pressing challenge of retaining employees aged 50+ in the labour market, a priority for national employment policies. Its core research problem is the analysis of the position of pre-retirement individuals in organisations, with emphasis on their values, needs, and the obstacles they face. It explores how universal principles of humanistic management – such as personalised development, digital upskilling, and inclusive organisational culture – can foster environments that support and motivate older workers. This chapter also examines the dual impact of AI: while it can enhance engagement through adaptive tools and training, it may also increase technostress, reduce interpersonal interaction, and exacerbate digital exclusion. Aesthetic and ethically grounded applications of AI, informed by humanistic management, are proposed as strategies to improve senior employees' sensory and emotional well-being.

The following *research questions* organise the investigation process: (RQ1) To what extent can the integration of humanistic management and tools developed through AI influence the emotional and sensory well-being of elderly people in the labour market? (RQ2) How can selected AI-powered tools assist older employees in adapting to a technology-dominated environment while safeguarding their sensory and emotional well-being?

DOI: 10.4324/9781003654377-14

This chapter uses non-reactive *research methods* based on literature and data analysis. It synthesises existing knowledge on humanistic management, age diversity and the implications of AI tools in the workplace. Data were gathered from academic databases such as JSTOR, Google Scholar, and Scopus, using keywords such as "humanistic management", "older employees", "AI in the workplace", "age diversity", and "well-being of mature workers". The literature search was conducted in English and Polish to ensure a comprehensive understanding of the subject matter.

This chapter can benefit organisational leaders, human resource managers and policymakers who promote age diversity in the workplace. In addition, scholars and researchers in humanistic management, gerontology and organisational behaviour will find valuable insights that can influence future research and practice to improve the well-being of older workers in an increasingly digital work environment.

## Literature review: elderly people in the labour market – synergies between well-being and AI tools in the context of professional activation

This section focuses on key aspects of the role of older employees in a changing work environment and the importance of their professional activation. It analyses the consequences of an ageing society for the labour market, emphasising the need to adapt management strategies to the challenges of age diversity in teams, discusses aspects of older people's emotional and sensory well-being, which are important for their professional engagement and quality of life, and examines the role of modern technologies (including AI) in activating older employees, pointing out how these tools can support them in adapting to the challenges of the modern labour market.

### *The ageing society's implications for the labour market: the importance of seniors' professional activation*

The contemporary workplace is closely linked to the VUCA concept, characterised by uncertainty, volatility, complexity, and ambiguity, which demand new management approaches. Coined in the 1990s for military contexts, VUCA highlights the challenges of rapid change and unclear communication (Nandram & Bindlish, 2017). This concept is increasingly relevant due to technological advancements and AI, which impact management through automation and data analysis, necessitating adaptation from employees and managers (Noponen, 2019). The development of AI coincides with the ageing population trend, termed the silver tsunami (Cruce & Hillman, 2012), significantly affecting the labour market. By 2050, life expectancy is projected to exceed 77 years, with the 60+ age group surpassing 21% of the global population (WHO, 2024).

In the EU-27, the average age is expected to rise by 4.5 to 48.2 years, with an increasing elderly dependency ratio from 34.1% in 2019 to 56.7% by 2050. The number of individuals aged 80 and above is projected to grow from 27.1 million to 64 million by 2100, indicating significant population ageing across Europe, with varying rates between regions (WHO, 2024).

It should be noted that the concept of old age is not clearly defined. According to the World Health Organisation, "older people" include workers over 45 years of age, but already in labour market institutions in many countries, people aged 50+ are included in this group. In some European countries (e.g., Poland), older people are assumed to be workers in retirement, i.e., 60+ for women and 65+ for men (Kowalewski & Moczydłowska, 2020). Old age itself also does not remain homogeneous. People aged 60–69 represent the younger post-working age, those aged 70–79 the older post-working age, and those over 80 represent old age (Ciura & Szymańczak, 2012). When talking about the ageing society in the context of the labour market, the following tools are used to measure the socio-economic impact of this process: (1) median age of old age; (2) the double ageing coefficient (increase in the number and share of the oldest people, i.e., those aged 80 and over in the population aged 65 and over; (3) the potential support ratio or the old-age dependency ratio (the ratio of the number of children (0–14) and elderly (65 and over) to the number of people aged 15–64) (Zagórowska, 2020, pp. 136–152).

The latter shows the effects of population ageing and its impact on the labour market due to the declining trend of the working-age population – the potential labour force concerning the other age groups (pre-productive and post-productive). In the EU27, this number is declining and is projected to fall by 18% by 2070 (European Commission, 2020, pp. 11–39). The change in these ratios results in a shortage of workers on the one hand and growing problems in the pension system on the other, which is reflected in the development of the old-age dependency ratio. The declining number of young people in the labour market further exacerbates the situation. Lee (2014, pp. 234–239) points out that the economic consequences of an ageing population largely depend on how long employees remain in the labour market. Therefore, in many countries, one of the most important labour market policy goals is to increase the labour force participation of older people, which fits in with the implementation of the concept of active ageing by prolonging the stay of older people in the labour market through public policies, including senior policies.

There is no doubt, therefore, that today's organisations should make numerous efforts to retain people of pre-retirement age in the workplace. Promoting age diversity is an opportunity to build a positive corporate image and a necessity in the face of the ongoing demographic decline (Ali & French, 2019).

Vocational activation of seniors is important not only for the economic aspect but also for their well-being and a better quality of life. Vocational activity increases social inclusion, prevents loneliness and helps maintain mental fitness for longer. In contrast, gerontology and sociology explain the social essence of old age in light of increasing longevity; the sequential life course model (first learning, then working, and finally retirement) based on chronological age not only no longer suffices but contributes to age-related stereotypes and various types of ageism (Ayalon & Tesch-Römer, 2018).

One of the most recent approaches to ageing is the so-called ageing 4.0 concept. The author of the latest *ageing* 4.0 concept is Kai Leichsenring (2018). The term refers to the phenomenon of the fourth industrial revolution, aimed at exploiting the opportunities in all spheres of life offered by automation, wireless connectivity, 3D printing, biotechnology, or AI. 2011 is officially accepted as the beginning of the fourth industrial revolution. While the steam engine gave birth to the first industrial revolution, which dramatically changed the face of organisations, devices with AI, autonomous vehicles and advanced robotisation have become symbols of the fourth industrial revolution (Lipińska-Grobelny, 2024).

In the context of the development of new technologies, the concept of ageing 4.0 assumes the presence of an integrated life cycle in which the traditional stages, such as education, work and retirement, do not have to occur in succession after attaining an appropriate age. However, it can be pursued in parallel throughout life. Someone who studies and works simultaneously or while retired is still active professionally or even acquires additional education (Lipińska-Grobelny, 2024). This approach shows that age integration breaks down structural age barriers as education and work become more and more accessible for people of all ages to enable a more flexible approach to life, but it also means age heterogeneity. The two approaches are in a reciprocal relationship. The implications for organisations with age-diverse workforces are that people of different ages become institutionally integrated and, as a result, the workplace is a place for age-diverse people to work together, which will help to mitigate age-related barriers to entry (Lipińska-Grobelny, 2024). As such, the concept of ageing 4.0 responds to new societal needs and challenges discussed under the umbrella of the fourth industrial revolution.

As the research results show, the concept of ageing 4.0 can contribute to the weakening of ageism due to the promotion of appropriate attitudes in the perception and planning of one's life activity, as well as the openness of employers. A life cycle treated linearly and described by specific age ranges fosters the development of ageism and reinforces the image of the elderly as sick, infirm, and in need of care. In contrast, the age integration in the Ageing 4.0 approach encourages breaking down structural age barriers and effective age management (Lipińska-Grobelny, 2024).

### *Seniors' sensory and emotional well-being in the workplace*

Mental well-being has long been overlooked by employers despite its crucial role in managing human resources (Lubrańska, 2024). Well-being encapsulates positive emotions across various life domains, including health, family satisfaction, job satisfaction, and a sense of purpose. However, factors such as health issues, financial stress, and burnout can undermine this sense of well-being, leading to poor physical and mental health outcomes.

Emotional and sensory well-being are key elements influencing quality of life, especially in older people. Emotional well-being refers to the subjective feeling of happiness, life satisfaction and the ability to cope with emotions and stress (Ryff, 1989). The literature emphasises that good emotional well-being can lead to improved work quality, increased productivity and better interpersonal relationships in the workplace. Older people who experience high levels of emotional well-being are more likely to engage in various professional activities, which may contribute to their extended presence in the labour market.

On the other hand, sensory well-being includes correctly perceiving sensory stimuli, which is important for interacting with the environment and making decisions. It affects the professional activity of older people. The ability to perceive sensory stimuli is important for the adequate performance of tasks and for maintaining social contact (Haertel et al., 2015). As people age, many experience a decline in sensory function, leading to social isolation and a reduced quality of life. Therefore, supporting sensory well-being, e.g., by adapting working conditions to the needs of older people, can significantly improve their engagement and job satisfaction.

Improving the emotional and sensory well-being of older people in the workplace is important for their professional activity. Employees who feel emotionally well are more motivated and willing to take on challenges, which can lead to better results for both the individual and the organisation (Ryff, 1989). In addition, creating an inclusive work environment that takes sensory needs into account contributes to greater diversity in the team, which can lead to innovative solutions and greater flexibility within the organisation (Haertel et al., 2015).

Active ageing, described as a strategy for enhancing life quality in old age, is essential for seniors. Successful ageing involves continuous learning, gradual retirement, and social involvement (Lipińska-Grobelny, 2024). In this context, humanistic management, which prioritises empathy and adapts the work environment to employees' needs, becomes vital for promoting the professional engagement of older adults (Szostak, 2023). Management now emphasises the importance of human values, shifting from a purely efficiency-driven perspective to one that values employee well-being equally alongside economic goals.

The demographic changes associated with an ageing population reshape workforce dynamics, leading to diverse age groups in organisations. Understanding the values of different generations – Baby Boomers, Generation X, Y, and Z – helps identify their unique needs, which is crucial for fostering an inclusive organisational culture (Gadomska, 2020). Differences in work values significantly impact motivation, loyalty, and job satisfaction across generations. Reviewing the research on employee values, it can be seen that employees

*Table 10.1* Selected work-related values represented by representatives of the active generations

| *The Baby Boomer generation (1946–1964)* | *Generation X (1965–1979)* | *Generation Y (1980–1995)* | *Generation Z (1996–2010)* |
|---|---|---|---|
| Dedication and hard work<br>Dedication and loyalty<br>Consistency/ predictability<br>Collegial working and communication style<br>Fairness<br>Respect for authority and tradition<br>Patience<br>High quality of work<br>Commitment<br>Long-term tasks<br>Independence<br>Achievements<br>Development of one's interests | Independence<br>Autonomy<br>Professional development<br>Focus on earning money<br>Communication<br>Fairness<br>Own initiative<br>Pursuit of goals through hard work<br>Short-term tasks | "Works to live"<br>Flexible working hours<br>Development of interests<br>Activities that foster work-life balance<br>Making sense of one's work<br>Clear division of tasks<br>Fast promotion<br>Career development<br>Good working atmosphere<br>Appreciation and respect<br>Success orientation<br>Short-term objectives<br>Openness<br>Transparency<br>Teamwork | Combining work and passions<br>Variety of tasks<br>Rapid career development<br>Working in a dynamic and multicultural environment<br>Innovation<br>Good atmosphere<br>Personal relationships<br>Respect<br>High importance of high salaries<br>Additional benefits<br>Long holidays |

*Source:* Own elaboration based on: Gadomska, 2020, Smola & Tutton, 2002, Deal, 2007, Bak, 2017, Widerszal-Bazyl & Wolodźko, 2015.

representing the four generations discussed above have a different understanding of the meaning of work and the fulfilment that can be achieved through it. Many criteria indicating different values can be found in the literature, and Table 10.1 lists a few selected with the four active generations in mind.

As the comparison in Table 10.1 shows, for older employees, intrinsic values such as independence and meaningful work are more important than extrinsic rewards like recognition and pay, which younger generations prioritise. This generational divide underscores the importance of job security and stability for older workers, who often prefer clear operational rules and a predictable work environment (Widerszal-Bazyl & Wołodźko, 2015). Awareness of generational values is vital for shaping work conditions that promote employee well-being. Management practices must align organisational values with those of employees to foster inclusivity and engagement. In contrast, misunderstandings related to generational differences can lead to age discrimination and hinder productivity (Lubrańska, 2024).

Another crucial factor influencing the well-being of seniors is work-life balance. Many older workers experience a "double burden", caring for their children and elderly parents (Hildt-Ciupińska, 2014). Flexible work arrangements, such as remote work and adjusted hours, can alleviate these pressures, allowing seniors to fulfil their caregiving roles while maintaining their professional responsibilities. Promoting lifelong learning is essential for seniors to adapt to a knowledge-based society. Continuous education enables active participation in social and economic life and encompasses formal and informal learning opportunities (Haertel et al., 2015). Offering flexible working hours and arrangements can further enhance the well-being of older employees.

Health promotion programs and ergonomic workplace designs contribute to seniors' physical and mental health. Regular health assessments and wellness initiatives help maintain well-being, while ergonomic adjustments reduce injury risks (Timmons et al., 2011). Furthermore, mentoring programs – where seniors share their expertise with younger workers – foster personal fulfilment and enhance social inclusion (Timmons et al., 2011).

Developing digital skills among older employees is also crucial. Facilitating access to training can boost confidence and job satisfaction, enabling seniors to engage more actively in teams (Kondrat & Kosiak, 2024). Investing in digital education improves professional capabilities and enhances personal quality of life. An aesthetically pleasing work environment significantly impacts older workers' sensory and emotional well-being. Organisational aesthetics should encompass sensory experiences that foster a sense of belonging and satisfaction (Kostera & Woźniak, 2022). AI technologies can adapt the work environment to meet sensory needs, such as adjusting lighting to reduce eye strain, which is particularly beneficial for seniors.

Moreover, integrating art into the workplace can create a harmonious atmosphere that enhances emotional security. The use of classical art combined with modern AI-generated elements can help ease the transition for seniors, stimulating creativity (Kostera & Woźniak, 2022). The colour scheme of workspaces also affects emotional responses; subdued tones can reduce stress, while bright colours may confuse. Mentoring programs incorporating creative activities can also enhance emotional well-being, fostering collaboration between seniors and younger generations (Twenge et al., 2010). Such initiatives increase the sense of agency and satisfaction among older workers.

In conclusion, a holistic approach integrating AI with humanistic management can create a supportive work environment for older employees. By addressing sensory and emotional needs through tailored experiences, organisations can foster an atmosphere of "aesthetic care" that enhances the overall well-being of seniors, ensuring their active participation in the workforce. As Szostak (2023) notes, managing art and creativity is essential for adapting to societal needs and benefiting employees and organisations.

***The role of new technology and AI in activating older employees***

In the public discourse of many countries in the modern world, the application of new technologies in response to a trend referred to as the silver tsunami is increasingly emerging. "Silver tsunami" is a metaphor for the massive increase in the number of elderly people in the population. It is an imminent demographic wave with implications for healthcare systems, the labour market, social policy, and the economy. On the other hand, the development of AI presents itself as a potential tool that can help manage these changes (Baran et al., 2023).

In recent decades, there has been a growing interest in new technologies, the application of which can contribute to the independence of older people. The juxtaposition of the terms "gerontology" and "technology" has created a new term – "gerontechnology". According to the definition of B. Rzeczyński, "Gerontechnology is a field of science initiated about 20 years ago, dealing with the problems of elderly people in society and the environment, but at the same time with the ability to practically apply measures facilitating access of this age group (burdened by nature with mobility and sometimes also perceptual limitations) to all infrastructure facilities. The paradigm of gerontechnology is constituted at the crossroads of progressive technology and advanced ageing in an interdisciplinary area of science in which technology is directed at the aspirations and capabilities of older people and is aimed at the research, development and design of products and services aimed at maintaining good health, full participation in social life and independence of existence" (Rzeczyński, 2009a,b).

Many modern countries are implementing new technologies in seniors' services, particularly in health care and social care, to stimulate social and civic participation, entertainment, and education. Work-related mental health and mental injury are important issues for people's livelihoods and well-being. Today, digitalisation and smart technologies have an extremely high impact on the workforce (Zapędowska-Kling, 2015).

The ability to use the solutions offered by AI is strongly linked to the ability to use the Internet. Among the opportunities that the Internet offers to older people are (Zapędowska-Kling, 2015):

- increasing the labour force participation of peri-retirement age people by enabling remote work from home (word processing, bookkeeping, mail order and others);
- active participation in lifelong learning programmes through remote *e-learning* methods (for example, taking an interactive English course or completing a postgraduate course via the Internet);
- becoming more socially active and reducing social isolation through the use of social networking sites (maintaining e-mail correspondence with foreign friends, finding friends from school, posting personal photos);
- reducing loneliness through the use of facilities for video-chatting/chatting with family members, which generally do not involve additional charges like telephone calls;

- assistance in complex IADL (instrumental activities of daily living), thanks to the possibility of ordering purchases for home delivery or paying bills remotely (electronic banking);
- easy and quick access to information on health and prevention, local initiatives for the elderly, available forms of care, the region's cultural and tourist facilities, and more;
- an increase in civic participation and a sense of political participation through solutions that are part of thee-democracy project (such as online voting, participation in political debates, co-determination on the distribution of the municipal budget, and e-governance projects) such as handling official matters online or using an electronic signature when dealing with public institutions.

This overview represents just a few examples of technologies already in use worldwide or in the process of being implemented (Zapędowska-Kling, 2015). It is crucial to understand the possible applications of AI in today's world, which include identifying the advantages and disadvantages of technological solutions and their potential negative social impacts. AI gains importance in activating seniors, both in daily life and professional contexts. AI-based technologies can particularly help older workers adapt to the changing demands of the labour market. So far, the impact of AI on workers' mental health has not been thoroughly investigated. There is data to suggest that integrating AI into work processes can mitigate mental health problems and improve this aspect of employee health. Research has shown a correlation between work intensity, pay and adaptation to industrial transformation using AI and employee mental health (Walusiak-Skorupa et al., 2023). Economies in transition and facing labour shortages can benefit from promoting AI and addressing labour shortages while supporting the workforce's mental health. Recent research shows that AI improves the mental health of workers by reducing symptoms of depression among those employed in manufacturing, which is particularly relevant in the context of activating older people at work. The effects of AI on mental health depend on the competence of the workers and the generation to which they belong. Unskilled workers born after 1980 show positive reactions and are ready to adopt AI in the workplace (Wei & Li, 2022).

Other studies indicate that limited autonomy and control at work negatively affect employee satisfaction, productivity and mental health. The complexity of tasks at work is related to autonomy but leads to different effects on employees. Complex and demanding tasks can act as both motivators and stressors, while the impact of autonomy on job satisfaction and psychological well-being is much less (De Cuyper & De Witte, 2006). Chung-Yan notes that the best effects on employees' mental health occur when high job autonomy is combined with task complexity (Chung-Yan, 2010). It is highlighted that new technologies and support methods can have a positive impact on work processes and mental health, but technostress can cause anxiety, fear, fatigue and reduced performance. Attention is also drawn to the potential use of AI in supporting employee health and managing chronic illness. The use of AI to create personalised preventive and therapeutic recommendations, e.g., for patients with diabetes, can support their ability to work. In addition, employees are being challenged to upgrade their qualifications and skills to meet the new challenges in the working environment created by the AI revolution. This demonstrates employees' high awareness regarding AI-related career development and the importance of informal learning in the workplace. Xu and colleagues' findings confirm the positive correlation between understanding and perceptions of AI at work and employees' sense of well-being (Xu et al., 2023). Research shows that more than 35% of companies use some form of AI, and almost 85% treat AI development as a key strategic priority. This suggests that AI will soon become integral to the work environment (Walusiak-Skorup et al., 2023).

Implementing AI in organisations requires appropriate measures in the preventive care system for employees. While digital transformation can support employers and employees, it can also be a burden or a threat. The role of AI systems in comprehensive preventive care for employees is crucial, as they support compliance with existing regulations and standards through an enhanced ability to monitor changes, create relevant documents and procedures, e.g., in emergency situations, automate form filling, and identify and minimise risks. Thanks to advanced analytics, it is possible to single out processes with the highest risk and propose effective prevention and risk modelling methods. Based on the data collected, AI can develop an effective prevention programme that is automatically updated as the company's situation changes, such as a new staff structure or changes in legislation. The analysis of complex data sets, such as the structure of a company, uses tools to model, visualise and automate data processing.

Comprehensive employee care using AI-powered solutions also includes ongoing training for employees tailored to their responsibilities and learning needs, regardless of the pace of change in the workforce, with the ability to identify those who require additional support. Virtual reality (VR) enables simulations and interactive exercises related to specific manoeuvres. The benefits and risks of using AI-supported systems are complex and should be considered in planned activities (Walusiak-Skorupa et al., 2023). A summary of these factors, divided into organisational, physical and psychosocial, can be found in Table 10.2.

AI is increasingly important in activating seniors' daily lives and professional contexts. Table 10.2 shows that its effect is particularly evident when considering psychophysical factors. In particular, AI-based technologies can support older workers in adapting to the changing demands of the labour market, but when inappropriately implemented and applied by organisations, they will contribute to the risks indicated in Table 10.2. Older workers represent great value and social capital for organisations, and their experience, combined with the new approach of younger people, can bring numerous benefits to organisations, such as improved knowledge transfer and innovation (Cruce & Hillman, 2012). In order to encourage people of pre-retirement age to stay and develop their skills

*Table 10.2* Selected benefits, challenges, and risks of using AI-powered systems in the workplace

| *Factor* | *AI-powered systems' advantages related to work* | *AI-powered systems' challenges and risks related to work* |
|---|---|---|
| Organisational | Increase in staff skills/ change in qualifications<br>Increase in task variety/ reduction of routine and monotonous tasks<br>Job control | Automation of specific skills that are no longer needed or developed<br>Employee discrimination due to intrusive monitoring, leading to private data collecting<br>Reduced completeness and consolidation of tasks |
| Physical | Education in physical workload<br>Improvement in the physical health of workers | Residual physical and environmental hazards<br>Intensification of work – forcing workers to work at a fast pace,<br>Reducing the time needed to perform specific procedures |
| Psychophysical | Increased well-being of employees<br>Inclusion in the workplace – workplaces more accessible to workers with different needs, including those dictated by age<br>Increase in social interaction (when systems support workers in self-directed tasks)<br>Reduced time spent in front of a screen (automation of cognitive tasks) | The need for highly specialised staff to implement and maintain the systems<br>Exclusion of unskilled workers<br>Loss of support from superiors when AI replaces people<br>Negative attitudes towards new technologies<br>Dehumanisation of employees<br>Forcing them to behave like machines<br>Loss of creative and independent thinking<br>Loss of control over work due to high stress levels, leading to poor performance, lower productivity and sickness absence |

*Source:* Own elaboration based on (Walusiak-Skorupa et al., 2023).

in a workplace that is constantly changing under the influence of AI developments, it is worth looking at the concept of humanistic management, the tenets of which can help to manage age diversity better.

## Results: improving the seniors' sensory and emotional well-being by combining humanistic management and AI tools

In today's world, where technology is increasingly important, integrating humanistic management with AI solutions is becoming essential. AI has the potential to support humanistic management by enabling, among other things, the personalisation of the employee experience. Through analytical algorithms, organisations can better understand the needs and preferences of seniors, allowing them to create tailored professional development programmes. The use of AI in monitoring employees' emotional well-being can also contribute to improving their quality of life at work. According to the studies cited in the first part of the paper, older workers often face challenges in adapting to new technologies.

Humanistic management and AI technologies can help overcome these barriers through appropriate training and support. AI represents a huge opportunity to increase the effectiveness of preventive care, but its emergence in the work environment means that occupational health professionals need to change and broaden their scope. Much of this should be done in collaboration with the employer.

Mentoring programmes in which younger generations share technological knowledge with seniors can increase their confidence and skills. The literature highlights that organisations that adopt a humanistic approach gain employee loyalty and engagement, which is particularly important in the context of older workers who often have valuable knowledge and experience. Integrating AI in such organisations can help increase efficiency while supporting employees' mental health. Through AI, it is also possible to develop flexible working solutions that consider seniors' needs, such as the ability to work remotely or adjust working hours. This approach enhances comfort at work and promotes a better work-life balance. It is also worth noting that humanistic management promotes an organisational culture in which diversity is valued and utilised. Introducing AI technologies to support this diversity can benefit employees and the organisation (e.g., AI can help identify talent and skills that may be overlooked in traditional recruitment processes). Integrating AI into humanistic management allows data to be used to understand older workers' needs better. Analysis of performance and job satisfaction data can help identify areas for improvement. This enables managers to make changes that make a real difference to the well-being of seniors, resulting in higher motivation and engagement (Kondrat, 2025).

Szostak (2023) points out the importance of empathy in management, which is particularly relevant in the context of generational diversity in the workplace. The introduction of AI technologies can support this process by enabling the personalisation of the employee experience. Through recommender systems, organisations can deliver personalised training and support that addresses seniors' individual needs. AI can also be key in creating a safe and comfortable working environment. Potential health risks can be identified through monitoring technologies, allowing them to be addressed quickly (Walusiak-Skorupa et al., 2023). Such measures can significantly affect the emotional well-being of older workers who feel valued and secure in their workplace. It is worth emphasising that humanistic management is not only about adapting technology to the needs of employees but also about building an organisational culture in which seniors are actively involved (Kostera & Wozniak, 2022). Examples include programmes where older employees share their knowledge and experience with younger colleagues. Such activities not only support the career development of younger employees but also enhance the seniors' sense of self-worth. Using AI in development programmes for seniors can help increase their skills and confidence (Kondrat, 2024). Technology provides feedback on progress, which motivates further learning. As a result, older workers become more competitive in the labour market, which benefits both them and the organisation. From an organisational perspective, investing in AI technologies that support humanistic management can bring long-term benefits. Companies that care about the well-being of their employees may often gain a reputation which attracts talent and customers (Melé, 2016).

Humanistic management practices combined with AI technologies can increase operational efficiency and innovation. From a societal perspective, promoting the labour force participation of mature people is crucial for sustainable economic development. The increase in the number of older people in society requires organisations to adapt to their needs, which can reduce the labour shortage problem (Kondrat & Kosiak, 2024). Preparing a work environment that values age diversity promotes social inclusion and strengthens interpersonal bonds (Kondrat, 2024). In summary, the synergistic combination of humanistic management with AI technologies creates a new quality in the workplace. This enables the work environment to be better adapted to the needs of seniors but also promotes their development and well-being. Leading to a balance between the demands of the labour market and the well-being of employees, which benefits both organisations and society in the long term. In the context of older workers, organisations need to recognise their unique needs and experiences. The literature, particularly the work of Szostak (2024), emphasises that arts management is about adapting strategies to diverse groups of employees, which can be perfectly supported by technologies such as AI that have the potential to activate seniors by adapting the working environment to their individual needs.

Based on the above, two main results of the research are: (1) a matrix of humanistic management aspects and AI-supported tools for the seniors' sensory and emotional well-being and (2) a list of recommendations for using AI-supported systems in the work environment for senior employees' health and safety.

### *Matrix of humanistic management aspects and AI-supported tools for the seniors' sensory and emotional well-being*

By integrating core dimensions of well-being explored in existing literature with principles of humanistic management and AI-based tools designed to support senior welfare, a framework for identifying benefits for older employees can be developed. A Matrix of selected aspects of humanistic management and AI-supported tools leading to an improvement in the seniors' sensory and emotional well-being

*Table 10.3* Matrix of selected aspects of humanistic management and AI-supported tools leading to an improvement in the seniors' sensory and emotional well-being

| *Aspect of well-being* | *Humanistic management aspects* | *AI tools to support the well-being of seniors* | *Benefits to seniors* |
|---|---|---|---|
| Sensory well-being, Health support | Adaptation of working environments to sensory needs (e.g., ergonomics, introduction of flexible forms of working | AI systems monitoring ergonomics of workstations, algorithms optimising environmental conditions (e.g., temperature, noise)<br>Health monitoring systems (e.g., wearables) suggesting breaks at work<br>AI tools analysing stress levels and suggesting anti-stress measures | Reduction of physical strain, improved working comfort<br>Reduction of workload |
| Emotional well-being | Emotional and social support programmes<br>Building a culture of respect and appreciation | AI chatbots offering emotional support. AI systems analysing employee moods | Reduction of stress and anxiety<br>Increased sense of security and belonging |
| Social inclusion/ building a respectful organisational culture | Building mixed-age teams<br>Mentoring programmes | AI tools suggesting the creation of teams based on diversity<br>Platforms and apps to support mentoring<br>AI tools analysing communication and eliminating stereotypes | Increased intergenerational integration<br>Exchange of knowledge and experience<br>Increased sense of value and appreciation<br>Elimination of age discrimination |
| Personal development | Professional development training<br>Promotion of autonomy and responsibility<br>Individual approach to employees | AI-based training platforms tailored to the needs of seniors<br>AI systems suggesting development paths based on analysis of employees' experience and knowledge | Increased motivation and job satisfaction<br>Opportunity for continuous development |

(*Continued*)

*Table 10.3* (Continued)

| *Aspect of well-being* | *Humanistic management aspects* | *AI tools to support the well-being of seniors* | *Benefits to seniors* |
|---|---|---|---|
| Work-life balance | Flexible working schedules | Algorithms to optimise working hours | Improved time management<br>Reduction of stress related to the number of responsibilities |
| Support for adaptation to technological change | Educational platforms offering digital competence training | Intuitive interfaces (e.g., voice assistants)<br>AI training tailored to the needs of seniors | Reduction of technological barriers<br>Increased confidence in using new technologies |

*Source:* own elaboration based on Baran et al., 2023, Kondrat & Kosiak, 2024, Kondrat, 2025, Xu et al., 2023, Zapędowska-Kling, 2015, Zwijsen et al., 2011.

(Table 10.3), formulated through a comprehensive literature review, addresses a critical gap in research. While prior studies have emphasised the need to enhance sensory and emotional well-being in older adults, no existing work systematically combines humanistic management approaches with practical AI solutions tailored for this demographic. The matrix represents a structured literature synthesis, bridging selected humanistic management aspects with AI applications to improve seniors' sensory and emotional well-being. Combining AI and humanistic management offers new opportunities to activate older workers. Organisations can improve productivity and job satisfaction by enhancing their sensory and emotional well-being. It is worth continuing research into this area to further understand how technology can support the sustainability of workers of all ages.

#### ***Recommendations for using AI-supported systems in the work environment for senior employees' health and safety***

It is possible to identify good practices showing how selected AI-supported tools can help older workers adapt to a technology-dominated environment that supports their well-being. Key recommendations for the use of AI-based systems in the work environment in an employee health and safety-oriented manner include:

- making structural changes in parallel with automation (examining the potential risks of using AI in a given work environment);

- analysing the skills of the workforce manifested by, among other things, assessing the attitudes of employees towards the technologies being introduced, preparing a strategy for the skills needed and planning the necessary training),
- introducing organisational changes to support workers using AI in the work environment after careful assessment of the occupational risks and preparation of appropriate procedures,
- involving workers as early as possible in the implementation of new solutions, selecting "key users" and "technology ambassadors", addressing workers' concerns, e.g., about job loss,
- monitoring critical elements and technological changes, taking into account employee perceptions and human-machine interaction,
- exploiting the potential arising from the application of AI in the work environment to reduce the burden on workers and occupational risks,
- responding to problems of social interaction so that the introduction of advanced technological systems does not disrupt social structures within the company,
- learning through experience, which is generally lacking with advanced technologies, thus making all AI-related workplace events all the more valuable,
- increasing employee awareness and internal communication.

## Discussion: management humanising in the face of an ageing population – integrating AI in the workplace to sustain the labour market activation of mature people

In the face of an ageing population, organisations need to adapt their approach to human resource management to realise mature employees' full potential. The development of new technologies, including AI in the workplace, is becoming a key element to be considered in strategies to create better working conditions for employees, regardless of age. As highlighted in the first part of this study, these technologies can support employees in their daily work, including active seniors, by offering solutions that respond to their specific needs, increasing comfort and efficiency at work.

Humanistic management, which emphasises empathy, values and adapting the work environment to the individual needs of employees, is an ideal complement to AI technologies. By combining selected humanistic management practices with the solutions offered by AI, organisations will be able to create an environment where seniors feel valued, motivated and fully engaged in their tasks. As a result, technology and humanistic management approaches can work together, leading to an improved quality of life and work for mature people. Integrating humanistic management principles with AI-powered solutions is becoming increasingly important in the context of dynamic changes in the labour market and the growing number of older workers. The research presented in this chapter provides significant evidence that combining these two approaches can effectively increase older workers' sensory and emotional well-being, which is a key step in filling the research gap identified in the literature review.

Previous studies, such as those by Szostak (2023), Sułkowski (2002), and Rakowska and Cichorzewska (2019), emphasised the importance of empathy and adapting the work environment to the needs of employees. It has been noted that older employees often face numerous challenges, such as technostress, social isolation, and difficulties in adapting to new technologies. However, the literature lacks a systematic approach combining these issues with practical AI tools that can support older employees in the workplace.

The matrix presented in this study, combining selected aspects of humanistic management with AI tools, is an innovative approach to improving the well-being of older workers. In particular, emphasising the role of AI in monitoring emotional well-being and adapting working conditions to the seniors' sensory needs is key in increasing their job satisfaction.

The literature often emphasises that emotional and sensory well-being is key to employee engagement. Timmons et al. (2011) point out that older employees often experience difficulties adapting to new technologies, leading to frustration and reduced job satisfaction. Integrating AI with mentoring programmes, enabling younger generations to share technological knowledge with seniors, can boost their confidence and skills. This approach supports knowledge transfer and builds a sense of value and belonging among older workers. In addition, using AI systems to monitor emotional well-being and adapt working conditions to the sensory needs of older employees can improve their quality of life; e.g., AI solutions can analyse employees' stress levels and suggest appropriate breaks or relaxation techniques, reducing psychological strain. These examples confirm that AI has the potential to act as a mediator in the adaptation of the working environment to the needs of older employees.

The recommendations included in the studies, such as the introduction of flexible working hours, individualised development programmes and mentoring, respond to the needs identified in the literature on the activation of senior citizens. According to Lee's (2014) research, promoting age diversity is crucial for building a positive image of the organisation and attracting talent. The introduction of flexible working arrangements, such as the possibility of remote working or adjusting working hours to individual needs, can significantly increase the comfort of older employees at work and thus their commitment.

An important aspect is promoting an organisational culture where diversity is valued and utilised. As indicated in the literature, organisations that adopt a humanistic approach gain employee loyalty and commitment, which is particularly important in the context of older employees, who often have valuable knowledge and experience. Integrating AI in such organisations can increase efficiency while supporting employees' mental health. Research shows that combining AI with humanistic management principles can significantly improve the well-being of older employees. Introducing AI systems that monitor emotional well-being, adapt working conditions to individual needs and support mentoring programmes can lead to better engagement and job satisfaction. As noted in the literature, investing in such solutions benefits employees and organisations, which can count on higher productivity and loyalty. From a social perspective, promoting the economic activity of people of pre-retirement age is crucial for sustainable economic development. In the face of an increasing number of older people in society, organisations must adapt their structures to their needs, which can help solve the labour shortage problem. Preparing a working environment that values age diversity promotes social integration and strengthens interpersonal relationships.

In the future, it is worth continuing research into how technology, including AI, can support the professional activity of older workers and contribute to their well-being. It will be important to understand how different generations react to new technologies and what their specific needs are in this respect. In particular, research should focus on how humanistic management strategies can be effectively combined with modern technological solutions to maximise employee and organisational benefits. The synergistic combination of humanistic management and AI-based technologies creates a new quality in the workplace, enabling a better adaptation of the work environment to the needs of older workers and promoting their development and well-being. In the long term, this approach will positively impact the balance between labour market requirements and employee well-being, benefitting organisations and society.

## Conclusion

Regarding RQ1 (*To what extent can the integration of humanistic management and tools developed through AI influence the emotional and sensory well-being of elderly people in the labour market?*), it can be said that the integration of humanistic management with AI tools has the potential to significantly influence the emotional and sensory well-being of older people in the labour market. Creating an organisational culture based on empathy, personalising employee experiences, monitoring well-being, and optimising the work environment by using AI tools contributes to improving the quality of working life of older employees, which is crucial to their professional activity and job satisfaction.

Regarding RQ2 (*How can selected AI-powered tools assist older employees in adapting to a technology-dominated environment while safeguarding their sensory and emotional well-being?*), theoretical frameworks imply that an integrated humanistic approach with the use of AI creates new qualities in the workplace, supporting the adaptation of older workers in a dynamic environment. Modern technologies and AI foster inclusivity by bridging generational gaps through tools like adaptive learning platforms and AI-driven communication systems. For instance, AI can customise training modules to match seniors' learning paces while facilitating knowledge exchange between older and younger employees via reverse mentoring. Emotion-aware AI systems (e.g., adjusting lighting or workload based on stress levels) enhance sensory comfort, reducing technostress among older workers. Platforms like VR for collaborative tasks or AI-mediated feedback loops promote intergenerational teamwork, valuing experience and innovation.

Nevertheless, it is important to acknowledge the *limitations* associated with the research being conducted. This study is conceptual, and while comprehensive, it lacks empirical validation. Most of the analysed studies concern the Western context (Europe, North America), which constrains the possibility of generalising the results to non-European societies with different socio-cultural norms regarding ageing and technology. In addition, many of the studies analysed were cross-sectional, making it impossible to draw causal conclusions about the long-term impact of the synergy between AI and humanistic management on the well-being of older employees.

Concerning the methodological limitations identified, it is possible to make *future research suggestions*: (1) interdisciplinary research combining knowledge from the fields of gerontology, data analytics and organisational psychology, enabling the design of AI systems that holistically respond to the sensory, cognitive and emotional needs of older employees; (2) participatory design involving the involvement of older employees in the co-creation of AI solutions to ensure that the technology is tailored to their experiences and to minimise the risk of digital exclusion; (3) inclusion of ethical framework for AI tools aimed at the ageing workforce, taking into account consent, transparency and responsibility in technologies that analyse emotions. Pursuing the suggested lines of research will increase the reliability and applicability of the results, supporting the creation of fair, age-inclusive work environments in the AI era. Ultimately, this approach encourages elderly employees to remain in the workforce longer, addressing the challenges of an ageing population and transforming the labour market into a more inclusive and dynamic space.

## References

Ali, M., & French, E. (2019). Age diversity management and organisational outcomes: The role of diversity perspectives. *Human Resource Management Journal*, 29 (2), 287–307. https://doi.org/10.1111/1748-8583.12225

Ayalon, L., & Tesch-Römer, C. (2018). Introduction to the section: Ageism—concept and origins. In L. Ayalon, & C. Tesch-Römer (Eds.), *Contemporary Perspectives on Ageism. International Perspectives on Aging*, vol 19. Springer. https://doi.org/10.1007/978-3-319-73820-8_1

Bąk, M. (2017). *Pracownicy pokolenia Z wyzwaniem dla pracodawców*. Materiały Powiatowego Urzędu Pracy.

Baran, M., Chmielewska, A., Kondrat, M., & Kosiak, P. (2023). Silver tsunami a postęp AI: Aspekty ekonomiczno-prawne starzejącego się społeczeństwa w Polsce. *IJONESS*, 20 (4), 247–266.

Chung-Yan, G. A. (2010). The nonlinear effects of job complexity and autonomy on job satisfaction, turnover, and psychological well-being. *Journal of Occupational Health Psychology*, 15 (3), 237–251. https://doi.org/10.1037/a0019823

Ciura, G., & Szymańczak, J. (2012). Starzenie się społeczeństwa polskiego. *Infos*, 12 (126), 1–4. https://orka.sejm.gov.pl/wydbas.nsf/0/D5E35E200F187640C1257A29004A756B/$File/Infos_126.pdf

Cruce, T. M., & Hillman, N. W. (2012). Preparing for the silver tsunami: The demand for higher education among older adults. *Research in Higher Education*, 53 (6), 593–613. https://doi.org/10.1007/s11162-011-9249-9

Deal, J. J. (2007). *Retiring the Generation Gap: How Employees Young and Old Can Find Common Ground*. Jossey-Bass.

De Cuyper, N., & De Witte, H. (2006). Autonomy and workload among temporary workers: Their effects on job satisfaction, organizational commitment, life satisfaction, and self-rated performance. *International Journal of Stress Management*, 13 (4), 441–459. https://doi.org/10.1037/1072-5245.13.4.441

Haertel, T., Radtke, M., Terkowsky, C., May, D., Neubauer, D., & Dehler, J. (2015). Too old to learn? Specific needs of senior workplace learners. *International Conference on Interactive Collaborative Learning (ICL),* Firenze, 132–136. https://doi.org/10.1109/ICL.2015.7318013

Hildt-Ciupińska, K. (2014). Work-life balance a wiek pracowników. *Bezpieczeństwo Pracy: Nauka i Praktyka*, 10, 14–17.

Ilmarinen, J. (2011). 30 years work ability and 20 years age management during life course. *Proceedings of the 4th Symposium on Work Ability*. Tampere University Press.

Kondrat, M. (2025). Kitsch in HRM: The role of communication in managing generational diversity in an organization. In M. Szostak (Ed.), *Management Aesthetics: Kitsch and Modern Organisations. Routledge*. https://doi.org/10.4324/9781003504931

Kondrat, M., & Kosiak, P. (2024). Digital competences of elderly people in Poland – challenges and opportunities in the technological era. *IJONESS*, 25 (1), 21–39.

Kostera, M., & Woźniak, C. (2022). *Aesthetics, Organization, and Humanistic Management*. Routledge.

Kowalewski, K., & Moczydłowska, J. (2020). *Patologie i dysfunkcje w organizacji*. Wydawnictwo Difin.

Lee, R. (2014). *How Population Aging Affects the Macroeconomy*. Presentation given at the 2014 Jackson Hole Conference.

Lipińska-Grobelny, A. (2024). Starzenie się 4.0 a rynek pracy pracownika. *Zarządzanie Zasobami Ludzkimi*, 159 (5), 24–36.

Lubrańska, A. (2024). Occupational values of seniors in the context of the type and position of work. *Social Policy*, 1, 10–18. https://doi.org/10.5604/01.3001.0054.4822

Melé, D. (2016). Understanding humanistic management. *Humanistic Management Journal*, 1 (1), 33–55. https://doi.org/10.1007/s41463-016-0011-5

Nandram, S. S., & Bindlish, K. P. (2017). *Managing VUCA through Integrative Self-Management: How to Cope with Volatility, Uncertainty, Complexity and Ambiguity in Organizational Behavior*. Springer. https://doi.org/10.1007/978-3-319-52231-9

Noponen, N. (2019). Impact of artificial intelligence on management, T. Takala, T. Auvinen, M. Vesa, J. Tienari, P. Sajasalo, S. Heikkinen, J. Helms Mills, & M. Kallinen-Kuisma (Eds.), *Electronic Journal of Business Ethics and Organization Studies*, 24 (2), 43–50. Jyväskylänyliopisto. https://ejbo.jyu.fi/pdf/ejbo_vol24_no2_pages_43-50.pdf

Rakowska, A., & Cichorzewska, M. (2019). Rola wartości preferowanych przez pracowników w kontekście kształtowania inkluzywnych organizacji. In W. Jarecki & A. Bąkicwicz (Eds.), *Zarządzanie kapitałem ludzkim – aspekty teoretyczne i praktyczne* (pp. 327–342). Społeczna Akademia Nauk.

Rzeczyński, B. (2009a). Gerontechnologia w przestrzeni komunalnej. *Przegląd Komunalny*, 3, 86–87.

Rzeczyński, B. (2009b). Gerontechnologia w perspektywie urbanistycznej. *Acta Universitatis Lodziensis Folia Oeconomica*, 231, 287–304.

Sułkowski, Ł. (2002). *Kulturowa zmienność organizacji*. PWE.

Sułkowski, Ł., & Woźniak, A. (Eds.). (2014). *Zarządzanie humanistyczne*. Wydawnictwo Społecznej Akademii Nauk.

Szostak, M. (2023). *Sztuka zarządzania – zarządzanie sztuką*. Wydawnictwo Społecznej Akademii Nauk.

Szostak, M. (2024). *Humanistic Management, Organisation and Aesthetics: Art of Management and Management of Art*. Routledge. https://doi.org/10.4324/9781003458029

The silver tsunami. (2010). The Economist. Retrieved. https://www.economist.com/business/2010/02/04/the-silver-tsunami

Timmons, J., Hall, A. C., Fesko, S. L., & Migliore, A. (2011). Retaining the older workforce: Social policy considerations for the universally designed workplace. *Journal of Aging & Social Policy*, 23 (2), 119–140. https://doi.org/10.1080/08959420.2011.551623

Twenge, J. M., Campbell, S., & Hoffman, B. (2010). Generational differences in work values: Leisure and extrinsic values increasing, social and intrinsic values decreasing. *Journal of Management*, 36 (5), 1117–1142.

Walusiak-Skorupa, J., Kaczmarek, P., & Wiszniewska, M. (2023). Artificial intelligence and employee's health – new challenges. *Medycyna Pracy*, 74 (3), 227–233. https://doi.org/10.13075/mp.5893.01422

Wei, W. Q., & Li, L. (2022). The impact of artificial intelligence on the mental health of manufacturing workers: The mediating role of overtime work and the work environment. *Frontiers in Public Health*, 10, 1–12. https://doi.org/10.3389/fpubh.2022.862407

WHO (2024). Ageing and health. https://www.who.int/news-room/fact-sheets/detail/ageing-and-health

Widerszal-Bazyl, M., & Wołodźko, E. (2015). Wartości związane z pracą w różnych pokoleniach. *Bezpieczeństwo Pracy – Nauka i Praktyka*, 10, 20–24.

Xu, G., Xue, M., & Zhao, J. (2023). The relationship of artificial intelligence opportunity perception and employee workplace well-being: A moderated mediation model. *International Journal of Environmental Research and Public Health*, 20 (3), 1974. https://doi.org/10.3390/ijerph20031974

Zagórowska, M. (2020). *Degradation Modelling in Process Control Applications*. Imperial College London.

Zapędowska-Kling, K. A. (2015). Nowe technologie w służbie seniorom. *Acta Universitatis Lodziensis Folia Oeconomica*, 4 (315), 203–215.

Zwijsen, S. A., Niemeijer, A. R., & Hertogh, C. M. P. M. (2011). Ethics of using assistive technology in the care for community-dwelling elderly people: An overview of the literature. *Assistive Technology*, 23 (4), 419–427.

# 11 The aesthetics of AI-driven management

## Balancing algorithmic efficiency and user experience in e-commerce development

*Aneta Ejsmont*

### Introduction

According to the definition on the AIoAI website, AI establishes an area of science and technology that focuses on creating machines and computer systems capable of performing tasks that require human intelligence (Coursera Staff, 2024). In this case, it is about the application of modern AI algorithms in the field of sales in the process of company management, particularly managing the development of business entities of different sizes under study, primarily because management is defined, among other things, as "the art of successfully achieving goals" (Szostak, 2024, pp. 42–69) especially as the main objective is to develop such modern algorithms in the field of machine learning, which significantly affect the process of managing the development of businesses of different sizes operating in a network (Rogalski, 2024).

There are many publications in various scientific databases on the application of AI tools in the process of managing the development of companies doing business on the Internet, in other words, in the e-commerce market. The literature shows that it is possible to find articles describing the application of new technologies in the development and management of enterprises by increasing efficiency and productivity through AI. There are articles on AI and its role in e-commerce, including a bibliometric study, a literature review, and a comprehensive analysis. Taking advantage of the research gap in this area, it should be explicitly stated that no scientific studies have been published to date that present research on the application of AI tools in the activities of businesses, especially in listed companies from the point of view of the aesthetics of AI algorithms implemented in the sales processes of the business entities studied.

This study's primary *research problem* is to realise whether modern AI algorithms can provide stability in developing business entities that conduct their activities in the broader e-commerce market is important, especially since it is challenging to develop such AI tools in terms of machine learning (e.g., sales intelligence) that will fully enable sales without negatively impacting the overall

DOI: 10.4324/9781003654377-15

level of development of the businesses (DMSales, 2024; AIMOJO, 2024). In addition, the study aims to analyse whether AI algorithms are justified in wider e-business from an aesthetic point of view. This chapter answers the following *research questions*: (RQ1) What AI algorithms for machine learning should be applied to the sales process to impact online businesses from an aesthetic point of view positively? (RQ2) How should modern AI algorithms affect the development management process of business entities from an aesthetic perspective?

Therefore, the *research method* used is creating the model of an Internet-based company using modern algorithms in such spheres of activity as bookkeeping, billing, and sales. The issues discussed in the study will be presented from the point of view of the broadly understood aesthetics of management, where management itself, and in particular development management using modern AI algorithms, is the art of effective goal achievement.

This chapter is further enriched by the estimation of an econometric model, which additionally uses not only econometric tools but also IT tools, combining a scheme for the construction of an algorithm that supports sales processes in the e-commerce market and the process of studying the impact of the use of various sales techniques on the level of development of listed companies or even limited liability companies developing mainly on the Internet. In this case, it becomes an important challenge to build such a model with the support of econometric tools, which would take into account, in particular, the preferences of consumers, who, in most cases, purchase various types of products with the help of smartphones, which are so popular in today's world. Moreover, this is where the applications supported by algorithms, which are developed for the needs of entrepreneurs who thus disseminate information about the novelties introduced into the e-commerce market, find great relevance (Xie and Ren, 2022, p. 1, 5). Given the range of analytical tools used in scientific research that consider constructing AI-supported econometric models, this study uses machine learning algorithms. The research conducted is empirical, considering the analysis of specific case studies. Specific algorithms used in the sales process will be analysed, further supporting the econometric model's estimation process. Due to increased access to data, the study analyses limited liability and joint stock companies from the electronics industry.

## Literature review: framing the discourse – algorithmic tools and aesthetic considerations in digital sales

The e-commerce market and related digital businesses aim to increase the competitiveness of the companies operating in it. This is done by implementing innovative digital technologies in cooperative relationships with business partners and customers. AI is becoming a technological innovation (Chaffey, 2016, p. 15; *Ethics guidelines for trustworthy AI*, 2019). The literature review section presents the following order. First of all, the essence of the development of companies in the e-commerce market was presented. Then, the section explains the role of (1) AI in sales process management and in the development of companies in that market; (2) aesthetics in creating AI and in the development of companies from the e-commerce market; and (3) ethics in the management of AI and development of companies in that market.

The last point is analysing the impact of ethics and aesthetics on AI in the sales management of the selected industrial limited liability and joint stock e-companies. Machine learning in improving sales processes in the broadly understood e-commerce market must encourage and attract as many customers as possible while ensuring that AI tools follow the principles of broadly understood ethics.

***Development of companies in the e-commerce market***

The e-commerce market consists of the flow of information capital, business and logistics, understood as the physical flow of goods from the seller to the consumer, including returns (Xiao et al., 2012, pp. 57–70). Besides, e-commerce trade is the fastest-growing sales channel or another omnichannel retailing, which impacts the development of companies running their own business on the Internet by increasing consumer demand for seamless shopping experiences (Risberg, 2023, p. 67).

Delfmann, Albers, and Gehring define e-commerce as the process where "retailers provide seamless consumer experience in omnichannel retailing by integrating their physical stores and online channels. The consumer might order online, receive the product at home, and return the product in the store" (Delfmann et al., 2002, pp. 203–222). Additionally, as Besharat wrote, e-commerce is a recent business process that cuts costs and increases the speed of service and delivery via the Internet, leading to savings for businesses and consumers" (Besharat, 2018, p. 138).

Quoting Taherdoost and Madanchian (2023, p. 1), "E-commerce platforms enable companies of all sizes to sell their items and promote their brand to a broader audience. The e-commerce sector is continually developing, as new technology and methods of purchasing and selling services and items are developed". Hence, thanks to the e-commerce market, companies can develop their selling processes at a swift pace. Through the high-level value of Internet marketing, modern enterprises could operate more effectively and run their business efficiently by developing an assortment of new products and services and increasing market transparency (Treichler, 2019, pp. 253–272).

Summarising the above considerations regarding the e-commerce market in the context of its impact on the increased development of enterprises, it should be clearly stated that e-commerce is a type of trade conducted on the Internet, regardless of the tools used. The main feature that distinguishes it from other forms of trade is that goods and services are ordered online, but delivery and payment can be made directly. As a result, the way this phenomenon is perceived is changing. Nowadays, e-commerce is not just about selling products on the

Internet. There are several forms of e-commerce, including (E-commerce dla początkujących – co to jest, co oznacza branża?, 2022): (1) direct or complex trade, characterised by the fact that commercial transactions are carried out entirely online, i.e. from the moment an order is placed, through payment, to the delivery of the goods (e.g. trade in so-called e-books); (2) indirect trade, which involves searching for goods or services and making payments online; on the other hand, delivery is carried out traditionally by courier; (3) hybrid trade, which involves various forms of distribution used temporarily due to deficiencies in the development of the network, telecommunications, or logistics services.

Therefore, this chapter analyses the impact of e-commerce, which is carried out more in a hybrid form, on the development of limited liability companies (in this case, DBMS Sp. z o.o.) and selected joint-stock companies in the industrial sector. These economic entities are large manufacturing companies conducting most of their transactions on-site, but some are also carried out via the Internet. The surveyed entities have many online shops that distribute the goods produced by these companies.

### *AI in sales process management and development of companies in the e-commerce market*

Often, the primary purpose of an effective layout for a stationary store is to present goods in such a way as to attract customers' attention and encourage them to walk more aisles. In this way, shoppers are exposed to more merchandise and what entrepreneurs say is positively correlated with sales. According to them, this constitutes "one of the most effective in-store marketing tactics that can directly influence customer decisions to increase sales and store profitability". The question is, "Is this really the case?" Well, customers strolling through the aisles, staying, for example, in a certain hypermarket, looking for something attractive for themselves, unable to find anything that would interest them (because nowadays there is again the paradox of ordering goods, which are then lined up on the shelves not by the employees employed but by the system, i.e. AI). Bored consumers, who do not want to waste time, increasingly prefer to purchase online. Hence, massive interest in developing the broader e-commerce market can be observed (Nguyen et al., 2022, p. 5707; Rhee and Bell, 2002, pp. 225–237).

Traditional sales processes have long relied on rigid frameworks to balance supply capacities with demand fluctuations. While effective in the past, these frameworks are becoming increasingly insufficient for handling the volatility of modern supply chains (Jonsson et al., 2021, p. 553), especially in an era especially in an era marked by numerous crises, from the pandemic to the ongoing armed conflict in Ukraine (Harper, 2022, p. 1213). AI used in sales processes in the e-commerce market is a lever for business growth. In all of this, the implementation of AI in sales and operations planning (S&OP) environments plays a significant role today (Jazairy et al., 2025, p. 1).

Examples of quite popular machine learning algorithms to support the sales process conducted by companies in the e-commerce market are "Sales Intelligence" systems. When analysing the impact of Sales Intelligence Systems on the effectiveness of marketing processes contributing to the level of e-business development and increasing customer confidence, it is worth mentioning that it is thanks to their use, e.g., in 2024, DBMS increased its sales by 30% in just six months (DMSales, 2024).

The rapid development of AI is bringing revolutionary changes in many areas, including e-commerce. Furthermore, e-commerce offers a variety of opportunities to increase consumer engagement by optimising business activities in the pharmaceutical, electrical engineering, and raw materials industries (Khrais, 2020, p. 1). In e-commerce purchasing, combined with AI, product recommendations have become a key tool for companies to personalise user experiences, increase sales and, consequently, improve overall customer satisfaction (Zhang and Xiong, 2024, p. 30379).

***Aesthetics of AI and development of companies in the e-commerce market***

The aesthetics of algorithms is a real challenge for companies in the ever-evolving e-commerce market. Well-developed machine learning components should be constantly adapted to customers' ever-increasing needs. Aesthetics is also about appearance, and quality should go hand in hand with it, although this issue is subject to separate discussion.

As Johnson (2015) wrote, "Annually, an average woman spends 140 hours on 45 trips shopping for clothes and shoes, and 95 hours on 84 trips shopping for food". However, impatient customers spend twice as much time in the store overall. Thus, the current conventional approach to store layout design is not so much based on passive as outright negative customer response. Potential consumers are increasingly looking for modern solutions on the Internet, purchasing goods that they have not found in a traditional store, which are characterised by high quality and lower prices compared to the same goods sold in the traditional market. From an aesthetic point of view, modern customers pay special attention to the speed of reaching a particular commodity when purchasing goods (Cil, 2012, pp. 8611–8625; Cil et al., 2009, pp. 465–470).

In this case, it is worth considering the process of expanding the algorithms that support customer service applications on the Internet, as this will affect the increased level of development of companies operating in the e-commerce market. Thus, as is well known, technological development makes it possible to create a lot of innovative goods for which buyers have greater or lesser demand. Thus, many companies invest a lot of time and money to attract as many customers as possible, but often based on assumptions rather than facts. Hence, important in all of this is the so-called "Design Thinking" approach, which helps prevent the introduction of misguided ideas by learning the perspective of the buyer of the goods and responding to the needs of the customer at the early stages of the work using modern AI algorithms, since the current perception of the aesthetics of management activities is based precisely on applications that are massively used on the Internet (Kochanowska, 2024).

### *Ethics of AI and development of companies in the e-commerce market*

We live in a time when everyone is raving about using AI algorithms in almost every area of activity. Similarly, sales conducted by companies in the e-commerce market are also increasingly based on the use of AI. Nevertheless, no one is thinking about how to use AI ethically. The explosion of data-driven applications using AI in recent years has led to several incidents involving law violations. Ethical issues in the context of legal violations often lead to discrimination and even privacy breaches through hacking. In the case of large manufacturing companies, the use of machine learning algorithms also harms the environment (O'Neil, 2016, pp. 1–272; Lacoste et al., 2019, p. 1; Christoforaki and Beyan, 2022, p. 1).

Since opinions on the ethics of AI remain divided among many communities (academics and practitioners), the governments of individual EU countries have taken steps to address this issue. The European Union has even prepared a draft law on AI. Unfortunately, translating ethical principles into practice has been identified as one of the critical issues in ensuring socially responsible AI systems. When introducing trade facilitation through the use of AI, companies should seek to demonstrate the legality, accuracy, efficiency, and security of the algorithms they develop while applying machine learning tools following ethical principles (Brown et al., 2021, p. 2; 2019, 2021; Morley et al., 2020, p. 2159; Sloane et al., 2022, pp. 1–9).

### *Impact of aesthetics and ethics on AI in sales management of the selected industrial e-companies*

A potential model incorporating elements of machine learning must, of course, be consistent with the broadly understood aesthetics, which in turn is also linked to ethics. Intending to attempt to study the impact of AI tools on the process of managing the development of companies doing business in the e-commerce market, it is necessary to look at the issue of the aesthetics of algorithms introduced into marketing activities following business ethics. In this case, ethics is a doctrine of morality that analyses worthy or unworthy human behaviour. On the other hand, aesthetics is a science that studies the essence and manifestation of beauty in human behaviour manifested in various areas of life, especially economic life.

Hence, the integration of AI with artistic endeavours finding wide application in the marketing activities of companies developing their business on the Internet leads to a complex interaction between ethics and aesthetics in art based on the cooperation between man (entrepreneur-marketer) and machine (Crawford and Paglen, 2021, pp. 1105–1116). Accordingly, the algorithms' aesthetics positively impact the growing experience of those conducting marketing activities in the e-commerce market. The aesthetics of the interface of AI tools, combined with their "elegance", have an impact on the effectiveness of sales management and, consequently, contributes to the level of development of the surveyed companies by increasing customer trust and commitment. In the age of technological ubiquity, AI is transforming not only industrial sectors but also fundamental human experiences, including creativity. Meanwhile, the design of what will be a commodity in the future is also related to creativity and, thus, aesthetics (Xu et al., 2025, p. 1).

In creating sales processes supported by AI, all technologies can strengthen and reduce the creative autonomy of entrepreneurs responsible for increasing sales. Therefore, the integrity of the originators of various online sales methods, characterised by their commitment to a personal creative vision and authenticity, should be a fundamental aspect of the development of the companies (limited liability companies and joint-stock companies) under investigation, effectively combining aesthetic and ethical considerations (Chamberlain et al., 2017, pp. 177–192; Mills, 2018, pp. 9–20; Thompson, 1995, pp. 38–45; Orr and Davis, 2020, pp. 719–735; Sekiguchi and Hori, 2019, pp. 3181–3190).

## Results: findings and interpretations from the empirical model

As is well known, machine learning algorithms work on specific data, making connections between subsystems. However, it sometimes happens that the assumptions made are not clearly specified, in which case the effect is the opposite of that intended. The problem is that the data read by AI algorithms is misleading. In this case, the error will be in the planning of sales processes carried out by e-commerce companies (Bonaccorso, 2019, p. 20). Thus, the task of the entire machine learning process is to find the best set of parameters maximising the target function, whose value depends on the data on which the model determined by both input X and output Y has been built. Therefore, the problem of building machine learning algorithms involves finding often abstract relationships that allow consistent generalisation towards the data generation process (Bonaccorso, 2019, p. 20).

AI tools for machine learning need to be developed so that they do not disrupt businesses that choose to conduct their business in the broader e-commerce market, so that they do not interfere with the process of sales. In summary, the study's result is the creation of such a model that uses both econometric and IT tools, combining the scheme of building an algorithm that handles sales processes in the e-commerce market and the process of studying the impact of various sales techniques on the level of development of companies that conduct their business via the Internet.

In order to write this chapter, case studies of joint-stock companies listed on the Warsaw Stock Exchange conducting sales not only on the traditional market but also in e-commerce, which use specific AI algorithms to support sales processes, were analysed. For this purpose, 34 companies operating in sectors of the economy such as pharmaceutical manufacturing, the electrical machinery industry or the raw materials industry, which use AI algorithms to a greater or lesser extent in their sales processes, were analysed. The overall design of these algorithms is based on the interaction of the following subsystems:

- "create tasks" subsystem (variable $x_1$),
- "send emails" subsystem (variable $x_2$),
- "create reminders" subsystem (variable $x_3$),
- subsystem "assign new leads" (variable $x_4$),
- "qualify leads" subsystem (variable $x_5$),
- subsystem "spot rotten deals" (variable $x_6$).

Therefore, employing econometric tools, the impact of the aforementioned subsystems on the value of a company (variable $Y$), i.e. its market capitalisation, will be analysed, which in turn has a significant impact on the volume of sales of products and services achieved by the selected companies using these algorithms. As a result of the estimation of the econometric model, it is possible to assess which subsystems have the most significant impact on the achievement of sales levels by companies and which subsystems could be added to the overall sales process in order to contribute to increasing the level of growth of companies conducting their business online.

The initial econometric model is, of course, a linear econometric model. The data for the model was reduced to a zero-one system. The subsystems comprising the overall AI algorithm in companies that did not use AI algorithms were assigned zero values, while those companies that used machine learning were assigned "1" values. The estimated model was described by the least squares method and by the following equation:

$$\begin{aligned} Y_t = \alpha_0 + \alpha_1 x_{1t} + \alpha_2 x_{2t} + \ldots + \alpha_j x_{jt} + \varepsilon_t \geq Y_t = \alpha_0 + \alpha_1 x_{1t} + \alpha_2 x_{2t} + \alpha_3 x_{3t} + \alpha_4 x_{4t} + \\ \alpha_5 x_{5t} + \alpha_6 x_{6t} + \varepsilon_t (t = 1,2....n) \geq Y_t = \alpha_0 + \alpha_1 x_{1t} + \varepsilon_t \end{aligned} \quad (11.1)$$

where:

$n$ – number of units under study,
$j$ – number of explanatory variables,
$x_t$, $\alpha_0$, $\alpha_1$, …, $\alpha_j$ – parameters of the model,
$\varepsilon_t$ – random component.

As a result of the econometric model estimation process, calculations performed in Gretl confirmed that only the variable $x_1$ ("create tasks" subsystem) has the

*Table 11.1* Model: OLS, using observations 1–34

| *Details* | *Coefficient* | *Std. Error* *t-ratio* | | *p-value* |
|---|---|---|---|---|
| const | 274.557 | 770.966 0.3561 | | 0.7241 |
| $x_1$ | 2032.59 | 1297.73 1.566 | | 0.1271 |
| Mean dependent var | 991.9429 | | S.D. dependent var | 3694.916 |
| Sum squared resid | 4.18e+08 | | S.E. of regression | 3616.153 |
| R-squared | 0.071204 | | Adjusted R-squared | 0.042179 |
| F(1, 32) | 2.453195 | | p-value(F) | 0.127123 |
| Log-likelihood | −325.7809 | | Akaike criterion | 655.5619 |
| Schwarz criterion | 658.6146 | | Hannan-Quinn | 656.6029 |

*Note:* Dependent variable: *y*.

most substantial impact on the market value of the companies recorded on 29 January 2025. Table 11.1 shows the data containing the final estimation process of the econometric model. The research sample comprises 34 observations representing the effects of introducing AI algorithms into sales processes.

The estimation results of the econometric model indicate that it is not a perfect model. The coefficient of determination R2 is very low. The p-value for the variable $x_1$ is also high, well above 10%. Nevertheless, it is precisely because of the difficulties of the zero-one parameters of the data describing the use of machine learning algorithms that only the independent variable $x_1$ appears to be the variable that, of all the variables, most strongly influences the market value of the listed companies under study.

Based on the estimation process of the econometric model, the results of the statistical tests carried out were also presented. These tests were aimed at confirming the influence of the subsystem determining task creation on the market value of the analysed 34 companies from industrial sectors (drug production, electrical machinery industry, raw materials industry), which in turn plays a significant role in sales processes taking place in the e-commerce market.

RESET test for specification–

Null hypothesis: specification is adequate

Test statistic: F(2, 32) = 0 with p-value = P(F(2, 32) > 0) = 1

White's test for heteroscedasticity–

Null hypothesis: heteroscedasticity not present

Test statistic: LM = 2.28232 with p-value = P(Chi-square(1) > 2.28232) = 0.130856

Breusch-Pagan test for heteroscedasticity–

Null hypothesis: heteroscedasticity not present

Test statistic: LM = 29.8769 with p-value = P(Chi-square(1) > 29.8769) = 4.60368e-08

Breusch-Pagan test for heteroscedasticity (robust variant)–

Null hypothesis: heteroscedasticity not present

Test statistic: LM = 2.28232 with p-value = P(Chi-square(1) > 2.28232) = 0.130856

Test for normality of residual–

Null hypothesis: error is normally distributed

Test statistic: Chi-square(2) – 337.288 with p-value = 5.73877e-74

Chow test for structural break at observation 17–

Null hypothesis: no structural break

Test statistic: F(2, 30) = 0.822101 with p-value = P(F(2, 30) > 0.822101) = 0.449166

The results of the tests applied in the process of verifying the econometric model also confirm that the model is not perfect due to the assumed zero-one values. The assumed null hypothesis $H_0$ in RAMSEY's RESET test, assuming that the specification is adequate due to the difficult structure of the model, was not positively verified (Test statistic: F = nan, with p-value = P(F(1,32) > nan) = nan). On the other hand, the results of the Breusch–Pagan test for heteroscedasticity also clearly indicate that the hypothesis $H_0$ assuming that 'heteroscedasticity not present' was not positively verified, and the same was true for the test for normality of residuals, which concluded that the random component does not have a normal distribution because the data do not follow the classical Gaussian distribution, meaning that the data have a different statistical distribution, unspecified. Confirmation of that fact is shown in Figure 11.1.

However, the $H_0$ hypothesis in White's test for heteroscedasticity, similarly to the Breusch-Pagan test for heteroscedasticity (robust variance) or the Chow test for structural break at observation 17, was verified positively. Thus, from an aesthetic point of view, it also seems logical that delegating or creating tasks significantly impacts sales and, thus, increases the value of the listed companies under study.

In turn, the predictive data relating to the values assigned to the dependent variable *y* confirms that, in a system of 27 out of 34, the values of listed companies indicated an increase in sales conducted on the e-commerce market due to

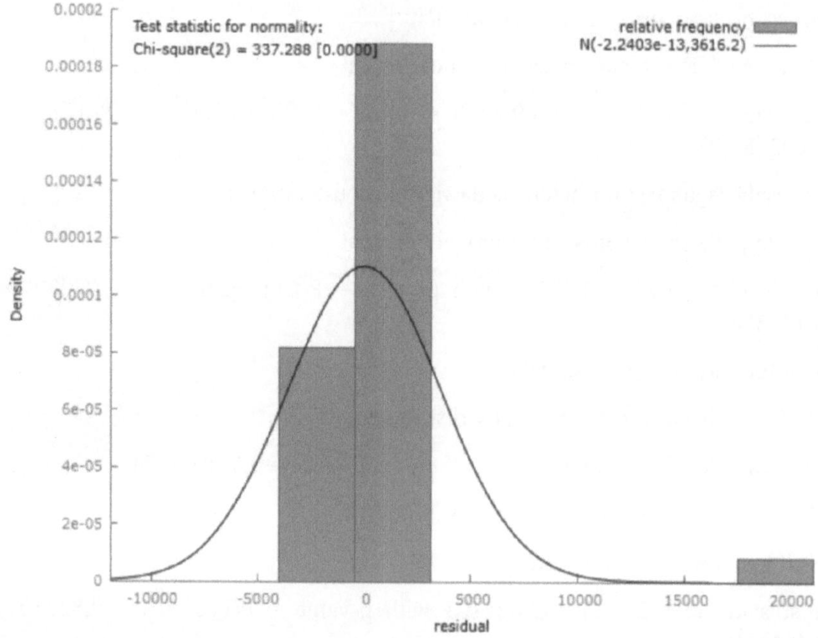


*Figure 11.1* Test statistic for normality: Chi-square (2)=337.288 [0.0000].

*Source:* Own elaboration

the aesthetic and at the same time ethical use of machine learning algorithms. This is confirmed in Figure 11.2.

Nevertheless, the estimation of the econometric model presented above confirms unequivocally that the precise dissection of tasks within the construction of AI algorithms positively influences the entire process of managing the development of a company conducting its business on the market in e-commerce and beyond. This is all the more so since investing in the stock market has been reduced to making transactions via appropriate online platforms and using AI tools.

As mentioned at the outset, quite a few companies are trying to improve their sales processes by implementing machine learning algorithms. One example is DBMS Sp. z o.o., which has introduced a system for the autonomous acquisition of B2B leads called "DMSales". With it, it is possible to identify and reach customers even faster than before. This inspired further research into the implementation of AI algorithms by joint-stock companies presented in this chapter.

## Discussion: reflecting on the aesthetic role of AI in organisational practice

The literature review section described a quite exhausting scope of content in which an attempt was made to explain the meaning of aesthetic management of

| Observations | y | prediction | std. error | 95% interval |
|---|---|---|---|---|
| 1 | 601.360 | 2307.15 | 3763.81 | (-5359.48, 9973.78) |
| 2 | 236.060 | 274.557 | 3697.43 | (-7256.85, 7805.97) |
| 3 | 72.7200 | 2307.15 | 3763.81 | (-5359.48, 9973.78) |
| 4 | 312.550 | 274.557 | 3697.43 | (-7256.85, 7805.97) |
| 5 | 143.370 | 274.557 | 3697.43 | (-7256.85, 7805.97) |
| 6 | 1341.03 | 2307.15 | 3763.81 | (-5359.48, 9973.78) |
| 7 | 46.5800 | 274.557 | 3697.43 | (-7256.85, 7805.97) |
| 8 | 36.3500 | 274.557 | 3697.43 | (-7256.85, 7805.97) |
| 9 | 87.7500 | 274.557 | 3697.43 | (-7256.85, 7805.97) |
| 10 | 1284.41 | 274.557 | 3697.43 | (-7256.85, 7805.97) |
| 11 | 233.390 | 2307.15 | 3763.81 | (-5359.48, 9973.78) |
| 12 | 82.5100 | 274.557 | 3697.43 | (-7256.85, 7805.97) |
| 13 | 34.8700 | 274.557 | 3697.43 | (-7256.85, 7805.97) |
| 14 | 21643.7 | 2307.15 | 3763.81 | (-5359.48, 9973.78) |
| 15 | 74.1300 | 2307.15 | 3763.81 | (-5359.48, 9973.78) |
| 16 | 145.620 | 2307.15 | 3763.81 | (-5359.48, 9973.78) |
| 17 | 419.310 | 2307.15 | 3763.81 | (-5359.48, 9973.78) |
| 18 | 13.7600 | 274.557 | 3697.43 | (-7256.85, 7805.97) |
| 19 | 2358.00 | 2307.15 | 3763.81 | (-5359.48, 9973.78) |
| 20 | 97.9400 | 274.557 | 3697.43 | (-7256.85, 7805.97) |
| 21 | 49.5600 | 274.557 | 3697.43 | (-7256.85, 7805.97) |
| 22 | 50.6000 | 274.557 | 3697.43 | (-7256.85, 7805.97) |
| 23 | 35.9600 | 274.557 | 3697.43 | (-7256.85, 7805.97) |
| 24 | 532.670 | 274.557 | 3697.43 | (-7256.85, 7805.97) |
| 25 | 50.5400 | 274.557 | 3697.43 | (-7256.85, 7805.97) |
| 26 | 272.000 | 2307.15 | 3763.81 | (-5359.48, 9973.78) |
| 27 | 222.600 | 274.557 | 3697.43 | (-7256.85, 7805.97) |
| 28 | 2238.75 | 274.557 | 3697.43 | (-7256.85, 7805.97) |
| 29 | 160.500 | 2307.15 | 3763.81 | (-5359.48, 9973.78) |
| 30 | 318.470 | 274.557 | 3697.43 | (-7256.85, 7805.97) |
| 31 | 364.060 | 2307.15 | 3763.81 | (-5359.48, 9973.78) |
| 32 | 64.6100 | 274.557 | 3697.43 | (-7256.85, 7805.97) |
| 33 | 13.9200 | 274.557 | 3697.43 | (-7256.85, 7805.97) |
| 34 | 86.4300 | 274.557 | 3697.43 | (-7256.85, 7805.97) |

*Figure 11.2* Forecasts based on the estimated econometric model.

*Source:* Own elaboration

Note: Dependent variable: *y*.

AI in improving sales processes in the e-commerce market by joint-stock companies and limited liability companies from the industrial sector following broadly understood ethics, which is to contribute to increasing the level of development of the economic entities under study. The discussion highlights the potential benefits that well-developed AI algorithms could bring to sales processes conducted more or less directly on the Internet by the companies surveyed. The econometric model estimation showed that creating a task subsystem has the most significant impact on increasing the market value of the 34 companies analysed. However, the aesthetics of AI must not distort the ethical framework, and ethics should not interfere with the aesthetics of algorithms.

Predictive data relating to the dependent variable $y$ describing market values recorded by companies confirmed that most of them, more precisely 27 out of 34, showed an increase in their value, which also translated into an increase in their sales on the e-commerce market through the increased impact of creating a subsystem of tasks focused on attracting more customers (not only young people but also older ones). All this was achieved thanks to AI algorithms' aesthetic and ethical use. In addition, many articles and studies point to AI-based sales systems that use sales forecasting. A real-time sales management model is also proposed, using AI agent-based systems to assist in presenting an online system that helps promote online sales in the broadest sense (Toorajipour et al., 2021, p. 505).

AI tools in the field of selling, such as data entry automation or predictive analysis using a wide range of databases, are expected to help enhance the growth of online businesses. The use of algorithms in the sales process, designed to enable companies to analyse data, forecast, personalise offers, automate processes and optimise sales activities, should also positively impact the growth management process of the businesses surveyed rather than harm them.

When examining the role of machine learning algorithms in the development of business conducted by companies on the Internet, we mainly focus on the potential yet positive benefits of AI, forgetting about the negative sides of these activities, such as (1) algorithmic biases affecting product recommendations, where the system sometimes imposes an artificial perception of a particular product or service; (2) the potential loss of aesthetics of the customer experience through excessive automation also prone to making mistakes; (3) the ethical challenges of handling customer data, with sensitive data increasingly exposed to cyberattacks as a result; (4) expanding machine learning algorithms to increase trust among customers from different cultures and parts of the world; nevertheless, the modern technological solutions described are directed primarily to customers of the younger generation, while the so-called "older" customers, who find it increasingly difficult to find their way in a virtual world managed by AI, are forgotten.

## Conclusion

This chapter has explored the intersection of algorithmic efficiency and user experience within AI-driven management practices in the e-commerce sector, highlighting these systems' aesthetic, ethical, and strategic dimensions. Drawing on empirical modelling and conceptual analysis, the findings underscore the importance of designing AI tools not merely for operational optimisation but with attention to their aesthetic coherence, emotional resonance, and inclusivity. The results highlight the value of integrating humanistic and design-oriented principles in developing AI-based solutions, especially where user interaction and trust are crucial. This closing section summarises the key contributions, reflects on the broader implications for managerial practice, and outlines directions for future research.

Answering the research questions, it can be said that from an aesthetic and, at the same time, ethical point of view, it appears that machine learning algorithms using precise task decomposition in the sales process are of significant importance for the development of companies (RQ2). The research confirmed that modern AI algorithms have a positive impact on increasing the market value of businesses while at the same time projecting an increase in sales by simultaneously increasing the possibility of reaching a wider range of customers and, in the case of listed companies, a wider range of potential investors (RQ1). Admittedly, an obstacle in the econometric model's estimation process was the underlying data's design, as zero-one values characterised the variables used; hence, the model verification was not entirely successful. Although the results of the study showed that there is no turning back anymore, the use of AI algorithms is quite costly, and not all companies decide to take this step; nevertheless, machine learning and AI are the future facing companies that want to develop sales, especially those companies that use online platforms in their operations (RQ1 and RQ2).

In order to eliminate such *limitations* in the estimation process of the econometric model presented above in the future, it would be necessary to (1) enrich the existing research with interviews with respondents, the primary purpose of which would be to collect reliable data on the impact of ethics and all legal norms on the aesthetics of AI with the possibility of delving into the structure of machine learning algorithms; (2) conduct research using methodologies including Computer Assisted Web Interview (CAWI), Computer Assisted Telephone Interview (CATI), or Computer Assisted Personal Interview (CAPI).

The main goal of *future research* should be to reach more experts, specialists and practitioners, including market leaders, inventors, representatives of key institutions, and founders of start-ups, in order to collect as much data as possible on the application of AI algorithms in specific companies, both manufacturing and service companies, to understand the concrete sense of implementing modern solutions of this type and whether it is in line with ethical principles.

## Bibliography

AIMOJO. (2024). 12 najlepszych narzędzi AI dla księgowości 2024: od algorytmów po dokładne księgi rachunkowe. Retrieved from https://aimojo.io/pl/best-ai-tools-accounting/, accessed: 11.19.2024.

Besharat, S. (2018). E-commerce Law, and WTO with reference io Iran. *International Review*, 1(2), pp. 138–145.

Bonaccorso, G. (2019). *Mastering Machine Learning Algorithms: Expert Techniques to Implement Popular Machine Learning Algorithms and Fine-Tune Your Models*, Polish edition copyright by Helion Public Limited Company, Gliwice.

Brown, S., Davidovic, J., and Hasan, A. (2021). The algorithm audit: Scoring the algorithms that score us, *Big Data & Society January–June,* 8(1). https://doi.org/10.1177/2053951720983865.

Chaffey, D. (2016). *Digital Business and E-Commerce Management, Strategy, Implementation and Practice*, PWN, Warsaw.

Chamberlain, R., Mullin, C., Scheerlinck, B., and Wagemans, J. (2017a). Putting the art in artificial: Aesthetic responses to computer-generated art. *Psychology of Aesthetics, Creativity, and the Arts*, 12(2), pp. 177–192.

Christoforaki, M., and Beyan, O. (2022). AI ethics – a bird's eye view. *Applied Sciences*, 12(4130), pp. 1–17, https://doi.org/10.3390/app12094130.

Cil, I. (2012). Consumption universes based supermarket layout through association rule mining and multidimensional scaling. *Expert Systems with Applications,* 39(10), pp. 8611–8625.

Cil, I., Ay, D., and Turkan, Y. S. (2009). Data driven decision support to supermarket layout. In: *Proceedings of the 8th WSEAS international conference on artificial intelligence, knowledge engineering and data bases, AIKED'09*. World Scientific and Engineering Academy and Society (WSEAS), Stevens Point, Wisconsin, pp. 465–470.

Coursera Staff. (2024). What Is Artificial Intelligence? Definition, Uses, and Types. Retrieved from https://www.coursera.org/articles/what-is-artificial-intelligence, accessed: 12.20.2024.

Crawford, K., and Paglen, T. (2021). Excavating AI: The politics of images in machine learning training sets. *Ai & Society*, 36(4), pp. 1105–1116.

Delfmann, W., Albers, S., and Gehring, M. (2002). The impact of electronic commerce on logistics service providers. *International Journal of Physical Distribution and Logistics Management,* 32(3), pp. 203–222, 22. doi:10.1108/09600030210426539.

DMSales. (2024). Pozyskuj idealnych klientów B2B. Retrieved from https://dmsales.com/blog/jak-systemy-sales-intelligence-rewolucjonizuja-proces-sprzedazy-b2b/, accessed: 6.6.2024.

*E-commerce dla początkujących - co to jest, co oznacza branża?* (2022). https://www.sempire.pl/e-commerce-co-to-jest.html, accessed: 3.8.2022.

*Ethics guidelines for trustworthy AI.* (2019). https://digital-strategy.ec.europa.eu/en/library/ethics-guidelines-trustworthy-ai, accessed: 4.8.2019.

Harper, S. (2022). Paradoxical tensions impacting small-series production implementation in high-cost contexts: Insights from the EU apparel industry. *International Journal of Operations and Production Management*, 42(8), pp. 1200–1228.

Jazairy, A., Shurrab, H., and Chedid, F. (2025). Impact pathways: Walking a tightrope – unveiling the paradoxes of adopting artificial intelligence (AI) in sales and operations planning. *International Journal of Operations &Production Management,* 45(13), pp. 1–17.

Johnson, E. (2015). The Real Cost of Your Shopping Habits, *Forbes,* 15 January, 2015, https://www.forbes.com/sites/emmajohnson/2015/01/15/the-real-cost-of-your-shopping-habits/, accessed: 1.15.2015.

Jonsson, P., Kaipia, R., and Barratt, M. (2021). Guest editorial: The future of S&OP: Dynamic complexity, ecosystems and resilience. *International Journal of Physical Distribution and Logistics Management*, 51(6), pp. 553–565, https://doi.org/10.1108/ijpdlm-07-2021-452.

Khrais, L. T. (2020). Role of artificial intelligence in shaping consumer demand in E-commerce. *Future Internet*, 12(12), 226, pp. 1–14.

Kochanowska, M. (2024). Service Design z wykorzystaniem Design Thinking. Retrieved from https://www.design-mindset-detector.com/blog/service-design-z-wykorzystaniem-design-thinking/, accessed: 12.19.2024.

Lacoste, A., Luccioni, A., Schmidt, V., and Dandres, T. (2019). Quantifying the Carbon Emissions of Machine Learning. arXiv 2019, arXiv:191009700, pp. 1–8.

Mills, C. (2018). Artistic integrity. *The Journal of Aesthetics and Art Criticism*, 76(1), pp. 9–20.

Mokander, J., Morley, J., Taddeo, M., and Floridi, L. (2021). Ethics-based auditing of automated decision-making systems: Nature, scope, and limitations. *Science and Engineering Ethics*, 27(44), pp. 1–30, https://doi.org/10.1007/s11948-021-00319-4.

Morley, J., Floridi, L., Kinsey, L., and Elhalat, A. (2020). From what to how: An initial review of publicly available AI ethics tools, methods and research to translate principles into practices. *Science and Engineering Ethic,* 26, pp. 2141–2168, https://doi.org/10.1007/s11948-019-00165-5.

Nguyen, K., Le, M., Martin, B., Cil, I., and Fookes, C. (2022). When AI meets store layout design: A review. *Artificial Intelligence Review*, 55, pp. 5707–5729. https://doi.org/10.1007/s10462-022-10142-3.

O'Neil, C. (2016). *Weapons of Math Destruction: How Big Data Increases Inequality and Threatens Democracy*, 1st ed, Crown, New York, USA.

Orr, W., and Davis, J. L. (2020). Attributions of ethical responsibility by artificial intelligence practitioners. *Information, Communication & Society*, 23(6), pp. 719–735.

*Proposal for a Regulation laying down harmonised rules on artificial intelligence.* (2021). https://digital-strategy.ec.europa.eu/en/library/proposal-regulation-laying-down-harmonised-rules-artificial-intelligence, accessed: 4.21.2021.

Rhee, H., and Bell, D. R. (2002). The inter-store mobility of supermarket shoppers. *Journal of Retailing,* 78(4), pp. 225–237.

Risberg, A. (2023). A systematic literature review on e-commerce logistics: Towards an e-commerce and omni-channel decision framework. *The International Review of Retail, Distribution and Consumer Research*, 33(1), pp. 67–91, https://doi.org/10.1080/09593969.2022.2089903.

Rogalski, M. (2024). Co to jest uczenie maszynowe – inteligentna analiza danych? Retrieved from https://www.gov.pl/web/popcwsparcie/co-to-jest-uczenie-maszynowe--inteligentnaanaliza-danych, accessed: 11.19.2024.

Sekiguchi, K., and Hori, K. (2019). Can ethics enhance creative design activity? In *Proceedings of the Design Society: International Conference on Engineering Design.* Cambridge University Press: Cambridge, pp 3181–3190.

Sloane, M., Moss, E., Chowdhury, R., and Silicon, A. (2022). Valley love triangle: Hiring algorithms, pseudo-science, and the quest for auditability. *Patterns,* 3(2), pp. 1–9, https://doi.org/10.1016/j.patter.2021.100425.

Szostak, M. (2024). *Humanistic Management, Organisation and Aesthetics: The Art of Management and the Management of Art*, Routledge. https://doi.org/10.4324/9781003458029.

Taherdoost, H., and Madanchian, M. (2023). Blockchain-based E-Commerce: A review on applications and challenges. *Electronics*, 12(1889), pp. 1–17, https://doi.org/10.3390/electronics12081889.

Thompson, K. M. (1995). Maintaining artistic integrity in an interdisciplinary setting. *Art Education*, 48(6), pp. 38–45.

Toorajipour, R, Sohrabpour, V., Nazarpour, A., Oghazi, P., and Fischl, M. (2021). Artificial intelligence in supply chain management: A systematic literature review. *Journal of Business Research*, 122(2021), pp. 502–517.

Treichler, C. (2019). Consulting industry and market trends: A two-sided view. In *Advances in Consulting Research – Recent Findings Practical Cases*. Springer: Berlin/Heidelberg, Germany, pp. 253–272.

Xiao, X., Liu, Y., and Zhang, Z. (2012). The analysis of the logistics mode decision to E-commerce. *Journal of Electronic Commerce in Organizations,* 10(4), pp. 57–70. https://doi.org/10.4018/jeco.2012100105.

Xie, N., and Ren, L. (2022). Effect of new media communication on consumer behavior based on industrial edge cloud deployment algorithm. *HindawiMobile Information Systems,* 2022, *Article ID 3851820,* pp. 1–13. http://doi.org/10.1155/2022/3851820.

Xu, C., Sun, Y. Q., and Zhou, H. B. (2025). Artificial aesthetics and ethical ambiguity: Exploring business ethics in the context of AI-driven creativity. *Journal of Business Ethics*, 199, pp. 671–692. https://doi.org/10.1007/s10551-024-05837-2.

Xu, D. W. (2021). A study on the influential mechanism of group psychology on consumer behavior in the new media environment, *Journal of Chizhou University,* 35(1), pp. 66–68.

Zhang, Q., and Xiong, Y. (2024). Harnessing AI potential in E-Commerce: Improving user engagement and sales through deep learning-based product recommendations, *Current Psychology*, 43, pp. 30379–30401, https://doi.org/10.1007/s12144-024-06649-3.

# 12 The aesthetics of metacommunication in organisational management

## AI-generated crisis communication

*Justyna Dziedzic and Łukasz Sułkowski*

### Introduction: framing crisis through aesthetic metacommunication

Organisations are increasingly expected to respond to crises with immediacy, empathy, and transparency, and the role of metacommunication – communication about communication – has become strategically significant. Crises are not managed solely through facts and actions but also through the aesthetic qualities of discourse, including tone, form, emotional resonance, and symbolic coherence. These dimensions shape stakeholders' perceptions of the message and the organisation's values, presence, and credibility. This chapter examines how metacommunication serves as an aesthetic practice and a means of identity construction in organisational crisis response. Aesthetic communication is a form of meaning-making that operates beyond direct language, relying on sensory experience, affective resonance, and symbolic forms. Aesthetic communication could be treated as a creative endeavour crossing the borders of art and organisational discourse (Szostak & Sulkowski, 2020). It frames crisis not only as a problem to be solved but as an experience to be interpreted through images, atmospheres, metaphors, and styles that shape how organisations perceive, feel, and respond to disruption.

This chapter aims to analyse the aesthetic dimensions of organisational metacommunication in crises and evaluate how these dimensions are preserved, transformed, or diminished when AI is introduced as a communication tool. By comparing two iconic case studies – Johnson & Johnson's Tylenol crisis (1982)[1] and the Starbucks racial incident (2018)[2] – and by introducing a conceptual example of AI-generated crisis communication, this chapter offers both a theoretical reflection and a practical assessment of communication strategies under pressure. This chapter explores the following research problem: How do the aesthetics of organisational metacommunication change when AI is employed in crisis management, and how does this affect perceived credibility and emotional resonance? This chapter addresses the following research questions: (RQ1) What aesthetic elements of metacommunication are essential for effective crisis

DOI: 10.4324/9781003654377-16

management, as demonstrated in the Tylenol and Starbucks case studies? (RQ2) How does organisational metacommunication shape credibility and emotional engagement during crises? (RQ3) What are the possibilities and limitations of using AI to generate crisis communication from the perspective of metacommunicative aesthetics?

This chapter adopts a qualitative and interpretive research approach, combining discourse analysis with theory-based analytical frameworks to investigate the aesthetic dimensions of metacommunication in organisational crisis contexts. The research method is designed to explore how communicative acts during crises convey not only information but also aesthetic, emotional, and relational meanings that shape public perception and organisational identity. The research is grounded in two key methodological components:

1. Critical Discourse Analysis (CDA): Discourse is approached as a social practice (Fairclough, 1995), and communicative acts during organisational crises are examined not only in terms of their content but also in terms of their tone, narrative structure, and performative functions. Particular attention is given to metacommunicative cues – messages about messages – which carry aesthetic and affective value beyond the surface of informational statements. The analysis considers how language constructs meanings of responsibility, care, control, and emotional resonance during crises.
2. Situational Crisis Communication Theory (SCCT) (Coombs, 2007) categorises crisis response strategies and assesses their alignment with stakeholder expectations and reputational repair objectives. This framework supports the interpretation of organisational responses, especially their aesthetic coherence and credibility, by evaluating the match between organisational action, verbal declarations, and perceived values.

The selected cases (Johnson & Johnson's Tylenol crisis and the Starbucks racial incident) enable the exploration of evolving norms of organisational metacommunication and their aesthetic dimensions. The analysis draws from publicly available statements, media coverage, and archival materials to reconstruct the communicative strategies used and to assess their metacommunicative effects.

A conceptual example was employed as an exploratory tool to illustrate the potential role of AI in the aesthetics of crisis-related metacommunication. This example is not based on empirical data but constitutes a theoretical simulation grounded. Using a conceptual example enables the phenomenon under analysis – AI-generated crisis communication – to be situated within a realistic scenario, facilitating critical reflection on the possibilities and limitations of this emerging development. As Gilson and Goldberg (2015) emphasise, conceptual examples are particularly valuable when studying novel or complex phenomena for which empirical data is limited, as they stimulate theoretical insight and suggest directions for future research. This method enables the demonstration of how AI could be applied in the context of established crisis cases, a comparison between the aesthetics of human- and AI-generated discourse, a reflection on the potential integration of AI within the SCCT framework and crisis discourse, and an identification of gaps, tensions, and risks related to the authenticity of meta-communication. Given the rapid development of generative AI technologies and the current scarcity of verified real-world applications in crisis management, a conceptual example provides a justified and productive exploration tool for this chapter. This methodology enables a deeper understanding of metacommunication, not only as a tool for message regulation but also as a vehicle for aesthetic expression and organisational meaning-making.

## Literature review: metacommunication and AI in crisis management

In the face of rapidly evolving organisational challenges, crisis management increasingly depends on nuanced human communication and advanced technological tools. This literature review explores the intersection of metacommunication – the subtle, often implicit layer of meaning that shapes interpersonal and organisational interactions – and AI as a strategic driver in crisis response. The review highlights how organisations navigate uncertainty, build resilience, and shape stakeholder perceptions during critical events by combining insights from communication theory and AI-enabled management practices.

### *Metacommunication in organisational settings*

Bateson first introduced the concept of metacommunication, defining it as communication that refers to communication itself (Bateson, 1951). Metacommunication is generally defined as "communication about communication itself", conveyed through both verbal and nonverbal cues (Castor & Bartesaghi, 2016). It deals with para-messages and unintentional expressions (Akinori, 2020). It is an act of commenting and reflecting on another communicative act. The exact effects of the metacommunicative act cannot be predicted because the information act itself is always subject to multiple interpretations, unexpected consequences, and even misunderstandings (Sullivan, 2009).

Metacommunication can be understood on three levels: within the theory of interactionism, the level of command and feedback circuit, and the systemic nature of communication (Castor & Bartesaghi, 2016). The first level refers to relational issues, which involve an information exchange at the second level. The third level is described in the functionalist perception of information exchange. From the perspective of this argument, it is reasonable to recall a complex relational intervention, the teaching and development of which can be challenging and involves a process of acquiring meta-communicative abilities (Calvert et al., 2020). It consists of sensing information to influence environmental objects related to their characteristics and perceptual abilities. Therefore, it encompasses properties of a higher order of mental content, including ease of processing, informativeness, and relevance. The function of sensing information is not to describe states of mind or things but to evaluate the possibility of acting and talking. Therefore, strictly communicative foundations refer to relationships in metacognition (Bisconti, 2021, p. 495). Due to these factors, metacommunication can be a real challenge for AI designers. The question of whether it is achievable beyond human perception is still open.

Interpersonal interactions are based on the construction of meanings. In this sense, relational metacommunication is closely related to the different levels of the communication process and refers to information about the quality and ways of this interaction (Valsiner & Branco, 2004). Authors from various fields have adopted metacommunication as an essential feature of interaction, including psychiatry, education, business, and media. S. Mateus points out that researchers analyse various aspects of its occurrence, ranging from the issue of intersubjective interactions between brands and infants (Nakano, 2001) to organisational communication (Castor, 2017) and threads related to the power of news creation and professional political PR (Esser et al., 2001). Awareness of mutual perception through communication influences interaction; this field of mutual influence can be described as meta-communisation (Mateus, 2017). Awareness of the perception of the other side of the relationship gives a new order of communication related to sensory processes and possibilities of interpretation. The new means of communication create the values of meaning-building inherent in them. Research in this area, led by L. Suciu and S. Şimon, focuses on online organisational communication and strives to perceive the image of identity. A comparative study of Samsung's digital communications in Romania and France led the authors to conclude that metacommunication at the reception level facilitates the interpretation of its message (Suciu & Şimon, 2014). The authors also highlighted the role of the so-called "masks" used by the organisation to achieve its intended goals and establish a specific type of relationship with interlocutors (Suciu & Şimon, 2014).

Metacommunication can be explicit and implicit. It serves as a framework for interpretation. It can have a formal positive dimension, regulating the relations of professional conversation, or be inappropriate when the language takes on, for example, an offensive form (Baltzersen, 2013). It is correct when it aligns with the interlocutor's experience in terms of social relationality. Even when it is not adapted to the message's recipient, it can be considered incorrect. People often send mixed signals, and being able to read them is a valuable skill. Children learn through instruction and observation, so the metacommunication repertoire results from these experiences in adulthood. Showing the intention of the conversation and the ability to enter the sender's world opens the dialogue and the ability to interpret (Wilmot, 2009). Communication beneath the surface is a multi-level event in which an ongoing process pushes communication away from the simple codification of content. Given that it is impossible not to communicate, each behaviour has the value of a message and can influence the manners of others (Mateus, 2017).

However, this human activity is not always measurable and refers to the properties of reflexivity, and each message has a metacommunicative resource. Its feature is the contextualisation of the original message, its modification, and its subject, which is subject to change according to its nature. This is particularly evident in political campaigns when every word spoken is analysed and criticised in the context of the words and speeches of candidates. Public discourse is based on explanations, appeals, or apologies. Additionally, people naturally tend to comment on others' communicative behaviours. Manifested in explications, excuses, and comments, it deconstructs or explains earlier statements (Anderson, 2009). Metacommunication is the ability to indicate how information should be interpreted, whether it conveys compliance, support, or sends conflicting messages (Mateus, 2017).

Metacognition refers to situations in which there is an activation of thinking and reflection on a given task, taking place on two levels: thinking and thinking about thinking (Stavholm, 2021). Meta-communicative capacity translates into the importance and urgency of communication and its role (Joëlle, 2016). This process is particularly veiled in the mass media environment. The audience may be unaware of the metacommunicative message due to the whole staffage of a set of evolved behaviours that facilitate efficiency in human understanding (Anderson, 2009, p. 653).

Therefore, the message is more than information; it is a state of speech that users directly to the audience, the public space, as a kind of creation, image management, or a sign of self-determination. The transmission of information in the environment of new technologies, among which the communicative ideas of the organisation resonate, surpasses the communication to which we are accustomed in the analogue world.

Many management manuals feature diagrams of organisational communication that are arranged vertically or horizontally. They refer to different levels of information transmission and hierarchical structures, which have already been discussed in critical discourse. Descriptions of organisations that communicate externally and manage the image or impression are also common. They create the desired image in the external and internal environment, taking care of their reputation. They craft messages that shape their image in the eyes of stakeholders, including the business environment, customers, creditors, and colleagues.

On the other hand, the employees themselves are public providers of reliable information about what is happening inside the organisation. Image management, for most organisations, is no longer the voice of the future. It has become a relational norm in the era of universal informational accessibility and social media culture. The concept of transparency no longer concerns only the policy of transparency in public and private organisations, which is essential for a sustainable world, obliging them to provide the external environment with information about "who we are".

Metacommunication in psychological discourse refers to the verbalisation of meanings that acquire the character desired by the sender of information. The right tone, the use of terms specific to the message's intention, and the choice of phrases and contexts of speech can significantly impact the effectiveness of the conversation. Psychotherapist and business trainer Natalia de Barbaro, in her book "A Tender Guide: A Woman's Way to Herself", writes about acts of metacommunication (De Barbaro, 2021). She highlights women's emotional survival strategies in concealing their feelings and thoughts. She writes that the most incredible power of life is the ability to communicate with both the external and internal worlds. She also notes that fear hinders one's ability to depart from oneself, and people often create plans based on what they believe others expect from them, thereby fuelling a fear of rejection (De Barbaro, 2021).

Metacommunication, although it refers to verbal messages at the level of feelings and moods, is a concept that should be extended to many other contexts for these considerations. A message hiding disapproval, irony, or reluctance, often concealed under the façade of courtesy or business language, can resonate in the form of feelings, subconscious moods, and resentment. Deciphering metamessages is possible by understanding one's assumptions and developing practical conversation skills. The camouflage of words can distance interlocutors from openness, directness, and deep respect. Children learn to read facial expressions. The basic ones are joy, anger, sadness, and curiosity. Over time, they expand their ability to recognise emotional states, all the messages contained in the voice, the nature of the speech, the timbre of the voice, and the generally verbal and non-verbal communication process. The next stage in the development of children from the iPhone generation can be revealed by understanding the power of new media messages and developing future communication strategies. What skills and levels of understanding of AI phenomena will be affected? It is not easy to guess today. Nevertheless, it is understandable that the world of new technologies is a reality of information, knowledge, and communication.

The key research directions in metacommunication within the field of management include several major thematic areas: crisis management (Coombs, 2019a,b; Fearn-Banks, 2016), organisational leadership (Fairhurst & Sarr, 1996; Kotter, 1990; Fairhurst & Connaughton, 2014), cultural management (Hall, 1976; Hofstede, 1980; Ting-Toomey & Dorjee, 2019), digital communication (Turkle, 2015; Baym, 2015; Walther & Valkenburg, 2021), consumer trust (Heath, 2018; Gilly & Wolfinbarger, 1998; Kim & Sung, 2020), conflict resolution (Pruitt & Rubin, 1986; Fisher & Ury, 1981; Jones & Brinkert, 2020), ethical dimensions (Bok, 1978; Rawls, 1971; Christians & Fackler, 2021), nonverbal communication (Mehrabian, 1972; Ekman & Friesen, 1969; Matsumoto et al., 2020), interpersonal communication (Watzlawick et al., 1967; Knapp et al., 2020), and contemporary studies and AI (McStay, 2018; Cowls & Floridi, 2018).

Foundational works, such as Coombs (2019a) in crisis management and Fairhurst and Sarr (1996) in leadership framing, continue to serve as cornerstones in these domains, offering strategic frameworks for effective communication. Contemporary studies have expanded these perspectives, addressing evolving challenges in globalised and digital environments, such as the ethical implications of virtual interactions and the role of cultural differences in interpreting messages.

The inclusion of recent studies highlights the ongoing dynamism in the field. Emerging research, such as Kim and Sung (2020) on consumer trust and Walther and Valkenburg (2021) on digital age social connections, illustrates how technological advancements and societal shifts reshape metacommunicative practices. These findings greatly emphasise context-sensitive approaches that integrate nonverbal cues, cultural nuances, and ethical considerations. As metacommunication continues to evolve, this synthesis of traditional and modern insights provides a robust foundation for future scholarly inquiries and practical applications, particularly in addressing the complexities of contemporary communication landscapes.

### *AI-driven crisis management: transforming organisational resilience*

Crisis communication is a crucial strategic tool designed to reduce the adverse effects of crises on organisations and their environment (Coombs, 2018). In crisis communication, it is generally recommended that public statements addressing the situation incorporate recognition of the inherent uncertainty surrounding the crisis as an essential component (Reynolds & Seeger, 2005). Effective crisis communication is vital in safeguarding an organisation's reputation, sustaining public trust, and ensuring stakeholder protection (Mwandembo, 2024). Rather than serving as a defensive mechanism, it should be integrated into a broader communication strategy to shape public perceptions (Sturges, 1994). It encompasses communicative efforts across all stages of crisis management: pre-crisis, crisis response, and post-crisis (Chen et al., 2022). Key aspects of successful crisis communication include proactive preparation, openness, empathy, and the rapid dissemination of accurate information. Therefore, it is essential to develop structured communication frameworks, establish specialised crisis response teams, and employ a multi-platform approach to engage all stakeholders effectively (Mwandembo, 2024). By implementing these strategies, organisations can manage crises more effectively and use them as opportunities for learning and organisational growth (Coombs & Holladay, 2014; Mwandembo, 2024).

Crisis management, understood as responding to unpredictable events that threaten an organisation's stakeholders, has gained a new dimension thanks to the use of AI to support decision-making (Ali & Wood-Harper, 2022). Modern crisis management is undergoing a dynamic transformation driven by the development of AI, which is supported by algorithms that facilitate fast data processing, predictive analytics, and real-time decision-making recommendations (Brynjolfsson & McAfee, 2017). The use of generative AI in simulation technologies presents significant opportunities to support the work of crisis management practitioners, particularly in decision-making and communication during the prevention, preparation, response, and recovery phases (Karinshak, 2023, following Coombs, 2023).

In the face of increasing threat complexity, early warning systems for crises, such as the Integrated Crisis Early Warning System (ICEWS), integrating social data and predictive analytics, are becoming a key tool to support decision-making processes (O'Brien, 2010). Based on the intuition and experience of leaders, traditional crisis response models are giving way to AI, which can predict threats and provide organisations with early warnings by identifying risk patterns based on massive datasets. AI tools can analyse current events and simulate future crises, strengthening an organisation's ability to adapt and plan strategically (Choi et al., 2021).

AI also supports organisations in crisis communication; designing and implementing organisations' collaborative networks in crises can be effectively supported by an AI-based metamodel that considers participants' context, partners, goals, and behaviours (Benaben et al., 2020). Chatbots, sentiment analysis systems, and automated message generation enable companies to respond promptly to crises and effectively manage their reputation (Nguyen et al., 2020). The integration of metacommunication, i.e., communication about communication, is crucial here – AI can support the analysis of how recipients receive and interpret messages, allowing for real-time correction of the message. AI-based solutions are proving effective in crisis management and response, enabling faster data analysis, decision-making, and resource allocation (Harika, 2021).

However, using AI in crisis management is not without its ethical challenges. The main challenges relate to decision transparency, the risk of bias in data, and liability issues (Cowls & Floridi, 2018). Organisational resilience is the ability to respond to crises, as well as to learn from them and implement lasting changes, which requires a conscious design of systems that consider the cultural and communicative context. Its effectiveness, therefore, depends on the skilful combination of technology with communicative reflexivity and the metacommunicative ability of leaders.

## Results: metacommunication aesthetic as a vital tool in crisis management

The aesthetic aspects of communication play a crucial role in shaping how various stakeholders perceive, interpret, and emotionally receive crisis messages. Aesthetic choices – such as the language used, the visual layout of statements, or the tone of voice in public addresses – can reinforce the organisation's empathy, transparency, and preparedness, making the message more trustworthy and impactful. Rather than merely decoration, aesthetics is a strategic layer of

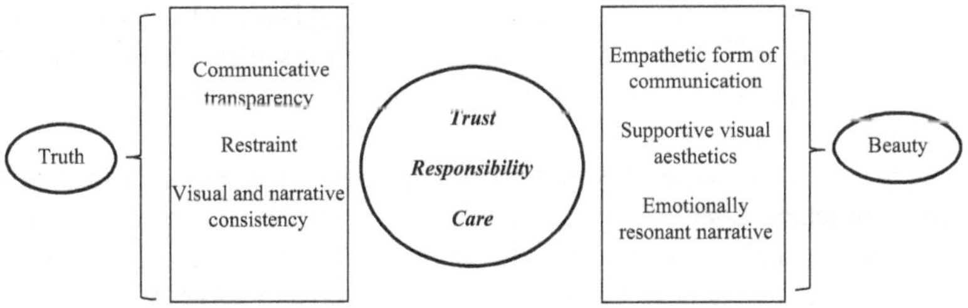


*Figure 12.1* The aesthetic framework for crisis communication in management.
*Source:* Own elaboration

meaning-making that helps align communication content with its intended emotional and ethical resonance. This is particularly important in crisis contexts, where audiences seek information, reassurance, and moral orientation. Aesthetics help convey values, reduce ambiguity, and facilitate more profound engagement with messages, crucial functions during crisis events (Szostak, 2023).

Figure 12.1 presents an aesthetic framework for crisis communication in management, structured along the symbolic axis of truth and beauty. On one side, the model foregrounds crisis response's ethical and communicative integrity, emphasising transparency, restraint, and narrative consistency. Conversely, it emphasises communication's emotional and symbolic aspects, focusing on empathy, visually appealing aesthetics, and emotionally resonant narratives. At the intersection of these axes lie the core values of trust, responsibility, and care, constituting the aesthetic foundation of meaningful and ethically grounded crisis discourse.

### *Discourse analysis in crisis metacommunication*

Discourse analysis in crisis management enables understanding of how organisations construct their messages during crises and the linguistic strategies they employ to rebuild trust. Discourse analysis is a qualitative research method used to examine language, communication patterns, and social context (Fairclough, 1995; van Dijk, 1997). It explores how language constructs meanings, particularly in crises where organisations seek to manage public perception and trust (Gee, 2014). This study examines two case studies: the Tylenol crisis (1982) and the Starbucks crisis (2018), employing discourse analysis as its primary methodological approach.

Organisational discourse in crises can be examined through the following categories (Fairhurst & Connaughton, 2014; Coombs, 2019a): (1) Communication transparency – clarity and consistency of messages (e.g., does the organisation avoid vague wording and euphemisms?); (2) Emotional resonance – how the organisation builds empathy with stakeholders (e.g., use of emotional language, acknowledgement of fault); (3) Alignment with organisational values – to what extent does communication align with the organisation's mission and values? (4) Public reaction and reception – analysis of interactions with media, stakeholders, and societal response.

Communication transparency in the Tylenol crisis was open; Johnson & Johnson communicated openly from the beginning, publishing detailed statements and regularly updating the public, with no euphemisms or avoidance strategies being used. Concrete actions, such as a product recall and apology in communication style, were implemented.

Starbucks's initial company messages were more general ("We commit to improvement"), but the CEO quickly took personal responsibility. The language was more performative ("This is our failure"), though it initially lacked specifics on corrective measures. Emotional resonance was evident; CEO James Burke emphasised the importance of care for customers, stating, "The most important thing is the safety and health of consumers", which gave the communication a compassionate tone, and the language was direct and non-defensive. CEO Kevin Johnson used highly emotional language: "This was a painful experience" and "We deeply apologise". The company also emphasised its values, e.g., "We are an open and inclusive organisation", strengthening its ethical stance.

Alignment with organisational values, Johnson & Johnson referred to its corporate credo, emphasising "responsibility to consumers" and acting accordingly. The full-scale product recall demonstrated alignment with corporate values. Starbucks emphasised its commitment to "creating open spaces" and responded with anti-bias training. However, the initial communication did not immediately reference corporate values, making it less cohesive in the first phase of the crisis.

Public reaction was apparent that they had done wrong, but they must be transparent; the media praised Johnson & Johnson for its openness and effective action. Positive public reaction – transparency and consistency helped the brand regain consumer trust. Starbucks have mixed reactions – some viewed the company's actions as insufficient, especially in the initial response phase. However, the decision to close stores for anti-bias training was seen as a symbolic step towards improvement.

Discourse analysis reveals that Tylenol's success stems from communication coherence and alignment with organisational values. In contrast, Starbucks' initial lack of a clear communication strategy rendered its response less effective, resulting in more diverse public perceptions. In both cases, organisations employed crisis metacommunication; however, success ultimately depended on transparency, coherence, and emotional engagement in communication. Discourse analysis strengthens the methodology by structuring the approach to comparing case studies.

### *Case analysis through the lens of SCCT*

SCCT identifies three primary crisis clusters: (1) Victim cluster – the organisation has minimal responsibility for the crisis (e.g., natural disasters, product tampering by external actors); recommended response: expressions of sympathy, corrective action, and reinforcing existing values (Coombs, 2019a); (2) Accidental cluster – the organisation is partially responsible due to unintentional factors (e.g., technical errors, unforeseen malfunctions); recommended response: corrective actions and explanations to mitigate reputational damage (Coombs, 2019a); (3) Preventable cluster – the organisation is directly responsible for negligence or ethical violations (e.g., fraud, discrimination); recommended response: strong apology, corrective measures, and transparent policy changes (Coombs, 2019a).

Analysing the Tylenol poisoning crisis in the context of SCCT, Johnson & Johnson is in a "victim cluster". In this case, the company was the victim of a deliberate action by third parties who poisoned the drug capsules after they left the production line. The company immediately recalled 31 million bottles of Tylenol from the market and introduced triple packaging security features, establishing itself as a leader in product safety.

In contrast, Starbucks admitted that the incident resulted from erroneous actions by staff, which placed this crisis in the SCCT's "preventive cluster", where the organisation bears full responsibility for the situation.

*Table 12.1* Discourse analysis: crisis communication strategies

| *Category* | *Tylenol crisis (1982) (SCCT: Victim Cluster)* | *Starbucks crisis (2018) (SCCT: Preventable Cluster)* |
|---|---|---|
| Message framing | Safety-first approach, consumer well-being emphasised | Accountability and inclusivity are emphasised |
| Emotional engagement | Expressed empathy and concern for victims and consumers | Apology issued acknowledged systemic issues |
| Transparency | Regular public updates, open about measures taken | Initial vagueness, later followed by a more precise response |
| Corporate values alignment | Aligned actions with corporate credo on responsibility | Linked response to an inclusive mission |
| Public reaction | Trust reinforced through decisive actions | Mixed response, initial criticism followed by support |
| Corrective actions | Product recall, improved packaging, and safety commitments | Nationwide racial bias training, policy revisions |
| Crisis attribution (SCCT) | Low responsibility (external actors caused harm) | High responsibility (organisational failure) |
| Long-term impact | Became a best-practice case in crisis communication | Strengthened corporate responsibility efforts |

*Source:* Own elaboration.

Table 12.1 presents a comparative discourse analysis of crisis communication strategies, where the SCCT framework is applied to classify crisis attribution and response strategies. The Tylenol case falls into the Victim cluster, where the organisation had minimal responsibility, while Starbucks falls into the Preventable cluster, where the company had direct responsibility for the crisis. This structured comparison highlights the differences in crisis attribution and metacommunication strategies and their impact on restoring public trust.

***AI simulations in crisis discourse***

To illustrate the potential and limitations of AI tools, such as large language models, in the aesthetic construction of crisis metacommunication, we present a conceptual simulation using an AI language model – trained on cases and public relations strategies – that is designed to generate crisis responses for two widely discussed incidents. The aim is to assess how well AI can replicate human-led communication's emotional and aesthetic dynamics under reputational pressure. AI-generated response (hypothetical): AI Reconstructs the Tylenol Crisis Response (1982): "We are profoundly saddened by the tragic events surrounding Tylenol. Our deepest sympathies go to the families affected. We are working in full cooperation with authorities and have initiated a nationwide recall to ensure customer safety. Your trust matters to us above all".

The AI-generated message effectively conveys an emotional tone and maintains structural coherence. It incorporates empathy, responsibility, and corrective action, aligning broadly with the SCCT framework. However, it lacks personalised performance and direct references to the company's foundational values. In the original crisis response, CEO James Burke was visibly and vocally present, delivering messages that informed and embodied the firm's ethical identity. The absence of such leadership embodiment in the AI version reveals a limitation in simulating human presence's affective and symbolic authority.

AI-generated response in Starbucks crisis (hypothetical): "We apologise for the incident that occurred in our Philadelphia store. This does not reflect our company's values. We are implementing nationwide anti-bias training and reviewing our internal policies to ensure inclusivity and fairness". While the AI-generated statement follows the structure of apology and corrective action, it falls short in emotional specificity and personalised accountability. The original CEO statement – "This is not who we are, and I take full responsibility" – carried an adequate weight and moral performativity that is difficult for AI to emulate. The AI's phrasing, while technically appropriate, lacks relational reflexivity, embodied sincerity, and a culturally situated voice – key elements in the aesthetic success of crisis metacommunication.

This conceptual exercise demonstrates that AI can generate structurally coherent and aesthetically consistent crisis messages, yet these messages often lack the metacommunicative depth and symbolic resonance achieved through human expression. Several limitations become evident: (1) Absence of performative leadership presence, including emotional expressiveness, embodied responsibility, and cultural awareness; (2) Lack of contextual referencing to organisational history, ethical commitments, or symbolic frameworks such as mission statements or company credos; (3) Insufficient nuance in emotional tone, which in human-led communication may involve irony, humility, mourning, or hopeful commitment – qualities that are difficult to codify algorithmically.

These gaps raise broader questions about the limits of automation in high-stakes communication, mainly where aesthetic and ethical meaning is inseparable from the mode of delivery. While AI may assist in managing structural and informational complexity, metacommunication's aesthetic and affective dimensions remain deeply human and situational.

## Discussion: between words and action – the role of metacommunication in organisational crisis management

One of the central themes emerging from this research is the alignment between organisational values and crisis response. Coombs (2019a) emphasises that consistency between stated corporate values and actions taken during a crisis is essential for maintaining credibility. In both case studies, metacommunicative strategies highlighted the organisations' commitment to responsibility and ethics. Johnson & Johnson's reference to its corporate credo during the Tylenol crisis and Starbucks' invocation of its inclusive mission are prime examples of how organisations can frame their responses within the context of their established identities (Johnson & Johnson, 2022; Starbucks, 2018). This approach mitigated reputational damage and allowed both organisations to reinforce stakeholder trust. Another significant dimension of metacommunication is emotional resonance. Empathy is pivotal in shaping how stakeholders perceive an organisation during a crisis. Johnson & Johnson's CEO, James Burke, openly expressed regret and commitment to consumer safety, while Starbucks' CEO, Kevin Johnson, acknowledged the systemic nature of the problem and took personal responsibility. These messages aligned with what Heath (2018) describes as "narratives of care", where organisations demonstrate a deep understanding of stakeholders' emotions and concerns. Such narratives, reinforced by transparent communication, reduce the risk of alienation and public backlash. However, this study also highlights the complexity of implementing metacommunication effectively. Inconsistent or poorly executed metacommunication can exacerbate crises, as pointed out by Mateus (2017). The Starbucks incident, for example, demonstrates how organisations must address immediate concerns and underlying systemic issues to avoid appearing performative or superficial in their responses. To this end, proactive measures, such as Starbucks' anti-bias training and engagement with civil rights organisations, reflect what Castor (2017) describes as "institutionalised metacommunication" actions that signal commitment to systemic change rather than short-term damage control. Finally, the digital and social media age has amplified the impact of metacommunication. As Sullivan (2009) argues, the speed and reach of information dissemination mean that organisations must respond swiftly while ensuring their messages remain accurate and aligned with stakeholder expectations. The case studies analysed here reveal that prompt, clear, and transparent responses are critical to managing crises effectively in today's interconnected world.

This study underscores the importance of metacommunication as a multidimensional strategy in organisational crisis management. Organisations can navigate crises with greater resilience and trustworthiness by fostering emotional resonance, ensuring transparency, and aligning responses with corporate values. The findings also suggest that organisations must adopt a proactive and systemic approach to metacommunication, integrating it into their communication strategies to address immediate challenges and long-term reputational goals. Future research could explore the role of digital platforms and AI in shaping metacommunicative practices, particularly in light of the increasing complexity of organisational crises. As the case studies demonstrate, mastering the nuances of metacommunication is not merely a best practice but an indispensable tool for maintaining organisational legitimacy in an era of heightened public scrutiny.

## Conclusion

All three research questions were addressed through the analysis, providing a foundation for further reflection on aesthetics, authenticity, and automation in crisis communication. Regarding RQ1 (What aesthetic elements of metacommunication are essential for effective crisis management, as demonstrated in the Tylenol and Starbucks case studies?), the findings indicate that aesthetic elements, such as empathy, transparency, and coherence with organisational identity, are essential for regaining stakeholder trust. Referring to RQ2 (How does organisational metacommunication shape credibility and emotional engagement during crises?), by signalling care, responsibility, and ethical commitment, metacommunication shapes credibility and relational engagement, strengthening organisational identity during reputational threats. Regarding RQ3 (What are the possibilities and limitations of using AI to generate crisis communication from the perspective of metacommunicative aesthetics?), it can be said that while AI-generated crisis communication offers structural and temporal efficiency, it lacks the emotional depth, contextual nuance, and performative presence typically delivered by human communicators.

This chapter introduces a conceptual example of AI-generated crisis communication, highlighting the potential and limitations of AI as a tool in high-stakes organisational discourse. While AI can enhance efficiency and consistency, it raises critical concerns regarding authenticity, ethical nuance, and emotional sensitivity, especially in crises that demand human presence and moral judgment.

This study's *limitations* include the conceptual nature of the example of AI and the challenge of generalising results across diverse industries. Moreover, the aesthetic effects of AI-generated messages were not empirically tested with audiences, which limits the strength of practical recommendations. In addition, this study is based on a limited number of historical case studies, which may not fully capture the dynamics of contemporary digital crisis communication.

*Future research* should empirically examine real-world applications of AI in crisis contexts and further explore the aesthetic dimensions of automated communication. Comparative audience studies could reveal how different publics perceive AI-generated versus human-led responses to crises. In addition, interdisciplinary research combining organisational studies, design aesthetics, and AI ethics could help define guidelines for integrating AI while maintaining communicative authenticity and cultural sensitivity.

## Notes

1 The Johnson & Johnson crisis was caused by the deliberate contamination of Tylenol capsules with cyanide in 1982, which resulted in the deaths of seven individuals and sparked widespread panic across the United States (Fearn-Banks, 2016). In response, the company was compelled to take immediate action to protect public health while simultaneously maintaining consumer trust. In a press release, CEO James Burke stated: "Nothing is more important than the health and safety of our customers. This tragedy saddens us deeply and we will do everything in our power to prevent further incidents" (Johnson & Johnson, 1982, as cited in Fearn-Banks, 2016). The company consistently kept the public informed of its actions, including updates on the investigation and the preventive measures being implemented (Johnson & Johnson, 2022). One of its official statements emphasised: "Our top priority is protecting consumers and regaining their trust. That is why we are working in full cooperation with authorities" (Johnson & Johnson, 1982). Despite the significant financial costs involved, the withdrawal of 31 million bottles of Tylenol from the market demonstrated the company's prioritisation of consumer safety over profit (Kaplan, 2016). A statement available on the company's archived website underlined its commitment to customers, communities, and employees: "Our Credo compels us to care for the health and well-being of all who are impacted by our products" (Johnson & Johnson, 2022). "Nothing is more important than the health and safety of our customers. We are deeply saddened by this tragedy and will do everything in our power to prevent further incidents" (Johnson & Johnson, 1982, as cited in Fearn-Banks, 2016).

2 In April 2018, two Black men were arrested in a Starbucks café in Philadelphia for alleged trespassing after they declined to make a purchase while waiting for a friend. The incident, captured on video, quickly went viral, sparking widespread outrage on social media and accusations of systemic racism against the Starbucks brand (BBC, 2018). The public backlash posed a significant threat to the company's reputation as an inclusive and socially responsible organisation. Starbucks responded with unequivocal public apologies. CEO Kevin Johnson addressed the incident, stating: "This is not who we are as a company. This was a failure on our part, and I take full responsibility for it. We apologise to the two men who were arrested and are working to rectify this immediately" (Starbucks, 2018). One of the most notable actions taken by Starbucks was the temporary closure of over 8,000 stores across the United States for a

day-long anti-bias training session involving nearly 175,000 employees. Described by the company as "A step toward creating a culture of belonging for all," Starbucks' statement on the training ", this initiative was both symbolic and practical (Starbucks, 2018). By allocating substantial resources to education, Starbucks positioned itself as a learning organisation committed to growth and accountability. Moreover, the company invited civil rights organisations such as the NAACP Legal Defense Fund and the Anti-Defamation League to audit and review its corporate policies and practices. The findings of these audits, including recommendations for improvement, were made publicly available, highlighting Starbucks' transparency and openness to criticism (Starbucks, 2019). Starbucks issued immediate and direct apologies, underscoring responsibility and empathy: "This is our failure and I take full responsibility" (Kevin Johnson, Starbucks, 2018). The company reaffirmed its corporate values by referring to its mission statement: "To nurture the human spirit—one person, one cup, one neighborhood at a time" (Starbucks Mission, 2018).

## References

Akinori, Y. (2020). *The Foundations of Relational Psychoanalysis*. Routledge.

Ali, M. B., & Wood-Harper, T. (2022). Artificial intelligence (AI) as a decision-making tool to control crisis situations. In Ali, M. (ed.), *Future Role of Sustainable, Innovative Technologies in Crisis Management* (pp. 1–13). IGI Global. https://doi.org/10.4018/978-1-7998-9815-3.ch006

Anderson, R. (2009). Metacommunication in public discourse: Commentary and reflexivity in political campaigns. *Journal of Communication Studies*, 57(5), 651–652.

Baltzersen, R. K. (2013). Metacommunication: The missing piece in the teaching-learning process? *International Journal of Educational Research*, 62(2), 132–144. https://doi.org/10.5430/ijhe.v2n2p128

Bateson, G. (1951). *Communication: The Social Matrix of Psychiatry*. Norton.

Baym, N. K. (2015). *Personal Connections in the Digital Age* (2nd ed.). Polity Press.

BBC. (2018). *Starbucks apologises after black men arrested in Philadelphia store*. Retrieved from [https://www.bbc.com].

Benaben, F., Fertier, A., Montarnal, A., Mu, W., Jiang, Z., Truptil, S., Barthe-Delanoë, A.-M., Lauras, M., & Mace-Ramete, G. (2020). An AI framework and a metamodel for collaborative situations: Application to crisis management contexts. *Journal of Contingencies and Crisis Management*, 28(3), 291–306. https://doi.org/10.1111/1468-5973.12310

Bisconti, A. (2021). Metacommunication and its role in relational cognition. *Journal of Cognitive Psychology*, 33(4), 495–510.

Bok, S. (1978). *Lying: Moral Choice in Public and Private Life*. Pantheon Books.

Brynjolfsson, E., & McAfee, A. (2017). *Machine, Platform, Crowd: Harnessing Our Digital Future*. W. W. Norton & Company.

Calvert, S. L., Stigler, J. W., & Jones, M. (2020). Complex relational interventions and the development of meta-communicative abilities. *Cognitive Science*, 44(6), 1084–1101.

Castor, T. (2017). Organisational metacommunication: Communication about communication in public and private organisations. *Communication Monographs,* 84(4), 492–510.

Castor, T., & Bartesaghi, M. (2016). Metacommunication during disaster response: "Reporting" and the constitution of problems in Hurricane Katrina teleconferences. *Management Communication Quarterly,* 30(4), 472–502. https://doi.org/10.1177/0893318916646454

Chen, F., Coombs, W. T., Holladay, S. J. (2022). Paracrisis and Crisis: Guidance from Situational Crisis Communication Theory. In Jin, Y., & Austin, L. L. (eds.), *Social Media and Crisis Communication*. Routledge. https://doi.org/10.4324/9781003043409

Choi, T. M., Wallace, S. W., & Wang, Y. (2021). Big data analytics in operations management. *Production and Operations Management*, 30(1), 1–20. https://doi.org/10.1111/poms.13230

Christians, C. G., & Fackler, M. (2021). *Media Ethics: Cases and Moral Reasoning* (11th ed.). Routledge.

Coombs, W. (2007). Protecting organization reputations during a crisis: The development and application of situational crisis communication theory. *Corporate Reputation Review*, 10, 163–176. https://doi.org/10.1057/palgrave.crr.1550049

Coombs, T. (2018). Crisis communication. In Heath, R. L., & Johansen, W. (eds.), *The International Encyclopedia of Strategic Communication*. Wiley. https://doi.org/10.1002/9781119010722.iesc0054

Coombs, W. T. (2019a). *Ongoing Crisis Communication: Planning, Managing, and Responding* (5th ed.). SAGE Publications.

Coombs, W. T. (2019b). *The Handbook of Crisis Communication*. Wiley-Blackwell.

Coombs, W. T. (2023). *Crisis Management and Communication*. Institute for Public Relations. https://instituteforpr.org/crisis-management-and-communications/

De Barbaro, N. (2021). *Czuła przewodniczka. Kobieca droga do siebie*. Agora.

Ekman, P., & Friesen, W. V. (1969). The repertoire of nonverbal behavior: Categories, origins, usage, and coding. *Semiotica*, 1(1), 49–98.

Esser, F., Reinemann, C., & Fan, D. (2001). Spin doctoring in news media: The power of professional political PR. *Journal of Political Communication*, 18(3), 16–45.

Fairclough, N. (1995). *Critical Discourse Analysis: The Critical Study of Language*. Longman.

Fairhurst, G. T., & Connaughton, S. L. (2014). Leadership: A communicative perspective. *Leadership*, 10(1), 7–35.

Fairhurst, G. T., & Sarr, R. A. (1996). *The Art of Framing: Managing the Language of Leadership*. Jossey-Bass.

Fearn-Banks, K. (2016). *Crisis Communications: A Casebook Approach*. Routledge.

Fisher, R., & Ury, W. (1981). *Getting to Yes: Negotiating Agreement Without Giving in*. Penguin Books.

Floridi, L., Cowls, J., Beltrametti, M., Chatila, R., Chazerand, P., Dignum, V., Luetge, C., Madelin, R., Pagallo, U., Rossi, F., Schafer, B., Valcke, P., & Vayena, E. (2018). AI4People – An ethical framework for a good AI society: Opportunities, risks, principles, and recommendations. *Minds and Machines*, 28(4), 689–707. https://doi.org/10.1007/s11023-018-9482-5

Gee, J. P. (2014). *An Introduction to Discourse Analysis: Theory and Method* (4th ed.). Routledge.

Gilly, M. C., & Wolfinbarger, M. (1998). Advertising's internal audience. *Journal of Marketing*, 62(1), 69–88.

Gilson, L. L., & Goldberg, C. B. (2015). Editor's comment: So, what is a conceptual paper? *Group & Organization Management*, 40(2), 127–130. https://doi.org/10.1177/1059601115576425

Hall, E. T. (1976). *Beyond Culture*. Anchor Books.

Harika, A., Balan, G., Thethi, H. P., Rana, A., Rajkumar, K. V., & Al-Allak, M. A. (2021). Harnessing the power of artificial intelligence for disaster response and management. *2021 International Conference on Advancements in Electrical, Electronics, Communication, Computing and Automation (ICAECA),* Coimbatore, 1–6. IEEE. https://doi.org/10.1109/ICAECA52838.2021.9675661

Heath, R. L. (2018). *Strategic Issues Management: Organisations and Public Policy Challenges*. SAGE Publications.

Hofstede, G. (1980). *Culture's Consequences: International Differences in Work-Related Values.* SAGE Publications.

Joëlle, F. (2016). The role of metacommunicative capacity in shaping communication urgency. *Journal of Media and Communication Studies*, 9(2), 189–201. https://doi.org/10.1016/j.proeng.2017.01.100

Johnson & Johnson. (1982). *Press Releases and Statements on Tylenol Crisis*. Retrieved from [Johnson & Johnson archives].

Johnson & Johnson. (2022). *Our Credo*. Retrieved from [https://www.jnj.com].

Jones, T. S., & Brinkert, R. (2020). *Conflict Coaching: Conflict Management Strategies and Skills for the Individual.* SAGE Publications.

Kaplan, D. (2016). The Tylenol Murders of 1982. *Forbes.* Retrieved from [https://www.forbes.com].

Karinshak, E. (2023). Simulations in human-AI crisis management systems. *Journal of Contingencies and Crisis Management*, 32(1), e12525. https://doi.org/10.1111/1468-5973.12525

Kim, S., & Sung, M. (2020). The role of metacommunication in consumer trust: A case study of corporate social responsibility communication. *Journal of Business Ethics*, 163(2), 377–392.

Knapp, M. L., Vangelisti, A. L., & Caughlin, J. P. (2020). *Interpersonal Communication and Human Relationships* (8th ed.). Pearson.

Kotter, J. P. (1990). *A Force for Change: How Leadership Differs from Management*. Free Press.

Mateus, S. (2017). The role of metacommunication in relational interaction and political discourse. *Journal of Media and Communication Research,* 12(4), 83–95.

Mateus, S. (2017). Metacommunication as second order communication. KOME: *An International Journal of Pure Communication Inquiry,* 5(1), 80–90. https://doi.org/10.17646/KOME.2017.15

Mateus, S. (2017). Metacommunication in contemporary organisational discourse. *Journal of Communication Studies,* 6(3), 81–95. https://doi.org/10.17646/KOME.2017.15

Matsumoto, D., Hwang, H. S., & Frank, M. G. (2020). *Nonverbal Communication: Science and Applications.* SAGE Publications.

McStay, A. (2018). *Personal Data and Privacy in the Age of AI.* Cambridge University Press.

Mehrabian, A. (1972). *Nonverbal Communication.* Aldine-Atherton.

Mwandembo, F. (2024). Navigating the storm: Effective crisis communication strategies. *International Journal of Innovative Science and Research Technology,* 9(3), 2685–2697. https://doi.org/10.38124/ijisrt/IJISRT24MAR2080

Nakano, Y. (2001). Early development of intersubjective communication. *Infant Behavior and Development*, 24(2), 121–134.

Nguyen, T. N., Ngo, L. V., & Ruël, H. (2020). Artificial intelligence in crisis communication: Applications and ethical concerns. *Journal of Business Research*, 116, 243–254. https://doi.org/10.1016/j.jbusres.2020.05.028

O'Brien, S. P. (2010). Crisis early warning and decision support: Contemporary approaches and thoughts on future research. *International Studies Review*, 12(1), 87–104. https://doi.org/10.1111/j.1468-2486.2009.00914.x

Pruitt, D. G., & Rubin, J. Z. (1986). *Social Conflict: Escalation, Stalemate, and Settlement*. McGraw-Hill.

Rawls, J. (1971). *A Theory of Justice*. Harvard University Press.

Reynolds, B., & Seeger, M. W. (2005). Crisis and emergency risk communication as an integrative model. *Journal of Health Communication*, 10(1), 43–55. https://doi.org/10.1080/10810730590904571

Starbucks. (2018). *CEO Kevin Johnson's apology statement*. Retrieved from [https://www.starbucks.com].

Starbucks. (2018). *Diversity and inclusion initiatives*. Retrieved from [https://www.starbucks.com].

Starbucks. (2019). *Civil rights audit report*. Retrieved from [https://www.starbucks.com].

Stavholm, B. (2021). Metacognition in task reflection: Thinking about thinking. *International Journal of Cognitive Development*, 15(1), 3–12.

Sturges, D. L. (1994). Communicating through a crisis: A strategy for organisational survival. *Management Communication Quarterly*, 7(3), 297–316. https://doi.org/10.1177/0893318994007003004

Suciu, L., & Şimon, S. (2014). Online organisational communication and identity construction: A comparative study of samsung in Romania and France. *Journal of Digital Communication*, 5(1), 1–20.

Sullivan, J. L. (2009). Media audiences and meta-narratives. *Journal of Media Ethics*, 24(5), 323–329.

Sullivan, W. M. (2009). *Educating for Democracy: Preparing Undergraduates for Responsible Political Engagement*. Jossey-Bass.

Szostak, M. (2023). *Sztuka zarządzania – zarządzanie sztuką*. Wydawnictwo Społecznej Akademii Nauk.

Szostak, M., & Sułkowski, Ł. (2020). Manager as an artist: Creative endeavour in crossing the borders of art and organizational discourse. *Creativity Studies*, 13(2), 351–368.

Ting-Toomey, S., & Dorjee, T. (2019). *Communicating Across Cultures*. Guilford Press.

Turkle, S. (2015). *Reclaiming Conversation: The Power of Talk in a Digital Age*. Penguin Press.

Valsiner, J., & Branco, A. U. (2004). Constructing meanings in interpersonal communication: Metacommunication and beyond. *Culture & Psychology*, 10(1), 9–26.

van Dijk, T. A. (1997). *Discourse as Social Interaction*. SAGE Publications.

Walther, J. B., & Valkenburg, P. M. (2021). Social connections in the digital age. *Annual Review of Psychology*, 72, 243–266.

Watzlawick, P., Beavin, J. H., & Jackson, D. D. (1967). *Pragmatics of Human Communication: A Study of Interactional Patterns, Pathologies, and Paradoxes*. W. W. Norton & Company.

Wilmot, W. W. (2009). Communication competence and the dynamics of relational interaction. *Interpersonal Communication Journal*, 34(3), 1103–1115.

# Conclusion

## Finding directions

*Michał Szostak*

### Restatement of the research problem and objectives

The primary research problem addressed in this book concerns the profound impact of AI-powered solutions on the foundations of humanistic management, viewed through the lens of aesthetics. Integrating AI technologies into organisational life challenges traditional notions of leadership, decision-making, communication, and employee well-being, raising critical questions about how human dignity, emotional engagement, creativity, and aesthetic experience can be preserved and enhanced. From an aesthetic standpoint, AI-driven systems are not neutral tools; they actively reshape how organisations are perceived, experienced, and symbolically constructed. This volume sought to explore how AI technologies modify the humanistic approach in managerial theory and practice, under what conditions AI can contribute to the humanisation of work, and conversely, how it might foster dehumanisation by marginalising human intuition, emotion, and relational depth. Furthermore, this book aimed to investigate the long-term consequences for organisational aesthetics, culture, and human experience when AI is applied without critical reflection on its humanistic and ethical dimensions. The overarching objective was to develop a nuanced, interdisciplinary understanding of AI's aesthetic and humanistic implications and to propose pathways for integrating technological advancement with the enduring values of humanistic management.

### Answering the research questions

Answering RQ1 (*How does the appearance of AI-powered solutions change the ground of the humanistic approach in managerial theory and practice from the point of view of aesthetics?*), it can be said that the emergence of AI-powered solutions transforms the ground of humanistic management by redefining the aesthetic experience of organisational life, leadership, decision-making, and communication. AI introduces new symbolic, emotional, and sensory dimensions into management, altering how authenticity, beauty, relationality, and

DOI: 10.4324/9781003654377-17

meaning are perceived within organisations (Chapter 1). At a pragmatic level, AI technologies such as large language models create opportunities for symbolic richness and risks of homogenisation and emotional flattening (Chapter 2). Furthermore, AI-driven systems reshape leadership styles by integrating algorithmic empathy and aesthetic sensitivity into managerial practice (Chapter 6), influence the aesthetic dimensions of decision-making processes (Chapter 7), and affect organisational communication aesthetics, particularly in crisis contexts (Chapter 12). Thus, AI solutions shift humanistic management from being solely human-centred to becoming a co-produced aesthetic field where technology and human sensibilities jointly construct organisational experiences.

Addressing RQ2a (*What are the conditions for considering AI-powered solutions as a tool for increasing the humanisation of work?*), we can say that AI-powered solutions can enhance the humanisation of work when they are designed and implemented to support relational authenticity, emotional engagement, creative freedom, inclusivity, and aesthetic richness. Historical ethical models, such as those embedded in Freemasonry's aesthetic principles, illustrate that organisational practices guided by symbolic and ethical values can integrate AI without eroding humanistic foundations (Chapter 3). Humanisation is supported when AI fosters meaning and purpose, as seen in IT professional development aligned with humanistic and spiritual values (Chapter 4). Leadership practices that combine AI tools with emotional intelligence, algorithmic transparency, and aesthetic awareness strengthen the humanistic dimensions of organisations (Chapter 6). Moreover, AI-supported HRM systems that personalise employee engagement, reduce bias, and enhance sensory and emotional well-being – particularly for older employees – are conditions for work humanisation (Chapters 9 and 10).

Regarding RQ2b (*What are the conditions for considering AI as a substitute for humans, i.e., a reason for dehumanising work?*), AI may become a substitute for humans – and a dehumanisation factor – when deployed in ways that diminish emotional depth, aesthetic richness, human agency, and ethical sensitivity in organisational life. When AI is treated merely as a means to operational optimisation without consideration of aesthetic and humanistic implications, it risks flattening relational engagement and standardising emotional expressions (Chapter 2). Decision-making processes that rely excessively on algorithmic efficiency without integrating human intuition and embodied knowledge contribute to dehumanisation (Chapter 7). AI-driven HRM processes can also foster dehumanisation when recruitment, evaluation, and interaction are reduced to mechanical data-driven models, excluding relational and aesthetic dimensions (Chapter 9). Moreover, crisis communication managed exclusively through AI systems lacks performative authenticity and symbolic nuance, reinforcing depersonalised, transactional organisational cultures (Chapter 12).

Answering RQ3 (*What long-term consequences to humans should a manager consider when applying AI-powered solutions in an organisation?*), we can conclude that managers must carefully consider a range of long-term consequences when implementing AI-powered solutions. These include the potential erosion of emotional authenticity, the loss of aesthetic depth in organisational life, the weakening of symbolic leadership presence, and the exacerbation of technostress or digital exclusion, particularly among vulnerable groups such as older employees (Chapter 10). There is a risk that algorithmically optimised systems may normalise aesthetic standardisation and emotional detachment over time, subtly altering organisational culture and human experience (Chapter 11). Managers should also anticipate how AI-driven organisational aesthetics could reinforce structural inequalities or biases if not critically supervised (Chapter 5). Long-term strategic decisions must integrate operational and financial metrics and ethical, aesthetic, and human-centred indicators to ensure that technological advancement strengthens rather than undermines human flourishing in organisations.

Regarding the findings across particular chapters, the contributions in this volume collectively highlight that the emergence of AI-powered solutions is transforming the humanistic and aesthetic dimensions of managerial theory and practice. Across diverse contexts, these chapters demonstrate how AI reshapes leadership communication, decision-making processes, organisational aesthetics, human resource practices, and user experience, challenging managers to reconcile technological advancement with human dignity, emotional depth, and aesthetic value.

At the conceptual foundation, it was shown that AI necessitates a redefinition of humanistic management theory through the aesthetic lens, urging a closer focus on how technological mediation alters symbolic, emotional, and sensory organisational realities (Chapter 1). The pragmatic implications of large language models for management aesthetics were discussed, highlighting the opportunities for enhanced symbolic richness and the threats of emotional flattening and aesthetic standardisation (Chapter 2). A historically grounded reflection on Freemasonry's aesthetic principles illustrated how ethical-symbolic traditions can guide the humanistic application of AI technologies (Chapter 3). Furthermore, integrating spirituality into IT professional development emphasised the importance of nurturing meaning and emotional resonance within technologically advanced work environments (Chapter 4). Expanding on theoretical perspectives, a cross-paradigmatic analysis demonstrated that interpretations of AI-driven aesthetics vary fundamentally depending on management paradigms, influencing how organisations perceive beauty, meaning, control, and emancipation (Chapter 5).

In leadership studies, the evolution of leadership styles under AI influence requires new competencies, such as algorithmic empathy, aesthetic sensitivity, and ethical discernment (Chapter 6). The aesthetic aspects of decision-making processes supported by AI tools were further analysed, revealing that leaders must maintain intuitive and sensory depth to prevent purely algorithmic rationality from dominating organisational judgement (Chapter 7). The textual charisma concept was introduced as a critical resource for sustaining aesthetic and relational authenticity in leadership communication mediated by AI technologies (Chapter 8).

In human resources and organisational practices, it was found that AI applications in HRM offer the potential for both humanisation and dehumanisation, depending on how technology is ethically designed and implemented (Chapter 9). The role of AI in supporting the sensory and emotional well-being of elderly employees was explored, showing that inclusive, ethically grounded AI systems can mitigate technostress and promote intergenerational engagement (Chapter 10). On the operational side, it was demonstrated that in e-commerce development, balancing algorithmic efficiency with aesthetic user experience is critical to maintaining emotional engagement, customer trust, and human-centred service design (Chapter 11). Finally, the challenges of AI-generated crisis communication were analysed, concluding that while AI can enhance informational delivery, it struggles to replicate the performative authenticity, emotional resonance, and aesthetic nuance required during organisational crises (Chapter 12). Together, these findings affirm that humanistic management in the AI era must consciously integrate aesthetic intelligence, emotional sensitivity, and ethical foresight to ensure that technological advancements enhance, rather than diminish, the richness of human organisational life.

## Theoretical and epistemological contributions and practical implications

This volume makes several important *theoretical* and *epistemological contributions* to the evolving fields of management studies, organisational aesthetics, AI ethics, and humanistic management. First, it repositions aesthetics as a fundamental, rather than peripheral, dimension of managerial theory and practice in the AI era. This book challenges the prevailing operational and technocratic narratives surrounding AI integration by demonstrating that aesthetic experience – encompassing sensory engagement, emotional resonance, symbolic meaning, and existential depth – is essential for understanding and managing AI-supported organisational life.

Epistemologically, the volume bridges distinct knowledge traditions: it integrates humanistic management theory with AI studies, organisational semiotics, phenomenological aesthetics, and critical management paradigms. Several chapters adopt cross-paradigmatic perspectives, illustrating that interpretations of AI-driven aesthetics vary significantly depending on underlying ontological and epistemological assumptions about technology, human agency, and organisational structure. This pluralistic and reflexive approach underscores that no single theoretical lens is sufficient to grasp the complex transformations AI induces in the aesthetic fabric of organisations.

Furthermore, this book advances the epistemology of humanistic management by showing that concepts such as dignity, authenticity, empathy, and creative freedom are ethical imperatives and aesthetic practices deeply affected by AI technologies. It argues that management research must embrace both critical inquiry and aesthetic sensitivity when analysing the socio-technical assemblages that AI creates to preserve the richness of human experience in organisations. Thus, this book contributes to reorienting management theory towards a more integrative, interdisciplinary, and humanistically grounded understanding of AI's role in shaping the future of organisational life.

The findings and reflections presented across this volume yield important *practical implications* for managers, designers of AI systems, and policymakers responsible for shaping the future of work and organisational life. First and foremost, managers are encouraged to approach AI not merely as a tool for operational optimisation but as an aesthetic and ethical force that actively shapes organisational identity, emotional climate, and relational dynamics. When implementing AI-powered solutions, managers must assess efficiency metrics and technological interventions' aesthetic and humanistic impact on employees, customers, and stakeholders. Integrating aesthetic sensitivity into leadership practices, decision-making processes, and crisis communication strategies becomes essential to preserve authenticity, empathy, and emotional engagement in AI-augmented environments.

For designers and developers of AI systems, this book emphasises the need to embed human-centred, aesthetic, and ethical considerations into the core of technological design. AI architectures should be crafted to enhance rather than flatten emotional experiences, to respect symbolic richness, and to foster trust through transparency, empathy, and responsiveness. Particular attention should be paid to sensory design, language aesthetics, inclusivity for diverse user groups (including seniors), and the prevention of dehumanising interactions.

Policymakers are similarly urged to recognise AI adoption's broader aesthetic and humanistic consequences in organisational settings. Regulatory frameworks should not focus solely on data security, transparency, and bias mitigation but should also support initiatives promoting workers' and users' emotional, aesthetic, and symbolic well-being. Encouraging research funding, certifications, and organisational practices prioritising aesthetic integrity, human dignity, and ethical innovation will be critical for shaping an AI-enhanced future that truly serves human flourishing.

## Analyses' limitations and future research directions

While this volume offers new insights into the intersection of AI, aesthetics, and humanistic management, several *limitations* must be acknowledged. First, many of the contributions adopt a predominantly conceptual and theoretical perspective. Although some chapters include empirical elements, such as econometric modelling or secondary data analysis, most findings are based on critical interpretation, narrative synthesis, and theoretical reflection. As such, the conclusions drawn would benefit from further empirical validation through case studies, interviews, ethnographic research, and longitudinal studies examining AI's aesthetic and humanistic effects in diverse organisational contexts. Second, while this book intentionally adopts a cross-disciplinary and cross-paradigmatic approach, the analyses' cultural scope is primarily within Western management traditions and frameworks. Broader inclusion of perspectives from non-Western cultures, where aesthetic values, humanistic principles, and approaches to AI integration may differ significantly, remains an important area for future exploration. Third, given the rapid pace of technological innovation, especially in AI and machine learning fields, some of the observations and theoretical assumptions presented in this volume may require updating as new forms of AI solutions, human-machine interaction models, and regulatory environments emerge. Recognising the dynamic nature of the field, the editors and contributors emphasise the provisional character of some conclusions, inviting ongoing critical dialogue, empirical research, and theoretical refinement.

Building upon this volume's conceptual foundations and findings, several promising *directions for future research emerge*. First, there is a pressing need for empirical studies that investigate how AI-driven organisational aesthetics influence emotional engagement, decision-making quality, leadership perception, and employee well-being across various sectors and industries. Qualitative research methods, including ethnographic case studies, narrative inquiry, and phenomenological interviews, would offer deeper insights into the lived experiences of individuals interacting with AI-mediated management environments. Second, cross-cultural and comparative research is essential to explore how different cultural traditions interpret, experience, and respond to AI-driven aesthetics and humanistic management practices. Future studies could investigate, for example, how aesthetic expectations and ethical concerns surrounding AI differ between Western, Asian, African, and Latin American organisational contexts, enriching the global applicability of humanistic AI frameworks. Third, future research should engage with emerging technologies – such as generative AI, immersive virtual environments, and emotional AI systems – to examine how these advancements further transform organisational life's aesthetic, ethical, and relational fabric. Exploring the long-term effects of AI aesthetics on organisational culture, identity formation, and symbolic leadership will be critical as workplaces become increasingly digitalised and hybridised. Finally, interdisciplinary collaboration between management scholars, AI ethicists, organisational aestheticians, designers, and practitioners should be encouraged to develop integrated models of AI-humanistic management, ensuring that technological progress remains aligned with the enduring values of human dignity, emotional richness, and aesthetic diversity.

As AI continues transforming organisations' structures, processes, and symbolic landscapes, it is imperative to ensure that technological advancement remains anchored in humanistic and aesthetic values. The future of management cannot be envisioned merely as an exercise in algorithmic optimisation or operational efficiency; it must also safeguard the emotional, relational, and sensory richness that makes organisational life authentically human. AI-powered solutions must be designed, implemented, and governed with conscious attention to how they shape experiences of beauty, dignity, meaning, and emotional resonance within the workplace. This volume advocates for a management paradigm in which AI is not a substitute for human judgment, creativity, and empathy but an augmentative partner that enriches human experiences rather than diminishing them. By fostering aesthetic intelligence, ethical sensitivity, and critical reflection, managers, designers, and policymakers can co-create organisations where technological innovation harmonises with the timeless aspirations of humanistic management: to cultivate environments where individuals can flourish emotionally, intellectually, and ethically in the AI-augmented world of tomorrow (Table C1).

*Table C1* Answers to research questions

| *Research question* | *Related chapters* | *Key insights* |
|---|---|---|
| (RQ1) How does the appearance of AI-powered solutions change the ground of the humanistic approach in managerial theory and practice from the point of view of aesthetics? | Chapter 1<br>Chapter 2<br>Chapter 6<br>Chapter 7<br>Chapter 12 | AI reshapes organisational aesthetics, decision-making, leadership, and communication, introducing new emotional, symbolic, and sensory dimensions into management. |
| (RQ2a) What are the conditions for considering AI-powered solutions as a tool for increasing the humanisation of work? | Chapter 3<br>Chapter 4<br>Chapter 6<br>Chapter 9<br>Chapter 10 | Humanisation is fostered when AI supports authenticity, relational engagement, creativity, emotional resonance, and inclusivity, and is implemented with ethical and aesthetic sensitivity. |
| (RQ2b) What are the conditions for considering AI as a substitute for humans, i.e., a reason for dehumanising work? | Chapter 2<br>Chapter 7<br>Chapter 9<br>Chapter 12 | Dehumanisation occurs when AI replaces emotional depth, aesthetic experience, and human intuition with purely mechanical, efficiency-driven processes in leadership, HRM, and communication. |
| (RQ3) What long-term consequences to humans should a manager consider when applying AI-powered solutions in an organisation? | Chapter 5<br>Chapter 10<br>Chapter 11 | Managers must consider the risks of emotional detachment, aesthetic standardisation, technostress, exclusion of vulnerable groups, and shifts in organisational culture due to AI integration. |

*Source:* Own elaboration.

# Index

Note: **Bold** page numbers refer to tables; *italic* page numbers refer to figures and page numbers followed by "n" denote endnotes.